LIPTON'S
A MARIJUANA
JOURNAL

LIPTON'S
A MARIJUANA
JOURNAL
1954-1955

NORMAN MAILER

EDITED BY
J. MICHAEL LENNON, GERALD R. LUCAS,
AND SUSAN MAILER

Arcade Publishing • New York

Arcade Publishing books may be purchased in bulk at special discounts for sales promotion, corporate gifts, fund-raising, or educational purposes. Special editions can also be created to specifications. For details, contact the Special Sales Department, Arcade Publishing, 307 West 36th Street, 11th Floor, New York, NY 10018 or arcade@skyhorsepublishing.com.

Arcade Publishing® is a registered trademark of Skyhorse Publishing, Inc.®, a Delaware corporation.

Visit our website at www.arcadepub.com.

10 9 8 7 6 5 4 3 2 1

Library of Congress Cataloging-in-Publication Data is available on file.

Book design by Giles Hoover
Cover design by Erin Seaward-Hiatt
Cover photo credit: Getty Images

Print ISBN: 978-1-956763-87-4
Ebook ISBN: 978-1-956763-88-1

Printed in the United States of America

CONTENTS

Introduction **VI**

Editors' Note **XIX**

Entries 1

  December 1, 1954 **2**

  December 8, 1954 **6**

  December 17, 1954 **14**

  December 28, 1954 **24**

  December 29, 1954 **26**

  December 31, 1954 **36**

  January 3, 1955 **47**

  January 20, 1955 **54**

  January 24, 1955 **60**

  January 25, 1955 **77**

  January 26, 1955 **87**

  January 27, 1955 **102**

  January 31, 1955 **107**

  February 1, 1955 **132**

  February 2, 1955 **151**

  February 7, 1955 **154**

  February 10, 1955 **183**

  February 14, 1955 **189**

  February 21, 1955 **203**

  February 22, 1955 **223**

  March 4, 1955 **233**

Correspondence between Norman Mailer and Robert Lindner 241

  Introduction **242**

  The Letters **247**

Endnotes 317

  Introduction **318**

  Entries **321**

  Letters **352**

Acknowledgments and Appreciations **361**

Index **363**

INTRODUCTION

The mid-1950s were a difficult time for Norman Mailer. His first book, *The Naked and the Dead*, a Pacific war novel, appeared in 1948, when he was twenty-five. It was critically acclaimed and a bestseller for over a year. But his second novel, *Barbary Shore* (1951), which devolves midway into a series of debates about the failure of the Russian Revolution and the nature of "true" socialism, was brutally dismissed. *Time*'s reviewer called it "tasteless, graceless and paceless," a description burned into his memory. There was, therefore, much at stake with his third novel, *The Deer Park*, which unfolds beneath the shadow of the Red Scare in Hollywood. Mailer felt it was his chance to redeem himself, to prove that he was not a one-hit impostor but a major novelist. Accepted for publication by Rinehart, it was canceled when Mailer refused to remove an opaque depiction of a Hollywood producer getting a blowjob from a call girl, less than three months before its scheduled publication date of February 14, 1955. The novel was already in page proof, and an ad for it had already appeared in *Publishers Weekly* when Mailer was informed. In making the decision, Stanley Rinehart, the firm's president, overrode his editorial staff, citing Mailer's refusal. Mailer was not completely surprised as the rejection came after protracted negotiations about the language of the novel.

It was during this period that he began a journal, titled *Lipton's* (tea = marijuana), which he described as "a wild set of thoughts and outlines for huge projects." The ideas "came so fast," he wrote, "that sometimes I think my mind was dulled by the heat." He began *Lipton's* on December 1, 1954, and made entries sporadically, usually on Mondays and Tuesdays after a weekend of smoking pot and going to Harlem jazz clubs with his new wife, Adele Morales. After thirteen weeks, he put the journal aside in order to begin a final revision of *The Deer Park*, which Putnam's—the seventh publisher to consider it—accepted for fall 1955 publication. When he made the final entry on March 4, 1955, the journal topped 104,000 words divided into 708 often mis-numbered entries.

Lipton's is Mailer's unsparing assessment of his intellectual resources, literary abilities, personal relationships, and psycho-sexual well-being at age thirty-two. It is also a record of the effects of marijuana, one similar to Thomas De Quincey's *Confessions of an English Opium-Eater* (1822) in its celebration of the salutary effects of a drug, and the drawbacks. Mailer drew on the cavalcade of ideas in *Lipton's*, some of them only partially birthed, and many delivered via the cumbersome jargon of psychology and sociology, for the remainder of his writing career. "The White Negro," his most celebrated and debated essay, published in 1957, was the first and perhaps most important outgrowth of *Lipton's*, but its influence can be seen in subsequent books as disparate as *Cannibals and Christians* (1966), *The Armies of the Night* (1968), *Ancient Evenings* (1983), and *Harlot's Ghost* (1991).

Smoking pot sanctioned and smoothed what Mailer called "the journey into myself," acting, he said, like an antispasmodic drug. It enfeebled his societal self and emboldened his instinctual self; or, put another way, it helped him marginalize the "despised image" of himself: "the sweet clumsy anxious to please Middle-class Jewish boy," and become a rebel with a cause, a "psychic outlaw." He found the drug both a means and an end, pleasurable in itself and also an enhancement of his sexual performance, his appreciation of jazz, and even his bodily strength. Without Lipton's, *Lipton's* would have been a thinner gruel, more circumspect. Yet, on occasion, Mailer found the use of marijuana, buttressed by Seconal (a barbiturate derivative), booze, cigarettes, and black coffee in various combinations, to be perilous. Some of the insights he gained while using Lipton's, particularly his vision on the evening of February 25, 1955, of a divided, vertiginous universe, were terrifying. Both madness and suicide seemed possible. "I don't think I have ever been so frightened in my life," he wrote.

Mailer's desire to explore his unconscious via psychoanalysis, a therapy more esteemed in the 1950s than today, also contributed to his writing of *Lipton's*. After years of writing about the social and political world in his first three novels, Mailer wished to travel

inward to the realm of dreams, repression, symbolism, Eros and Thanatos—to Freudian territory, in short—and then build a bridge between Freud and Marx, dreams and society, desire and history. This is not to say that psychological issues were ignored in his early novels, which is hardly the case, although under the tutelage of Jean Malaquais, his leftist mentor, Marx's *Capital*, the Russian Revolution, and its aftermath had been Mailer's course of study for a nine-month period: winter, spring, and summer, 1948–1949. After he and Malaquais grew apart, Mailer's reading skewed toward the works of Freud, including his correspondence and the insights of his biographer, Ernest Jones. Wilhelm Reich, who equated sexual maladjustment with the heavy hand of a puritanical society, was another of his favorites. Mailer was also familiar with the writings of others influenced by Freud: Karen Horney, Theodore Reik, Karl Jung, Edmund Bergler, Marion Rosen, Harry Stack Sullivan, and Alfred Adler. In *Lipton's*, he refers to many of the major figures in Freud's circle.

Mailer read Robert Lindner's *Prescription for Rebellion: A Reinterpretation of Psychoanalysis* (1952), Lindner's impassioned attack on the profession for encouraging patients to adjust rather than rebel. Mailer felt a shock of recognition when he read Lindner's contention that rebellion was humanity's instinctive response to societal repression. While honoring Freud and his followers, Lindner believed that psychoanalysts had misused and blunted the tools of analysis. Skepticism, unfocused anger, and a quiver of neuroses were assets not liabilities, and should be celebrated, not discouraged. Rinehart published Lindner's book, and Mailer was sent a copy. He read it right after it appeared in mid-October 1952, and wrote a long letter a few weeks later (included here, page 248), praising the book's thesis, but complaining that Lindner failed to identify with any precision what was wrong with society, what actions and inactions were inciting resistance. Both Mailer and Lindner were disheartened by the dull fog of conformity that was rolling over the nation during the Eisenhower era, but they didn't see eye to eye on what acts of intransigence might help to dissipate it. For example, Lindner did not recognize marijuana as a tool of liberation, while Mailer believed it was a magical drug that purged docility and opened up possibilities for movement and growth. Mailer asked Lindner to analyze him and was refused on the grounds it would destroy their friendship. Nevertheless, their correspondence burgeoned into a warm friendship. For several years they corresponded, talked regularly on the phone, and exchanged visits until early 1956, when Lindner died of congenital heart disease. Mailer sent Lindner chunks of the journal and Lindner sent back responses that further stimulated Mailer, who called their dialogue "inter-fecundation." It was one of the deepest friendships of Mailer's life, and Lindner's too.

Mailer's appreciation of jazz also added to *Lipton's*. While he was tone deaf and assigned the role of "listener" during primary school music classes, Mailer grew up listening to the jazz of the swing era. After World War II, he became a fan of bebop, and then the cool jazz of the 1950s. In the numerous jazz clubs of Manhattan (the Five Spot, the Village Vanguard, and the Jazz Gallery), he heard and savored many of the greats: Dizzy Gillespie, Thelonious Monk, Charlie Mingus, Miles Davis (on whom Mailer based a character in his 1965 novel, *An American Dream*), Dave Brubeck, Paul Desmond, Sonny Rollins, and Sonny Stitt. Like marijuana, jazz was a portal to the life force, which, toward the end of the journal, Mailer began to call "lerve." In *Lipton's*, and then in "The White Negro," Mailer links jazz to marijuana, sex, alcohol, and the disenthralled lifestyle of blacks in Harlem. During the period he was compiling the journal, he would accompany new friends in Harlem "on that happy ride where you discover a new duchy of jazz every night and the drought of the past is given a rain of new sound."

"For the first time in years," Mailer writes, "I am growing quickly again," and "I have to go on and make the attempt to be a genius." In *Lipton's* he reflects on the nature of genius, and considers a number of writers whose stature he hopes to attain: Freud, Marx, Joyce, Proust, Tolstoy, Dostoyevsky, Oswald Spengler, and to a lesser extent Mann and Gide. He also places Dizzy Gillespie, Marlon Brando, Charlie Chaplin, and Charles Laughton in or near the genius category (later in life he added Fidel Castro and Muhammad Ali). He states that he would prefer to be a genius than a saint, and he wrestles with the definitions of each, and also that of the psychopath, in dozens of entries. Mailer saw *Lipton's* as the prelude to a thousand-page "fuck novel" that would take years to write, a preparation for his attempt to become a daring Dostoyevskian novelist who will "make a revolution in the consciousness of our time," as he put it in *Advertisements for Myself* (1959). It is also a summary of all the societal forces and personal weaknesses that could impede his effort. Several times in the four-month period of composition, Mailer felt himself faltering, wondering if the journal was just a game, an illusion. At one point, when particularly disgusted with himself, he calls his daily Seconal dose "a pill for the swill."

Throughout the journal, Mailer points to the heaviness of his writing style, which he says is "about as sprightly as a German grammar teacher." Part of the reason for the crudity is the rush in which he wrote his entries—there is no revision, just count-er-thoughts in parentheses—and because he was bursting with ideas. These he set down in numbered entries, jumping from an insight about mystics to advertising, the connections among the atomic bomb and hipsters and black sexuality (later elaborated in "The White Negro"), the Holocaust, his imitations of Marlon Brando, orgies, orgasm, bisexuality, television, jazz, jokes, the Catholic Church, comedians, the hidden meanings of words (lots of these), the people in his life, bodily functions, literary style, and his first three novels. His relationship with Adele, and their sex life, is a constant in the journal.

In April 1954, Mailer married Adele Morales, who he began living with in mid-1951. She was much different than his first wife Bea, less independent and more involved in Mailer's roller-coaster emotional life. Mailer's first biographer, Hilary Mills, draws the contrast well:

Beatrice had in many ways been like Mailer's mother—strong, bright, Jewish, and intolerant of Norman's macho antics. But Adele was quite different: a dark, sensuous Latin, who at least initially, was a strong woman without a sense of her own strength. She had gone only to Washington Irving High School, and her limited education gave her a certain insecurity which permitted her to passively follow Norman's intellectual lead. Yet as an artist Adele had her own unconventional imagina-tion and she would learn to play Mailer's psychic games with innovation. Although these games would eventually get out of hand as Mailer's vision of the "orgiastic and violent" inten-

ADELE AND NORMAN.

sified, in the beginning Adele offered Mailer an exciting and mysterious departure from the dominant women he had known. "Adele's an Indian," Mailer has said, "primitive and elemental." Adele's responsive sensuality stimulated Mailer's evolving sense of freedom and his growing desire for the forbidden. "That early period with Adele was probably his happiest time," Wolf later said. "She opened him up."

Mailer's love for Adele is stated emphatically in *Lipton's*. Until November 1960, when he stabbed her with a penknife during a drunken argument, they were inseparable, although their relationship had begun to deteriorate at least a year earlier.

As the journal proceeds, the entries become longer and longer, essayistic and self-aware, reaching a crescendo in several linked entries written on his thirty-second birthday, January 31, 1955. He notes that the outflow on that day, twenty-four pages, is the most he has written since he produced at the age of nineteen the final forty pages of his first, unpublished novel, *No Percentage*.

Until *Lipton's*, Mailer's desire to create his own literary style was a distant second to his need to "disgorge" a mass of speculations, theories, and revilements. Uttering the big ideas is the main chance in *Lipton's*, but accompanying the blockbuster ideas is a stream of autobiographical comment coupled with an emerging interest in the language of self-presentation. As Richard Poirier, his most astute critic, has noted, until the mid-1950s Mailer "had not yet created for himself a distinctive voice or contrived his own ways of moving or shifting his own personal rhythm or sense of duration and momentum." His distaste for personal revelation can be seen in a comment he made to an interviewer in 1948, when *The Naked and the Dead* topped the bestseller lists: "I think it's much better when people who read your book don't know anything about you, even what you look like. . . . Getting your mug in the papers is one of the shameful ways of making a living." Mailer's later embrace of celebrity, his role as a public intellectual, is well-known, but he always had reservations about being too much in the public eye.

Lipton's is the beginning of Mailer's recognition that voice and public presence could be crafted, manipulated. "Literary style," he wrote in the journal, "is always the record of a war within a man." Adroitly deployed, such a style could convey his deepest concerns about a society that smothers. A personal style that reflected his *bellum intestinum*, he now began to see, could also be a means of communicating stances and moods too subtle for a straightforward argument of the formulaic kind essayed in scholarly journals such as *Dissent*. He also recognized that his obsession to complete one piece of work before embarking on another was a mistake; moving from project to project as the mood seized him would permit him to be more responsive to external stimuli and to keep all of his literary muscles toned. For the rest of his life, he was alert to the voice of his muse on what project to start or stop, and usually had a number of works in progress on his desk.

The new style ripened in January 1956, three months after *The Deer Park* was published, when Mailer began a column for the weekly newspaper he cofounded (and named), the *Village Voice*. He called the column "Quickly" (he planned to write each one in an hour or less), and took a nom de plume: "General Marijuana." "Quickly" and the equally irritable, irritating cartoons of Jules Feiffer were the tentpoles of the *Voice*, which became the progenitor of the counterculture press and the proving ground for a generation of new journalists. The new style was mercurial, generally sardonic, sometimes wounding, open to polyglot American parlance, or as Richard Poirier notes, not limited to modes "sanctioned by literary decorums." What modes did Mailer employ? Obscenity, sarcasm, fulmination, pontification, and ventriloquism are the first that come to mind, but also self-revelation. The new style is very much in evidence the following year when "The White Negro," an attempt to consolidate much of what was essayed in *Lipton's*, came out in the summer 1957 issue of *Dissent*, and quickly became the most contro-versial essay ever to appear in this reserved leftist journal. Two years later in *Advertisements for Myself* the style attained its full vigor. As Mailer noted in a 1976 preface to this collection of essays, reviews, interviews and excerpts from previous work, all stitched together by "advertisements" which directly address the reader, "Advertisements was the first work that I wrote with a style I could call my own." Mailer was also designing, by fits and starts, the template for a new kind of public intellectual, an independent, rambunctious, and unpredictable left-conservative (his coinage) who was interested, as he said in the fall of 1955, "less in politics as politics . . . than politics as a part of everything else in life."

Mailer comments in *Lipton's* that "to use the conceptual words of others is to maroon myself in pseudo-rational processes rather than to depend on my intuition." A new language, a "private jargon" was needed, and the journal is loaded with spontaneous coinages, some memorable, others not. The meanings of most the following can be easily construed: "startlings," "crankery," "lustility," "wombivity," "schlumperness," "hardonolgy," "limberology," "thingification, "smally," "viator," "mindish," "Liptoning up," "loverness." He refers to the entire journal, more than once, as a "fuckanalysis," and suggests that in the course of human progress, eventually, "history" will become "hissoul." Some of the more Germanic neologisms are central to the running argument in the journal that humanity is locked in a centuries-old struggle in every arena of existence between two forces, homeostasis and sociostasis. The former refers to life-giving acts and forces; the latter to society's efforts to maintain itself, arrest change by violence (which homeostasis also employs) and coercion, but also more subtle measures such as advertising and patriotism. Mailer quickly realized that homeostasis had a contradictory suffix and changed it to homeodynamism. Soon, however, he tires of typing these long words, and shortens them to H and S, which work for a time. Then he opts, inexplicably, for "sup" and "er," deriving from "superego." The homeodynamism substitute, "er," is related closely to "lerve," which Mailer prefers to libido. Writing *Lipton's* forced Mailer to become more alert to the shape and beat of his sentences. Before then, he said later, "I'd been someone who wrote for the sense of what I was saying, and now I began to write for the sound of what I was writing."

Lipton's is a hodgepodge, a lumber room of intellectual feints and fancies, arguments and insights, yet it hangs together. One

reason is that it is a psychoanalytic act. Another is that it is a dictionary of dualisms. The indubitable doubleness of all nature, all phenomena, is the centrifugal belief that supports every exploration in the journal. All the antinomies that Mailer had pondered since his youth come tumbling out. He works through a range of commonplace oppositions such as sun-moon, conscious-unconscious, heaven-hell, as well as bodily functions—orgasms and vomiting, weeping and laughter, intercourse as giving and taking—and dozens of others: choice-habit, antacid-analgesic (which he proposes as the title of his one-thousand-page "fuck novel"), expertise-intuition, revolutionary-mystic, romantic-realist, and energetic repetitions of the saint-psychopath opposition. He considers his sexuality, his addictions, his aspirations, and his deepest fears, and like Reverend Dimmesdale in Hawthorne's *Scarlet Letter*, practices vigils of self-examination.

> Looking at myself in the mirror, high on Lipton's, I saw myself as follows: The left side of my face is comparatively heavy, sensual, possessor of hard masculine knowledge, strong, proud, and vain. Seen front-face I appear nervous, irresolute, tender, anxious, vulnerable, earnest, and Jewish middle-class. The right side of my face is boyish, saintly, bisexual, psychopathic, and suggests the victim.

The ultimate claim to coherence for *Lipton's* is that the struggles and paradoxes of its creator are congruent with those of postwar America. *Lipton's* is a wellspring of ideas and stances that Mailer drew on—without ever quoting directly from it—for the rest of his life, and the closest thing to a genuine psychoanalysis he ever undertook. The major contradictions of the nation at that time (and our own) struggle with each other in Norman Mailer.

EDITORS' NOTE

When Mailer made the final entry to *Lipton's*, the journal topped 104,000 words divided into 708 numbered entries. Mailer numbered each entry consecutively, from 1 to 689, over the twenty-one days he wrote in his journal, from December 1, 1954 to March 4, 1955. Occasionally he would skip a number and likewise repeat one; some entries were repetitive, redundant, or ridiculous. The archival manuscript is rough, like a first draft that an editor might be privy to. It needed careful editing to present a cohesive, readable, and logical volume, as Mailer himself writes to Lindner on December 31, 1954: "As I read it over, there is hardly a note which could not be improved, or indeed expanded into an essay. So, the thing is very crude. But I don't want to stop to polish now. And I want the wild with what is less wild because some of the wild ones become less wild as I expand them subsequently." Adding this "polish" to wrangle the "wild ones" is the job of his editors, and the one that we have undertaken in this volume. We decided to approach editing *Lipton's* with two platforms in mind, the web and the book, each with its own intended users: (re)searchers and readers, respectively.

In the web, or Digital Humanities, version, the main users will be researchers looking for quick information, likely via Google or through keyword searches of the site. In the digital version of *Lipton's*, we decided to keep everything from the original manuscript to give researchers the most complete picture of the manuscript as possible, all browsable and accessible via search. All of Mailer's original entries have been renumbered, eliminating errors in the manuscript, and including his handwritten edits. Each journal entry has its own page, often with linked cross-references to other entries, and annotations are repeated to support a searchable, digital context. These annotations explain important people and events that might not be inferred from the text and often provide a greater intellectual and philosophical context for Mailer's thought, especially to users who may be unfamiliar with or new to Mailer's work. For more information about the digital project, see LIPTONSJOURNAL.COM.

This book version of *Lipton's* is designed for readers. We use the same numbering system employed for the digital version, but we were more selective in what we chose to include here, emphasizing readability and consistency. Therefore, numbers in this volume correspond with the digital version, simply skipping those entries we have left out. Entries, too, have been edited for clarity, but we have been careful not to use too much polish, which would change its raw and extemporaneous feel. Endnotes and annotations are used to clarify names and ideas, and, for convenience, they are numbered by entry and page, e.g. 4/3 meaning entry 4 on page 3. However, we have chosen to use blind notes, so no indications of an endnote interrupts the text. Finally, a name index allows for good, old-fashioned analog searches. As *Lipton's* is an important document that lays the foundation of Mailer's mature thought, we present a volume that we hope will be invaluable to Mailer scholars.

ENTRIES

December 1, 1954

1 PERHAPS THE ARTIST IS less sensitive than his audience. That is, he reacts with less emotion, less intensity, to experience than people who are not at all creative. His creativity (his need to synthesize) is merely the expression of less emotion, it being quite conceivable that emotion and language are antithetical. Thus the writer, seeing coldly, but able to see, touches upon matters which move him very little, and move his audience much. It is perfectly conceivable that the stupid man feels worlds of experience he can never communicate; he is actually far more sensitive than the intelligent "sensitive" man.

2 LIPTON'S SEEMS TO OPEN one to one's unconscious. Perhaps its brothers do too. Last night, for an experiment, I tried an overhead press with the 45 lb. barbell. I did it seventeen times, double what I normally do, and while I could probably do as much without Lipton's, I felt very little strain, and no stiffness this morning. Undoubtedly, our latent strength is far greater than our actual, and we become tired or drained because of anxiety. This would account for the super-human strength people exhibit in time of necessity. It is always there, but it takes the threat of death or something which is its psychological equivalent to quiet the anxiety and allow the full strength to appear. Perhaps this is why animals are always so strong for their size—their latent strength is always present.

3 FUCKING IS PERHAPS AN approach to the unconscious, which is why humans with the most elaborate conscious structures tend to be the most anxious and unhappy in their sex.

4 IN RELATION TO (1). The reason "insensitive" people very often react negatively to sex or shocking matters in books is because it is actually much more real to them. They are actually more "sensitive" to it. So, Stanley Rinehart. He must excise the presence of *The Deer Park* because he reacts to it more than I do.

3

5 THE CONCENTRATION CAMP NOVEL. A Lipton's insight I had last night. The German doctor has heretofore been too thin, too structural. Merely an unsympathetic character who comes to appear as sympathetic here and again until he is finally shown as more or less evil or at least utterly weak. But suppose I make the attempt to show him as genuinely sympathetic, suppose I let him get out of hand, let him convince the reader as well as the doctor. So that finally, even when he kills the children, he is merely thinking, "Sweet lovely children, this is how they pass from the world of insubstantialities into the world of the universe." Originally, he might merely feel numb; but as he is obliged to continue killing them, the mysticism arises.

6 ONE SHOULD ALWAYS LISTEN attentively to what children say. Because they are never burdened with the baggage we assume to be knowledge. That is why their questions are so difficult to answer. If there is a total unity, a sea from which we emerge and to which we return, then children are closer to it, it is less far behind them. That is why you cannot deceive a child about the state of your emotions. Language has not yet succeeded in severing it from the universe. It is also why children from nine to thirteen, let us say, are invariably so dull. They have learned language, they have lost their early instinctual apprehension of the universe, and so the child of ten is a caricature of the adult, all projects, all plans, all concerted emptiness. Particularly boys. Last night Susie said to me, "What is a scientist?" and indeed it is not a question one can answer easily.

7 HERBERT A. SAID OF Lipton's—"I think it may return one to a state close to the infant's where reaction-time is increased, and the senses swim in a peculiar mixture of passivity and exceptional alertness."

8 IN MODERN JAZZ, ONE feels a key to aesthetics. Because modern jazz consists almost entirely of surprising one's expectation, and it is in the degree, small or great, with which each successive expectation is startled, that the artistry lies. But modern jazz has risen to share the crisis of modern painting. It is a self-accelerating process for the audience's expectations are changed almost nightly (that is, the tight critical yeast of the true aficionados) and so questions of "beauty" disappear before the dilemma—last night's innovation is tomorrow's banality. What is suggested is a movement across the arts, each of them engaging the other in order to find new startlings of old expectations until the arts blend, possibly in mathematics, the only art where the expectations of expectations of expectations, etc. can approach infinity.

9 THOREAU'S BEAUTIFUL REMARK, "THE mass of men lead lives of quiet desperation," is said less well, but more accurately by "All of man is like chained tigers wild in the cage of society."

10 I UPSET HERBERT BY saying that possibly psychoanalysis is witchcraft. But it can so well be true. Scientifically, they have not even taken the second step of physics, the first being the concept of mass, or in psychoanalysis, the unconscious. But the one next step, that of measuring intensity of movement has never been approached, unlike physics. And a reason may well be that it suffers from the incapacity to see, to understand, of knowledge itself. Any scientist knows that an experiment, to be truly controlled, should be administered by people who not only are disinterested, but indeed do not know the purpose of the experiment. The more hypothetical, the less measurable by the objective test of nature, the more this is true. We may take it for granted that the wish to prove a theory alters a fact. But what of the facts, previous facts, which suddenly form in our mind to suggest a theory? What I've noticed in writing is how often my unconscious is ahead of me, creating characters who seem alien to me at the time, only for me to discover later that indeed they are part of myself. So it may be with theories. They can exist in the unconscious, prepared to answer tangible needs of one's social life, such as prestige, personality, position, etc., and while they exist there, previous to their appearance in consciousness, they may be altering the facts one sees, forming them to give credence to the theory when it will appear. This way, the "scientist" feels conviction; he has the illusion that the facts which support his theory are independent of himself.

13 IT SEEMS TO ME that the few occasions on which I have felt close to fainting were moments when I was abruptly face to face with the reality of a situation, where I saw the horror of it. So, last night, talking to Romain about Kafka, I was close to fainting because of the awful and meaningless gap between writing a book and what one must do to publish it afterward.

14 IT IS POSSIBLE THAT many kinds of major sensual experiences are sublimated into particular sports. For example, last night, with her across my lap, her body exposed and my hands conquering over it, I realized suddenly how close a woman's body is to a ski slope, and perhaps the fascination of skiing is due to a particular frustration of a particular kind of sexual experience—the great skier needs such triumph and does not have the psychic possibility of finding it in life. Hence he rides like a charioteer over a ski slope, a giant ascetic woman open to his fury.

15 ALL OF MY LIFE with Adele is as if we were making love, and as delicately and as broadly as she tricks and cozens and teases and gratifies my expectations, so does she act the same when we're out of bed. That's why we're bound so deeply, why it's impossible for us to break up—deep in us it seems as ridiculous as interrupting the act of love.

16 IF THERE IS THAT other world, that sub-stratum of "reality" which one has the impression of "tuning-in" on, perhaps love, the sexual act, the unconscious itself, are all entrances into that reality. Our tendency is for all mankind to join as brothers, but most can approach that only by loving one or a few.

17 LISTENING TO A CHILD. "Susie, why are there wars?" "Because people stay home, and after a while they get tired of staying home."

18 I ADVERTISE TO EVERYONE my Lipton's. It can only mean trouble and yet I persist. Why? I think it may not be necessarily self-destructive. There is a vast appetite in me to go to the end, to experience the particular thing to the full, and against that, against my peculiarly boundless enthusiasm for everyone to explain themselves to everyone (as if there can be brotherhood), considerations like caution have absolutely no reality to me. It is true that the person I'm talking to at a given moment seems more real to me, more "worth-while" than anything else, and so I'm perfectly capable of revealing the most disadvantageous things because of my bounteous faith that to reveal oneself to a person is to take away from them the desire to do one harm. I confess ten times as much to others as others confess to me.

19 SIX AND FOUR ARE close to one another. Six understands everything Four thinks as if Four thought like Six. And vice versa. So the closer people are to one another, the more fundamental must be their incapacity to understand each other.

20 KNOWLEDGE IS SYSTEMATIZED IGNORANCE. The expert is less capable of seeing the truth than a child.

21 A NOVEL IS SLOWLY emerging. Very mistily. A man and a woman are making love, and in the act a thousand pages must be written to cover it totally. Ridiculous. That's all I have that I can put on paper, and yet I think something may come of this.

22 IT MAY BE THAT the range of human consciousness is a circle, and we who are normal are merely a point on the circumference, judging everything in relation to our position, assuming automatically that the insane are "wrong," when indeed they may be far closer to the truth.

23 IN THE CONCENTRATION CAMP novel, the German doctor could have gone very far, so far that he could talk sincerely of his love for children, even describe the wisdom of his child (note **17**), and the Major could finally kill him because the view offered by the German is so horrifying to his complacency that he must destroy the doctor or alter his own life.

24 THERE MAY ACTUALLY BE such a separate entity as "society." It may be the sum of that part of everybody's unconscious which leads into action. Society is the sum of men's actions, and beneath the surface of life may be that stratum of the collective unconscious which connects men in a net of actions, "social and productive relations independent of their will." Marx is still perhaps the first and the only major psychologist.

25 EVERY WORD SETS UP its opposite echo. "Overlook" means to stare cruelly and nakedly from above—it also means in its common use to disregard, to fail to see. So the real world, my phrase for the "material world" may actually be quite unreal and composed of illusion just as certainly as "action" referred to in **24** may actually be the reverse of action. So far as we "act" to fulfill the needs of society, we are actually no more than a part of the net with which society keeps men from developing. We have the illusion of action, of motion; in truth we are merely lines of cord in the net.

26 TELEVISION MAY HAVE SOME extraordinary quality apart from, or rather, far deeper than the "hypnotic" effect peoples ascribe to it. It may be some sort of anti-spasmodic like Lipton's which opens one to the deeper "pulse" of life we all share. What confuses the character of it is that the values of the world are purveyed by it until the effect is headache—disturbance—one subsides more into the universe-world while more and more powerfully the real world beats upon us.

27 POSSIBLY THE SPASMODIC NERVOUS system is the physical concretion in us of society. Lipton's has its effect the same as any anti-spasmodic—it stills the part of us which is society and allows our instinctual senses to collaborate with our thought. We become free.

28 VOMITING MAY BE THE orgasm of displeasure. It is even possible that it could be pleasurable too if one were able consciously to see it as a pleasurable action of the involuntary system. But indeed the sexual orgasm and the act of vomiting are proscribed by society as opposites, and all the weight of our consciousness pushes us to believe one pleasurable, the other painful.

Perhaps this is even true of pain. I remember the time I was able to think in Reggie Moss's dentist chair that my tooth being drilled was actually enjoying the sensation, and indeed I succeeded in finding it at least half-pleasant, admittedly half-unpleasant.

29 No SAINT CAN BE a teacher. If there is God, and one arrives at Him, one has passed far beyond words, for words which are polar to meaning are the chains of society. To attempt to teach what one has learned is to return to words, to submit oneself to enslavement again, and so for whatever hint one gives of the direction one also adds falsehood upon falsehood. That is why mystical writers write so badly. What they seek to communicate is simply incommunicable, and the distortion into language properly punishes them by banality. What this means is that everyone must reach God alone. Even more difficult is that one must take the trip alone once one has determined to begin it. One cannot read one's way to Truth, nor talk one's way, one can only contemplate. The great artists are saints manqué—they return to teach; they are half-way posts; so long as one has not thought at all about becoming a saint they startle one into considering more, into thinking more, possibly feeling more, and so they encourage large renunciations of the world. But once one feels the other universe, there is no longer any help, only confusion if one looks for aid in books or other people. It is not a very human perspective, but perhaps man, somewhere, has lost the right to reach heavens of truth by brotherhood because brotherhood has been so abused, has been enlisted to the service of the world, of society. So one must go alone. Obviously, I never will. I am a teacher and a talker.

30 INFANTS MAY BE ENORMOUSLY wise. There is no way we can disprove it.

31 THE SAINT AND THE psychopath are twins. Each are alone; each are honest or rather cannot bear dishonesty. The saint looks for truth in the immaterial world; the psychopath in the world. If the psychopath kills a man because they have quarreled for ten seconds over who was first in line to go through the subway turnstile, it is not so much because he is uncontrollable as because he cannot bear the absolute insanity and indignity of two men quarreling over so insignificant a thing. The saint seeks to lead people away from the world; the psychopath wishes to destroy the world; each has a vision of something else. The saint is aware of how insignificant is the fiction of each envelope, each "individual" who is part of the whole; the psychopath, less far along the route, merely feels that he is no one person, but becomes this person or that person, slipping from skin to skin as the real world presents new situations to him. No wonder that I who at bottom am both can control them only by the apparently silly compromise of an over-friendly anxious boyish, Jewish intellectual—"seductive" and inhibited by turns.

32 NO ONE IS MORE unreligious, more lost, than the professional religionists, and their lay brethren—the statesmen, the executives, the entertainers, the academicians, the doctors, and the experts.

33 MEDICINE MAY BE WITCHCRAFT as fully as psychoanalysis. There is still no understanding of why the germ flourishes in this human and not in that at any moment. To say that the resistance is low is merely a fancy, societal, and untruthful way of describing X. But the idea of "germs" accomplishes much—including other things, it gives intellectual backing to the sexual inhibitions which society must generate to protect itself.

34 THE AGGRESSIVE INSTINCT, THE destructive instinct, anger, rage, the furies of the unconscious, etc. etc. may all be myths. The id may contain no such things at all. They may be created in man because of his pain at how fantastic and unreasonable the world is. The idea of them is the greatest aid for maintaining society, for if everyone knew that really there is no terror to the unconscious, only peace and bliss and wide love, then men would live freely and society would disappear.

35 PSYCHOANALYSIS, LIBERALISM, ETC. ETC., are ways to reduce men to zombies. Perhaps Bob's anger at lobotomies comes from the unconscious fear that with all his good will and his courage, perhaps he is making world zombies of his patients too. Is psychoanalysis perhaps no more than an ideational lobotomy to sever man completely from his deeper world, and leave him marooned, will-less, and adjusted (anger less) in the dead world of society?

The sterile land of relating, of conformity, of proportion—what is it worth to lose one's anger if we remember that anger is only the side result of frustrated vision. Children's anger is always violent, for children have visions destroyed every instant of their existence.

36 I HAVE LEARNED MORE from Susie and more from Adele than from anyone but myself. But what I must always watch in Susie is when her reaction is flat—that is when a scar is being made, and she is truly hurt.

37 IN THE DEER PARK after the accident when Marion Faye is fighting for consciousness, he could think at first of saving himself from jail, and then relapse with the thought that in jail, finally, he can begin the work of contemplation.

38 IF THE MORE SAINTLY people (and perhaps the psychopaths too) were to retire from the world, the world could no longer function, for all of society's most sensitive joints are filled with the abused and cruelly warped talents of the saints, the artists and the psychopaths (understanding the artist as the mixture of the two). The saint's vision, the psychopath's courage, and the artist's illumination of the two are what give the rigidities of society its little necessary flexing and bending. Without them, the world would simply snap.

39 IN A COLLIER'S ARTICLE, Mendès-France wrote about climbing a wall after he had studied it for six months from the window of his cell. Studying it that way he saw tiny crevices and cracks which would give him hand-holds up the vertical face. This is an active demonstration of the values of concentration, and the need to liberate oneself from the word. A "wall" means something one cannot climb. But suppose one approaches a wall with the idea that it is *climbable*. Immediately it is converted in meaning to its opposite—a road, an escape.

40 WORDS ARE NOT ENTIRELY bad. When we think of thought and of words, we can see that words are capable occasionally of trapping a thought, of penning it. Which mean that the next time we try to find the thought we can approach the cage of words and attempt to see through to the truth we have encircled.

41 DEATH MAY BE THE price we pay for not heeding our anger, which is a way of saying that we have not heeded our vision.

42 I KNOW NOTHING ABOUT semantics. They may be good, they may be dangerous. What I fear about them is that something bad, something ignoble, the worship of the word which would fall into disrepute if no attempt were made to save it, may in the future receive added worship—the Victorian chair becomes the foam rubber seat. We may accept the word again on the basis we are now beginning to loathe it—a question of good or bad taste.

43 TALK WITH RHODA L. We agreed that psychoanalysts are perhaps the greatest socially accepted psychopaths. The thing which characterizes the twentieth century is its absolute lack of common-sense, common-sense being finally the matter-of-fact understanding of a society (which is of course bad) but also is understandable. It is worldly sense, but worldly sense is no longer enough because the communication between individuals and society, the interrelation, is now broken. Society goes one way; men go another— but privately. So, the lack-of-sense of the twentieth century would never dream of asking what the common-sense of the 19th century (as exemplified by my mother) would question immediately: "How can a man listen to another human being and be both completely involved and attentive, and yet personally unmoved, capable of shifting his attention in the next hour to some other human and performing the same involvement and detachment?" The answer is that only a saint or a psychopath could do this. And since saints are not interested in their position in the world, which analysts most assuredly are, the answer I suspect with the most perfect glee is that the psychoanalyst is a psychopath masquerading as a quiet restrained "sensitive" mildly neurotic, middle-class-adjusted human being. No wonder they get nowhere.

December 17, 1954

44 THE SAINT AND THE churchman are polar in character. The churchman (by which I include most clerics and most church-goers) has a most definite idea of what God is. Whether he conceives Him as a superior person, a force, as love or justice or whatever, the conception is not something he worries about. He merely uses it to nourish his vanity. He believes in God, knows what and who He is, and then proceeds, usually quite practically to do the business of society. The saint is his opposite. The saint is consumed with the idea that God exists. Through all of his soul are the intimations of that. But what God is, he can but barely glimpse. And so his life, his way, his road are a search—he is the adventurer who never moves from a room. And that is where he is kin to the psychopath. For the psychopath is consumed with the desire to explore himself to the end, just as the saint is, but the psychopath conducts his search in the world. Indeed, that is the reason we find the psychopath so fascinating, and why the villain of a story carries our interest. Confronted with the collective soul of man (or whatever one wishes to call it) society can exercise the soul only be dividing it. So it says that saints are good, but of course we are all indifferent to saints. Then it brands the psychopath as evil, as the thing-to-be-destroyed, and allows us our fascination and terror of him. So society wins. The saint is ignored, the psychopath is shunned, and the purity of the human soul is concealed. We are returned to a world where we must be practical, mature, pluralistic, and confirmed in abysmal and false humilities—in return for agreeing to admit that we know nothing, we are offered the comforts, the securities, and the prestige of society.

45 THERE IS NO DEATH-INSTINCT. There is only anger, and we are not born with anger, not unless the mother is capable of communicating her anger to the embryo. What we think of as the death-instinct, which is applied almost always to the act which seems completely irrational and purposeless, is actually the anger of the soul at being forced to travel the tortured contradictory roads of the social world. The meaningless act is never meaningless—its meaning goes too deep. It is the cry of the soul against society, and it has a purpose—only the most irrational cries can appeal to the souls of others. It is the language allowed us. Only the soul can understand their meaning which is why we flee the impulse in ourselves and others, and call it the death-instinct. All words have their echoes, their deep contraries, and what we call the death-instinct is actually the life of the soul, its anger. But to admit it, to face up to it, is the most terrible revolution a human can undergo, for he loses not only all the vanities of his previous thought, his snobberies, his deceptions, but he is likely to lose his friends, his mate, his reputation, and even most probably his ambition.

46 WHAT WORRIES ME TODAY and other days is that I am playing an enormous deception on myself, and that I embark on these thoughts only to make myself more interesting, more complex to other people, more complex to myself. My vanity is so enormous. Perhaps I do all this to demonstrate to my audience that I too can create mystic spiritual characters. But on the other hand, these remarks can be merely my fear of what lies ahead. I love the world so much, I am so fascinated by it, that I dread the possibility that someday I may travel so far that I wish to relinquish it. What is important is that I think for the first time in years I'm growing quickly again.

47 SPENGLER IS A GREAT writer. His startling similarities are indeed similarities. More modestly I see the connection now between such things as jazz, bull-fighting and six-day bike races. Jazz is easy to understand once one has the key, but no one ever offers the key, and it is so simple. Instead of trying to understand the "beauty" of jazz, one should understand it as something which is constantly triumphing and failing. Particularly in modern jazz one notices how Brubeck and Desmond—off entirely on their own with nothing but their nervous systems to sustain them—wander through jungles of invention with society continually ambushing them. So the excitement comes not from victory which is the pleasure of swing (more later) but from the effort merely to keep musically alive. So Brubeck, for example, will to his horror discover that he has wandered into a musical cliché (society) and it is thrilling to see how he attempts to come out of it, how he takes the cliché, plays with it, investigates it, pulls it apart, attempts to put it together into something new (for in every cliché there is an ocean of truth once we truly look at it), and sometimes succeeds, and sometimes fails and can only go on having left his record of defeat at that particular moment. That is why modern jazz despite its apparent lyricalness is truly cold, cold like important conversations or Henry James. It is cold and it is nervous and it is under tension, just as in a lunch between an editor and an author: each makes mistakes and successes, attempts to expand the successes and turn the errors into smaller errors or even successes, and when it is done one hardly knows what has happened and whether it has been for one's good or for one's bad, but an "experience" (a communication between the soul and the world) has taken place. It is also why I find classical music possibly less exciting for that merely evokes the echo of a past "experience"—it is now part of society, one of the noblest parts of society perhaps, but still not of the soul. Only the echo of the composer's soul remains. And besides it consists too entirely of triumphs rather than of life.

48 SWING IN JAZZ IS different. Swing is a distillation of the competitiveness of social life. One follows the patterns, one loafs until it is one's turn, and then one is out and racing in a "jam" with victory as the only end. Is a mistake made? Does one falter? No matter; the purpose is not to turn back, to re-explore, to attempt to convert set-back into progress, but instead to go on, to "ride"— to "go." One is like an automobile driver in traffic who leaves the ensemble of cars and sets out to race, turning corners at hottest speed with no regard for whether a truck is coming the other way. If it is coming perhaps one can swerve at the last moment, but that is around the corner, and the road-race is on. So with bullfighting which is a tableau of the vast competitiveness of life.

49 WHEN SUSIE SPEAKS OF "war," she means strife. And strife is something a child understands very well, for a child is a human whose soul is being pinched, and so a child is always forced to enter the world of plans and manipulations where perhaps it may be able to save a piece here and a dent there of its soul, occasionally by strife, occasionally guile, and often by silence. So, "exile, silence, and cunning" were the tools of a genius who kept the child in him alive.

50 THERE IS A LESSON for me in the above. In a way I know more about jazz now after a month or two than aficionados can know in their lifetime. But that is not because I am exceptional, but because occasionally I have the gift of trusting my instincts and learning about something which interests me. So if I am interested, I can learn an enormous amount in a week or two weeks. If I am not interested I can spend years and never really learn the basic jargon. I have to heed what I have always been frightened of: my lack of caution. That is my special quality—I usually refuse to consider the consequences—and so I continue to learn. Caution is the high priest of society.

51 A REMARK ON WHY psychoanalysts have such difficulty in treating psychopaths. Apart from the dilemma of whether a psychopath with his special knowledge can really bear to enter the world is the other premise that the analyst is a concealed psychopath, and so in attempting to treat the open psychopath an enormous effect is exercised upon the analyst—dimly he senses that his own psychopathy will be revealed if he allows his sensitivity. So his sensitivity clams up, and with it his ability to reach the psychopath.

52 WHEN THE BUSINESSMAN THINKS of an embarrassing overture he may make which has a small chance of success, he thinks to himself, "After all, I'll try it. What can I lose?" And the answer, of course, is himself. But businessmen, most of them, lost themselves a long time ago. The rare ones who generally late in life are trying to come back always attract my sympathy. I realize now why I always like them so much.

53 PERHAPS THE REASON SUSIE was so flat with Millie is that she sensed how little soul Millie has, and Susie can never react nor open to a person with little soul. What I have neglected to say in all my writing about saints and psychopaths is that the psychopath has no soul, or rather has used all the energy and beauty of his soul to destroy the world with the tools of the world. Instead of being entire-detachment-of-soul from society, he is total-engagement-of-soul in society, so children turn away from him.

54 I UNDERSTAND NOW WHAT Danny meant when he said Bea has become a caricature of me. Wise Danny. He understands so very much.

55 THE WORD IS A flat non-conductor put across the infinite variety of experience felt in the fraction of a second. Crudely, very crudely, it is the equivalent of a cheap phonograph's rendition of a note to the sound in all its variation and multitude on hi-fidelity. Which is why many intellectuals abhor hi-fi. They prefer the flat passage of the word.

56 IN THE LARGER SENSE, *The Fifty Minute-Hour* is perhaps a modest book. It does not go far enough. But Doctor Lindner in his partial successes, is a vastly more stimulating, entertaining and important writer in his partial achievements than most psycho-analysts are in their successes. He is one of the very few analysts who, in my opinion, are creative, and this book, written properly around the edges of psychoanalysis, is not only fascinating for its stories, but encourages the mind to lose itself upon speculations and journeys.

57 THE STALINISTS HAVE SNEERED for decades at bourgeois writers, at their concern with mysticism, God, morality, etc. etc. And there is a curious half-justice to what they deride. For it is undoubtedly true that a man turns to such thoughts only when his needs are taken care of. That is the great promise of socialism—that it offers the possibility for everyone to engage in the mystic life, whereas now it is open to only a few. But what is vulgar and unjust is that the Stalinists deny the validity of the "experience" the great bourgeois writers undoubtedly have, and in denying the validity in criticism they proceed from having denied it in life. Orwell says somewhere that twenty years of socialism and everyone could have enough. He is right, but the difficulty is that we shall never be given the twenty years, not until the underground revolution takes place, not until men know in their bones that society destroys their soul, and literally kills them. (For again, anger is released as each arch of the soul is collapsed by the lead weight of society's bottom.) Until then, the bourgeois writers will continue to be blind to the realization that mystic revelation is always destroyed by the world until its opportunities are open to all men, and Stalinists will continue to war against cosmopolitanism, jazz, and, if it ever came up, bull-fighting. For such entertainments are the culture bearers of the hipster, and the hipster is the underground proletariat of the future, eating away at the husk of society.

58 MY CHARACTERS IN *The Deer Park* are called "unsympathetic" by everyone. And how unsympathetic they must be to the liberal pluralist who represents unhappily the best among editors. For after all, none of my characters go to Parent Teacher Meetings; they are not responsible members of the community; they do not debate whether their little good actions will make the world a little better. They are all psychopaths and saints and people torn between the two, and they wrestle for their souls in a most terrible society, and almost always lose them. Certainly, it is a depressing book, but they are not unsympathetic, my characters. They are souls in torment, and *The Deer Park* is a journey through torment. It would be a better book, a greater book, if the journey were even more terrible. I held back on Marion Faye.

59 EQUATIONS: MAN IS BORN with a soul which is part of the collective soul. Society is composed of the net of men's unwilled actions. It is opposed to the soul.

Each child enters the world with a pure soul (probably). (It is worse if they enter with souls already partially destroyed by their parents.)

Society attempts to destroy the soul in order to maintain its stability. The soul fights back. The war between the two is what we call the world which is the battleground between society and the universe (the collective soul—how inadequate are all these words).

Through history up to now the soul of the savage, which was all-soul, relinquished a part of its soul to enable man to battle against nature, for until nature was conquered, at least in its inhospitable manifestations, man was doomed to remain an animal.

The movement of man to find his soul worked its drama upon society, for as society (which is the concretion of the collective surrender of man's will) developed and altered men, removing them further and further from their souls, so did man fight back, occasionally altering society, the movement of his soul (with what endless waste) improving social structure. But usually losing his soul.

The twentieth century marked the point in history where society was ready to conquer nature completely. But the tragedy was that by then the majority of men had virtually lost their souls—they were psychopaths, and leaders, and *unfeeling*. So society instead of being finally conquered by men as was conceived in the original contract, instead drew away from men. The interrelation between man and society was broken. Society went its way, and man (those who had souls) retreated, or gave themselves up to being the machines of society. And the revolution never took place. And its only substitute, its echo, its polarity, was totalitarianism.

War is the symbolic collective act of man's anguish—"They got tired of living at home, and so they went to war." Living at home is not a home; it is a war against society, and when it becomes collectively intolerable, it is turned against society, but a false image of society—the enemy. It is also society's way of not allowing the battle against nature to be won by sheer development of technique. If man wants socialism, and from that, God, he must win it by revolution.

60 THE BIG NOVEL COULD be called *Antacid Analgesic*.

61 I LEARNED A PRACTICAL matter the other day. When negotiations are going on, the Order of Procedure determines to a great degree whether one will get one's point or not. It is critical whether one takes up first the items one is bound to win on or to lose on, depending on the psychology of the opponents and the totality of the situation. So in the U.N. when they argue whether a question is procedural or substantial, it is no mere waste of words among diplomats. They are wrestling for what makes the victory. Their sensitivity to manipulation is as acute as a hipster's ear for jazz. Essentially they are grasping abstract relations. So, too, for politicians, political leaders, athletes, etc. There is no such thing as a big or an important man who does not have some special sensitivity. That is why, try as we will, we are always obliged to respect big men.

No matter how corrupt, they have the special sensitivity, one way or another, which makes for greatness. That's why Bob always adores "name" people. It's far from simple snobbery. He recognizes their special sensitivity.

62 I HAVE ALWAYS HATED sentimentality: mother and children, church, the flag, the nation, the good man, the affirmative novel. And there is a reason. For these are society's bastardizations of what the soul knows. Sentimentality is the abuse of an abuse. It is the abuse of words which are already an abuse albeit a necessary one, so for good cause it was always intolerable to me. For what after all are the respective symbols above. They are (1) the mystery of the creation of life, (2) God, (3) the symbol of the brotherhood of men, (4) the brotherhood of men, (5) the man in possession of his soul, and (6) the vision. But only compare the "vision" to the average affirmative novel with its last sentence, "John stood up and walked up the stairs. Up there she was waiting, and the sun was shining."

I still think the psychopath is close to the saint. He is the saint turned inside out, his soul exhausted upon the world, but let him withdraw from the world (harder for the psychopath than anyone else, for the ghost of his soul which is the only "me" he can feel has to be chased through all circuits of the world), but let him withdraw, and the "dark magnificence" of his life is converted to its echo.

63 THE MEASUREMENT OF TIME is as necessary to society as the vision of space filled and space unfilled is to the soul. So Lipton's, which destroys the sense of time, also destroys the sense of society and opens the soul.

64 ADVERTISING AND TELEVISION AND radio and newspapers and movies, but especially advertising are society's war upon each individual. It is the place where advertising reaches deep into each man's soul and converts a piece of it to society. So there are good ads and bad ads but the good ads must always be studied for they sink deeply into the soul, and we receive them because finally material commodities are like petrifactions of love and of power, the two things the soul seeks for in life, legitimately, finely, the two things for which it entered its contract with society. (Power understood of course as the extension of one's faculties which is noble; but in society we can extend our faculties only by control over other people.)

So, too, do mass entertainers accomplish bastardy. They join men in false brotherhood, link them in sentimentality. But one hopeful sign is that the hipsters have entered mass entertainment, and preach anarchy and disrespect, à la Ernie Kovacs.

65 BECAUSE THE DESIRE FOR material things is natural to man, one can account for the peculiar crippled aspect of bohemians. They have rejected material commodities which is far better than to accept them unquestioningly, but they are warped and tortured with envy of the squares because most of them have committed a violence upon their natures.

66 ALMOST ALWAYS EXPERTS CAN never see the truth because the truth is always revealed by the soul (as a reward perhaps for heeding the anger of the soul) and the expert is a man who uses his talents and his intelligence for the service of society.

67 AT ITS BEST, MY mind is like a tiger. Something slinks through the far brush of my consciousness, and I'm after it on the hunt while sleepier minds go back to drowsing in their lair.

68 OVER AND OVER AGAIN, I discover these days that the big truths are to be found in the little things, and not the big things. So, with cigarette smoking. Dimly, it may be a spiritual experience. One has only to blow one's smoke into a shaft of light, and a universe of space is revealed with gas nebulae meandering through the universe and iotas of dust swimming like stars and planets through the cosmos. Dreamily, it leads one to suspect that in the microcosm, if one could only enter it, there are universes within universes, and within the atom, within the electron, there are still infinite subdivisions, universes, who-have-you. Perhaps for little enormous reasons like this, we find it so difficult to give up our smoking.

December 29, 1954

69 "VESTED INTEREST" IS ENORMOUSLY more powerful than we think. It is society's substitute for the soul, and the abstract man who lives totally in society has no identity, no "I" other than his vested interest. Which in its extreme case is an explanation of the totalitarian personality. It is vested interest which allows us to dismiss other people, to say of them that they are Negroes, Jews, homosexuals, anal-compulsives, hysterics, hicks, city slickers, etc. In effect by putting a label on a person we commit assassination, we cease to allow them existence in our minds. The echo of the word "liquidate" is "to petrifact," and that is what the Stalinist does.

He can kill by categories because the categories have become lifeless to him, no more than concepts.

71 THE GOSSIP IS THE great adventurer without courage to begin—feeling out the world, measuring its retribution, seeking to discover the ends of his own personality, but doing it in the world's way, spreading tales about the wildness of others, because essentially what the gossip wishes to discover is how the world reacts to wildness—whether it is indeed as dangerous to go off on the exploration of his own personality as he senses that it is. Much the same may be said of the person who is without caution—it is just that he is a little further along.

72 WORDS HAVE NOT ONLY echoes, but are many-faceted crystals, each of its phonetics a single crystal. If a crystal be altered or ignored then the whole gives off an echo, but in a different direction for each crystal.

73 THE CONCEALMENTS OF LANGUAGE: Perhaps under Lipton's we do not hear certain phonetics very well. Thus "royal purse" may sound like "royal pus," or "oil pus." But it is possible that each word says many things at once, and language, which is the manifestation of the social contract, contains in its phonetics whole parallel layers of meaning. So, man talks to man, and society talks to man through Aesopian sounds as well as Aesopian words. Perhaps that is why we laugh at the stammerer—the lisper—he is always revealing other meanings of words, and often they are terrible truths. So, by suppressing consonants and vowels, look what we get with Mother. Here are the echos: Other, Mither, Moher (More), Meter (Motor), Mothir, Mothe (Moth); Church: 'Er (Her), Chirch, Chuch; also Urch and Chur.

F.B.I. (of bee I) bee I, of I, of bee—or—be I? if I? if be? Altogether—(If it be I (who is Guilty).)

Cock: OK, Kick, Ok, Coc.

Cunt: Unt, Kint (Can't), Cut, Cun (Gun?).

Fuck: Uck and with different vowels—Fick, Fake, Fahk, Fack, Fehk, Feek, Fike, Foke, Fyuke.

74 THE SENSUAL IS THE soul's sense of the present. The spiritual is the soul's sense of the future. And society is man's sense of the past and of death, and a false vision of the future.

75 THE SENSE OF THE Past—All that is left to us is history which is the record of societies' movements, no more than the fossil remains of what was once alive, no more accurate than the fossil imprint is equal to the living heart of the animal which once was.

76 THERE ARE TWO KINDS of hatred—hatred of what we do not know and hatred of what we love. The first is the hatred we learn from the world, the second hatred is the rage of the soul.

77 THE POWER OF THE word Red in American political life. Americans put into it all their buried sensuality, especially Catholics. Red is simply The Flesh to them, and that is why they call Stalinists (of all people!) free-love atheists. Here we have the hatred of the soul, the hatred of Americans for the deep love they actually bear toward their misplaced idea of what Communism is—the irony is that deep in them they believe Communism, indeed especially Stalinism, is utopia, free-love, free-income, free communion, and all this is Red, it is forbidden, it is flesh.

Echoes of Red: Ed and Re. More significantly, Raid, Rod, Raad, reed, ride, road, rude.

78 THE KEY TO SERGIUS' character which I have avoided all through *The Deer Park* is that he is a *Catholic*. How else account for his impotence, his lust for Lulu, and his fleeing the world?

79 THE BREAKUP WITH LULU at Dorothea O'Faye's party: "And I realized that she was in the hell of knowing as so few people could know exactly what she looked like at every instant, it was cut into her memory by the hundred movies in which she had studied herself, and so she was forced with what pain I could understand only at this moment to see herself always in life as an image on a screen, and understanding this I could have wept for her since I could know that there was nothing for her to do but to criticize, and she was always forced to stare down upon her pleasures from a cold and lonely peak, and that even as she played at being silk and superficial, so she was also a soul in torment, and I had quit her, I had failed her, I had reminded her once again that no man nor any woman could ever satisfy her pleasures. She over-looked them, and stared down, searching for perfection, even as I would always wander and try to discover perfection. That was what we had shared or tried to share; we had looked for perfection together, as all loves do, it was what had kept us lovers so long. But I had understood with sudden humble grace that my idea of perfection was to be able to love everyone, and that was not her idea, not yet, not for a long time. So the illusion of a common search which is always the contract of loves was breached, and we were left apart, she on her mountain peak, I to wander the valleys."

82 IN ERROR THERE IS also truth. Truth is defined as completely by error as by truth. It is just that it is regarded from the wrong direction.

83 EITEL AND ELENA—LAST CHAPTER. What comes out is that in the fight with the analyst what she was worried about was that Eitel was not going anywhere, and Eitel senses with the self-honesty which was the last virtue left him, that now there was nothing for him but to hold her back, that in her inarticulate way she was a radical, she went to the root of things—which was why he first had been drawn to her, why he needed her now (for without Elena he would lose his honesty) and it was also why he could never truly permit her to grow, for if she grew she could only grow away from him.

84 DON BEDA. PERHAPS A scene with him and Marion and Elena. Not explanation. Just some view into his character, some sense of how he thinks, and what his battle is. For Beda is not merely a social satyr, he is also an adventurer.

85 INTERPRETATIONS OF PRESENT EVENTS once from our knowledge of how similar courses ended in the past. For example, knowing a man was a drunk, and died as a drunk, we say that drink is bad—but the bold spirit who drinks knows in some part of himself that the end, *his* end, is not known, and so he ventures ahead leaning on the private, the *unique* interpretation that human life is enormously various, and the end of his adventure may be different from all the ends which befell other men like himself who went off on similar adventures. What he believes is that tragic ends do not necessarily follow his actions. (Which is why the fall of such men is always tragic, for the heart of human endeavor is buried here.) What I have drawn above is the psychology of the saint, the artist, the criminal, the mad perhaps, the athlete, the warrior, the revolutionary, the entertainer, the libertine, the drug addict, the gambler, the alcoholic, the demagogue, and all the other varieties of the adventurer, the explorer. What characterizes them is that they have the boldness to believe that they are truly unique, and will not necessarily be punished like others because the world is not finite, the sun does not inevitably come up each morning, their actions cannot be interpreted in advance by the statistical end because truly, for them, there is confidence that the end is unknown.

Also true of the victim (who is the optimist), the victim who believes that he or she is unique and so will not be impoverished by the drunkard, raped by the sadist, murdered by the murderer. The victim is the passive complement to the adventurer. My mother as victim, my father as adventurer.

I, who have always been the adventurer (although enormously suppressed) have never been able to have love affairs with victims—they are too much like my mother. So I have searched out women who were adventurers—which is why virgins have never appealed to me. And all my affairs can be interpreted in this light. Those women who seemed adventurers but ended up in my mind as victims, I fled. Those women who were completely adventurers frightened me, as viz the Yipper. Bea and I broke up because she became too much the independent adventurer and that was intolerable to both of us. Adele and I have the big one of our lives because Adele who is half-adventurer like me, has wedded her sense of adventure to mine, and consents to be the victim because she can thereby find the most adventure. So the longer we are together the deeper is our bond.

86 MY FEELING ABOUT SEMANTICS may be correct. Arguing last night with Jean Malaquais I asked him if semantics are opposed to mysticism, and he said absolutely. Certainly as he presents it, they are.

87 ONE THING MUST BE said about the adventurer. He or she always has a very strong urge from the soul. Far from being superficial or undependable as they appear in life, their motivations always come from the deepest levels. See note **71**. The gossip is a passive adventurer.

91 WOMEN WHO ALWAYS HATE to have their make-up messed wish to keep a part of themselves inviolate—they do not wish to have *that* dirtied. Thus, ultimately, they can never be reached, and one does well to stay away from them, unless one is also inviolate, private, and insulated, and so seeks such a non-mate.

92 THE MORE KNOWLEDGE ONE has of one-self (soul knowledge) the more difficult it is to live in the world, for the more intolerable it becomes that the world is as hideous as it is.

94 THE SPY (ANOTHER ADVENTURER). The spy loves each half of his double life, and obviously could not live nearly as well without each necessary half. My love of opposites leads me to suspect that the side among which he masquerades is usually more real to him, more loved, than the side he is nominally working for.

95 ACTORS AND SPIES. WHAT is critical for the spy is to choose the right side, the victorious side, for otherwise he loses his life. For the actor, what is critical is the right part. But actors' lines are printed on *sides*, and we say of a part that it has twenty-one *sides*. In both cases, the spy and the actor, what is searched for is psychological victory, and their choices and actions have absolutely nothing to do with conventional morality.

97 "AM I BORING YOU?" someone asks, and *boring* has its two meanings, to be flat and to be piercing. What we really say is "Am I piercing you, am I not allowing you to live?"

98 So, BOREDOM, DEPRESSION, LAUGHTER, habits, are the camouflaged manifestations of the soul, and tell more about a person than rage, pleasure, sorrow, etc.

99 SAINTS AND PSYCHOPATHS. I had better define psychopath. The criminal psychopath, the assassin, is merely a special case of the psychopath. What characterizes the psychopath is that the present moment, the present person or thing or action which accompanies him is more real than anything which has gone before or will come later. The violent act is not so much the unfeeling act as the *present* act—one suspends all sense of consequence, one suspends one's view of society. So, there are psychopaths who will never kill a fly, but who must nonetheless wander through each experience without sense of the past or future, committed to the present experience, finding it more vivid than anything before or since. In a peculiar way, a bureaucrat, and his extension, a totalitarian, is a petrified psychopath—he gives to the office, the machine, the party, the enormously vivid sense of the present reality. Instead of using the present experience as soul food—the psychopath is always ravenous—the bureaucrat serves the present experience into the mirror of his soul, the office, and obtains his reaction from the way it bounces back. The saint is the opposite end of the spectrum—the present is insignificant to him—he sees all people and all things as part of the past and much more as part of the future. This spectrum, which I believe is the spectrum of the human soul, is present in all people in varying degree, surfaceness, and intensity. Most people have the saint-psychopath so deeply buried in themselves that they are for most of their lives or all of their lives simply social animals, and never adventurers.

100 LAUGHTER IS SPIRITUAL AND yet despairing. We laugh when we recognize a great truth and in the same instant conceal it.

101 THE PSYCHOPATH SEES THE present the way a saint sees the past and future. To the psychopath the present is enormous, all-important, infinite in its sense of the exploration, combinations, and discoveries present in even the exchange of a word.

102 SO THE HIPSTER IS the adventurer beneath the surface of society, the murderer who moves among social animals. And he is also the saint, but he dreams of a heaven on earth. So *predictions*: Hipsters are the proletariat of the future.

103 GIVEN MY INTELLECTUAL VERBAL mind, Lipton's was a great aid. To a poor bootblack, it probably can do no more than ease him from an intolerable existence into a cloudy nothingness. That is my great adventure with Lipton's. I will journey into myself with the hope that I, the adventurer, can come out without being destroyed. But I am terrified. I don't think I have ever been so frightened in my life.

104 A POSSIBILITY OCCURS TO me on *The Deer Park*. To wit, Marion Faye starts sending his journal to Sergius—in prison he has finally made it on Lipton's. So, when *The Deer Park* ends, Sergius appends an addition in which he says that now he is finished as author and must become editor. There is this flood of notes from Marion Faye, and he has not the courage to rewrite his novel in view of this new information. So he submits it to the reader who may have been bored, irritated, or enthralled by *The Deer Park* itself, and he invites the reader to read it, and if it interest him, to then reread *The Deer Park* and see it as Marion Faye would have seen it.

105 MARION FAYE NOTE. Two men created my mind: St. Augustine and the Marquis de Sade.

106 NOTE **103** COULD BE the last lines of Faye's journal.

107 MARION FAYE'S NOTE: RE: Teddy Pope, he's beautiful, the poor bastard. (Then an expansion of the note on the idea of how beautiful men go homo out of cowardice, because so much sex is open to them as heterosexuals and they have such sexual souls that they retreat into homosexuality where at least it can all go on underground.)

108 MARION FAYE ON EITEL: He wanted to be a celebrity and he wanted to be a great man, and the poor finch loved both so much that he ended by being neither.

109 MARION FAYE IN PRISON starts doing weight-lifting and gets his friends to smash his face. His aim when he leaves prison is to weigh 200 pounds, all muscle, and to have a changed smashed face. Then he can approach the world the other way.

110 SERGIUS IS MY BROTHER whether he knows it or not. That is why I send him my journal.

111 MARION FAYE JOURNAL. IT begins with following note: "I have finally started to make it on tea. Three cheers and over for the institutional life. Tea flows through this place like ice water in a first-rate hotel. And things are beginning to come clear to me. To really make it, I should put nothing into words, but I still want to try. I suppose what I suspect deep-down is that I'll never make it, but I want people to respect me for how close I came. I, too, am a slob."

112 MY JOURNAL AGAIN. ANXIETY is the noise man makes as he flees his soul.

114 MARION FAYE JOURNAL. THE last note. To the effect that he is frightened, but he is going to stop writing and try to make it. Last line: "I weep at night—I am so terrified I shall go mad."

115 (MY JOURNAL) ARROGANCE. To declare that one's previous works were bad is also arrogance for it assumes that one's present works are good. Yet, arrogance is better than indifference, for indifference is the drugged sleep of the soul, while arrogance is the record of a man's struggle against his soul, and by so describing it there may come the day when he will find it.

116 HUMOR IS MORE THAN wit, for wit appeals only to the intelligence, but humor goes to the soul, and the body shakes from it in horror and delight.

119 THE FEAR OF BEING ridiculous is the triumph of society and the secret of its strength. Our fear of being ridiculous puts our thought in defense, our bodies in awkwardness, and sends us clattering on the way of anxiety, fleeing our souls.

122 ANY ART-WORK WHICH IS considered by many to be good and by the rest to be bad must be either very good or very bad—it can hardly be mediocre.

123 "DO YOU KNOW, SERGIUS?" Lulu asked, "Underneath it all, you're really a very strong person."
I was of course tremendously pleased, but I have to admit I did not have the faintest idea of what she was talking about.

124 DOROTHEA O'FAYE COULD FIGURE prominently in Marion Faye's journal—thus closing the book with the same characters with who it began.

125 I AM GETTING WHOLE bodies of inchoate thoughts about Time, Time which is the conceptual chain of society, just as Space is the domain of the soul and the saint, and Force the arm of the psychopath. But it seems to me, as the transcription of the Lipton notes from last night will show here and there, that past of the crisis of the novel is that it uses society's concept of Time which means that the novel cannot liberate itself from Society and truly set out on what is its noble aim—to be the searcher for the meaning of human nature. When we condense Time, when we *select*—which is the word taught in all writing courses, we are using the trick by which society conceals the nature of man, we condense, we say of a man that he is a bad man, and fifty years of his life are put into a word. The movements of his soul with and against society are taken from us. Perhaps the secret to writing a great novel is to deliver oneself from Time, as I first dimly glimpsed it in my eight part novel—in other words we go beyond the limits of time by devoting a thousand pages, let us say, to all that goes on in a man in a day, an hour, or ideally, given sufficient genius, in an instant. That was what Joyce was working toward, and Proust, and in lesser degree Mann and Gide—and that is why we sense their greatness. But now to the notes of last night.

126 THOUGHTS. ALL THOUGHTS IN words are probably part true and part false. In other words there is no such thing as one person saying something about another person which is not true for them somewhere in their personality. Of course the person who declared the trait usually has it more powerfully than the one so described.

127 PEOPLE WHO MAKE LOVE without ever having a thought other than sensation (the psychoanalyst's dream "genital character") are not as healthy as they seem—they have a species of detachment; their minds cannot flourish with their bodies.

What we call the detached man is the man who fucks while he thinks of something else—neither the fucking nor the thinking is anything but second-rate, depressed, and uneasy.

But the man or woman who is unified sexually, creative sexually, thinks most brilliantly while they fuck most brilliantly even if all they are thinking about are the beautiful orgiastic permutations of fucking. Their body and their mind each fecundate (Bob's word) the other, and they soar upward on to stimulation beyond stimulation. Most of the so-called healthy people are actually only half-healthy, they can enjoy themselves only by suspending their minds. Once they are through fucking, they return to society. I believe that the "genital character" cannot be found in any person today who is highly developed and "sensitive."

128 GET A TAPE RECORDER for Lipton's soliloquies.

129 WORD ECHOES: WE HAVE had overlook and over-look, boring and boring (piercing). Now, fuck. Fuck means the act and it also means a nugatory word. We say of something that it is "No fucking good"—which also means that if there is no sexual experience or meaning within it, then it is truly no good at all. We say in a rage, "Get the *fuck* out of here"—It is our way of saying, "Get the sexual emotion, connotation, threat, out of my presence."

"What the fuck do you know?" If you don't know anything about fucking, we are saying, then indeed you know nothing at all.

And "The whole fucking world," because indeed the echo of the whole world are the only soul acts allowed man—his separate private fuckings, his soul communions with himself and with others.

130 ON THE UNDERSTANDING OF genius. We think of a genius as always succeeding during those times when he is creative, but actually the genius succeeds and fails, often in successive moments in that his genius is to do something new, to go farther than anyone before, and often he fails that and is merely mellifluous or skillful at a very high level. So the difference between the genius and the mystic is clear—the mystic succeeds or fails with himself or a very small audience; the genius contains his sense of his own soul and his sense of society (his skill, his craft) both at very high levels, and the torment of the genius is that he is so fantastically and variously organized that he can contain two such terribly antithetical elements in his character and succeed in combining them in works.

131 WORD ECHOES. MOTHER AND smother. But smother probably comes From God's Mother or 'S mother. Simply, the church, the high priest, the false saint of society.

Also success and successive. Success is that we break out of time and craft and go some place no one has ever been before. We set up the outward *succession*.

132 SERIOUSLY, TRULY, JUST SIMPLY, doesn't the great dancer wish to dance in the nude, and don't we wish to see him or her that way? Doesn't the great actor or actress wish finally to act before an audience the fuck itself, and indeed the great actor or actress always gives a sense of the fuck? (Marlon Brando, Tallulah Bankhead, Laurette Taylor.) Doesn't the great painter wish to convey the outside and then the inside of the act? Renaissance fabrics and textures and landscapes and nudes, and our modern non-objective art which is concerned with the variations of the soul in the act. Doesn't the great novelist always seek for ways to communicate his amazing knowledge of the sexual act?

But, now look, society prevents all these expressions in everything but the most degraded form. We are only allowed stripteasers for the dance, whores for the circus act, cheap drawings for the art, cheap pornography for the literature. Only in perversion is the sexual and creative soul of man allowed to express itself.

134 JAZZ IS MORE CREATIVE, more responsive to genius than classical music—but its origins are degraded and its expression is invariably degraded. Truly, only in degraded forms can genius express itself today. Jazz is to classical as the whore is to acting, the stripper to dancing, and so forth. It is degraded expression.

135 I USED TO BE outwardly a mild psychopath, inwardly enormously moral and severe on myself. Now, outwardly I'm moral (almost saintly I love my friends so much) and inwardly my mind races far, wild, and furiously like the psychopath stalking the present, letting nothing pass my ken. The tiniest most insignificant gesture or remark opens a world to me. (This could be a note for Marion Faye, too, who realizes that Lipton's left him unaffected before because he was afraid of the intellectual consequence—he would have to set out to be a genius or a saint.)

137 THE WORLD ALLOWS US to express our creativity only in perversion. Just as jail expresses the passions of life and its real buried tendencies.

138 MY AMBITION REMAINS MY contact with the world, and perhaps it is not all bad—I would certainly prefer to be a genius than a saint. That is why Bob is right about the petty Hitler in me. I have to do it all, all by myself only with Adele and Bob and Dan (and Malaquais and Devlin) if only they could come around, can I see a collaboration of love. With the others, I am competitive. Every bit of evidence I see, as in television, of hipsterism makes me worry, "My God, somebody may do it before I do it." No fear of me becoming a saint.

139 I THINK THAT THE new styles—in clothing—the short haircuts of women especially express the tendency (in the air) of all men and all women to love one another sexually, orgiastically, without regard of sex. Everywhere I feel the tendencies of hipsterism which is the euphemism for genitalism.

140 SEXUAL PSYCHOPATHY WOULD BE normal sex if the chains of society were broken—that is why society attacks sex so violently. Divorce is the first statement of orgiastic verity—so the church fights it. All churches say, "Be content." They are always opposed to change for they are the bastardization of the soul in society. Freud went very far, and indeed he started on cocaine I suspect, got his first intimations of the caverns below. He was a very great man, but no great man can do it all, and Freud stopped short for which one can hardly blame him. (Look what happened to Wilhelm Reich.) Freud stopped with the idea that society is good rather than that society is necessary until man conquers nature, but the society must in its turn be conquered or man will be destroyed.

141 WHAT I LEARN ABOUT *The Deer Park* these days. I wrote it in such depression because the whole book is a lie. I put my ideas, my real ideas in the most degraded characters. I made Beda a monster, and Marion Faye. Ah. Look. Marion, practically reads as Norman if one spells it backwards. All the letters of Norman are present with the addition of I. I really was saying I, Norman, and I kept wondering where Marion came from. *The Deer Park* is an attempt to deal with and to conceal from myself that my great enemy, my all-out enemy is the Catholic Church who has stolen the sexual soul of man. And Eitel—I tell. Teppis—The eppis, the skin, the man who is all society. The piss.

142 MOST CELEBRITIES ARE PEOPLE who have had talent or genius in some direction, and terrified of where it might lead them, for genius is *always* pitted against the world, they have cashed in their talent or genius for the rewards of the world. He "sold out" has deep meaning. It doesn't mean he sold himself as a slave—although that too is true—it means he or she has sold their substance.

143 MARION FAYE'S JOURNAL. HELL is the present. It is always here. It exists in order that man may find Heaven. But man-as-slob dreams of leaving Hell for no more than Purgatory which is Security—the false sense of the future as opposed to Heaven which is the vision of the future.

144 ANYONE READING THESE NOTES would exclaim at my paranoia which rides through these notes on a wave. Three cheers for my paranoia. It is the true measure in every man of great sensitivity—one's sensitivity to the wrath and retribution of society if one attempts to change it because one knows it is false, and does not suit the need of one's soul. Society's great lie is that man is evil and society protects men from one another's evil. All evil is created by society, and man is good.

145 AT THE POINT WHERE Eitel thinks, "Oh, how I'm degen- erating," there could come to him the thought of Marion Faye speaking over his shoulder, and saying, "No, my friend, you are beginning to grow, but you are much too terrified of that." All of *The*

Deer Park is the wrestle I made with myself to protect myself against quitting the values of the world in the false but nonetheless vivid way I held them. Thank God I lost. *The Deer Park* is a failure, but I have discovered myself.

146 THE UNIVERSE IS A vast puzzle, and man communicates in society as a code-maker. His soul allows him to be the great code-breaker. God is both.

147 IN NEW YORK, IF we want the time, we dial N E R V O U S.

148 TIME IS THE SENSE of society. Novelists are always *social*, or at least were until the 20th century. But the sense of time defeats the novel, and the substance of that struggle is what makes "literary style."

149 THE SO-CALLED DECADENT WRITERS are doing what I did in *The Deer Park*. They express their real ideas in degraded characters. They lack courage as I have lacked courage. Proust too lacked courage which is why his homosexual characters were invariably degraded. Joyce had courage.

150 WILD THOUGHT. THE ATOM bomb may actually have kicked off hipsterism. What I read about antibiotics gives me this wild speculation.

152 WHAT STALINISTS SEE IS the enormous lengths the world will go to stop them. That is their paranoia. It is not that they are wrong in essence but like all psychopaths they have no sense of time other than the present, and so they mistake the eventuality for the reality.

153 DON BEDA SHOULD BE a television producer. It is no accident that the balling crowd in New York revolves around television.

154 TIME AS THE SENSE of society. When we break out of time, when we are not regular in our habits, we have the exhilaration of fatigue or of being up all night. *The Naked and the Dead*

(After the storm wrecked his tent—"Goldstein felt the kind of merriment men know when events have ended in utter alienation.")

155 BOB LINDNER. AS HE reads this note, he is going to think I am sniping at him again, and he doesn't understand my feelings here. I am not sniping at him—if I were, I would not send him these notes, for my competitive feelings would say, "He may take them a step beyond you, and he'll get the credit." But Bob is one of the few people I don't feel competitive toward. I feel we could have a Marx and Engels relation, and leave the matter of who's Marx aside until we both have grown. But what I realized today in thinking about *The Fifty-Minute Hour* is that Bob's problems in creativity are the same as mine—his work, like mine, is the defense against letting go. For instance, I have come to realize that Bob's therapeutic methods and styles are comparatively as old-fashioned as his literary style. They are as heavy and inadequate to his sensitivity as is his prose. Bob, like me, is wild in his ideas, but conventional in his treatments of ideas. And what we both need is to loosen our treatment. So, after a bold beginning, with hypnosis, Bob has given it up, although a part of him is always drawn to new therapies, Rosen's, Reich's, etc. I wonder—this is wild—if hypnosis is actually not better than free-association. Analysts never gave it a chance, they were terrified of the consequences, because hypnosis which is what I believe I get in some form under Lipton's, opens man to his soul, immediately, powerfully, and perhaps *irrevocably*. Since few people have the situation or the resources to live with their soul, which means to war against society, hypnosis is indeed dangerous, but is it dangerous for the exceptional person? I suspect not. I suspect that techniques with drugs, hypnosis, group therapy, even orgiastic therapy, are inevitable for the future.

156 THE HOMO-EROTIC COROLLARY. THIS is for Bob Lindner. And with his insights he always goes smack like a wonderful comic figure (comic in the great sense) into the center of the problem, and then moves out again, or will until his Good Luck fails him, and Bob wants his Good Luck to fail him, and the Devil to take over. Kid, it's Verlaine and Rimbaud all over again.

I start with the premise that all men and women are bisexual. I believe this is natural. It is true for animals, and it makes sense, for love is best when it's unified (at last I find some agreement with the analyst although what a difference) and when we love someone we would make love with them if society did not prevent it or make it so painful. Given my premise, the pure heterosexual is a cripple—society has completely submerged one half of his nature.

And this is usually any originality of mind. So, too, is the pure homosexual—and I suspect that pure homosexuals are invariably very unfleshly. People like Gide, Ivan von Auw, etc. They are mind, they have denied their bodies, and sex is invariably painful to them, although in recompense their minds have saintly qualities. (Gide and Gertrude Stein).

But the bisexuals who have a very strong sense of sex in their souls, of the creatively sexual content or quality of their souls, which we describe crudely by saying this person is sexy or vital, or seductive, usually leads a life which is nominally heterosexual. Thus, I who am profoundly bisexual, have not had a homosexual contact since I was fourteen; so, too, Jonesie; so, Adele; so, Bob; so, Johnnie (I think); so, Adeline; so, Bea; so, Gandy; so, Miles and Barbara Forst; so, Mickey Knox. He fled the consequences of bisexuality.

On the other hand, there are many bisexuals who seem to be entirely homosexual. Toby, Mike, camps, queens, and athletes. Invariably, they are handsome men, who in their adolescence began to sense with inner terror what it meant of have sexual soul in a sexless society. It meant that their instincts to screw many women and, too, many men (*and the ease with which they could do it, given their beauty*), would bring them into outrageous conflict with society, violent conflict with society because *finally* the tendency of the bisexual person is to look for the orgy which at its best could be the physical expression of the communion of souls.

But in the world, one need only mention the orgy to see and feel the dangers. So, the bisexual who often choses homosexuality unconsciously because it is safer, despite its obvious disadvantages, than the open bisexual life, or even the wild heterosexual life, yet, and this is the core of it, the monogamous life was too unsatisfying for them. As homosexuals, as camps, they could have all the orgies, all the promiscuity their souls truly needed, their immediate sexuality demanded. And, this, I believe accounts for the great dichotomy in homosexuals which Bob Lindner put his finger on so exactly. There are monogamous unfleshly mindish "pure" homosexuals, and there is a larger world of frightened bisexuals who masquerade psychically as homosexuals because in homosexuality they can express their essential and unrootable desire for combinations, experiments, creativity, bright clothing, the ornamentation of love, and so on.

The homo-erotics are the true "gay" people, just as the "pure" homosexual is the "queen." He is an egg-head, an intellectual.

157 THE COROLLARY OF THIS is the Stalinist who in the better forms is a man with a soul which feels acutely the outrages of society. But the good Stalinist like Charlie Devlin cannot make the full repudiation of the world, it is too terrifying, and so he takes the half-repudiation of Stalinism, which with all its frightful restraints and smothering, because he is terrified that to relinquish the world completely is to mean madness. And this is society's last weapon, the one which indeed is working on me now. For the first time in my life I have come to realize that I, too, could go mad or commit suicide. I do not really believe it, I spend most of my hours in ebullience and enormous inner excitement, but there are moments at night when I am simply, soulfully happy that Adele is there, and that she understands me, and I can turn to her, and say, "Baby, I'm scared."

158 WHAT COURAGE ADELE HAS. She is as scared as I am, but she has faith in me. She knows I have to go this way, that I have to push to the end, that it is the basic expression of my character, and I tried to hide it in Croft, and in Hollingsworth and Lannie and McLeod, and in Lovett and Sergius, and finally in Marion Faye, and because I didn't succeed in hiding it, and have now discovered myself, I have to go on and make the attempt to be a genius, although all the odds are against that for any one person no matter how brave, no matter how talented. At least I have the conviction of my talent, but Adele has not yet found the conviction of her talent— which I've come to believe she truly has—and so she has nothing to sustain her but her magnificent love for me.

159 WHAT TERRIFIES ME IS exactly this: I am shoving off into a total reevaluation of everything, I am declaring to myself (because I believe it) that I must trust what my instincts tell me is good rather than what the world says is good. Our fear of the ridiculous is society's polite way, its subtle way of telling us, that if we go beyond the ridiculous and cease to be afraid of it, the second price may be death. So, I feel as if I am about to embark on the second Freudian expedition into the unknown, and so far only one man, Freud, succeeded without paying for it in madness, death, or prison. *But I feel optimistic.* I feel that I can do it, and so I'm going to try. For the first time in my life I feel that I can be a great writer—I never really had that confidence before. I thought *Naked* was an imposture, and in a way it was—I was hiding behind it. But my real nature has been not to hide, but to go forward, and this I'm going to do.

160 THE FUCK NOVEL, *Antacid Analgesique.* The form could be the Fuck, The Orgy, and the Masturbation, the Two, the Three, and the One. The man and the woman produce the child (the orgy as the dramatization and communion of the man, woman, and child) and then the isolation of masturbation which is solitary communion. And out of solitary communion comes the Fuck and the trip around the circle begins again, Two, Three, One, Two, Three, One, etc.

161 IF THIS RECORD IS to have any value, I have to be truthful, and today after a considerable New Year's weekend, I am definitely down. A reaction to too much Lipton's, too much fucking, simple and in combination, too many confessions, too many enthusiasms, too much talking, too much thinking—I feel exhausted, depressed, unpleasant, dirty . . . and relieved. Because although I'm depressed, the fear that my manic mood was a prelude to insanity seems to have gone. The world is around me again, problems, distastes, small worries, small revulsions, and mainly depression. But even as I'm writing this, my mood is picking up. For I had too much Lipton's last night, and by now I should know that too much leaves me with a bad hangover, and disgust at all the psychopathy I uncover in myself.

162 ONE OF THE CURIOUS effects of Lipton's is that it seems to take away my neurosis and expose me to all that is saintly and psychopathic in my character. Just enough Lipton's, and being alone with Adele, and the psychopathy is pleasantly expressed in fucking, and afterward I feel truly saintly and love everyone and am filled with compassion for mankind. But when I take Lipton's after being pretty strenuously fucked-out, especially if people are around, then the amount of psychopathy in me is frightening—I could fuck anyone, including my sister, I could go on an orgy with anyone, I feel cold and confident and capable of pushing anyone into anything, and of course like all psychopaths I become enormously convincing and hypnotic in my effects on others.

163 WHAT I DISLIKE SO much in myself today is that I'm no more than an intellectual demagogue—trying to rouse people to hysteric pitch in the cause of new wild ideas.

164 PERHAPS A MAN KILLS because deep within himself he senses that if he does not kill another, he will soon kill himself.

166 A PSYCHOPATH EXPANDS ONE element of the emotional spectrum to full size. For example he will see the bona-fide sexual content in everything, but he sees it virtually to the exclusion of all else, and he sees it paranoically, i.e., as filling the world, filling the consciousness of the item's creator, the item's audience, and of course, himself. In that sense, television is almost totally psychopathic, and that is part of its fascination. It creates such an enormous present.

167 ANY HUMAN SCENE, SUCH as saying good-bye, which is protracted beyond its due length, is of course just alive with sexual implication.

168 PRECISE SPEECH APPEALS ONLY to those who know what is being talked about, and are interested. The cliché, while it repels many people, actually has appeal across a vast spectrum. Precisely because it contains many meanings, and each can put into the cliché large portions of his own experience, the demagogue always speaks in clichés. I, as an intellectual demagogue, probably do no more generally than reinvigorate intellectual clichés. Man, am I down on myself today.

169 OUR FEAR OF GHOSTS and spirits may be our fear of all the truths (the human sensitivities) we have ignored in life— we feel we shall be punished for overlooking them. So the beggar we pass on the street may well become the monster in our dream. This is perhaps the deeper meaning of *A Christmas Carol.*

170 ON THE OTHER HAND, people who love spirits and ghosts and hope they exist are the people at one end of the sensitive spectrum whose sensitivities have been abused all through life.

171 THE SENSITIVITY SPECTRUM: To the poet, words are not only important, but he is even driven to tear up the individual word and try to find more meaning within. The general speaks in sentences so predictable that they are the equivalent of one word. For example: "Greater productive techniques are at the heart of delivering X bombs to Y target with maximum saturation, accuracy, and density." There are really only four words in the above sentence. Which occasions me to wonder if there has ever been a general in modern history who was also a decent poet. I believe not. Totally not. One kills individual people in order not to commit suicide, but one orders the deaths of vast quantities of people because life is always seen conceptually—in other words, the general has taken the life of the people to be murdered away from them by his mind, before he even gives the order. He is merely altering statistics. There have of course been writers like Malraux and Gary who have been good soldiers, but they were adventurer-soldiers, not bureaucrat soldiers.

173 ON TELEVISION, MANY OF the ads have their psychopathic appeal because the film is speeded up which makes the voice sound shriller. Listening to it on Lipton's, the voice is slowed down, but the high shrill-tone remains. There may be something to the whole business of frequencies, trebles, bases, fidelities, etc. In other words by altering electronically the quality of voices, advertising agencies may have discovered that better effects are produced. I think it's also probably true that psychopaths generally have subtly shrill taut voices—it's undeniable that hipster speech contains a fucking rhythm in it almost as powerful as music—I truly believe that I could fuck to the sound of a psychopath advertising anything, cleaning fluid, spark plugs, whatever, but apart from the meaning the rhythm of his voice is like a compelling beat. (Very syncopated speech.)

174 THERE IS ALSO THE possibility as a wild speculation that we are all of us receivers and senders of electric waves, and that our sensitivity, our response to others is indeed electric—we can tune in on some, we cannot on others.

175 LISTENING TO DIZZY GILLESPIE last night I thought he was a genius.

177 I SUSPECT THAT AN index to how close psychopathy exists beneath the surface may be taken from how readily a person takes to Lipton's the first time. The more they do, the more psychopathic they are.

178 Psychopathic love. Judging by myself, I would say that in the state of pure psychopathy, love is impossible, *but* the pure state is rare, and the psychopath in happy moods does borrow from the saint, and I have often loved in large sweet ways, overcome by the beauty of my mate, and willing to accept anything and everything in her.

179 Consider whether Elena after the car wreck could run away into the night screaming. "Why didn't you love me, Marion, why didn't you love me more?"

180 Sports and sex. The dive is the moment of orgasm, and the great diver is incapable of enjoying orgasm except in the sublimation of the dive.

181 Musicians. The saxophonist is the cock-sucker, the trumpeter is the ass-hole blower, the guitarist is the diddler, the bullfiddle man is the gooser, the drummer is the ass-beater, the pianist—??

182 Steve Allen talking while above his head girls walk by so that one sees them only from high-heeled shoes to the tips of their thighs. "If any of you folks have *eaten* in the last half hour I don't want you looking at the set." Right now he is giving a show in a pool at Miami Beach and the total effect is openly orgiastic.

183 I heard "The Star-Spangled Banner" sung by a chorus over the radio, and the music was so arranged that the total effect of the sound was like the anguish of angels in hell— which is certainly a far cry from the usual "Star-Spangled Banner." Undoubtedly, instinctively, some slick conductor did it that way to filter into people the patriotic agony of our time. Slick artists are geniuses in their insight into society (rather than into man). Anybody great at anything, even great at knitting, is the possessor of genius in that particular thing and has experiences different from anything we can know.

184 COMPETITION OF PERSONALITY MARKS the 20th century as the competition of economic interest marked the nineteenth century. Modern slick artists as well as serious ones have carried competition to a thing in itself, an artistry in itself.

185 NAME FOR A NEGRO. Washington O. Q. Lewis.

186 BE-BOP CHORUS. HEY HEY OO OO
You got me bee-bopping too.

187 WE MAY ALL HAVE a social image of ourselves, close to the despised image of ourselves. Thus, I always see myself as the sweet clumsy anxious to please middle-class Jewish boy, and socially I admire poise, coolness, manners, elegance. Many of our relations with people consist entirely of our admiration for their social face. Those are the relations where I remain fixed in certain kinds of habit and speech and never can express myself. As it used to be with Ted Amussen, Stan Rinehart, John Aldridge, and many others.

188 PERHAPS THE SECRET OF Marilyn Monroe's success is that she has a just-after-fucked look instead of a ready-to-fuck look. Thus she gives the feeling of sensual after-pleasure and *accomplishment*, rather than anticipation and uncertainty.

189 THIS IS THE AGE of anticipation rather than the age of accomplishment which was the nineteenth century. Thus, deep-down, what people seek today is the reverse of anticipation— simply, accomplishment, security, just as in the nineteenth century the urge among artists and exceptional ones was to rip up accomplishment in order to find anticipation.

190 MEMORY MAY BE A layer of the original actuality. Thus, memories are often sweet because that is the way a part of us (our souls) really felt at the time. As a wild extra, déjà vu may have reality—the soul may actually be capable of seeing into the future, especially if we see human life as extending not only in depth but across time.

191 THERE'S NO SUCH THING as a meaningless remark—at the very least it comes from something or it against something, it contains a psychological reality.

194 BOB TOLD THE PICKLE factory joke about the girl who was the pickle slicer. Its deep meaning is that essentially all production mechanisms employ the frustrated kinetic desires of people to do one thing or another, as the girl who wishes to suck and slice a thousand cocks a day.

196 OBSCENITY ECHOES. COCK AND Coke (Coca-Cola which comes in a phallic container). But coke is also dope in the south, and I have long remarked the "hipsterish" sensitivity of southerners who for close to a century now have been a psychically underground proletariat.

January 20, 1955

199 LOOKING AT MYSELF IN the mirror, high on Lipton's, I saw myself as follows: The left side of my face is comparatively heavy, sensual, possessor of hard masculine knowledge, strong, proud, and vain. Seen front-face I appear nervous, irresolute, tender, anxious, vulnerable, earnest, and Jewish middle-class. The right side of my face is boyish, saintly, bisexual, psychopathic, and suggests the victim.

200 THIS IS THE AGE of the war of the sensitivities. At a seemingly superficial level it is the battle of *Dissent* vs. *Partisan Review* vs. *Commentary*; or Carson McCullers and Paul Bowles and Truman Capote vs. Jones and Early Mailer. On a larger scale it is the deep and furious warfare between first Freud, Adler, and Jung now between Freudians, Reichians, Horneyans, etc. On an historical scale it was the *conflict of sensitivities* (the deep conviction of each that he alone saw the nature of reality) which set off the individual and collective murders in the contest of Lenin vs. Trotsky; Trotsky vs. Stalin; Stalin vs. Hitler—and now with the *Cold War*—the war of sensitivities becomes keyed to its full.

201 WHEN WE RUN ACROSS something we don't understand, and casually throw it out or ignore it, it is because we understand it much too well. This is true of all rejection.

As a corollary: What we erase is what we wish to emphasize. So the good writer crosses out the bad writing (the clichés) with which the ambitious part of his being had hoped to attract the public. Literary style is always the record of the war within a man.

202 THE TRAGIC AIR OF Mexico about which everyone can agree comes from the great need of the Mexicans to have heroes—for without heroes a culture and a civilization will perish. But to use Trotsky's style—Mexico arrives late on the stage of history in its attempt to found a civilization. So its heroes can never satisfy the Mexicans, for their cynicism is the cynicism of the world, and backward countries are equal to civilized countries in their cynicism, despair sets in, and sentimentality must follow to give the false rescue to despair. So the vicious circle revolves while the country slowly starves in its economic and political irreconcilables.

203 RICH BOYS ARE PROUD of being without money, middle class boys are not. The middle class boy who acts the poor life (such as bohemians) really wants to think of himself as aristocratic. Only working class is proud of wealth and power. Which is why the aristocrats admire artists, the middle class successful business men, and the working class admires politicians, racketeers, big trade union leaders and money-making athletes. But here again is the dichotomy of mind vs. body, spirit vs. flesh. There is the deepest significance in whether we make our living with our hands or our minds, and through history moves the myth and probably the actuality of the swarthy stocky sexy proletariat, and the languid slender tall neurotic mind-ness of the aristocracy and the part of the bourgeoisie which aspires to it.

204 "INSTANTS" AND "MOMENTS." THE *instant* when we look at a woman's lipstick on a cigarette butt and feel a moment (a flatness with a ring of almost intangible anxiety). The *moment* is our female identification with wearing lipstick and smoking.

205 JOHN WALSH IS A homosexual who genuinely is happy with "masculine warmth"—simply, the companionship of men. Thus, latent homosexuals of the order of Slim and Glenn and Clem who are masculine hard-swearing adventurers on the surface and who masquerade behind the joy of "masculine company" are drawn to the genuine desire in John.

A note on this is the type of the phallic narcissist who so very often has a name or *nickname* which ends in "n" or "m" or one syllable with a vowel in the middle. Thus, the company of Slim, Glenn, and Clem who look up John—all of whom (except John) call me Norm. Other examples are Jim Jones. I wonder if the general "m" sound at the end of the name is not an echo of Male and Nail. (Echo: Spike and Prick).

It seems reasonable that people in coteries are drawn together by the sound of their names—that is, people tend to like people with certain kinds of names. If the coterie aspect of the personality is strong enough, the coterie is joined which most satisfies the type of personality. But what I wonder is whether such coteries are not worth studying to see if there is a common denominator or several to the kinds and styles of names. Carried to its ultimate the attraction that's felt for the name becomes genuine love and we have The Snob.

206 IF I HAVE QUALITIES of genius, it is because in my case I have never found a home. I straddle many coteries and can never truly join any, yet I have a sensitivity and knowledge for each in myself. But that is why so many people see me as being tortured and nervous and obviously anxious. I have no home, no *roots*—I am indeed the orphan hero of *Barbary Shore* and *The Deer Park*—and so all my anxiety is evident whereas it is buried in other people. And that is why Adele and I were drawn together—for she is an orphan as much as I am.

207 THE PERFECT SECRETARY IS never the wife even though we call her an office wife. Rather, she is the Confidante, and what men seek in a secretary is the woman to whom all can be told. In proportion as the secretary is the perfect confidante so she is the perfect secretary.

As a corollary, I think it's probably true that the sort of high-minded marriage where the mates hope to be able to confide (word echo: confine) everything to each other usually ends in a sexual bust, for part of the nature of marriage, part of the excitement of marriage rests exactly in the fugue of mutual deceptions and mutual revelations which are constantly altering. We fuck to uncover a mystery—in extension it is truly the mystery of life—but in its immediate sense it is the mystery of personality, and there is something tasteless in fucking someone we know too well, which is why marriages which retain their sexual excitement create new elements of deception even as old ones are revealed, and that is also why a man and a woman who have been good close friends for years can rarely strike up a good fuck—they have become instead mutual boss and secretary.

208 THE NIGHT BOB SPOKE about Styron being through as a writer, I have the suspicion he was unconsciously talking to me directly, for I know he was deeply worried about me. Juan Bilbao talking to Bette Ford about Pat McCormick being through was actually warning Bette, and gloating over her future downfall with the part of him that hates Bette for all the abuse she gives him. As a general clue it might be worth noting when we hear a person talking over and over about how someone is through which of the people *in the room* (including the speaker) is really meant.

210 HOW MUCH REAL HATRED there is over sensibility. The person of less sensibility truly hates or loves the person of greater sensibility (or avoids him or her) because what is involved is one's close relation to a larger kind of life—and *it is most intolerable that we be deprived of that.* How much real hatred there is over sensibility. The person of less sensibility truly hates or loves the person of greater sensibility (or avoids him or her) because what is involved is one's close relation to a larger kind of life—*and it is most intolerable that we be deprived of that.* That is why I have always hidden my sensitivities from insensitive people. I was afraid of their genuine hatred.

211 WHAT WE DO ON the surface is a genuine expression of our personality, true for us at some level of our being. Thus if we are friendly to a stranger, and feel nothing consciously, nonetheless we love them with a part of ourselves.

212 IT IS POSSIBLE THAT we say the best thing we are capable of saying at the moment given divergent desires. It is probable that we always do the best thing we are capable of doing at the moment, kill in order not to commit suicide, commit suicide in order not to kill—the best thing we are capable of doing involves the true and false judgment of the psyche, the judgment of the soul and the judgment of society, so that in a curious way the murderer is closer to his soul than the suicide, for what the soul must always say is "Do the thing which will enable you to continue living."

213 OUR PERCEPTION OF OTHERS is never anything other than an exploration of ourselves. Those parts of society we know least about are indeed the parts to which we are drawn least—at any moment of development—and so we see them from the outside, we see *objectively, evaluatively.* The objective sense of society is dependent upon a *lack* of genuine attraction to the subject and insight about it. Somewhere along the way a curious game is played with the self—certain kinds of people take on work which is so alien to them, and yet so necessary in the defenses it provides, that they can be safe for their entire lives, if albeit a bit dead. Which is why academicians are dull—they have given themselves to a subject they are not close to spiritually—usually to hide some other deeper drive of their nature. They conceal the rampant murderer, lover, adventurer, etc. within themselves from themselves. Which would account for why so few editors know anything about books, why so few analysts know anything about human nature, so few sociologists anything about society, why so few anthropologists have a real feeling for primitive peoples, why so few historians have a poetic intuitive sense of history. But one could extend the list forever. The most obviously painful and pressing is the lack of real political understanding among diplomats and bureaucrats, the ignorance of war which characterizes most generals. Indeed, one of the great battles of the twentieth century is that more and more people are *attuned* to their occupations. People with a real feeling for law enter the law, analysts with real sensitivity become analysts, and there is a war mounting between the academicians and the ones with true vocation. The nineteenth century was built upon the solid obtuse blocks of the academicians—the twentieth century is torn by the desire to blast the bricks into dust and the anxiety to retain them.

214 WORD ECHOES. SON IS sin. Like the insane woman who tore off the cortisone label because it was saying sin to her.

January 24, 1955

215 WORD ECHOES. POSSIBLE WAY to handle obscenity. If we want to say lick the nigger's asshole—I could put it—lake the negre's sassoil or like the negra's sass-oil.

216 FRIDAY, SATURDAY, AND SUNDAY were all big days (Jan 21 to 23) and I had so many thoughts, feelings, etc. that I was almost flooded by them. Today, after a ball last night, and too much fucking and Lipton's I am still not depressed which is a good sign. Perhaps the Seconal I took with the Lipton's has a good effect. Anyway, let me see how much of it I can remember, recast, and state for the first time.

217 TO BEGIN WITH, ONE of the great divisions of personality occurred to me last night, and that is, one can divide people generally into takers and givers. Naturally there is an infinity of variations in the duality, and the giver always has his counterpart within himself of the taker, but it is best described by mentioning people. I am essentially a giver and not a taker which is why so many people see me as a bully. Adele is on the surface a taker rather than a giver—except in sex—but that is truly a defense against her great desires to give which would flood her away. Danny is a taker not a giver, so Malaquais. Devlin a giver. My mother is a giver—like me she cannot take, neither advice, nor presents, nor even in a funny way, love—she must give, give, give. Bob is one of those rare people who is both a giver and a taker—primarily a giver, but he can also take which accounts for his healthiness. Larry and Barbara are takers, my father is a taker. Generally, givers are "generous," bullying, dominating, somewhat overbearing, anxious, guilty, lively, self-pitying, compassionate, and apparently open. Takers are secretive, private, often sensitive—especially on what they receive—sly, greedy, subtle, envious, superior in their own eyes, passive, and just as the giver feels anxiety when it is a question of receiving, so the taker has great anxiety about giving. All performing artists are almost pure givers. People with a relaxed tweedy wit are takers. Givers tend to be sloppy or loud in their dress (the sloppy dresser and the loud dresser are the same thing)—takers are invariably neat. Givers express the masculine creative-destroying principle, takers the feminine conserving-principle. The irony is that givers open other people to their souls but takers are essentially closer to their souls. (Dave Kessler is a giver, Anne Kessler is a taker.) Susie worries me because while she is both a giver and a taker both are generally suppressed, and people who suppress both are in for a rocky road. Givers and takers always reveal themselves over things like picking up a check. Whenever I am threatened or have suffered some disaster I pick up every check in sight.

218 How I'm getting to love my journal. It is the refuge. A clean feeling of work comes over me at the thought that I have a full day to give to the journal and do not have to rush around. It is my way of moving from total giver to at least half-taker.

219 Spies are takers, as are snobs. Affected people are givers. There is that subtle distinction between the snob and the fop.

222 Wrestlers and boxers. Another great dichotomy in people. Givers are wrestlers—takers are boxers. It even carries over into love. Boxers are unisexuals, wrestlers bisexuals. The taker likes hard sharp fucking unless they are being done to— like the boxer's rub-down after a fight. The wrestler has his rubdown in the fight. I am a wrestler, and my idea of love is more the embrace, the love-play, the lingering and swelling, rather than the rat-tat-tat of hard fast fucking. And what I remember is that the first orgasm of my life (which was the best) came when I was thirteen and wrestling with a boy.

223 Homeostasis and sociostasis. I am going to postulate that here is not only homeostasis (which is the most healthy act possible at any moment for the soul), but there is sociostasis which is the health of society so that like people, but acting in the reverse direction, there is a sociostatic element in man placed there by society which resists and wars and retreats against the inroads of homeostasis which is the personal healthy rebellious and soulful expression of man. In the course of a human's life the child is born all homeostatic (unless the mother has communicated sociostatic components to the embryo) but generally the years of childhood are years in which the homeostatic principle or life-force is blocked, contained, damned, and even destroyed by the creation of sociostatic elements—the child is partially turned into someone who will serve the purposes of society. The essential animal-soul life is contained, forced underground, denied. But as people get older, there is this great tendency for the homeostatic principle to assert itself—middle-aged people kicking over the traces. Depression is the symptom of trench warfare between homeostasis and sociostasis. War in that sense is not the health of the state (Randolph Bourne) but rather is the desperate expression of sociostasis. Society chooses a terrible alternative, but it is the best alternative open to it, given the worse alternative of society disappearing (from its point of view of course, not mine).

224 WHAT I HAVE NOTICED is that over the years although I have spoken of society as nominally no more than a concept, the fact is that I believe there is such a tangible physical reality as society. As there is material man, there is material society. And I have even been one of the few to attempt to locate society—I have called it over and over the sum of man's actions. But as a wild speculation, I wonder if society does not actually have its material physical presence in life, in the very structure of atoms or molecules or even intra-atom structures. As a crude example, the total presence of building and structures in the world is an expression of society—it is part of the physical principles of society. In other words buildings do have a kind of life (and there is a basis, although of course, inaccurate in feeling ghosts in old houses). What I try to say is that a building is alive but it is not alive like animals or humans or even plants (I'm not at all sure of the last). In other words there are two kinds of life-forms in the universe. Animal forms and socio-structural forms of life, and they war upon one another. As a more stimulating example, I would say that the laws of physics for example are not something static and to be discovered for all time piece by little piece, but that just as man and animals, both homeostatic, evolve, *so too does physics evolve.* The physical laws of today are not the same as the physical laws of five thousand years ago, for example, and certainly not the same as the physical laws of five million years ago. I will put it crudely. Five million years ago one plus one might have been equal to one. Five thousand years ago one plus one were equal to two. Today one plus one is equal to 4? But the answer is certainly not two, thanks to Einstein. What is present in this, and intellectually enthralling is that man, Life, wars against the sociostatic principles of society (Other-Life) and of physics too. Said otherwise, man is not merely a creature of the universe—his concerted creative expression of the life-force alters the universe even as the universe alters him. So that, philosophically, we may be coming upon a time when the circle will be closed, or rather the spiral rounded and man will again see himself as the center of the universe, rather than as the victim of the universe. Put as the Grand Theory of Relativity it comes out thus: As man discovers the universe, so he changes the very laws of its being. I suspect Planck's Quantum theory would throw interesting lights on this if I knew anything about it. Also what Bob said about the nearness of the instruments to the experiment.

225 MY CHARACTER. I HAVE always been a philosopher masquerading as a novelist because philosophy was not a proper expression of our time. It had become the province of takers—scholars—academicians. Cut another way I am the boy sent out by God to do a man's job, the saint who must explore psychopathy. For the sociostatic principle protects itself in times of danger by trying to choose the man least fit to do the job (when it is a question of a human whose total life movement is rebellious, anti-social, essentially homeostatic). So I who was one of the worst soldiers ever to go into an Army, one of the people who had the least feeling for Army life, nonetheless was the one who had to capture the psychology inside and out of the Army. I, who am timid, cowardly, and wish only friendship and security, am the one who must take on the whole world (the small trumpet of my defiance). I, whose sexual nature is to cling to one woman like a child embracing the universe, am driven by my destiny to be the orgiast, or at least the intellectual mentor of orgasm. I, who find it essentially easier to love than to hate; I who could probably find more people to love in the world than anyone I know, am destined to write about characters who are conventionally "un-loveable." I, who in another time would have been the contemplative spirit which filled a cathedral with love, see my soul-duty as the man in the vanguard, the assassin in the night, the demolitioneer, the rapist, the arsonist, the murderer, the great destroyer. No wonder society chose me as the man to go to the end of the night—nobody could be more unfit for the job. Contrariwise, Bob is the psychopath sent out to become a saint. Yet, each of us takes our hard road. As I become tougher, more adventurous, more of a fighter, so Bob becomes more good. I am willing to bet he is a far kinder, more good person today than he used to be.

226 REMEMBER: THE FEAR OF being ridiculous deprives one of more knowledge than the desire to be ridiculous. Turn life on its head, see all the movies upside-down.

227 IN THE JOURNAL OF Marion Faye, the climax of the novel (novel?) should be a prison-break which is frustrated, and becomes no more than a hold-out war with hostages in the attempt to get reforms. The two movements of society—revolution and reform could be explored. Marion of course is the ringleader of the gang.

228 THE MOVEMENT OF MY writing. *Naked* is a saintly book, everything is understood and forgiven. *Barbary* is the attempt to do two things at once. The characters are psychopaths who think of themselves as saints and saints who have acted like psychopaths (McLeod). *The Deer Park* is a parade of psychopaths. I pretend to be condemning, but what repels most people from the book is that I am really saying Rejoice in these people—they are marvelous, they are helping us to destroy the world. *The Deer Park* is perhaps the first successful and almost-honest expression of myself as a saint writing about psychopaths and loving them. But the neurotic little boy clouded the issue and tried to make people think he was condemning.

229 I HAVE ALWAYS BEEN the romantic masquerading as the realist. That is what has given the peculiar tension (word echo peculair for peculiar—in the peculiar there is air, there is life) to my work. Now, as I become aware that I am really an enormous romantic my work may suffer tremendously for some time.

It is certainly true that the style of this journal is almost unremittingly crude mainly because I have so much to say.

230 To CONDEMN. TO CONDEMN. Or NM. Norman Mailer, or in society Mailer, Norman which is MN which is conde Mn. Or cunt and Mailer. I condemn because I see that as a masculine act, and in the past I have been trying to hide my cunt from people. Now I advertise my cunt because I have more confidence in my cock (Do I?) or are the defenses retreating? Anyway, as I expressed in an earlier note, the sounds of N and M are highly masculine, Glen, Slim, and John, etc. And the sound of 'r' is a very active masculine sexual word. It is Red, Rage, Ire, Choler, Rod, Race, Rough, Rail, Roil, Riot. In this sense there are good words and bad words. Words whose meanings and whose consonants and vowels are compatible—there is a *psychic onomatopoeiasm* to them. AngloSaxon is full of this and the focus of Anglo-Saxon-obscenities. Fuck, piss, cock, shit, cunt, prick, suck, . . . and luck. Luck is the loving fuck the universe gives one. And 'L' probably has psychic connotations of tenderness, clinging, fullness—to wit, love, lust, lewd, languish, lair, lie, lady, lass, etc. Now, P and S. Piss and Shit. But there may be a crossing here. Hidden and reversed onomatopoeiasm for Puh is close to the sound of shitting and sssssss is close to the sound of pissing. Thus the Ses and Pes get into words like Shut Up. (Stop pissing and shitting.) Naturally, everything I've said here applies only to English. In other languages there are undoubtedly profound psychic differences in the meanings of sounds because after all the consonants and vowels of foreign languages are never *exactly* identical to English. I'm not enough of a linguist to trace obscenities and nuances of other languages, but what occurs to me in a small way is that our R in English may be conveyed by the JO (pronounced Cho as in Hebrew) of the Spanish. For example angry is *enojo*, and red is *rojo*. Anyway, back to condemn and NM. This entire note came out of the curiosity I felt about leaving out the N in condemning as the last word of note **228**.

231 OUR RESISTANCE ABOUT CHANGING the spelling of the English language, and our teaching of new methods of learning to read by syllables rather than by letters may have profound meaning sociostatically. It may be a sociostatic retreat that the teaching of reading is changing, it may be a sociostatic advance. The little "curiosity" that English is spelled so unphonetically may be a very large and important actuality. I suspect that English more than other languages is very close to expressing psychic onomatopoeias. Therefore we muck it up with spellings which divert us from what is really being said. Thus receipt and deceat (I can no longer spell it)—deceit, and seat. If they were spelled reseet, and deseet, and seat, the echo of receipt—our rage at potential deceit—would be obviously deceit and seat, which is somehow, I feel, tied up with our asses and our ass-holes. It would all be too evident. Countries like France and Spain do not have such vast separations between society and soul—therefore, they can afford to spell more phonetically—their people aren't burning so to close the discrepancy. There may well be a material (that is bio-chemical) basis to such things as National Character—it comes from language. Even in America no one can convince me that Southerners and Northerners are not seriously different.

232 ROJO AND OJO. RED and Eye. Ire and Eye. Ire or Rage are the anger released at suddenly "seeing." We actually say, I saw red. And "rage"—it is the red of age—our fury at how society makes us die. Only man sees death as death. Animals see death as danger. Except dogs. Dogs seem to understand death.

233 MAN AND HIS DOG. Two neurotic beings. For the dog above all animals is capable of being domesticated, and seems to live with the same love-guilt-rage-sorrow axis as man. For the dog like man has two nervous systems—shall we call them *dog*eostasis and *master*iostasis? The dog is not only a dog, he is also his master. Biochemically, his master has gotten into him. That is why we have such contempt for dogs. We say, "What a dog," or "A dog's life." It is because we see ourselves in our tragic contradiction, cowed by society. Dog is God spelled backwards.

234 FOR THREE YEARS WHILE writing *The Deer Park* I felt as if I never had a new idea of any value. Now I have so many I can't keep up with them. My three year depression was indeed the muttering, the artillery rumble of the yeast bottles in my brain.

235 ROMANCE AND REALISM. *Naked* seems to be a realistic journalistic novel. But I was actually taking on the first crude statement of what will probably be the intellectual theme of my life. Those who are *Naked* (homeostatic) and those who are *Dead* (sociostatic). For underneath, as Laughton has been saying over and over, the men in *Naked* are Heroes, and *Naked* is the story of a group of men who each individually makes a terrible journey, a long journey. All of *Naked* is a Journey, structurally, thematically, symbolically. It was prophetic for myself—up to a point. The men (me) that is (Me—N) orman) (Norman—No man but for his R)—his red ruddy root.)

Anyway, Me, the Men, are mired in the jungle, the world, the contradiction, the depression—and then they are sent out to explore, to adventure—they end up climbing the mountain of Philosophy because their leader Croft (What is in his name?) (Coughed, roft—raft, rift, reft, ruft—coughed with rage—and indeed these days my cough is getting milder—Crift, Craft, (Kraft), Crowft, Cryft, Cruft, Crot (Crotch?) and Crof—I can't find anything which seems really revealing.

Anyway, because their leader Croft who is obviously the saint-psychopath in me, just as Cummings is the Affected sociostatic version of Croft and me,—anyway, Croft leads them up the mountain toward God. (Treating them incidentally like dogs, just as I in a part of myself used to treat the rest of me as if I were a dog.) But I couldn't resolve it at the point where I was then. The neurotic Jewish boy had to condemn and put in a degraded form the highest expression of himself—Croft, McLeod, Marion—and so I ducked out the back door, and left the mountain to God, and let the hornet's nest (What a symbol! I sure kicked it open with *The Deer Park*) chase the men down the mountain. Even Croft. But at least he knew that the mountain was Everything. The jungle is depression, the mountain is terror and exaltation.

236 THE SAINT AND THE psychopath are homeostatic rather than sociostatic. But there is one way—so long as there is history (one day we shall have *hissoul* than history)—there is one way the psychopath is superior to the saint. The psychopath is the giver rather than the taker—he may appear to take, to ravish, to steal, to cheat, but actually he is giving—he beats, he thumps, he prods, he wounds, he leaves *his* knife in the victim, he leaves his terrifying presence in the empty bank vault, he leaves his malice in the breast of the *sucker* (What a word. The sucker is always a taker). The saint, on the other hand, who seems to give (when he is so inclined) goodness and charity and works and hope, is actually taking in the psychic sense. He arouses goodness in people, he drains them of wrath, he takes from everyone around him, thereby enabling people to feel alive which is the same as feeling one is good. Hemingway saw it. He always says I felt good for I felt alive (Word echoes: Good and O God; Woe is me and Woman). But, fundamentally, the saint is taking from people, taking so that he may reach God. Which is why deep down we resent saints and admire psychopaths. For saints take from us (they are beyond words and so cannot give) and psychopaths always give. Which is why I like Jonesie. As I always said about him, "When he's around you get the feeling that things are going to happen, and indeed they often do."

237 IN THE SAINT-PSYCHOPATH SENSE, all of human history is the story of the movement of man from psychopath (giver) to saint (taker). If we reach Utopia which is God we shall all be open Takers communing with the Universe.

238 THIS IS THE BEST day I've had on the Journal since I began it.

239 I WAS DEEPLY INSTINCTIVELY right in *Naked* to go in for obscenity. Society fights obscenity because the truths of the universe are hidden in it. Sociostasis forces the truths of the universe to be hidden in all degraded froms. (I meant to say forms, but actually forms are *froms*-derivatives, substitutes.) Our fascination with evil does not come because we, humankind, are evil—it is because evil is the degraded expression sociostasis permits of the good, of the life-force. The abstract social contract (the contract where man abandoned simple forms of social cooperation—where every man knew every other man—the simple social contract) became frozen for Western civilization at least on the massive sociostasis of the Catholic Church which deprived humankind of sex and embodied sex in itself. For what the church said is that the Mystery (of the creation of man) is bodiless rather than body. It said that Life and the Good (God) comes from the joining of the Virgin with The Father, The Son, and *The Holy Ghost*. Man as soul wanted to say,

Fucking is Holy, but it's no Ghost. Society said: Fucking is no Ghost, but it is very evil.

240 Yet the course of human history reveals something else. Which is that homeostasis through the centuries has been on the advance. Indeed, it should be, for homeostasis accepted its enemy sociostasis in order that homeostasis might grow. (My God, dialectics.) But each victory of homeostasis created a new more highly complex form of sociostasis, more capable of dealing with the more alive and varied homeostasis. That is why Western man today is at the edge of the abyss—the war is at an incredible level of subtlety and enormity. Yet the hope is that the social forms do change as they retreat. Today saintly people do go into the Catholic Church, but they *bore from within*. The Church as it appears to get more flexible—and indeed its techniques amaze one with their variety, subtlety, power and insight—is nonetheless weakening. Saints and psychopaths are running wild through it, altering its sensibility. The church is being hipsterized. Television, Sheen, advertising, talk of the Pope's mistress at cocktail parties on the East Side, and in the arm of the Church, the F.B.I., they are getting paranoid sensitivity which is rendering the ridiculous to the liberal, and frightening to the conservative. The F.B.I. is just swept with the psychology of secret policemen who project onto the enemy their own enormous criminality. The result—for paranoids are usually right except that they have neglected the little matter of Time, they have over-anticipated—is that the F.B.I. is suffering from the most acute sense of being right, and yet to their horror, wherever they have scientific tests they discover they are more often wrong than right, even though they fight admitting it. The result is ferocious unbearable anxiety. The-anxiety-of-statesmen. One reads the word every day—a far cry from Victorian statesmen. So, there is hope. For even as homeostasis is tortured, so too is sociostasis. The mass-communication media are always in danger of getting out of hand, the hipsters spread and so does hipster sensitivity. Hipsters are generally takers, they are cool, but hipsters will take even action from Givers, and great Givers are growing.

241 For years, unknowingly, I talked like a bopster. Quickly, confusingly, one moment seeming to make great sense, the next moment bewildering, ideas knocking one another on the head, emotional currents of communication thrown out rather than precise wording, stumbling, stammering, racing, articulate and inarticulate often on the same word, and never going to orgasm, but trailing off so that I left my listeners excited, stimulated . . . and frustrated, irritated.

242 BEBOP. P AND B are sibling consonants, almost identical twins. Like T and D. So Bebop is be pop or pee pop—Go ahead father, piss. The trickling quality of the orgasm is implicit in the word, but so, too, is the subtlety, the lingering, the capacity to say many things at once. Man is at the point where the highest developed humans are starting to communicate on more than one level at the same time, and the words on bebop records can mean two or three things at the same time. It is absolutely conceivable that humans will speak in the style of *Finnegans Wake* in centuries or millennia or possibly much sooner.

243 WRITER'S BLOCKS EXIST BECAUSE the writer is in danger. His sociostatic forces are mobilized against where his homeostatic urges are leading him, and if the danger is great enough, *nothing* will come out. Life is pure depression. What is a more usual case is that the writer advances slowly against his sociostasis, burdened with depression. A novel is the record of a sociostatic retreat if it is a great or good novel. A bad novel is the record of a sociostasis advance (all this of course relative to the talents, the danger, and homeostatic energy of the creator) and the bad novel being the record of a sociostatic advance is written usually more rapidly and with more satisfaction until the hangover comes— the homeostatic urges (homeodynamic would be a much better word)—Now, I've got it. Homeostasis is not homeostatic at all. It is homeodynamism vs. sociostasis—The hangover comes because homeodynamic forces are enraged at the self and shame is felt. Thus, for people: Homeodynamic expression arouses emotions of guilt which are generated by sociostasis. Sociostatic expression arouses emotions of shame which are generated by homeodynamism. Thus guilt and shame are not close—*They are Polar.*

244 GOLFERS ARE PEOPLE WHO take their one ball and whack it a mile away; they are so angry their other ball was taken away years ago. Of course there are also putters who love to nudge their little ball lovingly. Iron shooters I don't dig although there's a lot in the word. Sand-blasters seem obvious, I think. They want to do a real big blast, but they don't want the ball to go *too* far away. Not to mention hooks and slices. They must be very painful to a one-balled man.

245 Put another way, the sociostatic mechanism in writers allows them each time to express their thought in the least dangerous way for society. So, depending on the kind of personality, the time, and the style and expression of homeodynamic urge and the sociostatic repression (in their philosophical extensions these are very different from id and super-ego)—mainly because Freud saw id as generally "bad" and I see it as generally "good"—I am turning Freud on his head just as Marx turned Hegel on his head.) Let's repeat: the sociostatic repression always allows the writer the least dangerous (to society) expression of his vision. The homeodynamic demands the most. Given conditions, the compromise, to wit the work, is always the best possible expression, the most efficient compromise. Which is why I say homeostasis is the compromise of homeodynamism and sociostasis.

246 But look at the philosophical results of this. It states that whatever we did in the past was the best possible thing we could have done and there is no use whatsoever in regretting our past actions. Indeed as analysts have discovered guilt is often used to keep from moving forward. And if people believed what I say here, sociostasis would suffer an enormous set-back, a great rout, for the expressions of homeodynamism would be more positive, more adventurous,—the cavalry, so to speak, of sociostasis would be dismounted, and the charges with the sword replaced. (As indeed unhappily they have been—by tanks (Psychoanalysts), which reminds me that in the 112th Cavalry all the ignorant Texans used to spell it Calvary.)

247 It also suggests that action, quite unlike society's view of it, is not single but double. Action is a compromise. It is the putting to rest of two irreconcilables, and no action is ever meaningless.

248 WHICH LEADS ME TO the one and the two. Society is always saying X is One. Man always knows X is two. For example, Society says crime is bad. Religion is good. Man knows that crime is bad but beneath the crime is goodness; religion is good but beneath it is death and evil. One is a unity. It is static. Two is infinity. That is to say in the act "ideationally" of moving from one to two we pass through an infinity of movements from the one to the two. 1.0000000001, 1.0000000002 and so forth. Stasis is one. Movement is infinite. That is why the novelist is so important. For centuries now he has been one of the few who keep saying in the good man there is bad, in the bad man there is good—he keeps us alive to the scope of infinity which does not diminish man but ennobles him. Society always wants one. That is why totalitarianism is its final expression, and its final victory it if could ever achieve it, but thank God I don't see how it can.

249 ENGLISH IS SO MAGNIFICENTLY blunt. It says GOoD and dEVIL. The Latin languages are far less direct it seems to me. But that's because the Church got a stranglehold on Latin.

250 TO GO BACK TO note **246**. The sociostatic repression allows the writer the least dangerous (to society) expression of his vision (homeodynamic urge). Therefore, style gives the clue usually to what happened in the soul. The great stylist is indeed a man who relatively does not have too much to say. There are geniuses like Joyce, Proust and Mann who said an awful lot, but the difficulties of their style kept them alive so to speak—they would have been hung if people had been able to understand them. To the other side are the bad stylists like myself who are just overflowing with ideas. My sociostatic defense is that I express them so badly that nearly everyone reading this journal would take me for a crank. My sociostatic defense (S.D.) at this stage is to allow the ideas to come in such waves that all is confusion. The S.D. (Social Democrat) hopes that I'll waste these ideas by throwing them away in the crudities of the style. But even this is dangerous for it. For years my brain was most alive when I was incapable of taking a note, or trapping the thought. And in my novels like *Barbary* and *Deer Park* where I had comparatively few ideas, I could reach them only through great pain, and the most stubborn depression and writing blocks. Yet I broke sociostatic things in myself. I have lost weight and with it depression. I am manic, alive, filled every day with the excitement and revelation of everything I see. Bergler, who has homeodynamic impulses so vast that he has to smother them in the most violent reactionary sociostasis, too violent even for his confreres, reveals great truths by the absurdity of his dictums. And once in a while he is magnificently right, despite himself. So I understand that he wrote that the writer writes away the defense in the course of writing. And that is so true. There is that wonderful line in *The Deer Park* which goes: "There was that law of life, so cruel and so just, which demanded that one must grow or else pay more for remaining the same." So the writer has to grow and the more his talent the more he has to grow. Which is why it is so awful and so exciting to be a novelist. Of all the art forms it is the one where one can hide the least, and in this country where growth is the most accelerated there is small wonder that American novelists die artistically very young. To be a great American novelist demands a superman. That is why great writers in America are not able to turn out work after work of equal value—the moment they do not continue to grow, the sociostatic defenses chase them back in a rout, as indeed they have to for the great American writer is living very dangerously.

251 JOYFUL THOUGHT. WHAT'S GOING to happen to Bergler? Whether he knows it or not he's in danger of blowing his brains out because the alternative would be to murder one of his Don Juan patients and Bergler is too sociostatic for that. I expect troubled days for the Herr German Doktor.

252 CHILDREN'S EATING. ANIMALS KNOW the food they need, simple animals. Rats in laboratories eating white powders at will and thriving better than their controls who are given the best administered diets. But that is because animals have a single nervous system. Children are born with a single nervous system, the homeodynamic, but the years of their childhood are the years when the sociostatic nervous system is set into the child. It is obviously a turbulent abrupt set of victories and defeats for the two systems, and so one is working and then the other. Therefore, simply, there are times when children eat exactly what they need; there are other times when their eating is completely sociostatic and very bad for them. Homeodynamic eating always preserves life. Sociostatic eating is to preserve society, lull rebellion, but in the process the body may be injured. Sweet poisonings for example coming out of the languorous libidinous frustrations of the wrestler-giver. Which is what fat people very often are—certain kinds of fat people, Adeline, Jenny Silverman, others.

253 ALL RIGHT, IF EVERYBODY is both male and female, heterosexual and homosexual—a commonplace—what isn't realized is that there are two kinds of sexual people—those who are essentially bisexual, and those whom I will call uni-sexual. Bisexuals make long clinging imaginative love passages, wanderings, where the orgasm is merely a regretted terminus rather than a climax. Uni-sexuals make short love, be it cold or hot, love which is harsh, active, emotional, rigorous, and oriented to climax. Analysts generally would call unisexuals healthy, bisexuals unhealthy, but I wonder. Because bisexuals are more developed and their lovemaking is a more painful but richer playing out of the id-superego conflict. Unisexuals have habits which enable them to suppress id or superego. So whether potent or frigid, love is over quickly and the mind of the unisexual is in hibernation while loving. The bisexual is stimulated, frightened, is at the edge of the mystery, is frustrated, comes back, flees, sweats cold, loses him or herself, has a great thought or perception, feels love, loses love, chases it again, and so forth.

The unisexual is all male or all female on the surface. Underneath, and deeply buried except as they reveal themselves in their *habits* is the reverse. So, a woman uni-sexual is apparently feminine, calm, capable, good housewife, efficient, motherly, light on make-up, likes the short brisk act, and acts unconsciously toward other women and men as a male. The unisexual male, if he is nominally heterosexual and healthy, is aggressive toward women in an easy way, has short quick acts, is decisive, executive, athletic, and is unaware of the woman in him, although he is subject to sudden aggressive and passive homosexual panics and indeed even actions. More powerful men reduce him to a psychic jelly.

Bisexuals are much more consciously aware of the male and female in them. They are therefore anxious, "sex-obsessed," orgiastic, and . . . stable. Because whether they make love to a man or a woman the man-and-woman in the bisexual makes love to the woman-and-man in the partner. There is always a quartet going on. Even if a bisexual makes love with a unisexual there is an orgy—at least three people are present and one is watching (the unisexual's buried self). Therefore, the bisexual may appear to have a great variety in the choice of partners but the bisexual is essentially making love always to the same partner—partners!—yet deepening the act by experience. Unisexuals are much more subject to real sexual anxiety attacks because the anxiety is more buried and the action is more compulsive. The bisexual is thus more "cool."

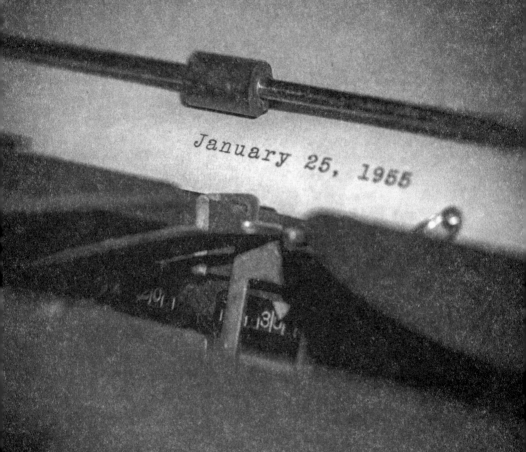

January 25, 1955

254 THE ADVANCES IN MEDICINE may well be an expression of the S. (I am sick of writing sociostasis. From now on S for that and H for homeodynamic). Put briefly, the increase in the war between the H and the S has rendered people so physically sick, their bodies so overcome by the false nutritions offered by S, that they are literally in danger of dying faster out of essentially nervous ailments. Sexual ailments—sex being the euphoria of the nervous system when it is satisfactory. Therefore more and more money has gone into research, and the antibiotics have come—without them mortality rates might have increased, and one of the strong advertisements society always has to offer is to say, "Look, because you obey us, you live longer. Medical research is society." The anti-biotics were lying around for years—penicillin was discovered back sometime in the twenties, but it wasn't necessary then—it is today. Uncle Dave would have died without cortisone, and he is one of the perfect examples of a man who was strong, capable, executive, dynamic, and then past fifty was suddenly ravaged by asthma—the rage of the soul at how he had not lived. But his case is not the exception. How, otherwise, can one account for the perfect obsession with cancer which runs through people, and the millions spent on research. I'm certain that when the cause of cancer is truly discovered, it will be psychosomatic.

255 THE PREDICTOR, THE PROPHET, and the gambler are cousins. The prophet has a saintly confidence—he is so certain he is right that he can afford to wait until he is dead before his prediction will be realized or confounded. The predictor is a gambler operating with social sanction. The gambler is a man (or woman) who feels in his bones that he is right and the whole world is wrong—but he also feels that he is wrong and the world is right. The uncertainty is so intense that he must make prophecies about events which occur in the next hour, for he must have the objective correlative. (In that sense he is a scientist.) I think Bob Lindner is right and yet not right in his assessment of the gambler playing with destiny—defeat one side, insanity the other. It may not be so desperate as that. The gambler feels his soul, he also feels society—he is essentially betting that his intuitions, his sensitivity, is greater than the world's. And the reason certain gamblers lose is not necessarily their fear that if they're right they will go mad, as the analysts would argue, so much as their fear that they will have to become all-out rebels and pit themselves against the world. So, painful as it is, they invariably lose. After all, the value of losing is that one can tell oneself that one was right except for bad luck. So one can remain a conformist and still maintain one's deep private respect for one's intuitions. But to win does not permit such ambiguity, such "double" profit. It lays down an imperative. "You were right," says victory, "Go ahead and rebel," which is why victory often produces deep depression. Certainly this is true of victories one has not sought—like my victory in having *The Deer Park* published. What I have said above applies mainly to the long-shot player, the man who roots for the underdog. There is the other kind of gambler who plays favorites, and his psychology is also fascinating. Victory tells him the world is right which is what he wants to hear because he suspects the opposite. Defeat is unbearable because it tells him he was wrong; such a man often flies into a rage. Yet, I wonder if he is not secretly thrilled by the underdog defeating his favorite. He would not be a gambler in the first place if he were not unconsciously obsessed with the whole business of the soul's insights against the world's insights. He gambles *malgré lui* (despite himself), he is drawn into it cautiously, slowly, reluctantly. Gambling on favorites is his defense against gambling on underdogs, gambling on his own intuitions. Men who bet on favorites are invariably successful men who are beginning to be deeply dissatisfied with their success; long-shot players cover a great range of what seems to be cranks, sneaks, weird-o's, rummies, whores, junkies, etc.

256 THE ABOVE NOTE. I did not have a deep depression when Putnam took the book, I had a half relief and a half depression. Because I was gambling two ways. The bet was hedged. On the one hand I didn't want a house to take it, because then I could have gone all the way. On the other hand I wanted a house to take it because I sensed that if I published it myself and won (as I felt

I would) my life as a gambler would be established. I could hardly turn back.

257 Bob is the dishonest man who was sent out to come back with the truth. I am the honest man who was sent out to explore the lie. That is why each of us were immediately fascinated with the other, and why each of us have exciting lives. An exciting life is to be sent by one's vocation across the extreme of one's personality. Doing that, one crosses the spectrum of humanity and outlines the architecture of the world.

258 I wonder if one doesn't choose a mate who accommodates the particular combination of our parents which the H and S need at a given time. So Bea who was like my mother in her strength, her confidence, her bold grasp, and her lack of deeper understanding combined with the essential non-conformism of my father. Essentially I married my mother (who is masculine) because I felt womanly, but I chose the particular mother-substitute who could remind me of my father (who is delicately feminine) but also a rebel. I married a woman who was a feminine rebel in a masculine way. But I grew in masculinity, and our marriage became intolerable to both of us. (One subtlety of Bea is that she acts like my father in times of stress—she pulls out of the situation, she becomes passive and inert.) With Adele I found the lovely sensitive woman who was always in my father, and Adele whose sensitivity is deep like my father's also plays the fool like my father. He says pompous things which repel one; she says silly things which make one ridicule her. But while the woman is dominant in Adele, the masculine element (my mother) is present. In times of stress—quarrels between us, etc.—Adele puts her head down and slugs it out toe to toe, just like my mother. Her rages are strong, her affection is strong, her loyalty is essentially constant but she plays with her loyalty to me, she examines it with the sensitivity of my father.

What I have tried to outline here is that we do not marry mother-substitutes or father-substitutes, we marry (especially if we are bisexual) mother-father embodiments. But we choose the embodiment we are best able to deal with, and for that matter admire—which is a way of saying what the world will approve of most. But there is no escaping it. When we find a mother-father embodiment who my God corresponds closely to what we truly need (given the particular H vs. S imbroglio we can hardly escape her or him). Weird marriages one must always attempt to understand, for they are the marriages of people who are very close homeodynamically (the word is just frightful—I've got to get something between that and soul).

260 HERR BERGLER (WHAT'S IN a name?) wrote a book *Divorce Won't Help.* No doubt he sees himself as a giant holding his enormous lever in the machine so the wheels can't turn. People are static and bound forever in their characters. Only Bergler can let them see their characters and accept them. But this is crap, and deep-down he knows it. People change. *People change.* It is part of their magnificence. Just as the body changes every instant of our existence, so too do people. And the H and S never remain static although they may be locked in the depression of trench warfare for a decade and then another decade. We change, and as we change we need another mother-father embodiment, one who is closer to us. So divorce can help, and often it does.

261 WHAT I WROTE ABOUT Sergius and his father is true for my father and me. "He was a workingman all his life, but he wanted to be an actor." "Once he confessed to me that my name was not really O'Shaugnessey at all, but something which resembled it remotely in Polish or Hungarian. There is nothing in the world like being a false Irishman." But I was saying it so directly. My father was born in Russia and has pretended to be born in South Africa for so long that he believes it himself. And our name is not really Mailer but something which resembles it remotely in Russian or Jewish. Truly, there is nothing in the world like being a false *Englishman.* Which is what my pop has been all his life, and what I have been. That's why I always get so nice-nelly and affected and talk with an English accent when I'm with Englishmen, American society people, or even the genteel rich-poor who live in Connecticut and Vermont. And this is true for my sister as well.

262 THIS JOURNAL IN SO far as it is a piece or a record of my Lipton's self-analysis has had one objective correlative. For in a way this Journal is a great big wager—I am betting that the under-dog (the H in me) is going to score. That I am going to come out of this bigger than I went in—successfully analyzed. And today before I started writing, I spent four hours with my father, and we talked, and it was the first talk we ever had in our lives, and I was able to tell him that I love him. And for once I was able to give him what he needs, to tell him what a great guy I think he is, instead of hitting him with all kinds of shit and making him feel like a piece of dirt. In a way, for the first time I understood him, understood him from inside himself and I was close to tears all the time, not tears of pity for him but tears of sorrow for myself and the way I had acted, and tears of pride at how marvelous he is really, and how his gambling was an expression of his artistry, and how now at the age of sixty-three he isn't ridden with cancer or asthma or heart trouble or rheumatism, but instead looks hale and hearty and handsome, a dapper little guy who's always been a gentleman and never hurt anybody except as he was forced to reluctantly in expressing his artistry. And I really got the feeling that he's going to grow in his old age, and find pleasures in play.

263 I REALIZED SO MANY funny things about Dad. He is the frustrated giver who has developed his giving to a high artistry. For one of the paradoxes about him (and be it said a paradox is never a paradox if we can only grasp it) was always the contrast between the sensitivity he would reveal at rare isolated moments so that I always knew he understood me better than mother—his sensitivity against his daily pompousness and ability to say nothing interesting were understood by me. For his pompousness was always the echo of mother's "bourgeois" sentiments. He overdid it. Unconsciously, he made her sound ridiculous. It was his private way of encouraging me to be a rebel. Her dictums made a certain practical common-sense. To rebel against them would have made me feel too guilty. But there was my father, repeating what she said, exaggerating it, multiplying it, until the sheer human nonsense of bourgeois values rang in my head, and then I would turn on him, and instead of showing his wonderful sensitivity and adroitness he would keep repeating what he had said. I remember that when I was eighteen he used to keep saying me, "Norman, either get a haircut or we'll have to buy you a violin." From deep within him, he meant it, he was warning me, he was saying, "Go out, son, be a rebel, because if you're not a rebel you'll end up a pompous fool, ignored, and the subject of people's contempt." So I loved him today; I wanted to kiss him and hug him because he did so much for me, and he was always so good to me in the cramped way permitted him by society and by my mother, sturdy society-substitute with all of society's sensitivity for danger. But finally he was smarter than her. He mocked her all through those years, saying, "Really, Norman, why don't you look decent for once," to which I would respond by opening my collar and yanking down my tie. And though he would pretend to look pained, there was always that little grin on his face. No wonder. He's scored a point for respectability which satisfied the top of his brain, and confirmed me in my rebellion which satisfied the rest of him. A man who can do two opposed things at once for all of his life against great difficulties has a kind of genius. And like all geniuses he looks mighty good in his old age. But what I should say is his nominal old age, for as he said today, and he talked to me as well as me to him, "You know, Norman, I still feel young."

264 SINCE I STARTED THIS Journal I have been feeling happier than I have in my whole life. So much has been released and so much created—because for me release and creation are parallel expressions of the same thing. But underneath it persists a feeling that I am going to die soon which perhaps is why I entrust each installment of the journal to the mail. I even caught myself thinking just now that perhaps I would write at this journal for the next year or two, and there would be thousands of pages, and then pop I would go—which makes me sad rather than depressed because for the first time in my life I really want to live—how I want to live. But anyway I then thought, "There must be literary executors," and I thought of Cy and Adele and possibly my sister, and Danny Wolf, and very much my father, and as chief executor, Bob Lindner of course. And then I thought of how that would pain Adele and yet it would be necessary, for so much of this journal would be painful to her, and so she could not exercise her genuine literary taste.

But what also occurs to me is that Bob too has feelings about dying early. Perhaps the emotion has no bodily significance—it is only the retiring cannonades of sociostasis which with its cunning knows that people who are highly sensitive and put trust in their sensitivity are most prone to the suggestion of death for they believe what their brain tells them. Only I suspect for both Bob and me that it's the S part of our brain which is talking and not the H. The H is giving the happiness now—it knows I'm going to live to a healthy old age like my father.

265 THE SENSE OF TIME. A person with a highly developed sense of the past and a careful sense of the future (in other words, fear of consequences) who puts little value in powerful emotions of the present is essentially an S man. People like myself, who at this moment is putting so much into the present, believing that what I discover each second will be true for the future, are H people. That is why I can now understand psychopaths and their sense of the present. But I wonder if I wasn't wrong about saints. Maybe they too have an enormous sense of the present. They believe what their heart tells them at any instant. Perhaps the difference between a saint and a psychopath is that the saint knows it is his heart which talks, and the psychopath knows nothing, feels only the compulsion. But there is much more to say about this difference, and I am not satisfied with it yet.

266 OLD PEOPLE DON'T SLOW down mentally. What happens is that they lose their powers of concentration because so much H resentment is welling up in them constantly. Society has handed out this myth that people slow down in order to lull them from their rage. A person who reaches old age with H triumphant over S can have an active mental life.

267 TO CONTINUE **265** I wonder if the difference between the saint and the psychopath is that what the psychopath feels for only a moment (but feels strongly and acts on it), the saint feels more or less permanently. As an example would be the love I felt for my father this afternoon. If it makes a permanent change in our relations, at least in my attitude toward him (by which I do not mean that there will be no ups and downs, but rather that the "average" of my feelings and expressions toward him is different) then I was feeling saintly emotion. But if it's all gone in a few days and I slip back into feeling the old things about him, then it was a psychopathic expression. In other words, it is not that psychopaths are "heartless" but that the bidding of their heart is isolated. So they love and hate in isolated apparently contradictory "bursts." The saint is almost always in communion with his "heart." Therefore he always loves. He loves because finally hatred is always *always* the frozen echo of love, and the saint is aware of the love he feels and has dissolved all hatred in himself.

268 THE INTERESTING CONFIRMATION OF this is that what we have always disliked about saints is that they are not haters. They love everyone. But this is intolerable to the social sense which consists of the spectrum of things detested absolutely to things admired absolutely. A saint has no discrimination we feel and so we get *fed up* with him. Psychopaths, of course, are always seen by society as hating everyone and everything. We speak of them as being filled with hate. And that is their connection to saints. They are truly saints reversed. But I wonder if hatred is not precisely the interruption, the severing, of the connection between the heart (the soul, the H), and the mind. Good old S in between.

270 RADICALS. PARTICULARLY SOCIALISTS. IT is no accident so many socialists come from the middle class in this country. They are almost all sociostatic in character. They hate our society, and the Soviet even more, if like me, they are anti-Stalinist leftists, then what leaves them so unappetizing and so unsatisfying even to themselves, as I was always so dissatisfied with the yawning holes in my intellectual structures, is that they wish to replace society by another society. Their imaginations, their creativity, their H is entirely devoted to the service of Sociostasis, and so their thoughts, programs, predictions, and analyses invariably have a square blunt building-brick quality. Even Malaquais, who is the best socialist thinker I have ever come across, thinks in finite blocks. His thought of course has the nobility of a cathedral, but he's filled every square inch of the cathedral with a tile, and so his new thought can consist merely of improving the total design. He can replace one tile by another. But he will never build a cathedral which dissolves into light. For all the beauty of his conceptions, a dank oppressive gloom breathes out of the doors and no one wants to enter poor Malaquais' cathedral. He is left the gloomy caretaker of it. One reason he cannot chase me away entirely is that I'm the village boy who wandered in one evening and stayed to admire the cathedral for many years, asking the caretaker every day, "Don Malaquais, tell me about the saints, and why this stone is this color?" I was a naughty boy and I was forever quitting his lessons to throw stones at the bats, but what he cannot bear, dear Malaquais, it the silence now that I am gone. Timidly, terrified, like a shy old miser, he is making the endless preparations necessary to go out and buy a new hat. He has no real hope he'll be detained in the village and find a place to build a new cathedral; he knows he'll go back to the old one and watch the bats multiply, but it is so gloomy in there. Even Fra Jean has to get a bit of air.

271 PROSE ON WINGS, TRA-LA, tra-la. What I started to say in the previous note was that radical socialists because they are sociostatic have ended up aiding society. They present tools of analysis bourgeois society unaided could never have come up with, but because socialists think sociostatically, so capitalists can turn their thought to their own advantage. Norman Thomas is always complaining that the Republican and Democratic parties have stolen his program, and indeed they have. Marxism for all its grandeur and its genuine revolutionary ethic—its ultimate anarchism which nearly all socialists have forgotten—approached the problem of society as a materialist conception. But capitalists are also materialists. So they could adapt Marxism to their needs, improve their sociostatic techniques, shore up the crazy house and keep the warped mirrors form cracking . . . yet.

272 So, MODESTLY, I SEE my mission. It is to put Freud into Marx, and Marx into Freud. Put Tolstoy into Dostoyevsky and Dostoyevsky in Tolstoy. Open anarchism with its soul-sense to the understanding of complexity, and infuse complex gloom with the radiance of anarchism. As Jenny Silverman said of me once, "The little pisherke with the big ideas." Pint-sized Hitler. Yes.

273 JEWS HATED HITLER VIOLENTLY because they knew that they were guilty too—of Jewish self-hatred. How else account for the wave of Zionism after the war? Hitler was a monster, but one should not hate monsters—one should kill them, I suppose, but kill them reluctantly, just deprive them of power.

275 I AM COMING TO believe that there are excellent therapeutic qualities to Lipton's if administered properly, especially when it is followed by Seconal for a couple of days. I had Lipton's last Friday, Saturday, and Sunday nights, and one capsule of Seconal on Friday, one on Sunday, two Monday night, two last night. For Monday, Tuesday, and today, my state has been one of enormous internal excitement and sensitivity without nervous tension. I find it hard to sleep but that is because my mind is so full of ideas. My insomnia instead of being depressed is elated, and if I suffer from anything it is an overabundance of ideas. I hardly know which ones to put down first, and for the last two days I have been working from five to eight hours on this Journal with no real fatigue, intense concentration, and great excitement—to my knowledge this is the first time I've been able to do mental work this way since I was an adolescent. Also, I have not felt driven—the most immediate expression is that I look at the clock sadly—I must quit work—rather than anxiously. Moreover, I have no desire these few days to take more Lipton's—I have all I can do to handle the sensitivity I have. What I suspect from having seen so many people take Lipton's is that a psychic process equivalent to the first six months of analysis (roughly) where the analyst must break down the patient's first resistance to the therapy seems to be accomplished in much less time. At least for me. Just as certain people fight analysis for a year, two years, so certain of my friends with very rigid characters—Danny, Jean, others—fight Lipton's. Others accept it quickly. One general theorem I suspect is that bisexuals take to Lipton's more readily than unisexuals, near-alcoholics, and heavy drinkers. These people have never to my memory been able to accept Lipton's. Indeed, I took Lipton's for the first time over three years ago and merely got ill—the five or six times I took it in the next three years were all unsatisfactory—I either felt anxiety so great it knocked me almost unconscious, or I became ill, or suffered violent paranoid experiences. But in Mexico, after that period when I had stopped drinking, Lipton's began to hit. It was also the time when I wrote my article for *One* magazine. Shortly after coming to New York I began to understand my profound bisexuality. Then bam with *The Deer Park*, and I was off on trying to understand myself. All this is preface to a Lipton's corollary: Alcohol makes one appear more masculine. Lipton's makes one feel more feminine. So men with a low threshold of active homosexual tendencies generally find Lipton's unbearable. Bisexuals like myself who are safely ensconced in heterosexual habits and express their feminine side in powerfully emotional friendships with men can accept Lipton's provided of course they are in a period where H is pressing powerfully forward and their S is crumbling.

For use in analysis I have the feeling that Lipton's used with certain people could speed up the analysis greatly, used both in and out of the analytic hours depending on results. For other people it could of course be disastrous, or at minimum time-wasting and ultimately S-enforcing. The above is very sketchy but at least it is a first approach to the problem.

276 I HAVE NOTICED IN analytic case studies that there is the recurring phenomenon of a period of early euphoria. Most analysts including Bob consider this as a general feeling of relief now that ventilation has been achieved. And nearly all analysts proceed to talk of the problems which follow next, the depressions and anxieties which come back, the plateaus, the "hangings." I wonder if this is not due to the fact that psychoanalysis is S-oriented. I have the feeling that my present euphoria is more than just ventilation. I may retreat of course because it is frightening. I may suffer all of the above setbacks, but I wonder: I am analyzing myself in order to become a real rebel, not just an adjusted rebel. (Notice the just in adjusted.) And so I have the confidence that my self-analysis may be less painful and that the euphoria may not be lost entirely. What I suspect is that in most analyses, the initial successes (whether they come in the first two weeks or only after three years) are the genuine thing, the S is weakened, the H is encouraged. But afterward, the analyst locked in his S-concepts, begins—whether he realized it or not—to fight the H and encourage the S. No wonder the patient gets so balky and suffers so much. The patient has been given a glimpse of heaven only to have papa take it away again. Returned to the sensuous wisdom of childhood the analysand is required to grow up again, to become the loud concerted adolescent full of projects and plans with no more promised than the adjusted maturity, the world of S. Of course analysis is feeling its panic. The world of S is the world of the atom bomb. Society is destruction. Everybody *knows* it today. Just as the F.B.I. is losing its grip because it is being flooded with sensitivity, so analysis is approaching a crisis and rebel-analysts like Bob are popping up all over the place. In the very madness of a Bergler is the exacerbated desperation of what is really a very sensitive man.

277 LET ME PUT IT this way: One of the basic analytic concepts is that the id forces are repressed by the ego and super-ego because they are too horrible to bear. I think that is true only until the euphoric phase takes place. Thereafter, in a conventional analysis, a transfer occurs within the patient, it is the id or what I prefer to call the H (being more healthy) *which becomes the censor, the resistance.* Deeply it knows that it is being tricked, being called forth in order to be converted from H to S. So H forces censor the H. Of a sudden the patient does not want to give up his neurosis. Of course not. Beneath the S, the H is very alive in a neurotic. Over and over again most analysts are haunted by the suspicion that their adjusted patients have lost something very vital. Indeed, that is why there is not to my knowledge a single example of a talented writer who did better work after his analysis. The rebel in him was quieted too much.

278 I KNOW NOW WHY I was never able to study exhaustively things which interested me. Particularly psychoanalysis. I have always been a reader and a studier in bits and pieces. It is because deep within me I sensed the wisdom of the old saw reversed. "A lot of knowledge is a dangerous thing."—Norman Mailer. I am not pleading for no knowledge, nor too little knowledge, but to learn a subject exhaustively is to give oneself a vested interest in it. It makes it that much more difficult to see it in a new way, to be creative. No wonder critics are critics and novelists are novelists.

279 CLUES, MYSTERIES, PUNS, DOUBLE-ENTENDRES, jokes, paradoxes, affectations, secret societies, pompousness, word games, cross-word puzzles, charades are all folk expressions of the total violence done human nature for thousands of years. The H always peeps through the S, it is undeniable, it must express itself in no matter how tortured a form. The pompous man, the extraordinarily pompous man, is trying to teach people. He wears a mask which is the caricature of himself. Indeed *one's personality is always the caricature of oneself.* So the pompous man is at bottom a loather of society, a potential destroyer. He is so bound to society that he cannot express himself in another way, but a part of him is always saying, "Look at me, look how ridiculous I am. If you are taken in by what I once believed, then you too will look like me, and will be able to teach only by driving people away."

280 IN THIS SENSE, WE are all part of a total soul, and even as we seem to be hurting each other, we are helping each other, instructing, aiding. Adele's mother loved life, was frustrated by early marriage, and in her own way she loved Adele. Deeply she loved Adele so much that she made life unbearable at home for Adele so that Adele would go out into the world and not have the bitch of a life Consuela had known. And this is true for Adele's father too. Society has so perverted us with its notions that we are always brooding about the damages other people have done to us. But everything is a double, and as we feel something one way in ourselves so its opposite echoes in another part of our being (H vs. S). Love contains the echo of the trap and of death; hatred offers a ticket to romantic places, a trip into life. That is why today at a time when society is changing and adapting every day, becoming almost as sensitive as life itself since human needs are so great, the majority of people consciously feel hate, and love is a sticky word. How true. Love sticks. Hatred flies. The human wisdom buried in the cliché. For the intuitive sensual life wisdom of the H can express itself in society only in degraded forms. So the wisest things are said in jokes, in obscenities, in clichés, in faulty art-works, in parables and paradoxes. Great art-works are enormous sociostatic defenses against H-forces. No matter how radical or revolutionary the writer may be, or the artist, his work is less radical than his H. Art is a homeostatic excretion, and in the faults of an art work, the shoddy passages, the scenes which did not come off, or the overblown prose, is concealed the soul of the artist.

281 IF THE ABOVE SOUNDS very fancy (the pompous man, the nasty mother) let it be remembered that animal life poses enigmas unless understood this way. The gentle pussy cat slaps her kittens away, the dove throws her fledglings into the air, and so forth. Life invents, life adapts, life fights stasis. In a hostile environment life must be aggressive to remain alive. A commonplace, but the same cat defends her kittens when danger is near. In the hostile environment of man's life, the pompous man drives away his children in order to give life to them, yet also defends them. The reason I found it hard to love Susie when she was born is that I was such a sociostatic radical (in my top drawer) that I wanted the State to provide for her.

282 SOCIOSTASIS AND SOCIOSTASIS. SOCIETIES leave behind them a homeostatic record (H vs. S) which we call history. Each death of an H vs. S leaves us a truth. Human life is not a circle but a spiral. When the spiral returns to the point where it was an age, a century, an eon ago, what was once an H may now be an S. Reason which is part of man's soul was once an H-instrument which put S in retreat. (Arbitrarily, the French Revolution.) But S is part of life too; it is Other-Life, and so in defeating an H it absorbs it. Reason has now become Rationalization (in the large sense of the word). It is one of the bulwarks of society. So the H turns to the illogical, the intuitive, *the irrational*. One symptom of this is what everybody is calling the plague of irrationality. Small communities refuse the fluoridation of water, although rationally fluoridation prevents tooth decay and does no *known* harm. McCarthys spring up and have to be defeated at what cost to the rational nervous system of the State it is difficult to contemplate. Demagogues are on the march, painting deserts the representational—to wit, the rational. Poetry ceases to communicate to large audiences. Billy Grahams electrify the staid English, Aldous Huxley, the last in line of a great intellectual family takes a drug and writes a book about it. The demagogue is everywhere. Millions give themselves to the gibberish of television. Be-bop floods America after the war, and it is the artistic expression of double-talk (ultimately the expression of many things at once). Monsters in uniform murder in the name of the state until finally the state itself is caught in contradiction. It is killing its own. It is killing the very people it needs for production which is its health. What then am I saying? The state has appropriated reason. With reason it is attempting to destroy life. So life responds by bewildering the state with monsters and mystics. At this moment in history, the State can handle anything rational, can adapt itself to anything rational, borrow from it, use it. The State has used Marxism itself in order to make super-states. So, life fights back by having people become monsters and mystics, the two things the State just cannot possibly handle. The hipster who combines both monster and mystic within himself is on Cloud Seven, and the psychoanalyst who is his social counterpart is merely in the chair.

In a curious cockeyed way, the concentration camps of the world were not an unalloyed monstrosity. They could have been worse, the world could have been destroyed. It is possible that in the long view of the historian centuries from now, the concentration camps will be seen as the warning which succeeded—the statement of life which warned people that the ultimate nature of the totally rational society is the monster. That if society is allowed total reason, it will destroy Life.

Once, in the Middle Ages mysticism and monsters were the province of society and reason was the expression of life. But we are half around the spiral, and it is possible that at this moment in history the irrational expressions of man are more healthy than the rational. For state-planners, and civic planners and community planners are always rattled, bewildered, rendered anxious by the totally irrational. McCarthy fucked up the confidence of the American State more completely than a million Communist Party members could have. Perhaps we fail to see the signs. Perhaps the crazy reactionaries and the tabloid papers and the comic books (I see what Bob means) and television and advertising even in certain ways, all the monstrosities are eating at the calm of the experts, fuddling the bureaucrats, expressing against Other-Life, the warped twisted but nonetheless assertive H permitted man today. And on a higher level, a century or three or five from now, the spiral may be completed (it will of course go on) and Reason, Higher Reason will return to the H and monsters and mysticism to the S.

283 So in that sense I am the rational saint sent out to find the good in monsters and psychopaths.

285 I have to face something. Just as the pompous man encourages rebellion, so I wonder if I as the *enfant terrible*, the pint-sized Hitler, the outrageous radical, am not encouraging conformity. I take out the Lipton's, and people who were previously drawn to me flee the house. Possibly, my mother planted her deep conservative seeds. Certainly, there is a vast conservative echo in me, and the expression of my S may be that I am now stating my thought in its most outrageous terms in order that other people conform. I think this is true, but I do believe in the predominance of the H. All the S can do now is hurt me, waste me, make me do foolhardy things. But since I am expressing things which have to do with life and with man's goodness so people who flee come back again. The only thing is that if I keep on the way I'm going, they'll have to come to visit me during jail hours.

286 Dialogue: Yesterday, Hiram Haydn called me and in his Abe Lincoln voice started to felicitate me on the Putnam deal.

Haydn: Congratulations, boy, you made it.

Mailer: You mean, *they* made it.

Haydn: (Pause) You'll have to forgive me, Norman. My manners are a little off today.

It was wonderful. A year ago I would have gone on for five minutes about how lucky I was, and how pleased, and I would have tried to show what a nice modest guy I am, all the while throwing shit on myself, and on *The Deer Park*.

288 Bob Lindner is in the dramatic electric intellectual situation he has been seeking all his life and which he approached in "The Jet-Propelled Couch." He has to wonder if I am going toward genius or psychosis, and with his fabulous intuitions he sensed dimly a long time ago that the heart of the enigma of life can be found here.

289 Let me try **283** again. I am the rationalist who is drawn to the mystery. I have no patience with exposition. Once I know something to my own satisfaction, I just do not have the enthusiasm to expound it, to go through the motions. That is why I have never been able to write a novel which I planned in advance. I can only write novels which I discover as I go. That is also why I was attracted to science and mathematics in my adolescence and started off to be an engineer. I was essentially a physicist at that time, for physicists (real physicists as opposed to academic physicists) are rational men who are attracted to a mystery. Engineers are their opposite. Engineers have confused minds which seek for certainty. The engineer is only happy when he can find the number, know the problem, state the answer. The physicist is only happy when he can quit the number, the answer, for the question. So my novels had to go forward and my audiences (at least my sympathetic audiences) diminish for I just could not go through the motions of describing how I had gotten to the point from which I start my characters. All my writing of that sort today is uninspired. I am interested essentially, creatively, in going on, and so my best characters in *The Deer Park* (for me) were the ones who were always mysteries to me before—to wit, Lulu, Munshin, and above all, Teppis. They are what lift the novel above the merely intelligent, sophisticated and cynical. They are glorious monsters. And Marion Faye is the character who leads me out of the book and has pointed the way to the next one, whatever it will be.

290 Now I COME BACK to word echoes and . . . letter echoes. And I am in something which is very difficult for me because . . . to be continued.

292 Now, BACK TO **290**. Something very difficult for me because I know so little about languages other than English, and one must know a language very well even to begin to do this since one must work almost entirely on intuition. But I do believe that the buried soul of man, the deeply suppressed H has always expressed itself in language, and this simply, so simply that no one ever pays attention. What I have to say here is true only for English. Other languages would have vastly different relations to consonants and vowels to the sex-soul and to the bodily functions, but if I'm right at all in English, such work is for others in other languages. Anyway, I have already discussed the quality of "r" which added to a work gives color, anger, movement, definition. For example "word" without the "r" is wod or what.

TH and D are related. D I believe has the connotations of death, TH the connotations of a thing, of Other-Life. For example, It is the combination of I (my self, my being) with (thingishness). D and T, A *debt* is a social death. TH and its relation to T, I don't feel yet.

But I'm starting in the middle. Let me begin with "I." It is the center of the universe, the center of language. It is the *eye*. It is the mediator between the self and the world, for of all the senses the eye is the one which bears the most direct relation to the world. (I believe that a similar study in all languages would have to begin with the equivalent of I except for Japanese and other such languages in which the I is not part of speech.) *I* is the giver. Me is the taker. Dialogue: To whom do I give this. Answer: To me.

Let me go back a few lines for a clue. It possibly comes from Ich in German. The German I is less assertive than the Saxon I. It is Ich, and possibly the Saxons borrowed *it* from *Ich*. Certainly Germans think of themselves (national character) more as (it)s than (I)s.

Back to I and Me. We also say, "May I take this?" and the answer is "From me?" On the surface taking and giving are respectively I and Me. *But*, the I initiates the action, and by initiating, by creating, the I is giving. The Me nominally giving is actually being taken from. What I get from this is that givers take even as givers, and takers give even as takers which is why strong givers have anxiety about taking and vice versa.

Very interesting. I made an error above. I meant to say givers give even when they seem to be taking; takers take even when they seem to be giving. I have a thing over this.

To continue: (despite all odds of my over-fecund brain) I believe intuitively that the rest of the vowels in English come from I. Eee we have already explored. It is buried in Me. It is the feminization, or better the feminine element in Me which contains both MMMMM (the grunt of the savage male) and EEEEEEEE (the delight of the female.) Ahhhhh, aaaaaaah, ohhhhhh, ooooooooo, ehhhhhhhh, ihhhh (the 'I' sound of it or give.) ayyyyyy (as g*a*ve) and the last vowel is 'u' that is the sound of YOU.

Before we go any further I want to say that from my slight knowledge of other languages it is obvious to me that English (or

Saxon—that is, English deprived of its Latinisms) is a very primitive language. It is exceptionally onomatopoetic, and therefore its spelling is so outrageous, for to conceal the obvious meanings of the sounds it was necessary that intelligent people, the very people who could go at the meanings, should be led astray by the spellings. This is one source of outrageous spelling. The other is that words were undoubtedly combined and fused letters separated. (For instance "s," I believe, used to be written as "f.") The connection between fucking and the piss-shit axis had to broken.

To go on. The primitive like the baby beginning to speak must first have conceived of I, and Me (I'm not sure in which order), then You, then It (a great discovery for his environment because less dangerous) then Give and Take—Take undoubtedly first from the point of the view of the baby, Give being the growing understanding of the world outside. One *gives* to locate the world which is why psychopaths are givers. One takes in order to understand the world.

294 ONE TAKES IN ORDER to understand the world. So the essential taker when he gives is attempting to dominate the world. Thus the boxer who takes three to give one, but the *one* will deliver him from his basic passivity, allow people to think of him as a champion, which gives him honorable sanction to be passive. One reason perhaps so few champion boxers defend their titles actively. They usually sit around for months.

295 BUT WRESTLERS WHO ARE givers, locators, finders, are attempting to find and crush the world. When they take, it is because they are weary of the constant expenditure of energy. They are begging to be thrown on their backs, because the only rest for the giver is to find a bigger giver. But the giver cannot remain in a state of passivity, he is up again, bouncing, ready to go. Tomorrow night he will wrestle again.

296 TALK IS CHEAP, ACTION is hard. So says the world and so I believed. But I was always at my best talking even though I was ashamed of my talent. Yet the way I write now is that I talk, I talk and talk, and I truly believe some of the things I'm coming across are important. Because talk is dear not cheap; in talk we express our real selves or come closer to expressing our real selves, and in work, in action, we express whatever of our self society will allow. Which is why Stalinists are often nice guys in the living room, tolearant—I meant tolerant but tolearant says more—to let(the)ear rant—perhaps all good words are combinations of words condensed, and bad words—JARGON—is but a single word. Anyway . . . Stalinists are nice guys in the living room, tolerant, sympathetic, and totally rigid in print. They are caricatures of the actuality. But a caricature is a dramatization.

302 ANT AND AND. FOR some time I have been wanting to write down a thought about ants. It is possible that life as it moves up the biological spectrum exhibits, like ascending octaves, socializations (highly developed forms of Other-Life) at certain levels which are highly complex, and then quits them to move to a higher level. Thus, ant society is highly elaborate. Cities are built, work-cooperation is intense. But mammals who are a far higher form of life as we classify them, and indeed they undoubtedly are, have until the level of the elephant and the ape almost no social organization beyond the most rudimentary social contract. This little mystery has made man uneasy of centuries. "And" is the peculiar word whose uses are enormous. It is a word of continuation, it has implications of death, for if we tell a story about a person and use *and* long enough, we will finally be obliged to say, "And then he died." But *and* also expresses the upward ascension. Perhaps its intimate relation to the past, the future, and its dramatic pendant present—we always interrupt the interesting or *boring* story to say, "And?" For note, be a story interesting or boring, saying "And?" makes it more interesting. So perhaps it is related to ant. *And* is alive, dramatic, partakes of death, and suggests life. The ant has the T at the end. It is close to being a thing. We are always a little repelled by the ant because its social organization is too high, too elaborate, for its life. It partakes too much of Other-Life.

303 OBSCENITIES: 69—*SOIXANTE-NEUF*. THE PROOF that we personify symbols as society would put it, or (H-wise) that symbols are clues to our buried H, our sexual souls. The typewriter is fascinating. Look at the symbols on top of the numbers. In order they are

```
" # $ % _ & ' ( ) *
2 3 4 5 6 7 8 9 0 -
```

304 JAZZ. Z AND S are sibling components. So are G and J. Transpose and we get GAS. Gas is the vapor, the cloud, the mystery—it is also energy, potency, drive as in GASoline.

305 AT THIS MOMENT I'M sick of word echoes. They depress me. Letter echoes are even worse. I begin to feel that I'm engaging in nonsense. To anyone but the most sympathetic reader it would seem that I'm psychotic.

306 BUT WHAT A COMPULSION. No sooner do I write it than I notice that I made a mistake in nonsense. I tried to write *nosese*. So, let's look at it. S and X are also sibling consonants. T think of sex and how *hex* and *cess* are echoes. I suspect cess as in cesspool and hex are words from the Middle Ages when the church was putting the hex on sex by making it cess.

307 I'M GETTING WEARY, AND I'd better leave word echoes and consonant relationships because I'm trying to go too fast, and so half the time I'm probably all wet. If I don't use some discrimination I'll be founding a sect halfway between the Rosicrucians and the Reichians. Bless Malaquais. He saved me years by teaching me that one does not necessarily have to act—that there are times when action is impossible. If I hadn't learned that I'd be setting up the letter-heads for the Mailerians. Anyway, one last thing about letters. I suspect that vowels are soul expressions of the self, shadings, colorings, of I. And consonants probably are more related to things outside the self, or to emotions which seem to come from outside forces such as rage for r, piss for p and s.

308 FUCK, PISS, COCK, SHIT, cunt. The world outer and inner can probably be constructed from those five words. One would have to bring in "eat" "sleep" "bleed"—all eee sounds, and incidentally socially acceptable. The ih, the ah, and the uh of my five four-letter words are obviously the grunts of love and defecation. And work or labor. And for that matter eating and sleeping. I bet the eee sounds came later, but first the savage had ih, ah, uh, Oh for wonder, and I. But perhaps "I" is the last of all to come, and is the abstraction of ih, ah, uh. With O and E thrown in. Possibly, like colors which when mixed together make white if they are lights, or gray or brown if they are opaque pigments, so if one could match tapes simultaneously of various vowel sounds, one could find the components of the rich and rather mysterious sound of 'I'.

310 WHEN I WAS A kid in college I wrote "The Bodily Function Blues" but everyone was repelled by it. Secretly, I never was. Here it is:

Ah gotta pissssss
Ah gotta ur-ri-nate
Piss, ss, ss, ss, sssss

Ah gotta shit,
Ah gotta de-fe-cate
Oo oo ee oo ee oo oo

Ah gotta bleed
Ah gotta menstruate
Trickle trickle, trickle trickle.

Ah gotta eat, alimentate, etc.
Ah gotta sleep, somnambulate, etc.

Ah gotta fuck
Ah gotta cop-u-late
Too late, too late.

Oh, what am I gonna do?
I got those blues, I got those blues.
I can't eat, I can't sleep, I can't shit, I can't fuck.
Ah got those bodily function blues. Dad a de dad a.

Exit blues.

311 MY POMPOUS MAN AGAIN. We say, "What a pompous prick." His pompousness pricks us. There are a dozen other things one could add but I am tired.

312 IT SEEMS OBVIOUS THAT insanity is the result of irrecon-cilable S and H. The obvious case: burning sexuality in a terribly severe conscience. Which relieves me about my own sanity. For my S and H are comparatively compatible. For years the H has battered away at the S forming rationalizations which were close to the actuality of myself. There is hardly anything I could discover about myself today which would be unbearable. I think that is why, instead, I am feeling generally so much aliveness and lack of depression. The H finally made it, but by slow stages.

314 ARISTOCRATS ARE USUALLY TAKERS (wits, fencers, collectors, drug addicts, they even marry within their families. They take and hold the family name). Some of the first English boxers were lords. Marquess of Queensberry rules. Boxers are proud.

Workers are usually givers. They give work, they brawl (wrestle). Wrestlers are jovial. They drink.

I am tired. Further examples fail me.

January 27, 1955

315 As was evident in the notes yesterday, I was moving toward a depression, and it came on me during the evening. I felt very tired, and rather disgusted with myself. It seemed to me as if I'd been indulging in mental masturbation for quite a few days, playing word games, playing at being a genius, playing at being at the edge of the psychotic, and I noted that the letter which was to accompany some notes I was sending to Bob which I had half-consciously written almost psychotically had been left out of the envelope. I was going to throw it away (crumple it into a ball), and then changed my mind and just stuck it in with carbons of old letters. I felt disgusted at harassing Bob like that, swindling him into giving a free analysis, not directly of course, but still drawing him in. What preceded the depression were some half-realizations of a very personal sort about my sister and Adele, and I suppose I drew back from them.

316 But what is also interesting is that I welcomed the depression. It was reassuring in a way, it was almost pleasant to return to the old neurotic state which I think signifies for me the state of work, hard work, depressed work, but of course honorable work. I don't know whether to take this journal seriously. At times I think I'm getting into wonderful things, other times I just wonder if I'm losing my grip and bathing in clichés and other people's ideas. We went to a party last night at Malaquais', and in the cab I said to Adele in a very profound voice, "You know, when people go away on vacations, it's not a casual act—it's of deep significance. They're hoping that something will happen which changes their lives." And Adele after a moment of shock at the seriousness I gave it, said, "But, of course, darling, everybody knows that." Perhaps it is just that she has known it all her life, but I was startled and upset. It had seemed such a perception to me. I had been thinking of the peculiar frozen look almost all people have when they come into a resort hotel and their baggage surrounds them with the stamp of the novice. And how relieved they are when they find friends, and the terrible depression under the surface if they cannot cozy up to new acquaintances. Like a repetition of the childhood trauma-adventure of moving to a new neighborhood.

Anyway, for the first time in many weeks I had a lot to drink at Malaquais'. Not to excess but four or five ryes on the rocks which I enjoyed. What I really enjoyed was the old neurotic tension of a party with its fatigues, its aggressions, its enthusiasms. The old depression with the feeling of "force" beneath it, of *masculinity*, was reassuring. We came home, had one of our enjoyable mock-spats for Adele drunk is always full of beans, and fell asleep. I woke up about four hours later, and had a deep perception which I can barely remember, but it made me realize the beauty in myself and in Adele, and I decided that the extraordinary contradiction of my personality, the saint in morality, the potential psychopath sexually was what gave me my strength as a writer. Sort of: the greater the contradiction in a person, the wider the range of his potential experience and intuitions. Only it was very beautiful as I saw it, so beautiful that I woke Adele up and we made love which was very pleasant, and then I almost fell asleep but didn't, and finally got up with four hours of sleep, and have been moving slowly all day, feeling drained, or more exactly drawn to too fine a pitch. Part of it is getting off Seconal which I had taken three nights in a row. Anyway, the obvious occurs to me which is that S forces contain a great deal of their strength because they conserve the body too, or give us the illusion that they do. When the H is open and riding for several days in a row there is exaltation but there is also terror—one feels close to death all the time. S gives me feelings of depression and force, as I have written above.

317 WHAT I DISTRUST OF course is that I'm looking for shortcuts, for magic. Undisciplined, lazy, half convinced of my talent, half doubting it, I feel even in my greatest enthusiasm that this journal may be no more than a game I play with myself to have the illusion that I can do it all alone, that I don't have to follow the rules, that my limitations can be dispelled because I postulate a good old H force.

318 ON THE POSITIVE SIDE, however, I had lunch with my mother today and she took the idea of my father quitting work very well, and the lunch was very pleasant. Again I was moved almost to tears when I spoke of what a good guy he is, and how bad I had been to him. And I thought of my sister and how the only way she is psychopathic is that she is psychopathically compassionate. One cannot tell her a sad story—a real sad story, not an ersatz one—without tears welling into her eyes. And yet all the while I was talking to my mother I had the uneasy feeling that I was acting a little bit like a man who feels death is coming on and so he must get all his affairs in order. (How interesting is the double use of the word "affairs" in English. Hints of the basic orgiastic desire do seem to appear everywhere.) Now a few notes.

320 FOR SOME TIME I have wanted to write a note about the Negro prejudice of Southerners. I wonder if their rage at Negro advancements is due to the unconscious belief in the myth—which may well be right—that the nigger has a happy sex life, happier than the white, and so the Negro is recompensed for his low state in society by his high state in the fuck. The scales are balanced. Therefore, to the white southerner, an improvement in Negro rights is to tip the scale in the Negro's favor. Status-anxiety so-called may consist essentially of the unconscious drawing up balance sheets in which people of lower status are considered to have equal status when the private benefits are added in. So, members of a high status group—to use that monstrous sociological jargon—feeling anxiety about a lower status group crawling up on them, are actually feeling the more intense anxiety that the lower status group is rising above them.

321 THE BUSINESS OF PUTTING magnificent ideas in one's notebook at night. The reason it always seems so flat in the morning is that the idea which may well have been beautiful—and dangerous, for the sense of beauty is umbilically linked with the sense of danger—was put down in cliché form in one's haste to trap it. Normally, one might expect to be able to expand it in the morning. But the S had been alerted, and so when one reads the note, the S drowns all the H sensitivity, and the note seems ridiculous. S is always telling us, "Pay no attention to what happens at night."

322 COROLLARY. WHENEVER ONE READS old notes or old manuscripts of one's work, the S is invariably extremely watchful, which is why old notes seem so flat. We may think we are relaxed, but we are actually deadened by the S which knows its danger.

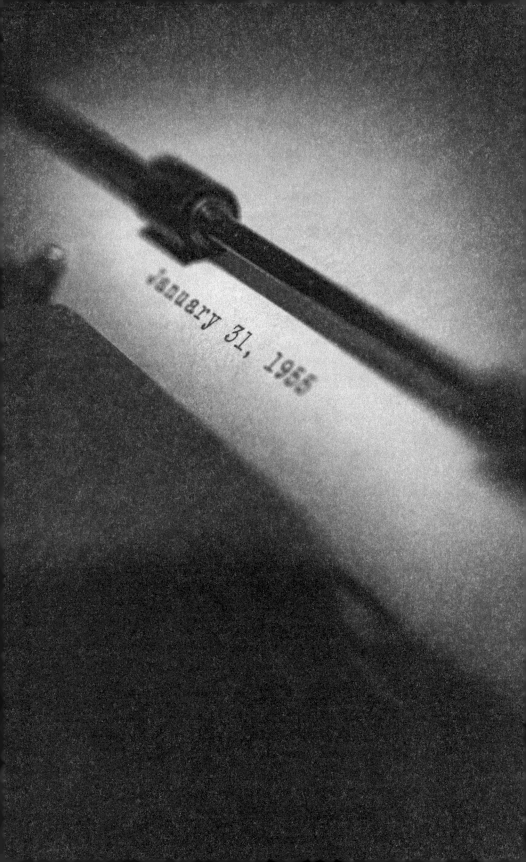

323 My birthday today. Let's give myself a present of a nice fat installment. My weekend will have bearing on this, but I have many ideas crowding me at this moment, and I would rather pick that up later.

325 Give-and-take. It is the life process which dominates, which characterizes every living movement. A static universe would be void of give-and-take. The essence of life movement is in the give-and-take. Naturally, this must be seen in all of its complexity. No human alive—not to mention other kinds of life—is ever simply a giver or a taker, but giving and taking predominate in various parts of the person. So it's suggested that the fat man for instance takes but cannot give in certain emotional ways. Basic kinds of emotional energy cannot be expended. The result is that it is stored as fat. As a corollary of this, the act of going on a diet bespeaks a profound desire to alter one's approach to life. For implicit in all I've written up to now is the idea that the psyche knows the state of the body, knows why a part functions well or badly. And a diet works or does not work in proportion as the person is profoundly ready or not ready to alter their condition. (A very frustrating thing here. As I sat down to write the note, my ideas were much bigger, much more exciting, than what I have put down here. At the last moment they deserted me. One thing I noticed over the weekend is that my S is beginning to work overtime.)

326 The possibility of other psychotherapeutic techniques. Generally, the patient gives gives gives—the analyst takes takes takes. Occasionally, this is reversed. But I wonder if this works well for everybody. Most people, despite their resistance, probably find it easier to talk about themselves, and the projection they put on the analyst is a subtler secondary thing, picked up by intuition. I wonder if certain kinds of neurotics, particularly aggressive "stupid" "insensitive" patients for one example, might not best enter the analysis with the instructions from the beginning to talk not about themselves but about the analyst. This would have to be done by feel of course, but there is a kind of top-heavy righteous man who is made to violate his nature when he is asked to attempt to free-associate. Far better for "cranks" and "reactionaries"—whose ranks are conspicuously absent among analysands—such as McCormick of the *Chicago Tribune* and Winchell—say to lie down or stand up or sit up and deliver themselves in the early weeks of exactly what they think of the analyst. Encouraged to say more and more and more the remarks will very quickly become a giant projection, and it seems to me the time will follow more or less shortly when they realize that. Stunned and terrified, they will then be ready for free association, because simply they will now need to go into themselves. The energy to strike back, to project, which is the character defense, has become over-extended and exhausted.

327 THE VOICE OF RADIO and recordings. It is a commonplace to say that the ear selects sounds, and it is almost as common to recognize that we select those sounds we wish to hear. The S is the inhibitor on the ear, and the reason "takers" are invariably more sensitive listeners that "givers" is that takers accept S more than givers—therefore they can afford to "hear" more. Freud, one of the great givers, could never enjoy music.

328 BUT, CARRY THIS A step further. I suspect that the first impact of the radio was that the ear was given "unselected" sound. So, sound effects. Paper rustled near a microphone sounded too loud. Who is to say it does not sound too loud in life and we merely suppress it? Elements of the voice which had been buried before became more evident to people—naturally at an unconscious level—it being understood as a basic premise through all of these notes that I see the unconscious as not one unconscious, but a whole series of unconsciouses, conceivably infinite, each more buried—and therefore closer to the essential H—than the one above. So put in this light, the voice of radio penetrated more deep into the unconscious layers than the human voice, face to face, where many interferences were present. Therefore an immediate fascination (as Bob says—attraction and repulsion in one package) was the result. The radio was actually conveying more reality *in its details of course* than normal human intercourse. But much more can be said. (There is great interference to my thoughts today. I work along at a dragging rate, instead of racing like last week.) On radio we notice certain qualities of the voice—it never sounds the same close to the microphone and far away. On tape recorders, which are cruder, this is even more true. Every effect of the voice bouncing off objects and walls *seems* to be magnified. I wonder if the truth is that a part of us, deep within us, actually hears aural experience this way. What I wish to emphasize is that S encourages us to hear the voice as one. We think of people as having a voice, not voices, but indeed a person never has the same voice exactly. At every distance we exercise our vocal cords differently from the way we exercise them close up—we are communing through all the filters of the situation in a slightly different way. In crude forms I've known this always without labeling. The voice of one's mate in one's ear is vastly different from the "same" voice calling across a room. And, indeed, because the discrepancy of recorded voices and "live" voices seemed too great, the sound effects man and the recording engineer were born. Their effort was to bridge the gap—the same may be said for movie lighting. The attempt in both is not only to increase "verisimilitude"—an S concept, for H always sees the individual experience as multiple—but to censor part of the actual reality. In the films, it is not merely a question of improving the deficient "seeing" qualities of photographic emulsions, but also a business of warping the final achievement.

329 ONE'S OWN VOICE. HERE the greatest discrepancy appears. Almost always a person is deeply shocked hearing their own voice. I know for me there seems almost no relation between my voice as it sounds to me and as I hear it over a tape recorder. One hears one's own voice naturally from the H—that is, we feel the real panic if we are scared, the exultation if we are excited. Heard as a play-back, it is invariably flattened. (Part of the art of the actor is to accommodate his inner feelings to correspond to the outer voice. Same for the singer.) But, listening to myself on Lipton's last night, hearing my voice on the tape recorder, I noticed that a voice is like a face—all the elements on one's personality exist in the various tones. On the surface my New York Jewish earnest sincere friendly patronizing voice—underneath much more complicated psychic-sexual elements were being communicated.

330 ONE OTHER OBSERVATION. IT was the first time in years that I spoke into a tape recorder. What happened was that I spoke very slowly. But indeed everybody except rare birds like Winchell speak slowly over the radio or television. The S is fantastically on guard, because it recognized the great danger one is in. So, that accounts for the fantastic pompousness of celebrities who have little to say, and the unbearable earnestness and suppressed anguish of the creative person when he speaks over a program. Everything in the self becomes slowed up as in Lipton's. Only, with what a difference. One speaks in a state of deep receptivity to social danger.

331 MIMICS ARE ALWAYS PSYCHOPATHS—GOOD mimics anyway. And a person who does parlor imitations is expressing his or her psychopathy, but it is psychopathy under a neurotic protection which is why they are not professional entertainers. What characterizes saints and psychopaths is that the S is comparatively non-existent in them. It is the difference in their H which separates them, and this I don't know how to define yet.

332 LAST WEEK I WROTE that the radical rebellious H of reason which was true from the Middle Ages until the nineteenth century has now become the rationalization of the state. And the hope for the future lies with the monsters and the mystics. To wit, the seemingly irrational, for only the irrational can fuck up the progress of the state. Monsters and mystics is of course merely a way of saying psychopaths and saints. But I wonder if the waves of psychopathy which every sensitive intellectual feels are not the generating life expressions of the only way to keep the H alive and healthy in people. In other words, psychopathy may be healthier than we think. It is an expression of the H which can find its understanding only by the mirror image of the S (here is one essential difference between saints and psychopaths), and therefore psychopathy always appears as a greater or lesser monstrosity, but what is important is that at least it is an H, and even appearing as an S (all genuine artistic expression today is degraded human expression) it is undigestable by the State (although unfortunately less undigestable than it used to be—society even seeks to rehabilitate the criminal) and therefore dangerous to the plans of the State.

333 I HAVE THE FEELING these days that I could make a remarkable businessman. The reason is that I feel close to the buried appetites of people in a way that is not the talent of the "creative" businessman. He senses the buried needs of people— perhaps not consciously—but the psychopathic intuitive is close to the surface. What keeps him from having our admiration is that the businessman is a good businessman insofar as he is all psychopath and no saint. He uses intuition for his own enrichment with no qualms about the social ends of his work. "Social ends" is of course an S. It is the social perversion of the brotherhood of man (a genuine H expression deep out of the self which knows we are all a part of the whole) but even as a perversion it reflects the echo of the H. One other difference between psychopaths and saints is that the psychopath's H is deficient in the knowledge of the brotherhood of man. The psychopath has an intense sense of his own needs, but cannot understand the needs of others because that part of his soul is deficient. Why, why it has been crippled, is something else, and I don't know the answer . . . yet.

334 A GREAT DEAL OF this journal first manifested itself in my Tarot readings. Even word and consonant echoes. What occurs to me about my character is that I used to be a condemning and highly moral neurotic with intense psychopathic drives. As my "analysis" goes on, I have the feeling that I move from psychopath to saint or mystic in my H because my S is in retreat.

But when I used to give Tarot readings, the extraordinary emanation I "knew" I gave off was because the psychopath and the mystic were evident to everyone in the room. It was the herald of what was coming.

335 JEALOUSY. BUT WHAT A mountain is to be uncovered here. The key is that degraded expressions, as I keep saying, express in perverted form, the true nature of man's needs. So, simply, jealousy is the degraded expression of the deep desire for the brotherhood of man. If jealous emotions give us pleasure—as is true for most bisexuals—it is not because one is expressing one's "latent homosexuality" which is the vulgar *condemnation* analysts generally put upon it, but because, as a practical matter, it is the only way one can feel "close" to another man. (We can feel close to other women by fucking them.) I remember that once with a girl I loved considerably, I got into an orgy (a quartet) and when she came while the other man was making love to her, I came too just watching—actually receiving the experience. I was horrified, horrified at her, at myself; I loathed the other man. But that was obviously defense against "taking." I could not admit the other man into brotherhood. But from deep in me, although fundamentally I'm still quite incapable of doing this with Adele, I suspect that there is great joy in giving one's mate to another man—there is genuine brotherhood at the heart of it. Which is why Reich with his incredible instincts and courage was so right about The Sexual Revolution. One cannot have a libertarian egalitarian society until one has the orgy accepted as a genuine part of life. For note, the orgy as I have said before, is the repetition of the family situation—but our first sense of brotherhood is given us by the family, and indeed in the socialized bastardized sense the brotherhood of man is given social sanction within the limits of the family—my mother for example is completely selfless within family limits, she would literally die for one of us. That is why she has so much life; she has gotten away with expressing her H all her life under cover of the S; it is why I will always love her, for in that sense she is truly good. The orgy is a reflection of the family, but the family is the first primal shock "in human language," that is, conceptually, to the infant. It is the first understanding that the I is the We, the first apperception of the brotherhood of man, the communion of all souls.

336 THE CYNIC. HE IS the incomplete honest man, the man who cannot accept S but has nothing to substitute for it, for he distrusts even himself. In that sense the cynic is *modest*. He will not compromise his hatred of S, but he cannot express H, so all the balked H energies go into constructing a rationalization of his H needs, in reverse of course. He attacks everything because he must— only by diminishing the level of the outer world can he breathe at his own self-despised level. But he is still better than most for at least he is an honest man; he has not tried to mutilate the small part of himself he can feel. He is the saint-and-psychopath (in varying degree) enslaved by his intelligence which is the mental part of human creativity completely appropriated by society. Finally, he is the echo of the *genius*, the pale counterpart, as I will try to describe below.

337 THE CONSERVATISM OF THE female element applies even to heaven. The woman, reaching heaven, is content to stay there. The male element demands to go on—"Is it possible," he asks with curiosity, "that beyond Heaven there may be Hell. If so, we have to take a look at it." This is the essence of genius, and provides a clue to why there have been so many more men geniuses than women—leaving social considerations aside—finally women did not rebel against their suppressed social role for so many centuries because it was not that essential to them, and indeed much of their "social liberation" is due to the efforts of men, the radical rationalists of the nineteenth century. The genius is a person who cannot bear the answer—like the physicist (and in science one finds the most geniuses because science is the most social of the arts, so social that it is nominally called knowledge, and therefore it receives the most sanction). But to repeat, the genius cannot bear the answer; he must go on to pose a new question. So, no matter what nominally he is doing, he is journeying deeper and deeper into the H, for the H contains all wisdom possible at any age to man since it is a part of life. But to do this, the genius must make a voyage which is opposed to society. No matter what his own notion of it, he is always attacking society because he is always carrying further our knowledge of the Self. (Note, word echo: Knowledge is now—ledge. It is society's use of soul-intuition. It is the present ledge, the present petrifaction of what the souls of the past have given us.) But to go into the self is to go against society which demands as the condition of its being that people be as self-less (not unselfish—a very important distinction) as possible in order that they be more malleable. So, the genius always carries with him the fear of Hell which is society's most poetic symbol of the punishment it gives for above all symbols, even above Heaven which is misty to people while Hell is concrete (this is true even for organized religions and Stalinism and Hitlerism which make Hell concrete, and leave Heaven to take care of itself). So, as a poetic symbol, Hell is capable of speaking to the deep self. And the genius moves into beauty—which is danger, and into exaltation—which is terror. The genius is a man, therefore, who is tormented all of his life by doubt whether he is a saint or a psychopath, good or evil. He is the gambler carried to divinity, for the genius wagers every creative instant of his existence that he is going to heaven and not to hell, and therefore he must be obsessed with feelings of terror and danger. It is a bet to take one's breath away—not to know never whether one goes to Heaven or Hell, and to be always aware that either is possible. What makes a genius is his incredible courage, for he is a man who lives always in fear, and yet continues.

338 WORD ECHOES. BREATH, STRIPPED of r and h becomes bet. The bet is the social action which is the concretion of the life process—breath—give and take. I tried to write "true" above but my fingers wrote *ture* which is tour. So truth is not the point, the static, the absolute, but the voyage, the tour, the changing.

339 EXCEPTIONAL PEOPLE. EXCEPTIONAL PEOPLE are people who go across a spectrum. The whore who becomes a lady (Eva Peron); the dishonest man who becomes honest—Bob Lindner; the artist who becomes a bourgeois—my father; the adventurer who becomes a rationalist, legalist—Cy Rembar; the lady who becomes a whore—any society nymphomaniac; myself, the bourgeois who goes toward the saint-psychopath; and so forth and so forth. Truly exceptional people, people who go down in history, are people who complete more than half of the voyage. Most people turn back. The mass of people hardly ever started. But it is natural to go across one's social nature, it is healthy, it is an expression of the desire to complete one's soul. For it is probably true that the most essential parts of oneself are the most buried. In infancy and childhood, the child begins to realize that whatever it offers to the world is taken away from it, made something which is no longer its own. So what it really wished to keep, it buries. Later in life the health of the body itself demands that what is buried be expressed, and exceptional people who are always people who are intensely alive (even though like Malaquais the conflicts may be so tremendous that they live in intense depression and in a tangential life expression—Malaquais is the poor Jew who wished to become a king—and settled for the tangential expression of being the most aristocratic of the radicals), exceptional people being extremely alive have to move on or they will die. So they begin, inevitably, step by step—in society's view they are people who start to deteriorate or take on airs. Sooner or later, for most of them, comes the crisis. The breakdown, the dead-end, the rout or the trench-warfare of H vs. S, and so they flee to the analyst. The analyst in his social function with rare exceptions is the man who turns people back to their starting point. So, in a case like my father's, a good result would have been achieved perhaps—the small artist in him would have emerged in small ways. I would probably have been turned back if I had had a bad but powerful analyst, to the bourgeois in me. The reason a successful analysis gives generally more comfort and less creativity is that the H is utilized to justify the S. One accepts society, not oneself—the advertisements of the analysts to the contrary—and so one emerges "contented" but always the prey of "stabbing" regrets. Did one lose something is the recurring obsession of the successful analysands. But for the analyst to do the opposite—to make the S accommodate itself to the H, rather than vice-versa, is to set the patient off in his own small way toward becoming a genius. Which means beauty and danger, exaltation and terror. How many people can bear that? Far better, reasons the analyst in his social cowardice, to take the H uncovered and turn it upon oneself. Implicit in conventional analysis is the idea that the unconscious is dirty, petty, childish, ugly, aggressive, disturbing—the social brute animal which must be cleansed . . . and tamed. So each H which reveals itself is seen through the eyes of S (as people we sense everything both in S-ways and H-ways, usually simultaneously, but with one or the other in predominance) and seen through the eyes of S by both analyst and patient. Therefore, a more elaborate social defense, a more flexible S, is devised "by ear" between patient and analyst to "handle" this "drive." Successful analyses, that is conventional successful analyses, do nothing for the H except confuse it, but they do give a wonderfully flexible and sensitive set of S-defenses. Which is why successful analysands always have that "pious" quality. They can name anything you do. They are to the soul, as the pious man is to real religion—a caricature of it, a diminisher, a reducer. Did you do something for a great, grand, and novel reason—they ascribe it to your desire to piss on people. Which is why I had to fight Elliot Kammerman. And that is why totally successful analysands (a theoretical concept) can never love people, they can only love society. So their successful marriages are always social marriages—they marry the "ideal" partner which means the socially ideal partner. I am willing to bet that geniuses always have wacky marriages—marriages which seem socially incredible on the surface. The successful analysand is the middle-class caricature in miniature of the perfect Stalinist citizen. And analysis is to blame. It entered the soul, but given its birth and social needs, it quickly became "socialized," and so it never saw the real good noble if warped qualities of the H—it could only condemn them. I am willing to bet that nearly all analysts are people who sensed more or less dimly that if they did not become analysts they would become rebels, terrifying rebels. Analysis is the best personality defense of them all for it is the graveyard of rebellion unless one is a genius.

340 WHICH BRINGS ME TO Bob Lidner. The "twist" in Bob is that he entered psychoanalysis not as a rebel essentially but as a manipulator, a con man, a crook. He was going to learn more about people so he could use them better. But that was the top of his soul, and the basic Bob who is the honest rebel has been emerging more and more. Despite himself, his analytic position becomes progressively more radical, more dangerous. He is travelling the spectrum of himself—as I wrote before he is going from the dishonest man to the honest man, and what a world he crosses. Analysis, practicing it, living with it, is a catalyst for him where it is a corset for most analysts, because analysis enables him to express his true being whereas for most analysts it allows only the suppression of the self. So most analysts get more depressed, more unpredictable in their tiny wild actions (Herbert Aldendorff) and Bob gets more open, more amiable, more loving, more delighted with himself and with others as the years go on. And that is why people (practically all my friends) find him so nice, so attractive, are so drawn to him, and then are disappointed in his books. It is his books which still represent the social part of him, the "crook," the con man of ideas who throws out things only to hide them—the hand is quicker than the eye.

341 PAGE **100**. IT BRINGS back to me the feeling I have always had about writing. If I get to a hundred pages it has always meant that I would finish the book. And so I always feel happy when I get to page one hundred.

342 STIMULANTS. MY IDEAS WHICH started slow this morning are now again coming so fast they are almost out of hand. The surface reason was Seconal and black coffee. I had Lipton's last night, quite a bit, and then Seconal to bring me down, and then black coffee to bring me up. But I didn't have enough, I still felt sluggish, so two and a half hours ago I went out to have more, and since then I've been flying. But what are stimulants? Given the incredible complexity of modern life, the deeper and deeper awareness of the H, the more and more elaborate construction of the S, trench-warfare is the condition of the soul. (As a wild speculation it opens the idea for an historical inquiry or thesis to the effect that each war which expresses the total of deep collective truths of the soul is the clue to the time which is to follow. So the trench warfare of 1914–1918 is expressed today in the psychic state of the average sensitive intellectual. And the spiritual life of the future, say 1984, may not be 1984 at all, but rather the wild, anarchic, intermittent, destructive and sudden liberating movements of the second world war. But this is a wild one, for the moment anyway.) To go on: The only way we can liberate enough H energy to do good work—for society's weakness is that it cannot defeat H entirely for if it does, society will become totally static and then deteriorate—is to take stimulants and sedatives—one giving more life, one giving more peace, but both opening the H. Yet society cannot allow real sanction to this for too much of the soul might be uncovered. So liquor is tolerated when it must be—marijuana which I understand is less harmful than liquor and considerably cheaper is illegal, sedatives like Seconal are considered the refuge of a weak spineless over-nervous person, and even coffee is frowned on. How many times have we heard people say, "He drinks too much coffee. It's not good for him." The wilder drugs like cocaine, heroin, and I predict, mescaline, are hounded and persecuted. What I have noticed in myself is that I need stimulants and Lipton's less and less over the whole than I have before because a breakthrough has come. But I still need them a great deal. However, I have found part of the secret. It is society's condemnation of stimulants which we carry in ourself which does at least half of their harm. Reduce the

S and the body could take a lot more playing around with provided genuine enjoyments of mind and body were the result. It is the half-enjoyments which send us back again and again. We half-know there is something there which is calling to our self, we half-despise ourselves. To wit: fascination.

343 FASCINATION KEEPS US ON the saint-psychopath spectrum. Without it we become either saints or psychopaths depending on whether pure attraction (saint) or pure repulsion is felt toward the outer thing (be it person, idea, object, etc.). So, the genius is always *fascinated*, which is why a genius always expresses himself in work. Work as the product of H vs. S is also the product of attraction vs. repulsion. So it is good in a way that I have my retreats, my depressions over this journal. *They are what keep me working.* This journal is the record of my attempts to overcome my disgust for these pages. So the journal has grown, and ideas which were crude and banal in the early pages develop into more satisfying insights later. But continually new crude "wild" ideas occur. Those give the hint to where I'm going if I can continue working, that is, continue being repelled, rather than just take off into saintliness and be shriven of repulsion and the desire to work. But I feel a real crisis for me as a novelist. My novels have always been explorations. I can never stop to expound the idea once I have it, I have to go on. And where now could I begin a novel? I have the unhappy thought that the insights of these pages have taken away from me ten years of solid novels. I hope not, but I suspect yes. Perhaps now I do have to go back to science which I quit when I was an engineering student because engineering, I knew in my bones, was merely the passive exposition of an idea handed you by another man. Ah, well, Malraux moved on, maybe I can too.

344 WHAT I NEGLECTED TO say about Winchell in the notes on radio and voices is that the secret of his success is simply, very simply, that he talks fast on radio. In life I suspect he talks much more slowly. Given the "ear" into one's H that the radio provides, vital experience is longed for. But instead come the sonorities of celebrities, announcers, and advertisements (1939 style, say). So Winchell as the liberal and Winchell as the reactionary still had an audience, even if it wasn't the same audience. He spoke quickly, he gave "electric" communication. Now, he is less important because the principle of speed has been used more and more by television. Announcements are given at top speed and so work better. The comedian of the present is a racer going faster and faster, doing more and more.

345 HALF-WAY STATIONS. I WAS the romantic sent out to discover realism—which is *Naked*. But once the realist, I had to become the realist going out to understand the romantic which is my present state. So, like a boomerang which we hold with both hands we throw ourselves forward, and when we land the boomerang is now us and we the boomerang.

346 JOURNALISTS—ANOTHER VARIETY OF PSYCHOPATH. They are dishonest men whose dishonesty is the defense (the turning-back) against their desire to know and to destroy. That is why they are so unpleasant. They have to get the story—it is their great compulsion—but of course once they get the story, they never write it. They write a lie instead. The worst of these are the political analysts, the "serious" journalists. They cover themselves with expertization, they penetrate into the crevices of society, and feed out social pap. At least the scandal writers, the murder writers, and the columnists occasionally do give out a bit. (The word bit really means in the slang—a bit of truth.) Underneath the pious tones with which call girls are written about—in the *Post* which is a forward paper socially—the pious tone is the tone of the social welfare worker who has everything clocked, rather than a conventionally moral tone. He or she *knows* that the sexy call girl is really rigid. (Only if this were truly so instead of half-true; why do they hate call-girls? Especially female social workers.) The *Life* and *Time* boys are the Harvard variety of the journalist, the man who must learn the truth in order to lie. Possible insight: the compulsion to get the story, to know the truth, can be a reflection of the anxiety that if the "truth" is not known, one cannot lie efficiently—by accident one may tell the truth.

347 AN INTERESTING CONFIRMATION OF the S-eating process. While I was having lunch, I stopped at a newsstand to buy a paper. A white-haired lady of sixty-odd was talking to the newsdealer. They were talking about the passing of the *Brooklyn Eagle*, and in a voice of shock and a little outrage, the white-haired lady said, "But it's over a hundred years old." I sensed immediately that it was deeply upsetting to her. She had the psychology of those old people who have been S all their lives. They feel that society should reward them which is why they often are so martyred in their air, and the fact that society changes too and venerable institutions which have become worthless like the *Brooklyn Eagle* are axed and buried by society itself, or so it seems to them, is terribly painful. Anyway, I watched her out of the corner of my eye. She wandered away, she came back to the stand, quiet, but close to being pathetic. Finally, after a little indecision and fumbling, she reached forward and chose a piece of candy from the rack. Truly, sweets are the great unrecognized drug, the one which cushions us against disappointment, but exacts the price of leaving the H inert. So, disappointment, fear, even terror are smoothed into depression and flatness by sweets.

I must say the scientist in me leaped when I saw her take the candy. I really feel a little these days like Einstein. I have the feeling that if I go far enough, I will be able to set up an experiment in advance, so to speak. One which might confirm or deny these ideas.

348 PRO AND CON—PRICK AND cunt. For and against. H and S.

349 THE CATHOLIC CHURCH IS the poet of society, using the warped tortured talents of its leaders and infantrymen to make society more capable of resisting the H. The Holy Mother Church is feminine, as is society.

351 WORD MIRRORS: (BETTER WORD than echo for reversals.) Be and ebb.

352 I CANNOT SAY IT often enough. In the tiny is the profound. Those things which are too insignificant to notice are always the doors od discovery. Every mistake I make on the typewriter now offers something. I just wrote od for of. The odd is the expression of satisfaction wed to the feeling of death. Ahhhh—dd.

353 HORSE-RACING. AN ARTICLE IN *Life* by a racing bureaucrat decries against horse-doping while giving a marvelous description of its benefits. We are against doping horses because if it works with horses why shouldn't it work with men? But that is too dangerous for society. Society accepts an innovation pressed by *reformers*, only when society is ready to adapt it to its own uses. So, it is perfectly possible that drugs will be used socially for people in twenty or fifty years or indeed in five. But society will then have elaborated the techniques of controlling the H thus released. It will use drugs in order to make people function more efficiently for its purposes. That is why I have instinctively been opposed to reformers and have always seen myself as a radical and revolutionary. As indeed I am. The reformer is the revolutionary turned back. His H turns back upon itself the moment it is in danger of going out too far—going to No-man's land. So the reformer delivers nothing—he merely offers language and analysis to society when it turns in its adaptations to what he presents. If he were not there, it would have done it more clumsily. That is why the Soviet Union is so ponderous, clumsy, and contradictory in its reforms, its very movements. It has to be since the reformer has nothing like the social sanction here. But I am a revolutionary because only by revolution, and probably not political revolution, can the S be set back on its heels and put into serious retreat, thus opening larger H gambits for future generations in which the S will never be as strong again. Although of course it cannot disappear until man reaches God which I suppose is the point of infinity.

355 WORD ECHOES. GOOD, GOD, Gold, and Goal. No wonder men pursue gold, and yet fear it. It is God, sensual pleasure, and death all in one word.

356 GOOD. GO TO D, Go to death—as society has used it. But if there is a God as I believe there is, his name should be Gol—Goal. Go to Life.

357 MODERN PAINTING. THE ABSTRACT painting reduces from life, condenses from life. It is essentially a social art, a diminishing art. But non-objective painting is the swelling up, the magnifying of a moment, a microcosm, it is the magnification of something apparently tiny or insignificant. So, it seems to have no relation to anything—except perhaps the hen-tracks and scratching of various electronic particles on photographic plates under the new microscopes. And indeed why could this not be true. Somewhere within itself the brain must understand the nature of the atom, know how it moves. But this is speculation. What is important is that non-objective painting is the first of the arts to move from society into the H. It goes beyond Time because it does not attempt *to condense Time* which is the essence of history, social understanding, reason, classified knowledge, etc. etc. etc. Instead it expands Time, it takes the moment and swells it into the creation. If I am ever to write more novels I shall have to take what is essentially a moment and swell it into a book.

358 THE KEY TO BILL Styron's nature is that he does not want a total involvement or commitment to anything or anyone. His strength and weakness as a man and an artist is in that. He was repelled by Maloney because Maloney insisted his friends go all the way with him, and Bill was not ready for that. Indeed, I would not have been either. One reason there may be few art works in the future is that we will be artists at human relations, give ourselves entirely to people in order to save them.

359 THE INTER-FECUNDATION IS STARTING. A letter from Bob says, "Occasionally . . . I find myself leaping ahead in my mind—or arguing fiercely as if you were present." It has to be. So many of my ideas are expansions of Bob's ideas—in turn many of mine will be expanded by Bob. Yet, I'm ashamed to say that I was not entirely pleased when I read the above. There's a part of me which is such a *holder.* I really hate to give up a part of me, and I usually give best when I will not be totally accepted (Bob was right about this). I'm so afraid things will be stolen—which of course is the way of saying things will be improved. What causes the rich man so much anguish when his joint is looted is that deep in him he suspects that the thief will enjoy his property more than he did. There is one other fear about Bob which is justifiable perhaps. I'm not at all sure he's the revolutionary—he is so capable of turning back to be the mere reformer. Which means my ideas will be abused. But this is quibbling. I have jumped on a stray lack of elation. The fact is that I would have been much less delighted, much more depressed if my ideas had not stimulated him because the modest part of me knows that everything created is a dead end unless it serves to stimulate the artist and others to go beyond. And Bob can go places I cannot go, just as the same is true for me. Once I get rid of more S, my H may be more content with being a part of the whole instead of the whole.

360 WHICH GIVES AN INSIGHT into the power-mad man. He is generally all S or some warping or new mutation of S with the most intense H beneath. All through his being he feels his difference, but he thinks conventionally, believes conventionally. So he can express his H only by being superior to everyone else, by dominating everyone else, by being right about everything. His drive to power is the homeostasis of his soul (homeostasis being understood again as the most effective compromise of H vs. S). Which would explain why power-mad men court disaster. They have to. They can never retreat. Which is why McCarthy went down although he was given every opportunity to compromise—indeed they finally had to squash him legislatively because they had become terrified of him—unlike other legislators he was not a social being—also true of all power-mad men. He was an animal. Which is what man becomes when his H—which is his greatness is expressed completely in S. But that also accounts for why he had his strength, may have it again, and why so many people including myself had a sneaking attraction toward him, not because of his ideas, but because of his person. The same is true for Hitler and the Germans, and the plan of the *Junker* generals to assassinate Hitler. How horrible is H when it appears on the surface as total S.

361 I AM ALWAYS INEPT at arguing when I feel myself in the presence of a powerful S mind. The reason is not so much cowardice as the preservation of H. (Why did I write S?—is it because I am so social that I don't really believe in H?) To attempt to deliver an H argument before it has developed is to ask oneself to relinquish the idea for years. Indeed, to enter an argument which one loses decisively is to encourage because one wishes to encourage a sociostatic advance.

365 A LOT OF THIS is probably concealed in the confusions and subtleties of prepositions. Never forget that 500 page book which was written on the subtleties of French and English prepositions.

366 A CORROBORATION PROOF IS that common people seem to have more of a knack for picking up languages than intellectuals although of course there are a thousand other things which enter. Takers are obviously better than givers for languages.

367 THE REFORMER'S LIBERAL IDEAS are his defense against his revolutionary impulses. So the journalist is to the novelist as the reformer is to the revolutionary, or should I say anarchist?

368 NAT HALPER. HIS WORK on the Joyce book proceeds so slowly because he is terrified he will go off on his own—into his own work. The *Finnegans Wake* analysis is his defense against his own impulse which is to be an original creator and not a follower.

369 MODERN ART. LIBERALS, SOCIAL democrats, analysands, etc. like abstract painting. It is a rationalization of the world. But non-objective painting they find a bit too "undisciplined" for their taste. Anarchists, cranks, rebels, wild-o's, dig non-objective painting because non-objective painting is the first expression of the H. Adele who has always been the rebel and anarchist who is secretly drawn to being the lady or the social-democratic equivalent of it possible for her, has this conflict in her painting. Abstract painting leaves her unsatisfied, but she is frightened of non-objective and cannot let go in it. Perhaps with my "new" influence, she may begin to.

370 ELENA IS A FAILURE in *The Deer Park* because she is a degraded image of Adele. I wrote Elena as my defense against loving Adele, but in creating Elena my defense was dissipated. That is the peculiar danger and stimulation of the artist, particularly the writer—as The Burglar says—he writes away his defense.

371 CANCER. I BELIEVE INSTINCTIVELY, intuitively, that cancer is the rage of the soul at not having lived properly, at not expressing the H. Its relation to cigarette smoking seems to be that cigarettes are not so much cancer producing agents as cancer accompanying agents. In other words, the smoker is probably an S man with rebellion very close to his surface. So he smokes, taking little sips of the tiny antiseptic penis with its red hot tip, and is both antiseptic-and-social and rebellious and orgiastic at the same time. He gets lung cancer if the H is never properly expressed. He is able to give up cigarettes if the H is waning, the S relaxing, and a state of comparative armistice arriving. So we gain weight when we give up smoking, we feel contented, we taste food—the S has prevailed. I wonder if one can give up cigarettes if the H triumphs over the S. Possibly. I have given up much of sweets and alcohol, I wish to eat less. But cigarettes—I'd have to have a very successful H analysis.

372 FOR *The Deer Park*—WHEN Elena cries out after the orgy, "I was the center of attention. I thought everybody loved me." That is, the last sentence should be added.

375 CONSONANT ECHOES: S. IT is the cross, the double cross, the erasure. A very difficult sound and letter. I don't feel it yet, I just have a hint.

376 THE CROSS WAS WHERE man was swindled. Jesus, the rebel, the anarchist, the saint, the compassionate, the life-giver, the kisser of feet was put on the cross and all his teachings were reversed. Christ became Christianity just as Reason became Rationalization.

377 ADELE'S QUALITIES. SHE HATED the portrait of Elena, it hurt terribly. She felt it was the way I saw her, yet she accepted it, she loves the book. Part of it of course is her despised image of herself, but more important still is the terrific woman in her who accepts my work no matter how painful it is to her, who is even capable of wishing only the best for it. It is an extraordinary human quality and yet she has a low opinion of herself. Once she comes to have a better opinion—based on what she is and not on what she wished to be—she's going to be remarkable.

378 THE VOICE. MORE BASIC than any expression or sense of man, it is the link between the self and society. Before speech there was man but there was no society, certainly no abstract social contract. So much is buried in the voice. I have always had inhibitions about speaking to strangers for I felt deep in me that the moment I spoke I would be discovered, that my voice would reveal my Self. It is depressing to hear the adenoidal range of my voice on a tape recorder, but it is also reassuring. I am more social than I thought. My voice is like other voices. I wonder if it will begin to change soon. That would be one of the indices of my self-analysis progressing.

379 A NOTE ON MY Self-Analysis. I'm not doing it a la Horney. I do it in blocks. I do it by commenting on the world, by expressing myself, by Liptoning up, by fucking, by feeling. There is no formal analysis as such, yet I believe that if nothing else happens and this were all to stop tomorrow that my relation to my parents, and my way of seeing things could never be quite the same again. So, something is definitely happening. It suggests that I am doing my analysis in the way proper for me which is through creativity—taking into the self, synthesizing, and giving back. The analysand given to the conventional analyst is run through a stamping machine. The same technique like the bed of society (the bed of Bluebeard which stretched legs and chopped off feet) is applied to everyone. If there are differences among analysts, rebellions, they are immediately converted into mutinies, sects, cults, schools. But very few analysts are capable of employing different techniques, radically different techniques as a matter of course with every patient. Adele's analyst strikes me as being rather remarkable under his German sociismus front. He had her sit up—which basically is the expression the analyst gives when he is uncertain what the hell to do with this patient. Another analyst would have seen Adele as little Spic with despised image—try to make her accept herself, get a nice husband at her level, etc. Booth recognized that Adele was tortured, unique, and many things potentially, but what he just could not say. So he had her sit up, had her analysis go on "supportively." He did not want to make her go back to her beginning, but on the other hand he could not see her future. So he waited until I came along and then decided a headache was off his hands. But at the same time he did not try to ruin her, to direct her, deep in him he had a feeling for her.

381 WHAT-THE-HELL. WHAT WE ARE saying, "No matter what the hell which awaits us, let's go on because we have to do this." Shortened in life to "What the hell, let's do it." So true of Americans who have carried the English casualness into reckless casualness. That is why our heroes are always cool. The English gentleman is cool in stress, that is the great value to him—he sees death or a potential social disaster as the same thing. So English gentlemen were great on the battlefield; it was more a social situation to them than the end of their life. They had to be cool because to be cool is for the English the social imperative. But Americans are more primal; so for us to be cool in action is the basic thing. The Englishman sees death as a social situation. The American close to death and danger (dagger—danger) all his life for our greatness as a nation was the vividness of the H in us, sees the social situation as death.

382 WORD ECHOES. HER AND err. I'm beginning to feel the h. It has connotations of head, hair, has, his—in other words it puts a human connotation on an act, emotion, idea, etc. (For example—history. H . . . I story.)—the total human collectivity of my story.) To err is human, to forgive is divine. But man has always see her, 'er (One of these days I'll have something to say about Cockneys) as erring all over the place. Man puts onto the woman his own masculine strivings, desires, etc. When 'er errs, man is always delighted with a part of him because he wishes to despise the inconstant, the striving, the wandering since it is really his nature to do that were it not so antipathetic to society. H seems to give a general philosophical quality, erect to a philosophical generality, some concrete aspect of the spirit. Air and Hair of course seem to be the opposite. A very ambiguous letter.

383 WHAT I AM DOING with letters now is what I used to do with the Tarot cards. I believe I could give Tarot readings now if people were to choose letters of the alphabet. And indeed there are twenty-two cards in The Major Arcana. 1 to 21 and 0. The twenty-one consonants—this is sheer shit, just this bit— and 0 for the cipher, the fool who is mankind, I. But The Major Arcana to the side, I think I might have a go at letters. I'll just ask people to choose a letter, tell it to me, or rather write it down, then choose another letter.

384 IS W THE WORLD? It appears in world, wealth (the w of health), wide, wisdom, (the w of is—dom) whole (the whole is a hole but for w), weight, etc. (the social measurement of ate, the increase of weight) while—(the world's idea of an isle) wait (the world w creates the antithesis of "ate"). Worry—(The w depression of 'urry) whir (w to her—again man's idea of woman.) (I assume in all this that man more than woman is the language-maker.) Mass— the male ass. Shit—hit—it. Ass in the Army was one's psyche. Shit was circumstance or society. Each provided for in mass ways. In mass life, truly one can only see oneself as an ass, and events, all events, as shit. Examples: Tough shit, when the shit hit the fan, chicken shit, bury me deep in shit, etc. Get your ass in gear, chew your ass, ass-hole buddy. (A buddy is a body, but the uh is closer to the I than the short ah. Or perhaps it's further away.)

385 SON OF A BITCH. The son of a whore. But a whore excites us because she embodies the orgiastic principle, just as an enemy (son-of-a-bitch is invariably used for someone who threatens us no matter how contemptible he may seem) excites our H, makes us feel alive, even if we are so S-ed up that all we can feel is anxiety.

386 SIMPLY, DIRECTLY, I EXCITED Stan Rinehart's anxiety. Dimly, he knew I was the enemy. I was bringing too much too close to him. He wanted me out of the house. No matter the cost. He had to do it because I was threatening him. In the privacy of his thoughts he probably thinks of me as "That son of a bitch Mailer."

387 ONCE IN A WHILE, in great admiration and love, we say of another man, "What a good son of a bitch he is." What a fine orgiastic life-loving man he is.

388 F AND V. F is fuck, v is some diminutive of it, some relation to it. V is in vice, vile, virtue, life and live, preference and perversion, that is prefer and pervert, vagina, vein, vain, (sister words) vain and fain. And so on.

389 I'M GETTING A LITTLE tired now. Interesting how the word and consonant echoes seem to come through at the end of a productive day when my guard is relaxed—the vowels are still mysteries to me really—and of course in writing the notes on consonants I get very tired. I suspect because I have something here. Nothing less than a new dictionary. I wonder if dictionary compliers are not actually scholars who are very close to this sort of thing, and conceal it in the most respectable work.

390 ANYWAY, I THINK I'LL finish with an expository chore. Describe my weekend. It has importance for this journal as background for the notes.

The weekend was a bust until late Sunday night. Bought a tape recorder for myself and hi-fi for the folks on Saturday. Two symbolic acts. Had Lipton's and made love Saturday night. But too much happened. For the first time I made love as if it were an analytic session and talked to Adele all through it, expounding her sexual character. She was a little repelled and frightened—so was I. I felt real potency deserting me for intellectual potency. But I was hot on the scent of what had long eluded me—why her past promiscuity always made me so hot, and I believe I found good reasons. For truly I recreate the past for her and make the past good. If her breasts were felt when she was fifteen and it was unsatisfactory thus driving her further on, I restore to her the fulfilled desire of how her breasts should really have been felt. And so on through all the parts of love. I love her sexual past because I can recreate it for her, make it better, and also feel identified with many men. So I was very excited intellectually while we made love, but I think she was repelled by what seemed unnatural to her—the Catholic is very deep and very basic in Adele—it's why she despises herself so. She feels if she doesn't despise herself, she'll go straight to Hell. Anyway, we were both left with great flatness which carried over to Sunday, and on Sunday morning I could remember nothing of the tremendous insights I felt I had on Saturday night. Again I felt depressed, and the *Dissent* meeting was hanging over me. That came on Sunday afternoon, and was deeply depressing. I felt I didn't belong there. All these bitter rationalists, with their rationalist talents—they would turn on me if they knew what an anarchist I am. And indeed Lewis Coser spoke approvingly of how Clara Thompson and the Sullivanites were riding

Reich out of business under the auspices of the Pure Food and Drug Act. (What a perfect title for a law for once.) The only time I felt understood was when Plastrik who is a vigorous meaty secretary (Radical parties may have the butcher boys for secretaries. Stalin, Molotov, etc.) said to me in passing, "Maybe you could do a piece on Serge Rubinstein." The oddity was that I had just been thinking the same thing. When I mentioned telepathy, their faces all got flat.

Anyway, the meeting was unbearably dull. I kept despairing of socialism. These people are all well-meaning, they are even courageous, but they are pale, they are scholars, bitter scholars, they are deeply middle-class, they are the essence of social-democracy even when they are to the left of it. They are socialists because they are all S—their socialism is not a desire for justice, a passion for equality, but merely—by now—the intellectual urge to order society. I kept feeling I should speak up, and kept deciding not to. It would have been disruptive, and I would have been defeated. After all, if I had won—which is inconceivable—I should have had to take over the magazine which I certainly don't want to do, and so I felt merely a spoiler, a wrecker, a renegade. I knew that I could stay with them only by accommodating my personality, giving articles to *Dissent* which would be stimulating for them because I would only go a very small distance.

Yet with Howe and Coser I get the feeling that they are deeply dissatisfied, that they wish to move on, and I expect more tolerance from them (father images again) (Father—let me rant in your ear) than from the others. Anyway, before the meeting was over I left—my only suggestion which was more than a joke being that *Dissent* covers remain the orange-red of the last issue—which was carried. But all afternoon first in the delicatessen—what else would Jewish socialists do before a meeting?—then in Plastrik's home, I felt a stranger and alien. I fled with Mike Harrington who is a Catholic Anarchist masquerading as a socialist, tried out a few of my milder ideas on him in the taxi, for which I got half-response, half-worry, and then home to Adele.

This has to be continued tomorrow, for a lot happens yet.

(24 pages today—To my memory the greatest number I've done in a day.)

February 1, 1955

391 TODAY MAKES TWO MONTHS since I started this journal. I started comparatively slowly, and have been accelerating steadily until now I give so much working time to it that I have no time to even write a letter.

392 LAST NIGHT, HAVING DINNER with Mother and Dad, I expressed my remark about journalists far better than I did in the journal. I said, "A journalist is a man obsessed with finding the truth in order to tell a lie."

394 WHAT APPEARS TO ME right off hand is that a compulsive liar is a man or a woman whose lying is a defense against telling the truth, the real truth, the truth which would destroy him. Very powerful H in compulsive liars as indeed there is in all psychopaths.

395 WORD ECHOES. (I SUPPOSE what I'm really trying to do with word and consonant echoes is psychoanalyze language.) Anyway: A Liar. The verb: to lie. Which also means to lie down. I accept the identity completely. A liar is engaging in a *passive* activity—no matter how much action he may appear to set off. The fact of the matter is that a liar is invariably punished, and lies with the desire to be so punished. For the liar, afraid of his H, is seeking the passive position where society will curb him. Like gossips, liars are adventurers afraid to begin. Their lying is their defense against action. Which is why it is so compulsive. Truly, there is a worse alternative—they will have to act, and that brings disaster.

396 ANOTHER WORD ECHO HERE: Lair. The lair of the liar.

397 THE BURGLAR AGAIN. ALL Herr Doktor wants to do is steal men's souls. His absolute social dictum is "basic passive masochism,"—"Case closed." Truly, he's so full of shit. He wants to make all men and women passive, because he is terrified of his own aggression, and deeply ashamed at how he has denied the rebel in himself. For the core of man is not masochism and passivity—if it were, all the world would be India. The heart of man is something allied to love and aggression—it is what I choose to call thrust. It is the incapacity to accept stasis. As Bob wrote—and I quote him more or less accurately, it is the desire to affect the environment and change it.

398 DISAGREEABLE AS IT IS to admit, Stalinism may be the child of Socialism—the mongoloid who grew out of the womb of the social-democrat couple. For apart from the very real and possibly insurmountable problems of socialism in one backward country, there was a time of alternative and choice. The Revolution of '17 opened more than economic perspectives of equality—it opened sexual equality. And from Lenin on down, the deeply bourgeois conservative social sense of the Bolsheviks were more than a little aghast at the sexual liberties which flowered. I quote Lenin from memory: "I wish some of these comrades would realize that sex is not the same as taking a drink of water." But of course sex is the same, or sex should be the same. Trotsky, with his extraordinary half insights, his extraordinary H which could never be completely contained in S-formulations so he was always overflowing into poetry and what seemed undisciplined enthusiasms, shrieked and shrieked and shrieked for the world revolution. He was of course not inclined at all toward a sexual revolution. Nothing consciously could have been more repellent to him. Yet I believe that dimly he sensed that world revolution might open the anarchist perspective. And Trotsky was spiritually an anarchist which is why he is tragic and beautiful—what figure could have been chosen more ironically to crush anarchism. (The Kronstadt rebellion.) To build socialism in a backward country surrounded by hostile enemies may have been impossible, but the one possibility of bringing it off, considering the incredible number of work hours and the poor consumer goods which would be given the proletariat for a decade and then another, was to allow them their H. Men can draw upon themselves far more endlessly if the H is permitted great rein. And they would have had genuine enthusiasm rather than enforced social enthusiasm. But the socialist mind is a bourgeois mind, stripped of H, infatuated with the proletariat because it believes (and not altogether incorrectly I would guess) that the proletariat has sex, has love, has life-energy which their own class has not. But the horror of socialism underneath its radicalism is that its bourgeois intellectuals who have written the commentaries on the great book, and have been its intellectual leaders as well as a great part of its political leaders, have always seen the proletariat with contempt. Their vision of the proletariat is to raise the proletariat in their own image, rather than be enriched themselves by the life of the proletariat. So the sexual revolution which was in the air, and actually in small ways in practice, was suppressed, was seen as the ultimate danger. And, in parallel, Trotsky was stripped of power, exiled, hunted, and slain. For Trotsky was the orgiast of revolution no matter how he tried to play at being the social builder. (I wrote play but torture is a better word. Play is the casual word we use to conceal torture.) And Stalin, the *nouveau riche*, the arriviste, built a bourgeois society the way only an arriviste can build one, laboring it with social ostentation, vulgarity, and outright cruelty. He was power-mad, a violent H in an unbelievably severe S, and so he was a leader, a monster, and a caricature of bourgeois society. He was the animal masquerading as a man, and the Russian people undoubtedly admired the Great Bear in him crushing everything with his powerful arms and his fat smelly seat. But the *nouveau riche* always come into bourgeois society with a fixed image of it, frozen be their childhood hungers. So arrivistes are vulgar because they are old-fashioned. They set in panoply the outmoded bourgeois taste of twenty years ago, fifty years ago. Stalin was obsessed with creating a society as all *nouveau riche* are, but his idea of society was Victorian society, and that is why Russia is so cumbersome, insensitive, and crude in its social methods. Socialism—let us read Stalinism—was built in one country, but it was built in the image of the nineteenth century, a throw-back, and a throw-back is a monstrosity, just as Joe McCarthy is a monster because he acts like a hanging judge in the Wild West, a man's man with the rope forever in his hands. (In this sense, the monster is to the rebel as a throw-back is to the creator.) (Note on McCarthy: The more I think of the image of the hanging judge the better I like it. The hanging judge always talks man-to-man to the wretch in the docket before he says, "Okay, boys, string him up.")

Anyway, what I have tried to outline is that Stalinism is the monster child of Socialism because Socialism being society-oriented could conceive of revolution only as new society, more rational society, and the result was an ape in a dinner jacket. The alternative: to have a sexual revolution which I believe was probably real to many of these Bolsheviks who were anarchists at heart was legitimately terrifying because the capitalist world with its profound anti-sexuality would probably have felt obliged to destroy it, or at least attempt to, and they might have been destroyed, but that was the gamble which should have been taken, and not the other.

399 I SUPPOSE THE LAST note is a filling-in on my reactions to *Dissent* and the *Dissent* meeting. What has to be said in favor of *Dissent* is that it is a magazine put out by socialists who have become—more or less consciously—deeply dissatisfied with Socialism. *Dissent* is their defense against an anarchist urge (rather than anarchist position) or what is the more real alternative, a return to bourgeois society and liberalism. So, there may be more than just the reluctance to engage in time-wasting correspondence behind my depression at the thought of quitting the magazine. Perhaps I feel the hope that the tolerance of *Dissent*'s editorial position—it is more tolerant than any Socialist magazine I can remember—is due to the fact that Howe and Coser created it because they truly wish to let someone (X) rant in their ear. Their depression is due to the fact that they are still waiting for X. Once in a while I think Howe suspects it may be me. But this could be sheer vanity.

400 To FINISH NOTE **390** on my weekend. I came home, Adele wanted to go to the movies, I wanted to stay home and have Lipton's. She accepted. First we made love, then took Lipton's. (I was repelled a little by how I had abused the act of love the night before by using it for fuckanalysis-with-Lipton's, so I wanted to do without it.) After love-making which was a touch flat for us, we took Lipton's—(by God, I call it Lipton's because my lip delivers tons of words)—and merely felt passive, dopey, and flat. First time that had happened, and I realized the reason. When there is sexual energy in me, Lipton's makes me creative. It floods my intelligence with sexual energy. But when I am temporarily sexually depleted, Lipton's merely fuddles me. Which would account for why Dan always sinks into a semi-coma when he takes Lipton's. His sexual energy is forever low because he must use it to maintain the intolerable contradictions of his personality. Anyway, we lay around, watched television which was mildly pleasant but not stimulating in the insights it gave me as it usually is, and then just as we were about to go to bed at eleven, I felt energy returning, and we took Lipton's again. This time I was full of energy—my sexual energy seems to take about two hours to return—and I got out the tape recorder, and Adele and I had an uproarious half-hour making a mock Tex and Jinx program, a *Break The Bloody Bank* program with the SixtyNine Dollar question, and so forth. I gave my Brando imitations. (Listening to them the following night, I found *Waterfront* and *Streetcar* disappointing, but *The Wild One* was extraordinary.) Then Seconal and to happy bed and sleep. Yesterday, once I got going, I worked with incredible energy and speed. I believe that for work Lipton's followed by Seconal is ideal albeit over-stimulated. The reason: I would guess that when I take Lipton's alone, I spend the night with my S working like mad to destroy everything H has liberated, so I wake up depressed and stunned. But when I add Seconal—which seems to quiet both H and S, but certainly S—long before Lipton's I had noticed the feeling of well-being Seconal gave me the following day, provided I hadn't been taking it too often—when I add Seconal, the S is unable to criticize all through the night, and H remains alive if resting, so that black coffee in the morning stimulates the H with just enough S discipline to keep it from being totally unruly. The result: elation, work, and a feeling of inexhaustible energy. Even when I get tired after hours of writing, I have only to allow myself the relaxation of thinking, "I will rest for a while," and the thought itself seems to provide enough rest for me to continue. (Which opens a half-wild speculation to the thought that concepts rule our energy output. Crudely: to believe we are tired is to make ourselves tired; to believe we cannot sleep is to render sleep impossible; to believe we will rest is to provide the restoration of rest—all this of course finally ruled by the actual bodily overall need, so that even the insomniac finally sleeps, and the tireless man rests, the inert man moves. But, someday soon perhaps I may be able to liberate myself from the tyranny of needing eight hours sleep to do a day's work.)

Anyway, yesterday was incredible for output if not for quality. I wrote more pages than I have ever written in my life, except perhaps for one night when I was eighteen and wrote something like forty absolutely awful last pages of a novel. Then, since it was my birthday I went over to my mother and father's, and because I was in a good mood, I put everybody else in a good mood. I enjoyed my birthday for the first time in years, I enjoyed my presents, I loved everybody there more than I normally do, and I was tickled pink when my father told me that he had won six bucks from Jack Alson in gin rummy. *My father had never won a game before from Jack.* (Jack is the sort of pompous cigar-smoking hearty self-made business man with buried aggressive sensitivity who has always buffaloed my father in the past.) I knew Dad was delighted, and I was delighted too—apparently the four hours we talked did a lot for him. He told me that he was fighting his office on the report they had made on him, and was preparing a letter where he was going to sock them back.

The whole evening went well. I enjoyed myself with my family which I haven't experienced so well in years, and after supper I played the first attempt at the alphabet game, the results of which I will list here later. During supper Barbara and I had a big fight over whether the meat thermometer was right or wrong (meter as mentor?) I saying, take the roast beef out, don't trust the thermometer, Barbara in a fury at me. We were each half-right. The center was indeed too rare, but the outside was done well enough so that we all had slices and were able to eat. Reason was right theoretically—I felt that I was right practically—we ate a half hour earlier than we would otherwise have eaten, and nobody had a piece too rare for them. But the big thing was the basic argument Barbara and I were having. I made her a rationalist over the years—I took her sensitive delicate nature and hammered my harsh reasoning mind into hers. No wonder she's furious at me now that I say Reason is bad, Instinct is good. She feels it, I suspect, as a betrayal. For what was her nature warped if I now tell her the warp is wrong?

Then we drove home with Larry and me playing endless fugues on his taking my old tape recorder for nothing. Larry is almost completely conscious of how completely he is the taker and how guilty it makes him, but he is still bound. He feels he always has to pay exact measure for taking—he is put in a rage (always expressed as depression for him) when he has to pay even a cent too much for what he buys, takes. "Spend money," I said to him at one point about something else, "it's good for the soul." What a tzaddik I am. But on the drive, I said to Barbara my line about being a saint who must explore psychopathy, and she understood immediately. She said in her slow thoughtful voice, "You know, I think you're right." I wonder if the same is true for her, but deeply suppressed, so only the saint appears, and the sweet bourgeois college girl, all reason, all brisk-ness, all pertness, while deep in her she always feels so unworthy and dirty, frightened by what she considers her evil impulses when actually they are not evil, they are the urges to explore her nature across the spectrum.

401 ONE ADDITION TO THIS. I have come to realize how much I am a leader. When I am depressed, I make others depressed. When I'm happy, people take on my mood, unless like Dan they are wrestling with me for their souls, or for Dan jabbing back. So I have a responsibility which I shun—that's what keeps me from being a leader. For a leader must take in one fundamental way. He must take responsibility.

402 BACK FROM LUNCH AND a walk and black coffee, and I am very excited because I think I've come up with something. I think I can clarify for myself the difference between the saint and the psychopath, particularly a species of psychopath I have hardly touched on up to now, to wit the criminal psychopath, the homicidal psychopath. What has been throwing me off all this time is that I have been holding in certain ways to the conventional view of the criminal psychopath—which is that he has no social sense. It is absolutely false. The reason a psychopath, a criminal psycho-path, is so dangerous is that he has a total view of society. His S is altogether developed, completely authoritarian, and constantly punishing. But in a sense he is schizoid—the war of H vs. S never meets in compromises the way it does in more normal people. (I am of course talking of the imaginary total criminal psychopath.) He sees and feels nothing but his H—the S is merely present as a sort of Holy Ghost, converting every one of his life impulses into a self-criticism which becomes so intolerable that he must demean everyone, see the enemy in everyone, suspect goodness no matter how or where it appears in himself or in others. So, even to talk to him is exceptionally dangerous, and if I were ever in prison as a prisoner I would be in danger of my life every instant I opened my mouth, for the key to the criminal psychopath is that deep within him he worships society like a graven stone, only the stone is in his heart. Essentially, he believes that everything about society is good, perfect, immutable, *churchly*, absolute and total. Psychologically, his hatred of himself, his hatred of others is his passport to heaven. Once accept himself, once accept anything radical to society, and at the instinctive level he feels himself doomed to go to hell, for that is real heresy. So, as Bob told me, prisoners will kill each other for being told they are mother-fuckers. You-do-not-fuck-your-mother is the first commandment of society. You-do-fuck-your-mother is the first commandment of H. Between them the epic-or-tragedy? of man's existence is played. But the criminal psychopath has the absolute S-taboo, he is cut off, amputated, from the source of H-satisfaction, and so his H must become more and more exacer-bated, more violent, because each of his actions are the attempt to flee the more and more pressing H-imperative to the orgy (the orgy being always a variant of the fuck-your-mother drive.)

Just as the sadistic cop is the criminal reversed—the cop, identi-fying with S can allow free play to the worst of his H, or put another way the cop sees all H as bad unless it is used in the service of S—which is why the cop sees the crook everywhere, so the criminal identifying with H but convinced H is bad, able to express his H only under the shadow of S, can never grapple with S because S is totally good to him no matter how he may believe he hates it, no matter how he may rail against it. Therefore, homicidal psychopaths are invariably reactionary in politics rather than radical—as are cops—to approach a homicidal psychopath when he is aroused and attempt to convince him that there is a good man in him is to court your own murder. Only the unrelenting approach of the priest or the hyper-moral minister can work—no reward can be offered, no hope other than the extended hope that years of punishment may bring surcease. To offer a reform, a concession to the psychopath is to open for him the possibility that he may be right. But if he is right, then he has denied God so Hell awaits him. (One further reason psychoanalysts have ducked homicidal psychopaths is that they would have had to come to grips with religion vs. sex and this they dare not do. They would become socially unrespectable again.) The prison lore of wardens and guards know that to give concessions to homicidal psychopaths—that is to depart from the original prison environment (be it hideous or comparatively liberal like Chino—Calif) is to encourage further trouble. The psychopath feels in his soul—and what a miserable maimed outraged soul!—that he has to be stopped or he doesn't make Heaven. So for every concession he must demand more until he is finally killed or stunned (life imprisonment). Ironically, I would guess that once given life imprisonment with no hope of parole, knowing he is totally immured against the mother-fucking urge, he probably quiets down, branches out, even becomes a useful member of the community. Lifers make good trustees.

So, what a prison problem! For what I have outlined above is true for only a small percentage of the prison population, and that not even totally true for no man is completely a type. So, for the radical urge of some, the reformist demands of many, and the total imprisonment essential for a few, the attempt is made to simmer them all in the same pot with only the crudest separations, and above this stands the warden—a man more and more traveling the spectrum from the cop-bureaucrat to the criminal psychopath, so his sympathies are divided, his anxieties contradictory, tormented by the unconscious knowledge that he half longs for the day when the prison population will dynamite the wall and destroy him.

403 A COMMENT ON THE above. When a "mad killer" is on the prowl, probably nothing can work. Because at such moments all his tortured life force is finally expressing itself. His detestation of himself is so intense that the only time he can feel alive and "happy" is when he is in the act of committing some outrage. For while he worships the S he also truly hates it with the part of himself which has always wanted to live. So, in the temporary suspending of his idea of S-retaliation, he feels great release, great joy, in the act of murdering he is truly living. At such times nothing can stop him, for mangled as this is, it is still an expression of the life-force, and nothing, short of death, can stop the unbearable tension-to-go-to-completion of the criminal who is usually so isolated from his sense of life. It is only when this has spent itself, or half-spent itself, that the strong approach can work. And indeed in practice it is only several days after the initial riot that the priests and ministers enter with their black robes.

404 AT THE OTHER END of the spectrum is the saint. The saint (that is the total saint) has no S whatsoever, he is all H-expression, and so he is all goodness, all sensitivity, all-accepting, all-forgiving. To kiss the feet of a whore, to tell a parable to his flock, to be unafraid of all worldly—that is, social—power is always the same thing to him, merely another part of the whole, as natural as breathing, weeping, defecating, fucking, comforting, etc. But, of course, in life, with perhaps the exception of Jesus, no total saint has ever appeared that I know about—certainly no sexual saint, unless it was some unknown tzaddik of the Chasidim, some wandering beggar in Asia, some illiterate frontiersman preacher of the West. But it is unlikely. Society would have ripped his arms and legs off, stuffed his genitals in his mouth, driven spikes through his belly, and eaten his eyes. The saints who have appeared (that is genuine saints, three-quarter saints say, like Gandhi, St. Francis perhaps, Lincoln???? How can one ever locate them in history for their works are so few, and the legends about them so distorted—it is safe to assume that most of the Catholic saints were bureaucrats, psychopaths, monsters and half-mystics). What one can say is that there have been three-quarter saints, men (or women) who somehow—and this is a mystery to me—were capable of expressing their unexpressed sexual urges in other ways. They were free of society, they had the happy grace—and what a revealing word is Grace—on the animal raised to human stature, and so they were good. But they were never totally good, nor totally saints—they suffered from Temptation. Of course. Somehow they managed to avoid most of the sex-vs-society exhaustion, but one cannot avoid sex entirely, not without turning one's food to poison. One can only accept sex completely, and one day when there comes such a man, there will be a total saint. By which of course I don't mean that he will be fucking all the time. Simply—and how difficult—he will fuck when he feels like it with whomever feels like it, and rest when he is done.

405 THE CATHOLIC WOULD ARGUE, "You see, you admit a three-quarter saint who can do without sex. How do you account for that?" To which I would answer that it is a riddle although probably not insurmountable, but that it is certainly less of a riddle than that there is a God who gave Life but immediately ceded the dispensing of life and the life energies over to a Devil. That is the total contradiction on which S rests, but it is so exhausting, so static, that until H began to express itself as Reason in the early Renaissance, Western slumbered in shit—giving snores of torture.

406 I MAY HAVE A clue to the lack of sexual drive in the three-quarter saint. As I have gone through my self-analysis, perversions which once gave me great excitement now give less. They seem less dirty, more natural. Along with my general exaltation goes less sexual heat and less depression. It is the thing which has been worrying me. My sexual urge now seems to come out in the flow of ideas and the release of emotions. I don't believe this is totally natural nor totally healthy, but it may be that all of us who were born under the weight of a society which denied sex except as the dirty, can feel saintly emotions—as occasionally I do—only when we have purged ourselves of sexual guilt. But we bear the scar. Sexual guilt was the catalyst which opened sex to us. In other words, in the process of growing up, the dirt-sex identification became so engraved upon us that to wash away the connotations of dirt was to wash away much of sex. Perhaps that is the answer to the three-quarter saints. They could accept the whore, they could accept the dirt, and so sexual urge diminished, perhaps even vanished. But the real saint, the saint-who-has-not-yet-appeared, would not even bear the scar. His sexual urge would be joyous, and how joyous. Once in my life I had a taste of full orgasm. It was my first, and it was incredibly lovely.

407 WORD ECHOES. I'VE DISCUSSED jazz and gas. But *note*: *Orgasm*. What a word. I read: O the red spirit (gas) of man.

408 IF MY IDENTIFICATION OF red and r seems too pat, be it remembered that red is the color of blood, the color of the sexual organs, it is the color of life in rage (wounds being the result) and in love. And gas is vapor, clouds—the first intimation to the child and the savage that there is a Great Spirit we cannot reach.

409 GATE. AND R: GREAT. Or: Grate. The big and the little combine. Greatness always grates on others.

410 THE STRENGTH OF THE Church. I wonder if it is not due to the fact that the Church above all institutions is ready to accept the hatred of its flock. Mother Church is a rock, it says, throw mud at us, hammer upon us, we remain unchanging. (What a lie about remaining unchanging.) After all, like all institutions whose nature is to deprive, the Church excites hatred in its Catholics beneath the level of their love. *But it is not afraid of that hatred.* And when we feel hatred toward anyone or anything, and can recognize no fear in the hated one, we feel impotent, powerless, enslaved. (Which parenthetically is the heart of the dependent relation of analysand to analyst, and is why certain analysands are forever abusing the analyst. If they can arouse a response from the analyst—which for my money would not be a bad thing at all—the analysand would not feel so helpless, so useless, so dependent.) That is why the renegade Catholic can never shake off the hand of the Church—for although the Church hates back, it conceals its hatred by announcing and practicing its willingness to take back anyone, no matter what the crimes, or sacrileges, if they are only willing (just like an analyst). Indeed the Church is way ahead of Stalinism in this respect, although I "feel" that Stalinism is beginning to borrow this technique. Perhaps with Tito it will. That is also why the Church catches so many homicidal psychopaths in their death cells—all of their life has been a preparation for this moment. In the ultimate sense, the Catholic who murders is the best Catholic material of them all. Which is why the Church has always had a soft spot for murderers.

411 A NOTE ON MY father. I have been acting like an analyst toward him, but I have taken a gamble no analyst would have taken. I have made the bet that he is more artist than psychopath, and so he will not gamble seriously again because I have given him my love. But there is a big danger. For if I have had a fundamental misapprehension of my father, and it is crucial to him to despise himself (which I do not believe, but may be possible) then, given my tolerance, he will have to attempt to destroy it by striking out, by gambling seriously. But my instinct told me the opposite, it told me that he was enough like me so that he cannot repel love but instead is drawn to it, needs it, respects it so basically that impotence for him as for me comes from the specter of wounding seriously someone we love. Like me, my father wounds people who love him only in passing, reluctantly, lightly, teasingly. He has no real desire to cut a hole or smash a head.

412 AND NOW I UNDERSTAND Monroe St. and the hammer I got on my head. When the hoodlums wanted to crash the party, I was wrong and the others were right. If I had taken a firm line (firm is pious in Yiddish I believe) and told them to get the fuck out of here—it was precisely the fuck which they wanted to introduce into my party—then they would either have fought immediately or gone away. But I took a tolerant compromising line and that was intolerable to them. They had to find out, destroy or be destroyed.

Just as in reverse, the time I followed Adele down the stairs at First Avenue and she was being whistled at/insulted by two teen-age hoodlums as I came out was a moment where angry at her, a little drunk, and feeling aggressive, I shouted at the hoodlums, "KNOCK OFF," and to my amazement they did, one staying his distance, the other apologizing.

413 ON HOW I CAN'T destroy love. The one total impotence I had in my life was with R.P. shortly after I met Adele. I was drawn to R, I found her totally attractive socially, I knew she was drawn to me. But I was afraid of what would happen if it clicked with her, and I was full of sexual beans at the time. I was afraid I would desert Adele. To turn upon someone who really loves me has always been deep in my unconscious the unforgiveable crime. So I was impotent with R.P. the first time we tried, I had a panic to quit her. It was only when I came to realize how sexually frigid R.P. was that I could have sex with her, and even then it was the worst, anxious, semi-potent, and possible only on tons of liquor. What a time I gave her. Before I met Adele, I could never know in advance whether I would be any good with another woman. I think I could make full love to another woman only if I felt Adele no longer really loved me. In the old days before we were married, my heart used to sink every time I realized how much she loved me. It meant I could never be free. Today, I no longer wish to be free. So, I have been loving her. And, slowly, very tentatively, with deep suspicion, she is beginning to believe that yes, truly, I do love her.

414 ONE THING BOTHERS ME. I had a few intimations under Lipton's that there is some sort of identification between Adele and my sister. (Further proof of the mother-father embodiment—who but a sibling substitute could be better for a mother-father embodiment?) I don't like it, and I steer away from approaching it, but I suspect that I have to face it and tear into it because my sexual scar may be exactly here.

415 A LAY ANALYST. HE is a layman. The Layman is the fucker. The expert does without fucking. So, depending on taste, we are drawn to Layman X or Doctor X. But wed to the English language is the idea that the non-expert is closer to sex. And indeed he is.

416 I HAVE A HUNCH the next novel may be the worst of all to write because to do it I will probably have to quit Lipton's and go back to depression. If I don't it will all come too easily and be too surface. But to go with open arms back into depression! I don't see how I can do it. In other words I don't see how I can start a new book yet. At least, I will have the experience of tuning *The Deer Park* once again, and that may give hints and intimations of what to expect with and without Lipton's.

417 MY SEXUAL SCAR. THAT is, a part of me has always seen sex as a pussy wound. Mmmmm. I meant to write pus—sy. So, chasing the dirty I felt excitement and then guilt. Now, with guilt eased, there is less excitement. (Perhaps . . . this is only for the last few weeks, at most the last few months as a tendency.) In other words, once the dirt is taken out of sex, I see it as brother-sister relations. Platonic. Which is why I get dirtier all the time to apparently less effect. I just feel tender. Even in the last ball, I felt tender toward the other girl as if she were my child. But, I mustn't go too far with this. The few times we've made love in the last month without Lipton's were pretty Goddamn hot—and without even a trace of guilt afterward. The effects of brother-sisterliness come out with Lipton's. The only exception is the love we made Sunday night which was without Lipton's and comparatively un-hot. I may be reading much too much into this. On the other hand, one of these days I am going to sit down, lie down, and free-associate on it. For example, why in hell am I thinking more and more of a secretary. Why do I put out feelers to Barbara. Why the note a couple of weeks ago about secretary and wife?

418 DEPRESSION IS COMING ON, distrust of this journal, distrust of myself and my ideas. Again I worry—Is this all a monster rationalization? Am I full of shit? Also, I'm hungry again. I interrupt to go down for supper.

419 PERHAPS THE SEXUAL EXPLANATION is that I use up so much energy in this journal and doing my weight-lifting that there just isn't a hell of a lot left over. I notice that I start high on this Journal every day, or get high in the course of writing— *auto*-stimulation, and who was it that first called us authors?—and then wear out, feel the ideas become less sharp, the tone begin to wander, until finally in word echoes and consonant chasings I feel depression come on lightly.

420 JESUS, I'D RATHER BE a genius than a saint (but in my mind the sentence kept coming out reversed—I'd rather be a saint than a genius). The psychopath, I'm afraid reluctantly, I must relinquish—at least temporarily.

422 DECADENCE. I WONDER IF it isn't generally misunderstood, especially because decadent periods are periods dangerous to society. A decadent time always follows a prosperous time, that is, the decadence appears first in ideas, art-works, fashions, etc. and is only then followed by economic crisis, or a political reaction, or by revolution. But decadence is the natural, even inevitable growth which follows prosperity, and I believe it comes into being because the abstract social contract is no longer pressing; relatively— to its time—the mood to quit it has come. So a concern with man as a-thing-in-himself, rather than the concern with man-in- and-of-society is the result. But society always underlines such attempts as perverted, and so they can only appear in degraded forms. The inquiry about man becomes expressed by homosexuality (always seen and understood by Everybody to be the real meaning of the word decadence) artistic experimentation which leads nowhere, or seems to lead nowhere, bisexual fashions in dress, distrust of power, anxiety of statesmen, feelings of general impotence, and increase in hatred and disrespect of the lower classes for the upper classes, a mood of doubt, a refinement of comedy, and perhaps most significant a cutting across categories, so that hybrid arts like opera, or today—bebop—are born. Until now it has been impossible for what I believe have been the genuine and indeed highest probing of the human spirit—occurring precisely in the period of decadence—to gain acceptance or energy. Society is threatened, the time is not yet to dissolve the social contract, and so all the S forces are whipped up again. But the period of decadence we are in now is of the most profound sort. For what characterizes decadence is that it occurs more powerfully and for longer duration each time it appears, and each time the process of destroying it is less complete and more difficult. The real soul of man, I suspect, has always come closest to expression in decadent periods, but the expression was always degraded. There will come a time perhaps when a decadence less degraded will to everyone's amazement produce the greatest flowering.

423 THE ABOVE NOTE WAS written on a full stomach after supper. I wrote it with a style about as sprightly as a German grammar teacher, and this kills me because there was do much I wanted to say in that. If I don't bounce up soon, I'm going to quit for the day.

424 ECHOES AND OPPOSITES. THE child wishes to do something. It is forbidden. The child wished to express something. But, presto, as the words are on its tongue, it realizes that this too will be forbidden. So it requests a different object, less satisfactory but close to the original (an echo) or it requests the opposite. (The child wishes to strike its sister—it says instead, "I love my sister.") But the child like the psychopath lives in the enormous present, and living in the present is like being in the center of a giant drum—every whisper returns its sound, and it is difficult to separate the whisper from the reply. So the reply in time comes to seem more real to the child than its own whisper, and the child identifies with the reply, the reply is itself, the child is the mother or the father or the mother-father, and its own Self is banished to be persecuted later when the Self produces its own child. So to the psyche (which I use for H vs. S) every attitude has its refraction (its echo) or its mirror (its opposite), and the problem of what is the Self remains for most people exactly the Mystery.

Which is why everything must be turned on its head—at least for experiment—before one may be certain it is understood. Again I repeat—one comes closer to finding the truth-in-its-circuits by the desire to be ridiculous than the fear of being ridiculous. And the extraordinary person is extraordinary because the unbearable question of the child—Who and what am I?—has never been frozen into answers, but demands instead that one voyage for answers. (Echo: Answereers for engineers.)

425 THE SPECTRUM OF THE saint-psychopath. The infant, initially, is all H or virtually all H. The child is mainly H with great conversions into S being formed daily, being vomited back, absorbed again, shifted, etc. The saint-psychopath retains this quality of the child, and probably if I knew enough, and if it were worthwhile one could draw the spectrum. The homicidal psycho at one end—the total saint at the other. And petty crooks, gamblers, adventurers, certain kinds of businessmen, entertainers, reporters, artists, evangelists, psychotics, alcoholics, beggars, old maids and saints would fit in some order of development and H vs. S flowings (I prefer to avoid the word: structures). But what characterizes them and separates them from the other world of humans, the conform-ist-neurotic spectrum which inhabits the middle of society just as the saint-psycho occupies the top and the bottom (this is even more true psychically than by classes or status) is that the saint-psychos are spontaneous, apparently contradictory—since reality shifts for them all the time, their reaction to apparently similar stimuli may be vastly different on different occasions—fluid and mobile, subject to crisis, subject to recovery, generally givers, active and inert intuitive, manic-depressive, undependable in long-term love but incandescent for short love, the subject of gossip, the centers of attention, electric in quality, driven, shriven, and driven again, compassionate and selfish. They are creators.

The neurotic-conformist is the total opposite. They are dependable, stable, cautious, consistently honest, privately dishonest, expert at best, plodders at worst, socially affable, privately malicious, petty, and envious, takers, subject to attrition, mildly steadily active, dull for short-term love but good providers for long-term, listeners, mechanical in air, intelligent and practical once the scope is defined, analytical, helpless before problems of synthesis. They are professionally compassionate (charity and community work) and professionally selfish. They are critics.

These, naturally, are poles. And the majority of people fit somewhere in between although of course they tend toward the neurotic-conformist. But the tendency of society is to make all of mankind neurotic-conformist—the tendency of man, as viz his modern heroes and celebrities, is to liberate the saint-psychopath present to some degree in everyone.

Generally speaking we have come to the point in history—in this country anyway—where the middle class and upper middle class is composed primarily of the neurotic-conformists, and the saint-psychos are found in some of the activities of the working class (as opposed to the working class itself), in the Negro people, in Bohemians, in the illiterates, among the reactionaries, a few of the radicals, some of the prison population, and of course in the mass communication media.

426 THE ABOVE NOTE OUGHT to prove the ridiculousness of summaries and expositions. I've said all this before, only much better.

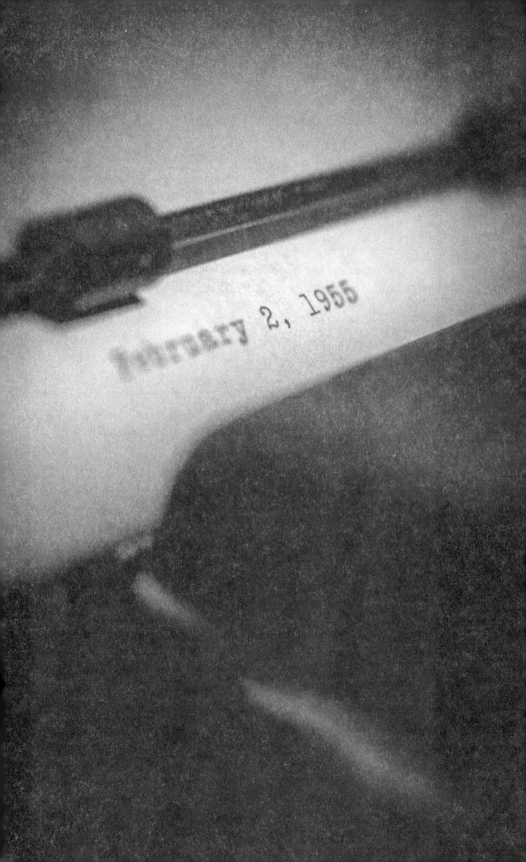

February 2, 1956

429 THE HORRIBLE THOUGHT OCCURS that all my letter and consonant theories may come out of no more than their propinquity on the typewriter keyboard. But on the other hand, those letters were arranged because they bore a certain relation in use and frequency, etc. It might be worthwhile to explore the theories of setting up letters on the typewriter keyboard.

430 THE ARTIST AND HIS paranoia. As I've written before, paranoia sees the ultimate danger in the trivial circumstance. The sense of time (which is either the same or very close to the sense of proportion) is deficient. But this is why artists are always paranoid. To be ahead of one's time, to see tendencies before others see them, is exactly the talent of the artist, and his insights are given by the racing terrified ultimate sense of paranoia.

432 IT IS REALLY INCREDIBLE that analysts have played with concepts like the death-wish for so many decades now, and yet have done no large work I know of on what are probably the two greatest abstractions for the mass of humanity, Hell and Heaven. How much of human behavior is motivated by this, and yet on the environmental accident (or could it have been possible anywhere else?) of psychoanalysis being born in German-Jewish rational circles where Hell and Heaven were considered old-fashioned, the problem relatively has been ignored. One of the most profound and ineradicable human attitudes—"If I hate myself even more, if I think of myself as being even more despicable than my despicable action, then I do not necessarily go to Hell." Why torture our understanding of life by trying to postulate a death-instinct. The explanation of self-destructive acts is right under our noses.

433 EACH OF THE CHURCH'S dictums reveal the opposite reality, the opposite thrust. So the Church making suicide a mortal sin confessed that the tendency of its total perversion upon nature was to drive its believers to suicide. Given the psychology of despising oneself in order to avoid Hell, the end of the road is the act of total loathing for the self—one's own death. But the Church could hardly permit this—no institution can last very long if its members advertise it by destroying themselves.

434 THE GAMBLER'S DEBT IS always a debt of honor. For good cause. Paying the money takes away the psychic sting of H vs. S which has been opened again by defeat.

435 I'VE SPENT THE LAST few hours re-reading the Journal and find it less exciting than I thought, and quite un-publishable in its present form (which had been at the back of my mind). But there is a lot in it. I just have to develop it. One thing I notice is that the wild mystical plunge of the early pages simmers down after a while. I think the early pages merely express the great relief of being able to use words like God, soul, saint, genius, and so forth—at last I was going to allow myself to revel in the cliché. But I write this note totally off everything. Off Lipton's—it's three days now, off Seconal—two days. Feelings of sexual vigor are returning, and with it more quiet confidence. One thing which bucked me up is that in going over *The Deer Park* I found that I could add sentences to it which had the nice literary style of the book. So, apparently, I'm not stylistically drained. What I felt as I was writing *Deer Park* lines this morning was the old feeling of fine tension, very strong H versus very strong S, so that the words seemed to come out like poetry to me.

I can probably generalize on the effects of Lipton's and Seconal. Lipton's releases of course—vast amounts of exciting material and trivial material with very little selection. It enables me to work at a tremendous rate, but everything is equally exciting to me. (Which is mystically, philosophically valid, but is almost impossible for a novelist to deal with—at least in my present stage.) That is, I could not write novels on it, although it might be good to turn to it when I got writing blocks. The Seconal is what is bad for it is beginning to give me bad letdowns and deep depressions. Except I know how to handle those too, now. If I can't sleep, I must just sit up and read instead of trying to fight myself into sleep. Enough for today. I think I'll lay off the Journal for a few days and fill up again.

February 7, 1955

436 THE OPENING INTO MYSELF occurred again over the weekend, and I have disgorged such vast masses of material and understanding that to develop them properly would take years, a lifetime. What I notice over and over again in these notes is that every single idea I have started with starts as a cliché. The early pages of this journal are ridden with clichés. What excites Bob and makes him believe that I am really "on to something," (Interesting phrasing—the crook in Bob sees knowledge as manipulation, power—which is why he goes forward, to become a better bigger more powerful crook—the irony is that the crook has the best understanding of honesty because he moves against it, and so in moving against it, in being a giver, he takes honesty—the giver as I have said before is the explorer seeking to locate the world. Once Bob begins to take, as indeed he is taking now—what characterizes him I am willing to bet is that in the old days he was completely, actively, that it is, a giver. Now, as the years go on, he takes more and more—so his dishonesty is converted to honesty.) What a long digression. There are going to be endless parentheses today.

I started to write, "What excites Bob and makes him believe *I'm on to something*"—that is, dominating it,—is that each cliché opens out. And as it opens I discover more and more. The wisdom of all of mankind is buried in clichés. The common people use them. More dominated, but less S-oriented, and quite un-verbal—H people usually are—the cliché for them opens them to their souls. The banal conversations one has in an elevator or in a restaurant about weather or how the days fly are the most profound conversations. They are truly philosophical if at a very low level. For weather is Nature which man must dominate in order to live like a king, and the calendar is Time, it is Society, which too man must dominate if he is to live like a saint-lover. (Another parenthesis. The perspective of a better future is that the saint-psychopath becomes the saint-lover. Lovers in the sexual act are always—by our growing understanding of the word—psychopathic. When one fucks, one is at the heart of the present. A good fuck suspends Time—it opens it into an enormous present where one is a king, a God, and one's mate is a Queen, a Goddess.) AP. (Which I use from now on as "another parenthesis"): The reason so many homosexuals are snobs and furnish their places in "period style" is that their relations seem to them in some deep part of them to be the relations of two kings, making concordats, entertaining one another in pomp. Which is why they're snobs, reactionaries, and aristocrats so often in their attitudes and manners—the fancy homosexual partakes of the monster—he is a throwback to the time when only a king could express the whims (which are the deep desires) of his soul.

437 ONE IDEA IN THIS opens another. I must stop trying to channel my ideas but let them flow so that they give birth better.

440 I HAVE TO EXPLAIN what I believe is true of the psyche and of dialectics. The part of Marx I always found least congenial was his dialectical materialism. It seemed an irrational mystical note in his supreme reasoning. And all the engineers of socialism have thrown away the theory for the practice, and converted Marxism to its vulgarization, the practice of socialism rather than the thrust to anarchism. Marx was a genius; he was even partly a saint, but he was both these things because he was not merely a realist and a rationalist, he was also a mystic, and dialectics are no more nor no less than the endless chain of give-and-take and take-and-give. Society and history are the projection forward of the projection inward. Man is not simply a conscious and an unconscious. He is many levels of consciousness, each the mirror, the reflection of a state in the unconscious which is more pure, more the thing-in-itself which is nothing other than the polarity, the double—AP: No thing in itself is a one but a two—the reflection in the conscious mind of an unconscious state. I believe that the unconscious of man is an endless chain inward, inward, inward to the point which is infinity. Put less crudely, put topographically, the conscious and the unconscious are the polarized "thing" of mind-and-body. As we plumb nominally, plumb the unconscious, states of consciousness appear—in the conventional analysis what invariably appears is the malice under sweetness, the passivity under aggression, the chaos under order. But that is merely the first level inward of the unconscious, and it is the level most suscep-tible to socializing because the "moral-ethical" sense is already in the consciousness—therefore we see the unconscious as dirty, evel—evil—what-have-you? But beneath the sweetness of the sweet person, is malice, beneath the malice is real sweetness, beneath the real sweetness is real malice, beneath real malice is real real sweet-ness, beneath real real sweetness is real malice, beneath real real malice is real real real sweetness—and so forth. On to infinity in every person alive. Which suggests that God when we reach him is God-and-Devil not God and Devil. Give-and-Take not give and take. For only through Give-and-Take, dialectics, is the world and nature advanced. Which is why the nature of man is both joyous-and-tragic. It is truly both, not one—the sentimental petrifaction into One of Society when it calls man joyous; nor tragic, also one, which is the social despairing of people who believe that man is one, all bad, all divided. What they sense is Good-and-Evil (Give-and-Take, And Take-and-Give) AP: the comma is the way we indicate a larger AND than "and." The comma sets up the "and" of equality. So good-and-evil (G-T And T-G) are the nature of progress, they are the nature of GO.

441 But I go at this in the most outrageous form. All the things I learned over the weekend went into the above notes. *I hate exposition.* So I detest going back over the ideas I had, they are already real to me, and I wish merely to cast them now into mathematical forms. (How lucky Einstein was! The universe really gave him a loving fuck.) But, to explain how I got here, I have to go back over the exposition, and I hate to waste the time. Nonetheless, for those hours in the week to follow when I am down from this peak, I'd better have less advanced and mystical remarks or I'll be repelled myself.

442 Besides I may discover more by going back. Exposition for me when it works always creates new ideas. Which is why I'm a writer. The act of writing is creative for me too whereas for people who are not writers it is merely crude exposition, cliché exposition, which is why the slick writer is usually safe—the exposition of his conception does not carry him further, does not get him into danger.

446 BUT, AGAIN, BACK TO give-and-take. Not yet. AP: Freud was the genius who like Marx placed most of his thought in the One. Against his enormous desire to be everywhere, do everything, understand everything he set up the enraged dictum of the One. In that sense he was a crank and a miser, husbanding his genius. To Theodore Reik he said, "Reik, you want to be a big man, make your mark, piss in one spot!"

447 Now, GIVE-AND-TAKE. IT IS everywhere, it is the life-process. We eat and excrete, our cells absorb and expel, our rhythm governs the health of our body. We fuck by give-and-take, we breathe by give-and-take, we walk by give-and-take. Tides are give and take, day and night are the reflection of the earth responding to the *steady* (The sun is the one of society.) light of the sun. (Which opens the wild speculation that day and night are the give-and-take which permit man progress.) That where a planet does not revolve it has achieved unity, absorbed darkness into light.) So, conceivably, the expanding universe is indeed heaven, and the multi-billions of stars (perhaps infinite or close to infinite) are the souls of those who made Heaven-and-Hell. When we die (this is close to the Hindus), we go back to earth to explore another existence, or we go into the Heaven-Hell of being a pure soul, a star. (Which may account for the primitive belief of some tribes that man when he dies goes to the sun. Primitives close to the knowledge of their own bodies but totally un-verbal can express their knowledge, their wisdom, only in superstitions. And a superstition is a folk cliché which has become outmoded because so much of man's H has been converted to S. But the interest in anthropology is a clue to the enormous reversal of history, Marx' swing of the pendulum, which is coming, and of which I feel I am a standard bearer.)

453 YET TO STAY ALIVE we must act. We must draw away from total acceptance of the self. We draw an enormous blank check upon the future, for man's nature is to subdue the hostility of nature, and therefore enable himself to live forever in life. (In that sense Nature is always seen finally as The End, as Death—

When an author finishes a book, he writes The End—he wishes to end this social concretion he has elaborated as the defense against discovering himself, and now deliver it to the reader's sensibilities, to the reader's self. He wishes the reader to take and to grow beyond him. So, when we act, we hurt ourselves in order to give to others. We deliver a blank check to the future.

457 PERHAPS THE CLUE TO all this, and the defense of the ultimate H-S conciliation is that man has not yet conquered nature and nature-substitute-which-is-abstract-society enough to become the lover and the taker. So, in the very horror of modern life may be a deep progression. We are not ready yet to take more, to fuck our mothers, we have to be frustrated in order to go on. That is why I hate the love I feel for people these days, and why when I become close to them distaste is behind it, I see myself as passive, loving, sticky—somewhere in me I sense that to love others and love myself is to deprive myself of further work. To go in and in and in, and never stop, as I am half-stopping today, by bothering to write what I think in the journal.

458 THE CROOK IN BOB Lindner. Until one understands this, one cannot understand Bob. The crook in him is what enables him to go forward. Like the journalist he seeks for knowledge in order to tell a lie. But the more truth he discovers the more creative become his lies, because deep within, no doubt because of his parents most directly, he learned early that to be truthful is to be destroyed. So, only by giving his honesty back to the world as dishonesty, can he find peace and safety and yet go on. That is why he always gets more pleasure from turning a dishonest buck than an honest one—why his books give him more pleasure than his patients, and why—what shocked me so deeply is now understandable—he was so drawn to the idea of opening the clinic where they would do lobotomies. It would be such a dishonest buck. He lusted after it like a hot bitch. But yet he could not quite do it. It was dishonesty at too low a level. So he had to tell me about it, because he knew I could destroy it. I could plumb it, I could say, "What the fuck do you want to give money to your kids for," and in saying it, Bob felt that I was right, that wasn't motive. So I took away his social justification, and he was left with the knowledge that to fuck this particular bitch was too crude a lie. I goose Bob to making his lies more and more finely drawn, until finally—in what horror—and torment he is going to tell the truth, just as Bob has given to me his deep sense of the validity of everything, because only the fine crook, the crook cubed can understand the importance of everything in the social world. "There's an angle everywhere," says the master con man.

A small example of this is his fury at the guy who made him give back the $250. Bob had been taken by a superior crook—the fact of the matter is that deeply Bob knew he'd been a crook to take the $250 in the first place. And Freddy Weisgal whose attraction is that he is an amiable healthy vigorous crook (who is only half-ashamed of his crookedness—most good lawyers indeed) was the mid-wife who got out the $250 from the psychopath's father—undoubtedly a miser. AP: The deep psychic folk tale of the crook who takes the miser. Bob was enraged. Like all crooks, he wants to give, he cannot bear to be taken from—not with money which is his Open Sesame to society.

459 SESAME. THE SEX OF me. What opens me to knowledge. Again I say: In the fuck is the mystery. There is where we discover our real selves.

460 BUT WHY CAN I understand the crook in Bob? It is because at a deeper level of the unconscious I'm a bigger crook than he is. Why else did I turn down the Pepsi-Cola show which so intrigued Bob. It's because the crook in me is at a lower level of the unconscious, more rarified, more honest on the surface. It shows in my reading and my ideas. I'm a synthesizer, just as a crook is. I cannot make the original discovery, but I can add the fabulous jewel to it at my best. So I dip into other books and other men's styles, take the ideas I wish, throw away the others, understand one facet of a person to the exclusion of the rest because what I want is the jewel in the suitcase—fuck the rest, fuck the furs and the bonds. I'll rip everything apart to come up with what I feel is the nugget. *The Deer Park* is an enormous lie. It was my crook's way of finding the truth. And so in my own way I came up with the jewel. Analyzers are honest but cannot give. Synthesizers are crooks (hence their scholarly footnotes—at least in the more socialized ones) and so they can only take partially, and that from wealth acquired by someone else. So, with my ideas. I love to give them, I love to steal complacency from my friends, torture them into finer states of being, make them know because I am alive with what they have missed, what they have renunciated, but as Bob said I cannot accept, neither their love nor their approval of my ideas. Let that happen and I am being taken—I have met a bigger crook. So, I always love Adele when she is in a rage at me because then I can steal a big thing from her, I can steal her rage—I was never so happy as when she poured the liquor on my head. But when she loves me absolutely then I become uneasy. No wonder. My creation is being improved. So she never gives me the absolute total acceptance. When my ideas really begin to fly and I tell them to her, she glows for a while, but then she deserts me, she goes to sleep, because deep in her she knows with her woman's wisdom that to give her love absolutely to me at a given moment is to make me withdraw—how afraid I am that she is a bigger crook than me. No wonder I get annoyed when she loses money or buys something that is over-priced. She's taken me, she's taken my crook's money which I stole Naked-wise from the very heart of society.

And that is why bad receptions for my books pain me so much. It means I can't steal any more, and so I have to go on, and try to be dishonest at an even higher level.

All of this is an explanation of why artists are so fascinated by crooks. And that is why as I get older and come to discover the value of the crook in me, I wish to make more money. It is making money which gives me pleasure. I stole it from the very heart of that world which can't keep up with me—and indeed what society can keep up with a first-rate crook. So, in that sense, John Huston is a crook which is why we were always so polite and far away from one another although we understood the mutual attraction. Neither one of us could decide who was the bigger crook and we were thus scared stiff. And suspicious.

461 After lunch, and how I hated giving up time for lunch. So many ideas I had while I bolted my food, and so many of them must be lost.

462 CROOKS ARE INTERESTED IN the trip, and that is why their loyalty is to the moment, to the particular idea, cause, person or valuable they are attracted to at the instant. (Some time examine the difference between instant and moment, it has to do with I and me.) Instant—I-and-not-society-take-and-not-take. Moment—Mother of me no take. Mother do not take. We take moments (we feel) we give instants by not taking them. For example: In an instant he was off the floor and at me again. (I did not feel the instant in which he was down, I did not go through the eternity of Victory (and defeat) while he was down, I was waiting for him to get up.) But the other example is: It was one of those moments in which one lives one's whole life. We would never dream of saying, It was one of those instants in which etc. So, the instant belongs to society, it is time, it is number. (Why o why do we call the unit of time a *second*?—Is it Sociostatic—that is to fuck up our primitive understanding of language?) But a moment is a part of being, it is Homeodynamic. The "ing" is always passivity, the state of something, the implication of everlasting life in the transient instant society allows us. That is why the feeling of loving always seems as if it will last forever at the instant we have it.

466 I'M ONE OF THE first novelists who was really a scientist. There were many novelists (like Zola and Norris and Farrell who were behaviorists who became scientists), but very few physicists become novelists and I'm one of them. Styron is a southern minister who became a novelist and that accounts for his strength. And his weakness. He feels such a responsibility. I have the happier irresponsibility of the crook-physicist. If this experiment blows up the lab, well I can always con somebody into giving me another lab. Viz. Rinehart and Putnam. viz. *The Man in The White Suit*.

468 THE ART OF THE playwright is to create types so finely drawn that they are begging for actors to fill their insides. For years I said actors were people without selves in search of Selfs. But the truth is that actors are pure being, pure me's looking for I's (that is, types), which to express the passive flowing nature of their sensitivity. Which is why as I continue to write, my characters become more and more elaborated types (my successful characters like Munshin, Teppis, Lulu, and earlier Guinevere and Hollingsworth) and I am drawn more and more to the theatre. But, also, I begin to act more and more. My inner sensitivity, my H, demands that I express much I cannot say by entering into others, others who we always see as types. I can imitate Adele less and less, create her personality less and less in writing because she is not a type to me, she is a Being, and to create a Being in a book requires genius, whereas to create or limn a type requires merely talent. I have so far to go as a novelist. Yet, the pleasure of my books is that through my types one feels the beating of hearts, the being of hearts.

470 GERMAN. THE GERMANS ARE philosophers; the Germans are the rationalists who set out to explore the types. So their monsters in the last war were social monsters, rationalized, mechanized—just as the total of all machinery expresses the total understanding to this date that society has of the functioning of the body. As we learn more about the mind we have IBM machines, calculators, automation, cybernetics. Invention comes from our deep penetration into the understanding of our body.

471 ANYWAY, THE GERMANS. THEY are philosophers, rationalists, societists,—even as monsters they insisted upon being all of the above three; even as mystics they wrote as crabbed rationalists— Kant. They are pompous because they feel the great seriousness of life, of what they say. A pompous style is the expression of feelings of deep seriousness with little sense or insight into what one really wishes to say. But great works have to be pompous—they should be. They are like symphonies, they are regal, they are the highest social elevations of the soaring Type. So the Germans always use capitals for their nouns. Indeed, they should. Capitals are the expression that one wishes to elevate a noun (which is always implicitly a type) into a Type. This note answers my dilemma about the concentration camp novel. I should place it in the past after the last war and have it a German camp rather than in the future in a Soviet camp. But, still, I wonder.

478 ER WOULD BE A far better word than id for H. But notice what society has done. To err is to be wrong. The state of existence, the passive taking ehhhhh and the active locating changing rrrrrr are denied, called bad. So to change id to er would be to change the bad qualities of id (I-death) (And Freud knew English) to the bad social qualities of er (taking-giving-being, wanting, desire, etc. is to err, to be bad).

479 SUPER. To SUP AND to er. To be er at a higher level of supping. Super-ego. And I thought that S could be called the sup. But we eat in order to deny the er, and yet we must eat. So we are bound to earth and dream of being supermen where what we eat, what we sup upon is immediately converted into making higher er.

480 I'M GETTING TIRED AGAIN. Like a clock, letter consonants exhaust me, mainly because they seem so cultish, so ridiculous, so far-fetched, and yet I am drawn to them more and more. For example: rear. Take away the "rr" and one has eeeeeee. To rear is to surround the passive taking state with the rage of having to give. (And at some part of them isn't that how all parents feel?)

481 BUT I HAVEN'T EVEN begun to scratch the enormous material of the weekend. Before I do, one thought on Bob and myself, and why he was reluctant to analyze me. Deep in him he felt the crook in me. And I as the crook (knowing the destructive and the creative power the crook gives me) was furious at the thought of being analyzed by any old analyst who would take all my marvelous crookery, the H permitted me by society, and convert it to pappish S, dulling me. What the crook always fears is the honest man because the honest man is static, if the honest man wins the crook's intense if crippled sense of life will be lost. His life force will be relocated in a higher region of the er, ergo a less sensitive region. Truly, he will be less a man. So, I as the crook did not want to be taken, and what I sensed in Bob for what amazed me when I invited him to be my analyst is that much as I liked him, and I liked him tremendously—what-the-fuck loved him—I didn't trust him one little bit. (I still don't trust him completely. Good old Bob, he doesn't even trust himself.) But what I sensed in him was a crook on the grand scale who would give me room to maneuver because he respected the crook in me—as viz his up-to-now perplexing and ambivalent feelings of helping and hindering me in the pursuit of JB. So, I invited Bob, it was a challenge to me to con a big crook and do it lying on my back. But Bob sensed that, and the crook in him was scared—Was he going to be taken, he had to wonder. So, our "analysis" continues via the hournal (H journal). (Hour and whore) (H is society's understanding of mystical concepts, or rather society's trapping. The our becomes the hour.) Bob knows the hour is crookery—it is a fifty minute hour, but the analyst takes ten minutes himself although he charges for that.

And the journal is the only way we can do it, because in the journal we can express our love for each other and our distrust— we can accept the crook in each other because we know the crook brings life.

482 ANY RATIONALIST READING THIS would exclaim, "What a diseased mind. What a fantastic and unpleasant imagination. What monstrous and fantastic *rationalizations* this Mailer sets up to justify himself." To which I would answer, "simply, dear old friend who is now an enemy, just tell me where the hell all this came from. Tell me why man is on earth, why there is life, why people are not rational when you know reason is most reasonable, why you want and even believe in a good society when you think people are insignificant, stupid, hopeless, cruel, and in need of order." In a sentence: I get these ideas from somewhere, something, be it myself or the universe, but these ideas have a psychological reality *which one cannot ignore.* For if one does, one enters philosophically into the most untenable position of all for the rational materialist, to wit, something (nonsense) has come out of nothing. And all rationalists believe in the conservation of matter, and the conservation of energy. One cannot be scientific if one does not believe this. So reason demands the mystical explanation. That in the one is found the other. That every Thing contains its Opposite.

483 FOR THE FIRST TIME I come to believe that Laughton may make a great picture out of *Naked.* It won't be the book; it will be on the cliché-parable spectrum, but it can be tremendous. And I don't know whether to tell him I think this or not.

486 LET'S START WITH ORGASM, frigidity, power and castration. Nobody understands these things. They are written and talked about endlessly, but they are never understood. And I think I have a clue to them. I am continuing on the premise that the essential nature of humans is bisexual. And I start from mother, the masculine other who we learn is a woman. Other "proof"

is the necessity of life itself to give-and-take, to act and to understand. My bisexual thesis is anchored in my entire concept of the
duality of everything. So, a step further, I make the postulate that
the bisexual nature is solidified, typed, set at a level, *a mechanical functioning except under stress*, and so decisions are made to
become a sexual type—so necessary to stay alive in society even
at a despised level like the fag—*but*, sexual typology is the loosest
and the least stable because it is the part of man society has insisted
upon burying. So, only with psychoanalysis and with Kinsey does
the collective sociostasis which is equal to society slowly begin to
recognize the great danger it is in unless it narrows the gap between
the sup and the er, for all violent expressions in and against society
are expressions of a great gap between sup and er—hence the
comparative deep contradictory violence of the Soviet Union as
opposed to the surface violence and crankery of the United States.
Well, I postulate crude sexual typologies and the social need to limn
(good old fleshing of the limb) the sexual type. And I'm the first to
make a penetrative contribution to it. How my conservation tricks
my anarchism, so that a hundred years from now I'll be a reactionary
whose ideas must be overthrown. Anyway, the essential decision
which is made and which of course alters according to other needs
and pressures and deep er demands is to take sex frontally as a
bisexual (the healthier course I believe) or to take sex unisexually
and gain the benefits and uncreative disadvantages of that. But that
once done, the orgasm is affected. I suspect with my intuitions that
the state of the sexual soul is close to the orgasm of the bisexual
which is less intense than the orgasm of the unisexual. (How we
give and how we take is of course a great part of this. To have a
truly good orgasm one must be able to take with the body.) Which
is why my orgasms are comparatively pissy except on Lipton's where
the time is extended—that is the time in which I take my orgasm.
To repeat, the state of the sexual soul is less intense for *instants* of
orgasm but the bisexual has sexual consciousness, and creativity,
imagination, etc. plus anxiety running through much more sup and
er. (That is, the bisexual is a more conscious human being because
more of his unconscious has become conscious.) In cruder words,
the limber dick and the stiff-dick-which-is-not-close-to-ejaculation
is the condition of the bisexual which is why he makes a better lover

generally. He can give more satisfaction as well as more anxiety to the woman, depending so enormously on the woman. (One obvious difference between unisexuals and bisexuals is that unisexuals tend to make love much more similarly with each partner than bisexuals who are at the mercy of the partner.) Thus, what I am saying is that orgasm, the fact that we have orgasm, is the indication that society is within us, society which teaches us from childhood that every action must have its culmination, every period of play must come to its abrupt stop, "Darling, put the toys away and come to supper." Action which is not purposeful, manly, *good*, is action which goes on endlessly says the S. So, the idea of erection rather than the limber dick of semi-excitation (note that limber comes from limb which is flexible. One's cock is truly one's third leg). And the unisexual who is usually action, self-confidence, manliness, executive, all the things of One-consciousness is subject to tearing depression, the terror before compulsive action, and . . . suicide. Bisexuals merely threaten to commit suicide. Bisexuals live in a state of semi-potency, semi-anxiety given the fact that S does not understand them at all—or does S understand and so generate self-hatred—so that bi-sexuals invariably despise themselves consciously, but at a deeper level of the er (I can only go down two or three steps but underneath this is always a progressive dialectical inversion and intensification) at a deeper level of the er, bisexuals have a capacity to live which amazes one. They always seem on the edge of a breakdown, their neuroses are in the air, but somehow they bounce back, they give, they are wrestlers with their er, er squared, and even er cubed flowing through them. (I must hurry up—it's close to quitting time.) Anyway, a good orgasm as such is an indication that the person can use the er in sup-approved ways. Which means the good orgasm is not found in creative people, for creative people are against society, and when it comes to fucking they cannot suspend their minds, they cannot play the social game of saying, "Well, this is all very fine and pleasant and I sure had a bang of a coming, but let's get going now." Or, "let's go to sleep." (I'm finding it a little harder to concentrate.) Instead, their (bisexuals) coming is reluctant, grudged, they hate this state of super-sensitivity to end. And in their sexual approaches, bisexuals express their deep bisexual nature, they either as men allow women to approach them or as women act masculine and aggressive about entering the act. (I'm talking of the first fuck between two people which is as important as a signature or as being born and giving one's first cry. The instant of meeting a person is the instant we must trust in most cases for we are never so sensitive to people again—I'm not sure of this.) Probably, with most people, the real understanding of the first moment is buried deep in the er. If we don't like them later, it is the er which furnishes the emotion it knew at the first instant, and vice versa. Probably, in varying degree, we respond mainly to people on first meeting with our S and only echoes of H are present.

487 To ATTEMPT TO GO on. So the orgasm, the hard on—The *excelsior!* of society, Hard and Onward (Excelsior is also waste stuffing) is the sexual benefit given to the healthy unisexual who needs some H communion in order to go on socially. And gets it from his delightful orgasm—when he is a healthy unisexual, of whom there aren't too many either. The healthy bisexual protracts the love-act and explores other parts of life, drama in sex-play, pornography, beautiful love language, dirty love language, lingering, subtle aggressions like controlled spankings, "perversions"—the basic one is always 69 with its great message that mouths are cunts and cunts are mouths, that cocks are tongues and tongues are cocks. Corollary—whether a girl or boy is bisexual or unisexual (at that stage) is probably indicated by whether they are drawn or repelled by soul-kissing. I, who can make love for as long as two hours, notice that when I go limber, I can get hard by talking or thinking of something dirty to me, something forbidden that is, I can project myself forward sexually as a rebel against society, and society responds by making me hard, making me hot, good old S trying to make me come so I won't discover too much. In this sense, premature ejaculation is the S-defense against discovering too much H; just as impotence is the expression of even greater danger. Impotence implies total absence of er-consciousness; premature ejaculation implies bisexual anxiety, bisexual and from that er-awareness. Just as the inability to come (which I've never had—not at least for the first orgasm) is a stubborn fixation, an H determination not to quit because if one continues, something essential will be discovered. I suspect that clinically inability-to-come is the most unstable of the sexual "impotencies." One either goes into total impotence, or one is able to some, or one stops sex (I have to check with Bob and other analysts on this).

490 So, IF MY PREMISE is granted for the sake of the argument, the essential nature of the human is to be bisexual, unorgiastic (not impotent) but tumescent, and the nature of society is to impose upon the essential being of man and woman's perpetual limber dick, the social form of the One—one is either potent or impotent—and looked at from the eyes of a Martian, the form of orgiastic potency of the unisexual is one of separate broken states of total erection and potency and total lack-of-erection and impotency. In the simple sheer sexual sense, a man who is capable of sitting at his desk and making decisions while his penis rests comfortably quietly and smally in the pocket of his pants is *impotent* at that moment. Naturally, this is merely society's view of it, the form from which it dominates and shapes matter and indeed is the only way society can understand it. (A very subtle but important nuance here is that form can only understand matter through the eyes of form—I am bequeathing sup-intelligence to form.) Matter can only understand form through its emotions. (Matter here stands for mind-and-body, er.) Hence, matter's understanding of form is always as the one who grants and the one who denies. One's mother implants upon the infant's sensate matter the first emotional apperception of form. And indeed for the artist, his unconscious sup-conception of form (for as I've said before—at every layer of the unconscious the sup exists in its sibling relationship to its appropriate er) directs him to proceed or to desist. (Which is why too tight a form strangles the ambitious novelist—so much material he wished to disgorge and leave as his petrifaction, his mark (Reik, piss in one hole) is denied by the sup-form which declares it unassimilable, dangerous, and wasteful.) In this sense, work-blocks like impotence are expressions of trench warfare between sup and er— the form simply cannot dispose, allow, or understand the matter which is seeking issue. It demands a lower, cruder, or a higher, more private expression.

491 I KEEP TRYING TO write about potency, orgasm, frigidity, and castration, and I seem to end up every time today discussing the artist. But I cannot force these things—my mind is deeply dialectical, my understanding of one thing creates its antithesis—beginning to write about A, I end up with an illumination of B. Which if continued would disgorge deep factual matter about C, which in turn would illumine D. This whole journal has been an expression of in-and-out, give-and-take, dialectical illumination and factual or theoretical (did anyone ever say that a fact is always a theory), it is no more than a frozen hypothesis accepted by everyone until a new hypothesis overthrows it and becomes fact in its turn. (Fact—fuck act, the f of act, the "beat" imposed on the continuum) factual or theoretical discovery. No wonder I buried in the last sentence of *The Deer Park*—"and nothing is so difficult to discover as a simple fact." Of course. The fact has no existence—it has merely sup-intelligence, Other-Life existence.

492 WHICH IS WHY I have such difficulty—up till now—writing articles and giving suitable endings to my books. For, beneath my rational desires, was the knowledge that there is no such thing as a fact or an end, but that one can merely "hook on" to the continuum as an artist, and "get out" as best one can. And what wouldn't the Freudian analyst have to say about "hook on" and "get out."

493 MOM. A CUNT O surrounded by two men—father and son. Both in the mother. Note: Capital M and little m.

497 SO, THE BISEXUAL IN society is both healthier (in that he expresses the relaxed safe state of the animal) and unhealthier (in that he is inefficient, anxious, nervous, temperamental, saint-psycopathish, inspired-depressed, and restless) in society than the unisexual. But because the bisexual exhibits the anxiety of living in a society of which he is very aware—nothing less in America than a unisexual-bisexual culture—he seems unhealthier. His troubles and discontents are always rippling over him. Yet, as must be remembered, the bisexual somehow endures, always lives longer than one expects, bounces back when one is least prepared—the unisexual caves in sooner or later before an inner crisis. Given their respective human and social natures, the unisexual (who is social) is better in action, no Hamlet he, better in war, better generally at succeeding, but he has in his rigidity no capacity to take the shocks of psychic life—so his body rots or breaks or dries up. The bisexual—often so inept in social life—is yet brilliant in it, and I say he lasts, he does not die of cancer nearly so often (not unless he or she is a bisexual who strangled half-consciously their nature, and enforced it into the unisexual mold—but that is the condition of half the Americans alive) and what is most interesting, is that the bisexual is now beginning to be successful in the business world, mainly because America above all countries I know (except Mexico perhaps) is developed and progressively more permissive to bisexuality. (Perhaps that is the secret of its "strength" as *Life Magazine* will always declare to us radicals).

501 I'VE JUST BEEN OUT for lunch, came up to work, felt not enough energy, went down for black coffee and now feel ready. Since I feel I have a great deal now to say about stimulants and depressants, I want to make one or two remarks and symbols to save time later. L-day will stand for the day or night I take Lipton's and follow it with Seconal. Lplus1is the following day, L plus 2 the day after, and so forth. L plus 2 is today, and what I notice is that L-day or just plain L is always full of insights so round, so enormous, that when I attempt to write them down they come out as clichés or paradoxes. L plus 1 because of the Seconal I believe has me working like a dynamo for long hours attempting to recapture the total mass of material uncovered, discovered, and . . . named. L plus 2 is the critical day. I usually take Seconal again the night of L plus 1—for two reasons: (1) I am still overexcited by the work on the journal, (2) I believe that Seconal seems to keep my "inspiration" from being attacked by the sup during the night. What I've noticed is that on L 1 and L 2 I wake up eager to go to work and full of ideas. But Seconal overused seems to bring on depression. So, L 2 is the critical day. My critical faculties are beginning to work just enough to give shape and cogency to my arguments—so at times the best notes seem to be written on L 2. (Parenthetically, I'm going to add L symbols to the dates from now on.) But, and it is a big but, the hangover, the repression, the rejection is in the wings, and by the night of L 2 I am usually depressed and disgusted so that L 3 and L 4 are the worst days of the week, the days in which the journal seems most idiotic to me. What happens, I think, is obvious. L releases deep parts of my unconscious and given the "cop" in me, I set out to track them down. They result in ideas. Note: the crook is the action, the cop is catching the crook makes the idea, gives word to the act. But the cop who is absent almost totally—except for his presence as a *passive* registering observer the night of the "crime"—is weak the next day. His essential love for the crook has him applauding in the wings. By L 2 however he has caught up, and we have the chase, with every action of the crook repeated by the cop so that the line of thought while less widely inventive is nonetheless registered in detail rather than in parable, parenthesis, or cliché. But by L 3 the poor crook has been caught again, and what a third degree he gets. All of the cop's rage at having indulged the crook rides and smashes onto the crook's ass (word consonants, cock and crook). But, of course, that cannot go on indefinitely either because a cop is dependent for his existence upon the crook—the crook is the initiator of action, the cop is the responding agent—so after a while L 5 or L 6 the cop is lazy again, complacent, enjoying the fruits and "promotions" of having caught the crook again. So, wham, a little Lipton's, and the process is repeated. But what gives me optimism is that I believe this journal goes forward, and that my ideas are better and deeper now than they were a hundred pages ago. Although of course they're less provocative for the quick reader.

502 THIS HAS ALL BEEN a preface to note **499** and my reactions to it during lunch. It seemed over-simple to me. What must be added, and what the mechanical analogy of changing gears clouded completely, is that people being infinitely more complex than machines, do not have the limited option of a machine. It takes much more to strip sexual gears than to strip automobile gears, and so the refusal to shift into higher sexual gear is very often partial— so many men and women are "hangers." They move from higher to lower gear and back again. There is a certain type of dame who for years is half-castrator half-wanton, castrating some men, being conquered by others, often doing both with the same man. One reason I fell so hard and so fast for Adele was that I sensed immediately how very little of the castrator she had in her, less than any woman I've ever known. And I with my delicate-wild (the opposition is consciously worded) sexual appetite am more than normally vulnerable to the castrating powers of women. Another man's hot fuck is so often my psychic castrator because this is one part of women that I am incredibly sensitive to, although I'm more than blind to so much in women.

503 AT ANY RATE, I still believe in the basic law or formulation. It is: A refusal to shift sexual gears drives a man into power conquests or impotence, and a woman into power castration needs and/or frigidity. One proof of this is that castrating women (and of course a great many of them can come which is what the vulgar psychiatric social worker or analyst never understands) always have a peculiarly characteristic sexual quality. I've never known a castrating woman yet who does not give off an aura of sexiness. It is usually glittering sex—they are the women who promise more than they deliver. And there's a reason for this. The capacity to deliver exists in them, the sexual energy and awareness is there—only the ability to overcome the sup is lacking.

506 BUT WHAT REMAINS AN enigma to me is what I called earlier life-force or life-energy or basic energy. And whether people are born with this—that is born unequally, or whether they develop it—that is, potentially, even actually, all infants or at least all sperm-ovule connections contain the same energy is almost impossible to even guess at. What I am afraid is true is that life-energy, shall we call it the lerve (libido I don't like—Freud has id I-death running through everything) is already conditioned to a certain extent by the parents. It makes more sense to me. If the condition of the body is a reflection of the psyche which travels through a social arena, how can one assume that the sperm itself should be unaffected. But here we're even closer to the mystery and so more ignorant. What is undeniable is that the lerve seems to be the determining thing in keeping people alive and functioning despite the heavy psychic armor they carry. A person with low lerve reaches the end of his or her possibilities much sooner, and so must take the next step or perish. Life myself. Paradoxically enough I probably have low lerve (comparatively, that is). But there is so much more lerve in all of us than we are ever able to use, that once we make even a little more available our energy becomes incredible—as mine is at the moment.

507 THE COP IS GETTING stronger by the minute. "What a two-bit crook are you," he is beginning to say, "you want to loot the bank of knowledge, and float bond deals for a new bank, when all you have is the brains of a college sophomore who can't even rob the fraternity party fund."

508 I'VE GOT TO SHAKE this off.

509 THE FAMILY DINNER. WHAT characterizes all family dinners is that everybody eats too fucking much. But there it is, obvious as hell. The analysts call it depression and anxiety, whereas really it's even worse. Everybody presents wants to fuck or murder everybody else, and they dull these feelings with mountains of food.

510 I DON'T HAVE THE patience to retrace my weekend, but what applies most directly is that Adele and I had a great fuck on Sunday night, just when each of us were beginning to worry about losing desire. And it was that—for we entered new territory, we shifted gears—which made me realize how so often in a couple who are right for each other sexually those little temporary slackening periods of a week or two (neutral) are invariably the coasting, the building up for an entrance into a new kind of sex. She was radiant yesterday, and indeed so was I. Dinner at my folks was again a genuine pleasure, and to my amazement Adele brought them a box of candy. Nothing she could have done would have been better proof to me that she loved me, for giving presents is still not natural nor easy for her, and especially to my folks. Barbara and Larry, however, did show up. They're scared of me now. I know it. But so guilt-ridden. Larry had to call me to ask for some guy's address. It is the trap of their lives. They can't do anything the way they would like to. Aggression has to be smothered in the propitiatory act, love pinched by the gnawing doubt.

514 FROM TIME TO TIME I worry: What if my ideas should be published and take root. In time the state would appropriate parts of them to function better. But actually this need only be a half-worry and half-possibility. For nearly everybody I know would be repelled by most of these ideas (deaths?), and their spread would certainly lag for decades anyway behind the course of events.

515 COURSE OF EVENTS: WHAT a suppressed pundit there is in me.

516 I HAVE POSTULATED UNISEXUALITY and bisexuality. It is enough in talking of people to communicate the idea that for life there is never a one, there is always at least a Two. But, actually, if I could carry it far enough, there would be a Three and a Four and so forth, until one could say people are potentially n-sexual or even ∞-sexual. As little examples, are the fragmentary sexual desires one senses vaguely at times toward animals, toward nature itself, and the concretions of nature. I know that to make love outdoors with the sun on my back is so exciting that I'm ready to come as soon as my pants are off. And it is not so much the illicitness of it as the sense of the sun and the space. Once, in the Army, alone on a guard post in the hills, I masturbated because I was so excited by the privacy, the isolation, and the presence of nature. So, shoe fetishists, and all the freaks, cranks, coocoos and queers in the pages of Ellis. Perhaps, poor bastards, they were more developed than us although in crippled ways given the total non-acceptance of S.

524 ACTS OF THE BODY. Walk, talk, fuck, pluck, suck, cluck, balk, buck, cluck, duck ache—If I go on with this I'll be busy for the rest of the day so many words open out. For example: fuck and fickle (the I in fucking who is never constant) suck and sickle (the I who does not speak while sucking but has nonetheless a sharp tongue). Some time when I'm worn out I'm going to play with all the simple variations of body verbs and the body nouns, and body actions like "bake" which come out of this.

526 WHEN AN INTELLIGENT PERSON comes up with a lousy idea it is the sure sign that the idea is a defense, a retreat, rather than a flaw of mind—and in a really intelligent person their lousiest ideas are the ones which leap ahead suddenly and become their big new ideas. I repeat: Thought like fucking is dialectic but directed. The ultimate end of the fuck like the ultimate end of thought is to comprehend the universe whole.

527 ADELE GETS FURIOUS THESE days when I talk about bisexuality. Why don't you become a homosexual, she flares at me, you want to anyway. The funny thing is that I don't—I feel less homosexual tension than I have ever felt—neither homosexual desire which for that matter I've never felt consciously, but more important no homosexual anxiety. The other day in a homosexual clothing store the salesman was giving me a covert feel while measuring the length of the cuffs. A year ago I would have broken out into a sweat. This time I stood there unmoved but feeling tenderly humorous toward him. (The two is definitely in toward. We go from one toward two.) The spelling conflicts with the basic instinctive pronunciation which is why so many illiterate people have a bitch of a time pronouncing that seemingly simple word). Anyway, I felt no anxiety. Instead, I thought, "Well, my friend, congratulations. A part of me always wanted to be a corset adjuster so I could cop quick feels (and isn't that just the sexual quality of the cop—he always takes as a stranger) and get away with it. And you on your side of the fence have made it.

528 ACTUALLY, THERE'S NO CONTRADICTION here. I have deep bisexual love with Adele, my sexual habits are formed around women as the envelope-object of pleasure. So, to "go" homosexual would be merely a setback to me at this time. I wish to explore the mountain of sex from the high vista I now have. To change camps, to go over would be to have to start again with new equipment, new guides, new mistakes. Besides, I have the feeling that if I were to find equal sexual pleasure with men and with women, which I postulate as the sex characteristics of the future, the ideal future, I would lose the tension which now furnishes thought. Complete healthiness is very close to complete passivity of the guilt-less sort—and one hardly lives in such a world. Actually, Adele is not worried about my going homosexual nor actively bisexual—what she's afraid of is that if I take the dirt out of sex I will find her less attractive. She's wrong on this I believe, but because we went along for years with that as the basic sexual starter in me—the dirty, I can hardly ask her to believe I am changing profoundly so quickly. And besides her despised idea of herself which diminishes every day can hardly believe that I would love her if I were healthy. So a part of her fights my ideas, a part of her accepts them. She also knows with her woman's sense that a man must have furnished to him over and over the masculine comfort of having conquered a woman, be it in bed or in thought, but unless the woman resists there is no feeling of victory. Which, parenthetically, is Bill Styron's trap. Rose—who is an enigma to me—is, at least on the surface, so accepting, so taking, so good, so loyal, so level, that poor Bill strangles in the rage he feels toward her which he feels would be monstrous to express. Or, maybe, I misread them completely.

529 BUT THIS OPENS THE peculiar understanding and lack of understanding of the analyst. Adele always yells at me, "If you talk about bisexuality so much, you must be feeling an awful lot of anxiety." I'm not. I swear I'm not. If there's anything I "feel" at fairly deep levels it's when I'm anxious, uneasy, suspicious of my motives. Unless this anxiety is buried deeper than any I've known— which I suppose is possible—it is the part of Adele's mind which is mired in analyst-concepts which is wrong. There is a paradox worth exploring in the analyst-patient relationship. As the patient free-associates, material comes up, H (er) material. Only the patient actually knows the intensity and the complex mysterious character of the actual emotion(s). The analyst either draws a blank, puts a concept—an S concept given their ideology—on the material, or empathizes. But the character of empathy is the most mysterious of all. For when we empathize we can never know if we're right. The fact that we feel certain we are feeling the same thing as the other person cannot be verified. If they say yes, particularly in an analytic relationship, it may be for a variety of reasons and can even be an outright lie. If they say no, they may be unaware but actually feeling that, or again they may lie. The mystery of empathy is whether it is valid or not—I suspect it is—but it may be valid in peculiar ways—er-conscious for some, er-unconscious for others. So, the analyst, except for the more adventurous ones find that empathy is very undependable and dangerous—they can never know if they are right or wrong and they get into terrible deep *accepting* waters. For to empathize is to admit weakness in the social sense—one is saying, "Yes, I have had that terror too." So, as a practical matter, empathy is in that dangerous illogical, irrational, socially and psychoanalytically condemned area bounded by paranoid projection and *telepathy*. Most analysts are frightened by it. Herbert Aldendorff is terrified by it because he has so much of it, and therefore Germanically, characteristically, he is resolutely passive in his analyses—his only defense outside of self-hatred from keeping him from taking a wild plunge off the Freudian board into the oceanic unconscious. Therefore, I would wager that most analysts, nearly all bad ones, and even most good ones depend upon S-concepts, Sup-understandings of the patient's er-deliveries. "I . . . er . . . want to say . . . er er er . . . you're . . . er . . . good guys . . . errrrr." (Maybe the Naa or the Hih or the Ugh would be better than the Sup as the opposite number to er—which I've now decided is perfect). (I just now wrote high for which, leaving out the w. Maybe the hitch is the word for the sup. Ah, well).

530 EXCELSIOR! HARDONS ONWARD. DR. Mailer, H.L.D. Specialist in Hardonology and Limberology. From now on I use Excelsior, abbreviated as excls (exclusive)! for to go on, to continue, anyway, etc.

531 EXCELSIOR: WHAT I'M GETTING at is that some of the analysts understand their patients some of the time, and none of the analysts understand their patients all of the time. They can't. Apart from the obvious human impossibility, there is a total conceptual barrier which is rarely passed, and in Freudian analyses, given the analyst as warden, taker, God, priest, no-give, there is the misery of a complex emotion which could lead one onward to discoveries being turned back by the analysts conceptual inversion of it. Which is why analysts so often mistake a patient's legitimate situation-anxiety for an illusory anxiety. As viz Bob's brother and the jealousy. So, too, the patient's guilt at er sexual desires (invariably some permutation of the bisexual) is all too often misunderstood by the analyst as bonafide shame.

532 Now, OF COURSE, AN analyst tries not to convey his attitude to the patient. An analyst will drop dead at a cocktail party before he admits that he ever directs a patient. But the fact is that they do. The analyst in most cases is a rebel who retreated, and that is a very uncomfortable position—very power-obsessed but with no vocational sanction to wield power. So, truly, in many cases, the analyst is sitting in a hotter seat than the patient. And the patient suspects this but cannot bear to believe it. Mother-father-embodiment must be strong or there's nothing left. Moreover, the super-sensitized relation of analyst-patient creates empathies, approaches to telepathy, and telepathy itself all the time. Like the wall of Mendes-France which was studied for six months and so became a ladder, the impassive face of the analyst or rather the impassive voice (for the analyst is seen usually only at the beginning and the end of the hour) reveals a whole gamut of reactions, and they are not all paranoid projections of the patient. The ridiculous assumption under Freudian practice is that the patient should be alone in a room talking to a dummy, a wax dummy. If the analyst "dummy" were actually a dummy there might be some justification to saying that all the patient's material and interpretation of the analyst was a projection, but given a human being no matter how determinedly impassive, the hyper-acute sensitivity and need of the patient penetrates the façade. So, analyses are directed, and the analyst consciously and unconsciously, by his silences as much as his speeches, is constantly giving approval or disapproval. He believes he is taking, but his taking is the defense, the *penance* for his rebellious beginnings, and beware of ex-rebels who are penitents—nobody is more S-directed. So, analyses go on, they go on interminably, the patients get better or they get worse, they deteriorate when the analyst expects success and vice versa, they also conform at times to the analyst's expectation. The analysis is over and the analyst if he is honest has to wonder, "Just what the fuck did happen in there?" As indeed the patient wonders.

533 YET, WE CANNOT DENY it. There seems to be some kind of general over-all benefit to psychoanalysis. Probably, it is so difficult to determine, more people are benefited than are hurt. If this be true, I have an idea why. In the very absence of meeting, in the essential square peg to round hole, the misapplied and erroneous S-concept of the analyst attached to the er-released matter there is a liberty for the patient to come to his or her own conclusions. I suspect that when the patient makes a poor transference, there are often surprisingly good results. This, at least, for Freudian analysts. What happens is that a self-analysis with an essentially unimportant but nonetheless not-to-be-ignored chaperone has taken place. The analyst says, "Dependency drives, castration fantasies"—The patient feels: and feels beneath words: "I know what love is, I know what power is, I know (and this is private H knowledge) that I am not as bad as I thought I was, but this I'm keeping to myself. If I give it to old Four-Eyes he'll tack it on his article board, put it under glass, and give it a name."

So, beneath the surface, a mighty ventilation takes place. On the surface there is guilt, hostility, pain, self-hatred—in the deep reaches of the er, there is shame, opening of rhythm, pleasure, self-love, and the suppressed H understanding and S admitting that one is not so bad after all. What characterizes the successful analysis is that the S has been dealt a blow, not the er. It isn't that one learns to control one's outrageous id, as Freudians would have it, but rather that the sup loses power, must take retreats, must admit some of its imposture. On the surface the analyst believes he has tamed the patient; what has happened is that the patient has out-foxed him. There was more than one girl I laid who said to me, "I'm not going to tell my analyst I've been sleeping with you until you leave town, because if I do, he's going to fuck it up."

534 I'm very dissatisfied with the above notes. On Lipton's I saw it all very clearly, and in a few words. Above, I just wandered, tried to find the handle, and passed away from the subject again.

539 The reason the common people read with such delight the stories and fables of unhappy kings is that it cozens them into accepting society. "Look," they must think, even if you have liberty, you're still unhappy, so I'm not so bad off." And that is why kings in their public pronouncements—even if they had to get their head out of their mistresses' twat long enough to get dressed—always speak solemnly of the cares of state. There'd be revolution if they ever hinted they have a good time.

540 And so the enigma of the King and Queen of England— they are always loved because they are always long-faced, sad, responsible, sober, industrious, unimaginative, in short the same as the gray lot of the English themselves. Get a ripper or a fag on the Throne of England and the PM starts the abdication apparatus.

545 I just realized that the reason I never could accept the Soviet Union even in the height of my Wallace days is that I could never believe instinctively that a good society could have sex repression. There was a time when I could have explained away 25,000,000 slave laborers I had such contempt for people, but I could never explain away difficult divorce laws. And in a way I was right. Today I would say that the slave laborers while more monstrous are less basic than the bad sex laws.

546 ANYBODY WHO'S REALLY A radical has to fight for greater sexual liberty. It is the acid in which the rebel is tested. Does he turn from blue to red?

547 I HAVE TO EXPLORE the idea of what it means to different people to go to Heaven and Hell. Probably one of the really good projective tests would be to have people outline for you what they believed Heaven was like, and what Hell was like. And I suspect that underneath the surface construction, once you could draw them out, would be projected a great deal of H-desire masquerading as S and vice versa. This is one of those common-places which ought to be explored more. The trouble with most projective techniques is that they work better for people on the college-to-expert express than they do for weird-os. Most projective techniques are quite inept, I believe, when it comes to doing more than recognizing that a particular person is very unusual.

548 HEMINGWAY'S PECULIAR WEAKNESS IS that he's a taker, his heroes are all Takers. His idea of courage is that you can take it. It never seems to have occurred to him once that courage might also consist of giving. Which is why he probably lives in a cloudy mystical state and reads universes into every cliché and half parable he writes.

549 DEPRESSANTS AND STIMULANTS: WHAT I've noticed—who could miss it?—is that Lipton's affects me differently from everybody else. It is nominally a depressant but I become more stimulated than anyone else. (Everybody passes through a brief period of stimulation on Lipton's before relapsing into passivity, but my stimulation lasts much longer and my passivity sometimes never comes.) Nearly all of my friends are Takers—the power of American conformity today tends to make sensitive people develop the secretive Taking powers rather than the more dangerous—if radical—giving powers. So, there are probably more Takers around than Givers these days. But more than that, I as a Giver surround myself with Takers. What Giver doesn't? And only a few friendships have been with Givers—First Devlin, the peculiarly intense restricted giver, then Malaquais (who conceals the Old Lady Taker in him), and Bob who is the easiest Giver-Taker I know. Plus Adele who gives sexually and emotionally.

552 I'M WRITTEN OUT, ALTHOUGH not depressed. I better put down no more notes or I'll throw them away in verbiage. Off to Baltimore (a visit to Lindner).

February 10, 1955

553 A NEW TYPEWRITER RIBBON—WHICH for me always means that my ideas are going to read better.

554 TODAY IS L PLUS 1—some Lipton's, one Seconal, and two bouts of love. But the lift is not tremendous today mainly I think because I took it too soon after the last time. Still, I'm not depressed either, and in reading over the last fifty pages of the journal I find many interesting, even fascinating things buried in the general incoherence.

555 BUT WHAT I WANT to try to get at now is the business of thought—what is thought? etc. Having gotten into the habit, particularly under Lipton's of keeping a very sharp sense of my "mental state," I have come to the conclusion that "thought" as such is without words. There is truly a razor's edge in the mind between the "thought" and the words—even though unsaid—which come to give it shape and one-ness. I realized this in a peculiar way. I found myself having the old fantasy of an electric pad on my brain which would carry my unspoken words into a tape recorder. And at that instant I realized that I was truly thinking without words, for what came immediately after—and the thoughts had been beautiful and very clear—was that to think of capturing the thought immediately aroused "words" in me, and though the words were good, and still nominally "thought" since I did not speak them, I could sense immediately that the thought had been chased away, and I was left only with word scraps. So, I want to formulate it like this: the universe which is always within us delivers matter—that is, a part of what we have "taken" floats into consciousness; with words we seek to give it form, we are attempting to convert what we have taken—and so long as it is still "thought" we are still "taking" it—into an "Idea"—something we may give. So, form, idea, word, are sup-things; matter, thoughts, feeling are from the er.

556 THIS CAN HELP TO explain the difficult condition of the novice writer. Over and over I've noticed that young writers, or old young writers, for that matter, cannot seem to understand why their work, which to the reader is banal, thin, and uninspired, is so magnificent and powerful to them. The answer is of course simple. Their work is highly un-social and private. What has happened is that they have mistaken the intensity and beauty of their thought for the drab expression in words. "He felt old and sad and alone," seems to them to convey the state of old-age as it has never been conveyed before. The sophisticated reader who demands that thought be trapped as closely as possible, or he will not respond to it with his own thought, considers the work puerile. Part of becoming a writer is to develop a more and more intense conception of the particular inaccurate word which is least inaccurate—at least for oneself; one can hardly estimate the value of words for others.

557 FOR THE ANALYST AND the analysand part of the same process occurs. The analysand is delivering thoughts—at the very best they are so concerned with the thought that the "idea" is completely crude—"I wanna fuck my mudder . . . er . . . I'm sorry . . . didn't mean it . . . What do I mean? . . . I feel dizzy . . . er . . . glass balls . . . er . . . Chevrolet for '55 . . . what a fucking quack you are . . . I'm sorry . . . didn't mean it . . . What do I mean? . . . I feel dizzy . . . er . . ." And so forth. As a literary production it is close to zero—yet the internal process has been intense. Yet the analyst would be super-human if he were able to remind himself constantly that these grunts and phrases far from revealing how stupid people are beneath the surface, actually show that we are all close to genius once we open ourselves to the er.

558 I HAVE COME TO a conclusion about work. Which is that I must desert my old obsession with not getting overwhelmed and doing but one job at a time no matter how slow and painful it was, and instead I must take on a number of projects, novels, stories, articles, books-to-read, etc., and whenever I feel bored or worn out with one, I must leave it for the next. That way I think I could tap far greater productivity. The key of course is to be concerned with the act of working itself rather than its issue or product. One reason I have gone at such a great rate in this journal is that I have not been much concerned with publishing it. If I ever decide to publish it which means revising, rewriting, censoring, etc. it will become slow hard and anxious work.

560 INVESTIGATING THE CONSONANTS I'VE found some fascinating material. R and L are the only consonants which combine with any frequency with other consonants at the beginning of words until one gets to S. S has many combinations. Sh, Sk, Sl, Sm, Sn, Sp, Squ, Sc, Scr, St, Str, Sw. No doubt about it, R, L, and S are the key consonants in English.

561 ON THE VOWELS, I'M beginning to feel other things. The hard vowels, I, ay, EEEE, Ohhh, (which is midway between hard and soft) and OOOOOOO seem to have more relation to giving, to society, to I as social actor. And the soft vowels are more from the er. Of course this is enormously complex and I haven't begun to feel it yet, but slowly I make progress.

562 I HAVE AN IDEA which I think is important. The problem of psychoanalysis has always been one of measuring intensity. There has never been an objective correlative. The variables in the patient have to be judged by the variables in the analyst. Which of course is the mathematical relation of all human relations. So the business of deciding just how neurotic the patient is becomes the riddle wrapped in a mystery and surrounded by an enigma. (AP. Neurotic—The no of erotic; also, the new of erotic. Also, the knew of erotic).

But there is one way we can go at it. A human is the combination of a human animal—God and a social-person. The link between man and society is Time which is society's concept and its building bricks. What may be said of any person who is highly socialized is that they grow up with a clock built into them. We have all had the experience of going to sleep without a clock knowing that we must wake up at some difficult hour, and always five or ten minutes before the time we stir and are ready. Just as a carpenter measuring spaces all his life can estimate to the quarter of an inch a length of wood four feet long, so civilized clock-chained man can measure time. But we have two systems of time within us. We have the social time which is accurate if not metronomic, and we have er-time which is cloudy and suspended—so that often on a flight of thought (not a flight of "ideas") we have no idea whether we have been "gone" for two minutes or twenty-two minutes. Our sense of time has broken down because the nature of the experience has been one of taking, and taking with its intensity muddies the count—the sense of time is dependent upon "even" experience. (Perhaps even the five-minute error in awakening is due to the three-second dream which seemed like five minutes.)

So, what I sense as a test is this: To measure the discrepancy between clock-time and subjective time through a range of passive and active experiences. This has been done by some testers I believe, but so far as I know it has been approached more as a stunt, as a curiosity, than as a serious investigation. What would be involved is to study first on a person their sense of time in standard characteristic activities—eating, reading a newspaper, going through a modest interview, etc. With very neurotic—that is half socialized people—the discrepancies would appear already, but they would at least provide a guide to the more elaborate tests. Then would come such things as listening to a piece of jazz, a piece of a symphony, studying a painting, singing a song themselves, watching TV, or better a part of a movie since TV has commercials to set a "beat." There I throw out as suggestions—undoubtedly better standard things could be chosen. Then tests of rhythm according to the best methods possible. By the time one was done, I believe that the give-take functions of the person would be revealed in their similarities and discrepancies to other people. For example any person who has already demonstrated a close sense of time in characteristic activities would reveal er-anxiety, passivity anxiety if five minutes of a symphony sounded like two minutes to him or twenty minutes might it have enjoyed it that much, or the same with two minutes—it was so good that they felt it was fleeting—but that in itself would reveal *attitudes* toward time, and given the battery of subjective-time responses there would be inner evidence to support the idea of special sensitivities or special anxieties. And if used at the beginning and end of an analysis, one could have a certain objective correlative to the progress and loss of the analysis. The great obstacle to this test is of course the one present in all tests—the presence of the tester who as society immediately alerts and dulls and thereby distorts the character of the one who is tested. But, probably, there is a great deal here, and maybe I'll get further ideas on it.

February 14, 1955

563 AGAIN I START WORK on the journal in a state of intense excitement (which from the outside is called mania) and indeed as all thought is circular to the conservative-rationalist and spiral to the radical-mystic, so I am thinking of a thousand things at once.

564 THE KICK-OFF WAS THE weekend in Baltimore. One interesting result is that I have a mock-cold this morning. That is, my nose is running—like allergy—and yet I do not feel the depression of a cold. It has set me thinking about the nature of colds, and the Roxitchitl or whatever the hell it is that Bob gave. I took a capsule last night, felt no effect, and so added two seconals and went to sleep. But the note on the box literature said that "nasal congestion" was sometimes a side-effect. This morning I have nasal congestion. I wonder if colds are not an expression of an S-victory necessary to relieve a too-intense conflict. The depression which accompanies my colds (except for today) is the sadness and anger of the er at being defeated again. Yet the cold may well be one of the basic homeostases—when one is feeling too much "tnesion" (nesion as nerve tension) too much er, the S relieves the conflict by knocking the body out—what is essential to the cold is that the er cannot win at that given period, and so S in its victory declares a punitive peace treaty. The roxyl drug is probably an S stimulant, an H vitiator—hence in people whose nervous systems react to S increments by a cold, "nasal congestion" is the result. Whenever I get a bad cold in the future, I am going to try Lipton's and see if it is a cure.

565 I HAVE NOT WARMED up yet this morning, but I feel that this journal today is not going to be very well-expressed.

570 IT CAN BE STATED as a philosophical proposition I believe that pleasure and idea are antithetical, yin and yang.

To have society man must be deprived of pleasure, for it is in the frustration of pleasure that reason (desperate to save the body from the bio-chemical poison of frustration) advances into the mystical unknown. So intellectuals are unhappy because their need is to convert thoughts into ideas, and the intellectual knows pleasure only when he has expressed the thought in an idea which is so elaborated, so "approximately" perfect that he may relax back into vague thought. For thought is the state of pleasure. It is only when we attempt to convert it to an idea that pain comes—the pain of birth, of separating an embodiment from the total. As our idea that "man is the measure of all things" has grown through history, so woman's child-birth has become progressively more painful. Child-birth now is an idea rather than a thought; an orgasm of pain rather than a swell of muscular ebb and flow.

Adele often comments in our bed, "Why are you frowning so? You look in pain? You look angry and tortured?" Every time she makes such a remark I am in the process of trying to shape a thought into an idea. I am trying to give birth. My mighty mother is in me, but I have books, ideas, projects, theses, etc., instead of birthing children.

572 "Stupid" people find thought painful, fucking delightful—at least generally, *typically,* they do. (Folk-lore and platitudes show the truth of this.) Intellectuals find thought joyous, fucking painful—again generally true. Rare people find fucking and thought joyous—usually orgiastic mystics who can dispense with the guilt of no-orgasm and the guilt of no-idea, no-work-accomplished. Balanced "healthy" people are people who can move from one to the other from the orgiastic mystic to the rational orgasm and back again. Contentment and depression are the lot of the "socially healthy" person—hard ideas and strong orgasms—a very rare bird by the way. But such birds pay by being relatively ordinary—they are not geniuses. Orgiastic mystics (the rarest birds of all) who are healthy orgiastic mystics have a rich inner tumescent universe, but seem pitiable, perverted, "crazy" and hopeless to society. The genius is the rarest of all for he contains both—his love and hate for himself, his er and his sup, his saint-loverness and social-critical oneness are both enormously developed. The genius is deprived of pleasure and deprived of real love of the one (One's mate) so the genius has his incredible insights into the nature of pleasure and pain, and when he loves a person is capable of loving them only by endowing them (as indeed every person understood well enough is) with all the nature of pleasure and pain, all the love and hate the genius feels for the universe. There have been very few total geniuses in history, but more and more I suspect that Joyce was one of them. If I can ever write *Antacid Analgesic* the way I conceive it, I too will be a genius. Until then I will merely give intimations and promises of genius together with a lot of qvatch.

I started this note on the thought that I can enjoy fucking only when it arouses creative thought (not detachment) which flows in and out and around and of the person or persons to whom I make love. Once it wells into words, ideas, the fucking loses its savor. Which is why Adele was so furious at me the night of the fuckanalysis. She knew that a joyous act had become a painful one for me; I was no longer thinking-flowing, but ideating—stopping and starting.

573 *Antacid Analgesic.* THERE ARE many elements in this. And and ant. Acid and alkali. Anal and by implication Oral. Already I could call it *Andalc Oralgesic*. The take and the cid (the beggar and the king) (Take from tac); Pain and pain-killer. Pain-killer provides pleasure, so pain and pleasure—the condition of existence. Even, very private, an al, an Al—from Brother Can You Spare A Dime—Don't You Know me, They call me Al, it was Al (hell) all the time. So Heaven and Hell. Gesic. Guess and seek. God—little e of self-society; I who is sic, sick. God and I guess and seek for the sick. (And the healthy.)

574 WHAT A TITLE. I bet I could locate (give) every theme, idea, thought and spiral and circle of this journal in *Antacid Analgesic*. How significant that I never read Joyce. I know when I'll read him. (That is I never read more than a hundred pages of *Ulysses*, and two or three pages of *Finnegans Wake*.) But if I write a great *Antacid Analgesic*, then I will read Joyce and be able to understand him as few or perhaps no rationalist has before me.

577 MY NOSE HAS STOPPED running. Why? I knew this was not a cold. But has it stopped running because the S is complacent, not punishing, because it knows that I am merely putting down in crude ideas vast thoughts which therefore will endanger it not at all so that in a few days when I reread this I'll think, "Oh, My God." (Oh, Society, please forgive me for such nonsense.) Or is it because I am happy, because my lerve is finally flowing again.

578 A TRULY GREAT MAN is a man who does not begin the freezing-making process until he is totally ready, until he cannot grow unless he begins to make and give. A crank, a fanatic, a dogmatist was a potential genius who froze too early, who made too early. Wilhelm Reich strikes me as being half-genius, half-crank. I know very little about his orgone theory, but I suspect that he was close to something truly tremendous, and perhaps terrified of going insane (which is the danger of growing when the road is too impacted with obstacles) he froze at the level of his orgone box, which haunts us, for we feel alternately and even simultaneously that it is a lie and a truth (using truth as something on the way to Truth).

582 LAST NIGHT TAKING MY Seconal I thought—"A pill for the swill." And I was flat (stunned) by the recognition. How I hate this journal, hate myself, hate Adele, hate my wild kick, hate the garbage I release, how I cling to society to knock me out, to stun my rebellion. If I ever go insane I'll not be a schizo. I'll be a manic-depressive. Adele will too. For we either love each other or hate each other, we are either all er or all S at a given moment. The lucky saving grace which makes us mates is that we almost always love each other or hate each other fairly simultaneously. So our hatred flows into love by being discharged, our love becomes hatred by being expressed in its fullness. And the longer we live together the deeper this becomes—although since it becomes more understandable, we grow over the whole closer and I believe stronger-if-more-vulnerable because we have more to lose. But my salvation is for my honesty to hunt the crook in me forever. Only through understanding myself can I come to create. By going in, I can give out. As I understand myself, and understand Adele (for whom sensuality is the equivalent of speech for me) so I can waste less time. These days I'm consumed with impatience which comes out in the barely suppressed pompousness and sense of rightness with which I talk even to dear friends—They must understand, there's no time to lose. I feel it so unbearably. And yet I must repel them even as I seek to bring them closer because if I bring them closer I find contentment and so must give up the attempt to be a genius.

Bea was a manic-depressive too, still is but now maniacal outside, depressed inside—she thickens her skin, becomes progressively more insensitive, and feels like death in her heart. Bea's trouble and mine was that one always zigged when the other zagged, and I always felt as if she always led the tune—whereas Adele and I take turns at leading one another. So Bea was a "castrator" and Adele is not. When I was tender and loving with Bea, she was cold; when I was frustrated, angry, and cold with Bea, she became a soft little child saying "Why do you hurt me so?" No wonder I hate her today—I think she was right in being afraid of me, I think I might conceivably have killed her if she had continued frustrating me. When I get angry at Adele I just want to smack her (smack—man sacks the female) and usually I do. Bea I rarely touched, but I used to feel like strangling her.

583 WHAT BOTHERED ME ABOUT "A pill for the swill," was that Adele and I had been so happy, so close, so loving on the train and the train trip seemed to take two hours, no more. We were very close. We held hands and felt our bodies flowing into one another. *But I exhaust everything when I feel intense.* So I spent my love, and realized in taking the pill that now my hatred was close. I have to recognize, accept, and more get the benefit of these swings of mood for I learn from each—and it is only when we try to suppress one aspect of ebb or flow, give or take, make or rest, challenge or response, love or hate, upbeat or downbeat—when we try to be simply happy, strong, loving, or whatever, try to freeze the rhythm into a straight line progression that we become frustrated, impotent, anxiety-ridden and restless. So, when I hate Adele I will recognize it from now on in myself, even as I will try to appreciate her when she hates me. Indeed I do. Drunk, full of beans, she often hates me, or rather feels general lustility for the world. After all hatred is not simply hatred. Hatred is valuable too. Hatred is the mover, love is the rest. Hate makes, love nourishes. A mother who simply loved her children would make nothing but contented cows. It takes the bull to make a bullfight, and when we have a Ferdinand in the ring, the crowd gives hate, the crowd rains pillows down.

When the bull hates and charges and seeks to kill, and the bullfighter shows his great appreciation and understanding of that hatred, then the corwd (crowd and cord) can love. And how it loves. It would kiss the feel, the (I wrote feel for feet—must explore this). feel, the feet, of the bullfighter, in order the ass, the genitals, the belly and the lips, it adores this taking loving agent of bullfighter who has shown the creativity which may be saved from hatred. And that is the value of the bullfight—it shows us that hatred too is creative, it is at the heart of the creative process—that hatred goes into love and love back to hatred. No wonder the Mexicans turn on their hero-bullfighters when they're bad. And no wonder El Loco was so extraordinary—for he aroused the maximum of love and hate, and aroused it in waves.

585 TED AMUSSEN CANNOT EXPRESS hatred—that is his sickness. Neither can Danny Wolf. If Danny doesn't take a smack at me soon, I've got to let up or I'll drive him into schizo-phrenia. The answer to Bob's question as to why I provoke the orgy with people like Dan and Rhoda, whom I don't desire sexually (and what a world of lack of understanding is buried in to desire sexually) is double at least. I want to enrage Dan to the point where he'll attack me. If he could express his hostility in physical aggres-sion he would feel wonderful afterward—I know that. I would like to make him scram at me, weep, rage, spit, and strike. Next day he'd wake up in a good mood. I know it. That's why I always try to touch off hatred in people—it's the only way to get back to love. When Bob came to India's I knew he was suppressing his hostility toward me (chassidility) (He was like a rabbi furious that his most talented disciple was wearing his tefillin) (And isn't Bob's talent to be a teacher who stimulates others past him?) and I also knew that the longer Bob suppressed his hostility toward me the more depressed and tired he would become. So I taunted him, insulted him, stuck needles in him, twisted writs and wrists (the Ritz is the Writs) provoked him until—and I really believe this—he scared us in turn when he drove the car. Granted the Lipton's had us paranoid. Nonetheless, Bob had a shit-eating grin when we screamed that we were scared. And after that, after that equality, after hatred met hated, we were close and warm the rest of the evening which was a fine evening—and Bob's energy, his enormous lerve was flowing. Because Bob is a lover. When he loves he is tireless—it is the source of his energy. He becomes flat only when he hates and cannot express it. But crook loves crook. And crooks know how to express hatred. So I shit on Bob, and he shit on me, and then we were brothers again, mutual leader and follower.

590 THE CURVE IS LIFE, the straight line is society. We believe we solve in a straight line—that is reason's assumption. The slovenly is the inchoate mass. To be simply a solver or simply a sloven is to deny oneself. One must be both. One must love disorder and love order, hate order and hate disorder. Yet, here is where I disagree with the Greeks and all the other Golden Meaners—there is no such thing as the Golden Mean in Life. It is only by welcoming the extremes of one's personality, tempering those extremes only— assuming of which I'm not certain that life here is better than life-after-death—tempering those extremes only by the knowledge that one must not be destroyed by them, that one goes on, one grows, one finds creative-destroying fulfillment. For no philosopher (artist, scientist, merchant man, chief) is ever simply a creator, no real good one. The essence of creativity is that it accepts the destruction implicit in its assertion.

591 CLASSICIST AND ROMANTIC. BOTH are in me. I write my philosophical propositions which are romantically wild to most people in their enormous magnification of Self in the stiff stone prose of an Aristotle.

593 MY THROAT IS SORE again. (I don't know why I wrote again). It became sore about an hour after my nose stopped running. For a while I was fighting it—I think I used to get sick so much because I was always fighting my body needs, fighting my sickness, loathing it. This time I will accept my sore throat, feel its soreness, relax in the very soreness, and I have the hunch (a sudden warping of the body-mind which is why hunches are forcings, premature predictions, lacks of patience) that my sore throat will go away if only I give myself truly to it.

594 PATIENCE AND IMPATIENCE. THEY are the polar expressions of society-and-man, man-and-society. Our impatience comes from our desire to fuse with the universe, our patience is our recognition that society impedes the way and one cannot do it *instantly*. But the two become reversed. The person s-oriented is impatient, impatient with delay, broken appointments, the inability to communicate, etc. (Etc. is the word symbol for infinity.) Etc. could be the title of a novel which ran a million pages out of trying to capture the total of a moment. The person who is er-oriented like Ivan von Auw has patience. They can wait. They know that everybody and everything comes to its fulfillment (if it will—which is what gives them their sadness. Sadness and Gladness) comes to its fulfillment if one accepts, if one takes. So, what happens is that the S gives its essential nervous quality which is time—patience to the H, and the H gives its impatience—fusing to the S. The two people within us affect one another. *Every man is a marriage within himself.*

595 THE REASON THIS JOURNAL goes is that I do not force it. I accept it. I give to it when I feel like giving, and leave it when I feel barren toward it. (A barren, a baron, a bar on—a barrier is a bar-wielder. Language personifies the outer environment. This all started with the and he. The is the thinginfication of he. It is the definite article. If I am right, all nouns are personifications of human ers. Again s. At the beginning of a word it is society generally—at the end it is plurals which are continuations. And English is rich, is bi-polared because English draws deeply and directly from two streams, the Druid blood sacrifices which gave Anglo-Saxon and the rationality of Latin.)

598 IMPATIENCE—PATIENCE. THIS, TOO, REVOLVES respectively around the Entering-Giving liaison, and the Take-Make liaison. Givers are invariably "insensitive" to people's receptivity that is patience-resistance. As viz myself and my mother. Takers are invariably insensitive to people's impatience. What may be said is that neither patience nor impatience are virtues in themselves. A man who is healthy on the patience-impatience spectrum is capable of waiting and capable of hurrying. His entering-leaving faculties are highly developed (what we mean by strong "sensitivity") and so he or she can be patient or pressing as they sense the relative activity or inertness (interness—unwillingness to accept) of the person, audience, whatever which surrounds them.

What I must develop is patience and the entering—taking aspects of my personality for I have always been able to make and to give. The others are what screw me up. I need never worry about losing my energetic impatience (I have so much of it) if I take on patience. It is just that I must stop forcing my personality into a One—I must accept the two—and when I do I'll really be able to go. I must stop being dogmatic, but be a dogmatic and eager follower as each demands me.

601 THE PHALLIC-NARCISSIST (JIM JONES) cannot take. The hysteric cannot make. The dependent cannot give. This is vastly oversimplified, and each category bears its relation not only to how the R-act of (Enter-Take—Make-Give from now on called the Etemege or its echo (Leave—Give—Destroy—Take) the Legedete. (Etemeges and Legedetes Unite and Separate) but the R-act also bears its relation to the L-act which is the rest, the passivity-activation of the self. The image of the movie is most adequate. I'll expand later—it's gobbledygook as it now stands. But to expand the beginning of this:

The phallic-narcissist (Jim Jones) tends to go directly from something entering him to making something. He does not "take" or digest it long enough. The hysteric goes from taking (which is strong in the hysteric) to giving (which is also strong) without making the product rich and various enough. Hence the "vulgarity" of the hysteric. The dependent goes from making to entering the other without giving. Hence they seem passive. Or sullen, or remote. Schizophrenics for example. The mystic cannot give—which is why his remarks are too cryptic for any audience. The compulsive cannot allow new things to enter, old things to go away which is why they are "constipated," academic, pillars-of-society, rigid, driven in their actions. Give and Take are *signals* to them rather than intervals for entrance and exit with appropriate rests.

606 LET ME MAKE AS assumption. Every human is born with the same er, the same soul or self which is capable of understanding All. But the second nervous system, the sociostatic nervous system gives us our warp, our "identity," and in the collaboration of the irreconcilables our capacity to enter the pool of knowledge which exists in all of us, is different for everyone. So, everyone apprehends Reality in his own way, through the filter of his own S. And therefore no matter how deeply we dip into our er, our collective wisdom, the "particular" insights we return to the world with, are colored by our S. So, we can never know All, never that is until all men reach God which is the point of infinity. Therefore, we cannot "know" the murderer driver around the corner, although we can come very close to knowing him, and so, total knowledge of the totality is impossible for us—at least while we live—we can only guess and gamble, exercise our free-will. Free-will is the manly substitute-attribute of Man who has not reached God. So we have Choice which is indispensable if we are to reach God. To postulate a rational world is to postulate a totally determined world. To postulate God is to postulate free-will. This is one of the most fascinating of the philosophical opposites. And I find that as I believe in free-will, so I am terrified. I was much more comfortable with determinism for it gave the solace that one could not make a mistake—that, so to speak, if one had not fucked-up the way one did, one would have fucked-up worse.

607 YET, THIS IS STILL true. The body-mind is a master chess player; it is capable of refining the choices to the best two or three possibilities. So, whatever we do at a given moment may not be the *best* thing we could have done, but it was at least the next-best thing.

608 WHICH IS WHERE AN understanding of habit comes in. Habit is the suspension of the gambling-faculty—— Juggler is given his sleep. To live in society demands habits. Otherwise, the Juggler would be overworked. (The Juggler works while we sleep, rest—generally—while we act and move. Each night the Juggler lays out the choices for tomorrow, makes the Great Debates, and judges them by his lights.) But the Juggler to conserve his energy frequently makes the decision to take the most irreconcilable, the most difficult-to-decide of the choices and freeze it, make it a habit, a habit which will not be broken until he decides that the health of the body-mind (homeostasis) *radically* demands it. Which could account for the over-determination of neurotic symptoms. Choice-energy must not be wasted. In order for Life to function amidst Other-Life in the Body-Mind, a day to day altering of habit will exhaust the lerve—Symbolically, a habit is to brain as a shell-fragment is to the flesh—to disgorge it is a surgeon's decision. Each "destructive" habit becomes more difficult to disgorge as one grows older and the lerve wanes—which is why we cannot carry the impediments of youth in middle-age. So, the over-determination of the neurotic symptom-habit is not really "over-determination." A habit must be placed beyond day-to-day questioning, for if it is not, lerve is wasted in considering it, debating, coming close to decision, and then retreating, and the waste of lerve (that is the continual expenditure of more lerve than is recreated) encourages bankruptcy and death. So the over-determination of habit reflects the need of the Juggler to conserve lerve.

609 I LOST WEIGHT ALL last summer and fall because I was generating the lerve necessary to change a good many old habits, habits which had grown to the point of strangling me. When I married Adele, I made the decision to change my habits. If I had remained as I was, I would have drowned in depression. So, I am still capable of adapting, and the knowledge that I can adapt gives me optimism again as well as a sense of greater fear, but fear with dignity attached, for I recognize that my old neurotic fears were disgusting to me because I could not understand the validity of them. My new fears I take on as a gambler. Which is why I "romanticize" myself, ergo infuriating all my rationally-determined friends. Every gambler is a romantic, he knows that life and death ride on every ball on every wheel.

But how much harder this would have been without Lipton's.

610 I WONDER IF ONCE smoking tobacco did not give a similar feeling like Lipton's. Especially when tobacco first introduced into Europe was regarded as a serious vice. It is only when we take on a serious vice that we are ready to explore. Our sense of vice, of danger and retribution generate the over-determination of paranoia which throws its searchlight into ourselves in order to understand the enemy society, and also casts its searchlight on the world in order again to understand oneself. Danger develops the extremes of one's personality. If I had not considered Lipton's such a gamble, I would have been left relatively unmoved by it. So it is not merely that physical action of a depressant or stimulant which causes new states, but rather the "over-determination" of paranoid lerve which creates the subjective effect.

611 THE RATIONALIST SAYS: WE can only trust objective data, for the subjective is a mal-proportioned exaggeration of the essential material phenomena.

The mystic says: We can only trust subjective "thoughts" for the objective data, the facts, are merely frozen theories, agglomerated habits of ideas which are mistaken for a Reality which may not even be Material.

And I shuttle back and forth, making a hundred trips these days. No wonder my thoughts race like a madman, and my ideas stumble in incoherent spasmodic brilliance.

612 WHAT I SUSPECT ABOUT Lipton's is that a great deal of its effect may be due to the concentration upon breathing, and the unaccustomed breathing we do. Our lives, our bodies, our existences "corporeally" rather than cellularly depend and exist upon our breathing habits. To learn to breathe "better" is probably the fastest way to improve one's health.

613 MY SORE THROAT SEEMS gone. Now, my chest aches. From cigarette inhaling? Sigh-of-regret inhaling? Is a cigarette cough the bark of anger which is the echo of the sigh of regret? Vance Bourjaily once wrote that a penis was that "slippery bridge from which one of us tries to reach another." It's the best line he ever wrote. I wonder if a cigarette is not indeed the bridge of sighs which goes nowhere.

614 ONE HEALTHY THING I am doing these days. I am worrying less. Worrying less about my habits instead of fighting them. So I accept Lipton's and Seconal and cigarettes with less guilt and-or shame (I don't know quite which) than I used to. I give myself to them and find in the case of Lipton's and Seconal that I can relinquish them partially too. It is the business of extremes. To attack a habit properly one must let it alone for a time. Constant guilt nagging at the habit merely strengthens it, makes it more wary and resourceful—which is why compulsives have such incredible habits. Incredibly strong that is. So, to break a habit one must first "enjoy" it.

619 A THOUSAND THINGS YET to discuss, but I'm getting tired, and I'll obey my decision to respect the ebb and flow in me and not try to force a One on a Two.

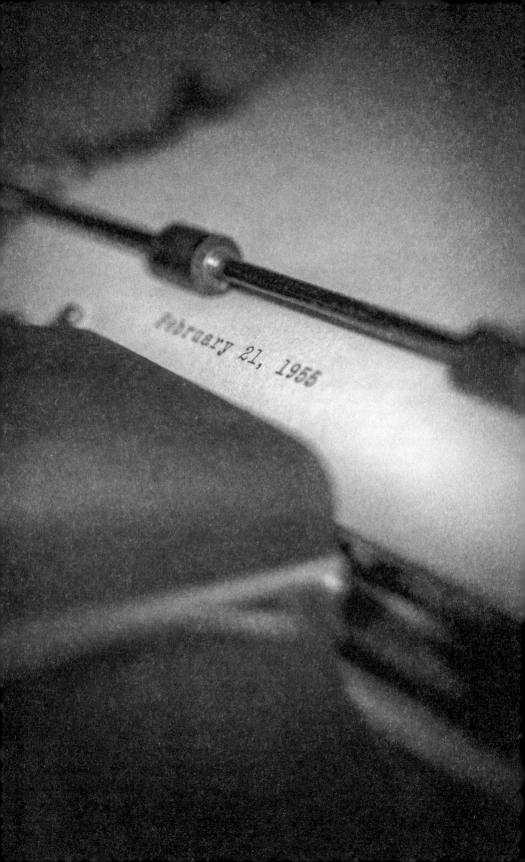
February 21, 1955

621 HERE WE GO AGAIN. A very good weekend, a very happy emotional exhausting and refreshing weekend, and what was good about it was that I allowed myself to go where I was carried instead of trying to force every single moment into what I thought it should be. Saturday night on Lipton's with Dan and Rhoda, and of course Adele—I think of her these days as part of me, we are so close—we had a Lipton's radio broadcast on the tape recorder, an hour of it, and while it's garbled and boring to a stranger undoubtedly, I found it fascinating. There are mountains of material in it, tons of laughter, oceans of piss, thunder ranges of shit, lustility and hoffection, and in a way I learned more about Dan and Rhoda in one night than I've learned about them in years. Interestingly enough, as a psychoanalytical session I believe it was truly valuable—elements of psychodrama, test situations, orgiastic connotations, working out of latent homosexuality—at one point I squeezed Dan's cock and taunted him to do the same to me—to my amazement, he did—which for Dan is an explosion. Anyway, I'm going to try to get a transcript of the hour. We acted out people we know, we sang (even me), we quarreled and bickered, we agreed—it was really incredible from the inside although to an analyst it might seem no more than release of tension.

622 OUT OF CURIOSITY I'VE started taking the Indian Roximyl or whatever it is. It does leave me in a pleasant state, sort of myself without Lipton's, but in a better mood and somewhat more sensitive. However its effects are extraordinarily subtle.

623 I TRULY HAVE THE feeling that my self-analysis will succeed in making me a happier more effective rebel. More effective because I'll be less afraid, more confident of my real stature. For example, for the first time in my life, I am becoming aware of how much effect I have upon people in my personality. Until now, ridiculously, I could only understand how people acted on me—I never realized how much I stimulate, frighten, warm and chill people around me. No wonder if my characters were always acted upon rather than acting. The secret to being a successful rebel is to feel in one's bones the wisdom of the two. Most rebels— for the rebel always has a strong sup—he would be a mystic otherwise. The only way he can accommodate the discrepancies of sup and er is to dream of a better society. So most rebels think in terms of a one. They think of what they should be, how they should act, and they attempt to force themselves—they give before they are ready to give, they refuse to take unless the taking fits the arbitrary (one) scheme they have set up for themselves. These days I wander, I allow myself to follow my curiosity—I read or watch something with absorption until I am bored, and the moment I am bored, I respect the boredom, it means I have taken enough of whatever has been given (more accurately: allowed to enter), and now I must stop trying to force it, but instead "digest," really take. So, from now on, so far as is possible, given the exigencies of outer life I am going to do what my body dictates. When I feel like exercising and not before, I will exercise; when I feel like staying up, I will stay up instead of trying to force sleep upon myself. My insomnia which used to be anxious, depressed and miserable, has been different the past few months—I do not sleep because I feel too active, my mind is too active, I am too full of life. Hence, I resent deeply forcing system upon myself. For insomnia like everything else is a double or more. The child's insomnia—or rather its refusal to go to bed— is a legitimate expression of its taste for life, and within reason (outer social exigency) one should not suppress it.

On the business of sleep one does well to obey that too. If one cannot sleep long enough (to fit the idea of the scheme) one should get up. If one can sleep longer—as indeed I can—one should, and then work longer. From now on, I will try to ease myself from the tyranny of the eight hours. There are times when I need no more than six hours of sleep or even four; there are other times when I must have ten. So be it.

One further note on my Lipton's fuckanalysis. It releases my paranoia, which is why I see far and always "exaggerate" the good or evil of my friends—paranoia is actually I believe legitimate perception, but it ignores social shaping—it leaps across time to see the end in the present, it seeks to grasp essential er character rather than er and sup character. So, for example, on Lipton's I realized suddenly that Dan has a monstrous unconscious—that he is a sadist, a Tartar muzhik king. But he also has a sup, a benevolent-oriented, rational, highly social sup. Hence his impotence in life, his weak body, his passivity. He cannot get physically strong or more active in life for fear that he will express his great potential cruelty. No wonder he ducks analysis. He cannot bear to enter the enormous hatreds and viciousness he contains. On Lipton's I realized this. The next day I realized in turn that beneath the Cossack is the little boy with the big sad brown eyes. But his journey would be too terrible to get back to that saintly loving little boy, for he's got to do it over the corpses of all the victims he's flayed with his Tartar sadism.

And in fucking, I learn also. One must not be ashamed of what one feels for one's mate afterward. These days I am rarely depressed after making love. The reason: I do not try to force my emotions while fucking any longer. If I feel aggression or hatred, I allow myself to feel it, I wallow in it—amazingly, feeling of love follows it, *and without guilt.* If I feel masculine (giving) then I give; if I feel feminine and passive then I lie like a woman and allow Adele to express her art, and I relish the passivity, relish it enough so that I arise refreshed from that phase of the continuing act, and enter the next phase where I wish to give. So our fucking gets better and better, and as it does we love each other more. What I must allow Adele is to be actually sadistic with me—it is buried in her, she represses it, just as I repress the masochist, the male-female terrified of outer aggression. If I were to allow her to whip me for example, I'd probably be less afraid of being beaten up—for my fear of being beaten up has always been—I realize now—that I would grovel before my beater. Hence the almost paralyzing anxiety I feel before a fight. And for Adele, it would soften her occasional spasmodic aggressiveness, her at times unreasonable temper. So be it again—I will look forward to getting my ass slapped.

624 THE REASON I BELIEVE in these things is that they work. By expressing my paranoia in Lipton's, I am less paranoid the next day, or by L-2. (Incidentally, my depression has not come on yet, and I believe that too may begin to diminish as I realize these things.) And when I am less paranoid, I am less anxious. I feel relaxed strength, the capacity to deal with more people than I ever have before. A curious confirmation of this came up today. The elevator man is a sly secretive ferreting sort of fellow, very tight-mouthed, very perceptive, but yet not a bastard considering all these things in him. For the last month through jokes, vague evocative remarks, and a certain psychic "recognition" between us, we've been getting closer, more respectful of one another without words being said. A few weeks ago, grinning, I said to him, "You know you ought to work for the secret service as a code breaker." (Service. Society—er—in the service of—vice.) He looked at me and said, "Why do you say that?" "Who are you kidding?" I asked him. "You know you could break any code." He clammed up. Today, he showed me a paper, and said, "You know, I don't show this to anybody." His picture was on the front page. He had won third place in the *Herald Tribune* Tangle contest (one of those word-puzzle contests). Two thousand bucks he won. I clapped him on the shoulder and congratulated him warmly. Part of my joy was in my intuition, the other part was in this poor aging elevator man with his sharp ferret mind, who by God had used it.

625 SAW *MUTINY ON THE Bounty* and some Keystone Chaplin films last night. What a genius Chaplin is. How he expresses all the body frustrations of sexual repression. He wipes his nose on a rag, wipes the rag on a dish, hands the dish to a whore in a dirty restaurant. He hitches his ass, he "*rolls*" his eyes, he strikes and is struck, and always, sex, sex, sex. We laugh in orar roars and waves. (roar, orar, horror, aura). And the captions which I may include later are incredible. In one skit, standing before his wife who dominates him completely, he grins sheepishly struts and says, "Every day I get better and better, but every night I get worse."

626 AND LAUGHTON. WHAT AN incredible sense of the homosexual sadist, the sex-repressing officer. *Mutiny on the Bounty* is the source of *The Caine Mutiny*, but with what a dramatic difference. For Fletcher Christian is the man who goes native, while Bligh, totally sadistic before sexual expression (the most minor infraction of discipline), is also the great leading mother-figure once he gets in the boat with the men (orphans, sex-denyers, that is sex deniers) who have elected to come with him. Now he knows sex will not be in the air, and so he can be a great seaman. (Semen.)

627 OVER AND OVER I come to discover that words which are spelled differently but mean the same thing, are indeed the same words. Words which sound alike are sibling in meaning. Elect which is eee-lect. Also de*lect*able—lect and licked. The sex denyer can stand great hardships—it is what he has denied sex for. The sex-expresser—at least in society—is capable of brilliance, insight, and warm intensity.

629 BACK TO LAUGHTON. HE might do a great *Naked* for *Naked* like *Mutiny on the Bounty* expresses the er-men and the sup-men. Those who are naked and those who are dead. Only I was so social when I wrote it that I had the arrogance to say, The fanatics are naked, and the dead don't care. Which is a kind of proof of the mystery of perception. Someone years ago might have read my book, and thought Mailer means the men who are alive and therefore naked, and those who are dead, authoritarian, etc. How disappointed in his perception he might have been, that fellow, if he read the interview where I said the second. But now he's right. Little does he know it.

630 A FEW WORD ECHOES:
       Negro. Knee-grow (Child, grow!)
      Nigra. Ni as deny; gra God's rah. As in rajah.
      Nigger. Deny God, but still it's god's er.
   Ferret. The fuck of er enraged into a thing. To ferret is to devote one's life energies to uncovering a tiny buried thing.

631 MY SORE THROAT. AFTER the installment of the journal last week, I came down with one of my terrible sore throats. For one day I stayed in bed, for another I took antibiotics. No effect. Then I decided it was psychosomatic and, more than that, valid. That is, I wished to have it, the juggler had given it to me in order to freeze a certain process. Well, one cannot force a process. So I accepted it, I ignored it, I made love with it which means among other things that I put my mouth wherever I wished—hang the germs!—and I got a little better. And then Saturday night I asked Rhoda about it for she had gone to a Reichian, and Rhoda said I should scream. So I practiced screaming into a pillow (very hard for me—I always have enormous tension in the throat), which is why savages rarely kiss and civilized people do. The sup relocates lerve in the mouth, the ass, the breasts, the hips, everywhere. (Savages particularly in Tahiti, which is very mild suppishly, undoubtedly get their sex much more directly from their genitals). Then we had *Tea-Time*, the radio program. Then later Adele and I made love. I woke up with four hours of sleep and my throat practically all better. Today it is just a tiny bit sore, but I don't mind it. I realized that I got my sore throats four times in the last few years, each before taking a big step forward. After the first I conceived *The Deer Park*, after the second Adele and I began to live in the same cold-water flat, after the third we lived together as nominal husband and wife in Mexico, that wild er country, and the fourth was last summer when we went to Mexico and were effectively beginning our real legal marriage. So I have hopes for this sore throat. The longer is lasts, the more may come of it. I am rather tempted to go to a Reichian for a little while, especially since there is no verbal psychoanalysis which would merely get me into an all-out war with the analyst.

632 I HAVE AN ENORMOUSLY tense body comparatively. Which is why I ideate so much when tension is released. I would not be at all surprised if muscular tension is related to frozen er thought, and as we release tension so we get ideas. For the idea is the mental act, just as physical motion is the relaxing of the tensed muscle. (There is a great deal in this I feel.)

633 CIGARETTE SMOKING. I HAVE a hunch (premature warping) (Lunch is the loving hunch—the social partition of the generalized desire to eat.) I have a hunch that smoking cigarettes is an expression of suppressed homosexuality (by which I always mean suppressed passivity, an enforced giving inflicted upon a readiness to take—among homosexuals the active homosexual uses that as his defense against the female principle which is to take; being understood of course that male and female are merely facts, frozen hypotheses, envelopes concealing mysteries. Before male and female there is merely give-and-take in the most primitive "sexless" forms of life). Among women who smoke, the same is true. Generally career women smoke more than happy housewives. The reason: they are fighting their desire to take, to be passive. Just as liquor drinkers are fighting their impulse to take. Nothing so characterizes the drunk as that he hears only what he wishes to hear and gives gives gives in long rambling talk upon that subject.

634 THE CIGARETTE IS SOCIETY's substitute for the penis. It is a cylinder of brown crapped in society's white (germless) (Sinlinder and cylinder and phallus) with the fiery end away from the mouth. But the tobacco (to back-hole—one's asshole), the tobacco is in the mouth. (Chocolate kisses for example). The English who are even more sex repressed than us except for their saving homosexuality—in extreme sup characters, some form (active or passive) of homosexuality is necessary to maintain sanity. At any rate, the English with their tight ass-holes like the tobacco removed tip of *Parliaments*. (In the Chaplin movie, Chaplin gave a parody of a statesmen who threw out his arms like a fuck and said, "I make a motion.") And now we begin to have filters. Our cigarettes are easy on the throat say the advertisements, a genuine homosexual concern I should think if one's going to have a cock in the throat all the time, but more than that it reminds one that although the cigarette is a tiny phallus it fills the mouth, *it reaches the throat*. And today coughing up some phlegm, I thought (realized) that the er in me had always enjoyed the phlegm of the cough. Only the sup with its idea that I must be manly, healthy, forthright, had hated the cough. (Healthy—healthy—hell hat three—what a sup I've had all these years. To be healthy, to be sexual was to go to hell.) Anyway, with the phlegm in my mouth (I was in the subway—the iron tunnel—the womb) I had a distance to go before I could expectorate it unless I wished to expectorate in my handkerchief—and over the last few years I've not enjoyed expectorating in my handkerchiefs which I'll go into in a moment. So, instead I decided to walk the two hundred yards to the entrance before spitting out the phlegm, and as I walked I allowed myself to enjoy it, to feel the phlegm coursing through me mouth (I wrote me for mouth—how much of me is my mouth) and I thought, it's like semen, and how nice semen is in the mouth. And indeed it is and should be if one allows oneself to enjoy is naturally. So the smoker's cough with its accompanying phlegm is the suppressed desire which finds its semen satisfaction substitute. Smoker's coughs without accompanying phlegm are something else. Maybe it's even stronger, it's accomp*nay*ing.

Anyway, I believe one lights a cigarette, or takes a puff in order to galvanize oneself from passive variety into one-giving. Which is why writers so close to the ocean of their passivity-thought smoke intensely while working. They have to in order to drive forward to their ideational-one-point. And we light a cigarette whenever we are disturbed—dist—er—bed—more and more I like er—whenever our wide er passivity is engaged but we wish to go on to a definite point. So an interruption, a conference, a party, a wave of external impressions makes us smoke furiously. Thus, people with exceptionally active er who have a very strong one-sup smoke a great deal. To stop smoking one must relax the sup, let two-consciousness and n-consciousness (n is vast number and nothing) predominate. Which means that to give up smoking, given such people, one must be less socially efficient or desirous of being socially efficient. Or else, the er must relax, even deaden, one's soul must become less vivid. Which is why resigned people smoke little, why homosexuals who accept their homosexually smoke little, why happy women who believe in sex and accept it smoke little—at least, that is, accept the female passivity of their natures. Tremendously repressed people, ministers, judges, social characters who have succeeded in whipping their er into submission are usually not smokers. Smoking is the state of imbalance between sup and er. I, for instance, will not be able to give up smoking until I become much more passive, but because I do not wish to become too passive, because I feel that I wish to give to the world, I shall probably have to smoke or else suck cock. And cigarettes all in all are easier on me.

635 A shit-eating grin. To eat shit is to express power. (The double idea. By undergoing degradation in private one may express power in public provided one isn't overcome by guilt in which case one is crushed or becomes sadistic.) A shit-eating grin is the grin of a man who has gotten away with it, who is wielding power without having had to eat the shit. As viz Bob Lindner in the car when he knew he had Adele and me under his thumb. So he had a shit-eating grin. But indeed as we all knew I had made him eat shit half an hour before and he was entitled now to redress the balance. Which is why, scared as I was, I didn't dislike him but instead liked him enormously at the moment. Not because he was making me grovel (or was it just that—safe groveling *?) Yes, it was. I wrote a * which to me is the puckering of pussy lips. He was making me a pussy at that moment. But, also, I like him because he could come back, he wasn't a pushover.

636 BEFORE I GO TO lunch, one further note. Handkerchiefs, snot, and semen. I realize that for years I have unconsciously identified the two. When I was an adolescent I used to masturbate into a handkerchief, a piece of toilet paper, or occasionally a Kleenex or a towel. Once or twice into the bathtub. And for years I carried around filthy snot rags—they were the years when I was always compromise-one-dressed. Baggy shapeless tweeds, loud clashing but dirty colors. Today I wear workmen's clothes when I feel like it, or I get dressed up neat as hell because I feel that way. But I'm sick of walking around like a schlumper, an apologetic lump. Fuck it if people don't like me, think I'm a dude. These days, more and more, I feel like I'm terrific, and about time. Anyway, today when I didn't want to spit in my handkerchief it's because I realized I think that semen is not snot, and thinking phlegm as semen, feeling it as such, I wish to dignify it by casting it away into the air instead of burying it in my pocket. (This whole thing is weird. A pocket is a cunt—do I really think cunts are dirty smelly things. Gawd. Which reminds me that the pair of slacks I bought in the fag store have one pocket within the other, a practical arrangement, but I wondered why. Now I know. It's like two balls side by side.) Anyway, I feel that the desire to hold my semen was good. I meant to write phlegm. It's true though. I do prefer to hold my semen which is why I make love for over an hour so often.

640 LAST NIGHT I CAUGHT a piece of *Omnibus*. It was about reading. I'll come back to it.

641 TEARS AND SEMEN. COLDS are homosexual-repressions, passivity repressions. Which is why I used to get so many colds. And now don't. Now I start to get sore throats—the punishment I suppose for wishing to suck cock. We leak semen from our nose and eyes in a cold—the cold is always the expression of the need to be promiscuous and orgiastic (seen of course always in terms of what would be the next step). That was why I always hated my colds—I knew they were punishment, er punishment for what I did not do. Colds will be cured when sex is free.

For some time the analysts have been saying that colds are a form of weeping. But what are tears. They are the expression of child makes when a pleasure is cramped. An er expression is being mutilated. So a child weeps when it falls off a tree it is climbing. It weeps not from the pain so much as from the knowledge that the joyous expression of climbing trees is dangerous. So, tears express the sadness, the discharge, of frustration which comes from the outer environment. As we get older we cannot weep so freely, so we get colds more often, just as a child gets colds when it realizes that the thing it wishes to weep for will not be allowed by its parents. So, sexual frustrations, toilet training, etc., are the cause of colds in children.

But there seems some evidence that some of the substances in tears prevent or inhibit cancer. There is an enormous clue here. For tears, while usually a sex substitute a love-rage substitute, are occasionally philosophical tears and thus express a higher faculty, a more noble potentiality. We can weep for others—we can weep for them because we can recognize that they like us live in the terrible situation of man upon the anvil of society and that very little can be saved from the enormous effort of merely keeping alive. Like an army which needs three-quarters, nine-tenths of its men and effort merely to keep the one-tenth or one-hundredth in action, so human life demands that ninety-nine percent of our lives are used merely to keep alive, and few are the creators in a position to advance man. Such tears are noble. But to get back, tears express a love-rage substitute. As a practical matter one cannot always fuck, one cannot always fight, when one wishes to. So one finds substitutes, less satisfying but more safe. Tears are dangerous but necessary—dangerous because they are still close to what was denied, they keep it open; necessary because they are a body expression. Tearless people get cancer, people who deny the soft side of themselves (always relatively to the distance gone—a compassionate person who could have been a saint can also get cancer, although its less likely if he or she start refusing compassion). The principle in all this can be taken from a profound line by John Dewey: "A bad man is one, who no matter how good he has been, is getting worse, and a good man is one, who no matter how bad he has been is getting better." So for the sick man, the powerful man, the sexual man, the compassionate man, etc. One gets to be less of anything good—the compassionate, the sexual, even the developing of one's personal power as opposed to the dominating and manipulating of others,—one gets to be less at the expense of one's health. So in sex you either screw your own wife better, or you screw other women, or you do both, or else you get sick. Most men live in the condition of doing all four things half-assedly and so live in a state of doubt and conviction, depression and excitement, joy and gloom. But that's better than killing oneself with cancer, asthma, or one of the others. You have to grow or else carry more for remaining the same.

642 I REALIZED DURING LUNCH why I grow stimulated under Lipton's. Essential to my entire mechanism (psychic that is) is my essential basic and enormous passivity. Very deep in me is the sensitivity of the womb. And indeed, the room which is the Other-Life equivalent of the womb is the way I picture my brain—as indeed an enormous room with fantastic life going on in it. Given my passivity—which as a child was so great that I wouldn't go out of the house for days at a time—I have been able to overcome that wombishness (womanishness) only by being a giver. So whenever I sense the deep feminine element in me getting ready to receive, I start to give. I enforce a quick give on an enormous take. I smoke, I talk, I pace about, I wave my hands, I generate energy to keep me out of the womb. Indeed my sexual anxiety has always been the one of being able to go so far, so deep into sex, that I should never return. Cunts have never been frightening to me as cunts—they have always seemed appealing. To lick a cunt has always been a delight for me. The partial impotencies I had with various women and the psychic impotencies I had with others came from the fear that I would truly fall in, become the little boy of this giant woman. I was able to give myself to Adele because when I first knew her I had contempt for her social face—I figured such a woman could never hold me, so I could go, I could explore. But of course another part of me must have known what a woman there was in Adele, and today I can know that I love her because the thought of losing her, through death, through the army, through jail, through whatever, is unbearable to me. A void opens. I know that without her I would be a cripple. With her, able to nourish myself in the womb of our relation, but now finally accepting that need, giving myself to it instead of fighting it, I can act more decisively with other. (Incidentally, driving a car fast and long is a solution to people like me, or as I used to be. One gets in the womb and one travels—one does both at once. But now I have less desire to drive because I recognize the reasons.) Anyway, taking the clue that I give when I am terrified of the big take, my stimulation under Lipton's becomes understandable. It generates all my giving capacities in order to keep from becoming the enormous open mouth swallowing the universe. But there is a touch of the hysteric in me, the imperfect maker. Under Lipton's I make less well than otherwise because my giving tends to short-circuit the making process, the danger of great take is so intense. Truly, with perceptions I get in five minutes under Lipton's, I would have enough to make a life's work of books. Patience and an easy relation to time and work are the most difficult things for me to achieve because my entering and taking apparatus is so enormous.

But this gives a clue to stimulants and depressants. I am truly like a plane which has burst through the sound barrier and so has to use *reverse English* on the controls. Takes have become gives for me, gives are takes (I get my best thoughts from the act of the stranger in me talking to someone else—the friend I always see as myself). Thus, sedatives are often stimulants for me—I fight them by giving even more. Stimulants, once in a while, act as sedatives. I know that they are givers, so I can afford to accept my take. As viz the other night when, enormously stimulated, I went out for a walk at seven in the morning, had breakfast, had a black coffee, and then went home and fell right asleep. I think the idea of the coffee-stimulant in me relaxed the giver in me enough so that the taker of sleep could draw me in. But to be scientific I have to admit that I slept only four hours and that lightly. On the other hand, I was so stimulated, so excited, that I probably would otherwise have stayed up for another twenty-four hours.

643 PSYCHOANALYZING NAMES. I DO believe that a large part of a man's psyche forms around his name as an armature, and that people respond to his name, first name personally, last name socially, respectively er and sup responses. For example: Dwight D. Ike Eisenhower. I's in our. I's in hour. I's in power. Which would account for the affection so many people have for him. The Dwight D. and the Ike I don't feel yet.

Also Churchill—the church on the hill. How English. Nature and authority combined.

Truman: Honest Harry True Man.

Nixon: Nix on dirty old Communist sex. Richard the dick.

Adlai Stevenson. Adlai—the addled lay.

Stalin—the Russian for Steel.

Adele Morales. A dell, a death-hell. Morales: More or less? Morals? And indeed it was the enigma of whether Adele was morally good or morally bad which rendered her so fascinating to the moralist in me. For Adele, Morales also means More a Les(bian). Which of course is not true of her. She is deeply bisexual. Dikes are unisexuals.

644 HOMOSEXUALITY. I WOULD GUESS that the bisexual homosexual is relatively easy to turn "straight." The camp among men and the hysteric lesbian among women have a capacity to vary, given their bisexuality. But the unisexual homosexual, the cuff-shooting Lesbian, and the "pure homosexual have a state of balance already. The woman is a man in woman's envelope. The man is a woman in man's envelope—Toby for instance. So, in their own socially tortured way, they do have a legitimate er balance, for the er demands that one express the male and the female principle in oneself. Of all male homosexuals I would guess that the active unisexual is the most difficult to alter. Gore Vidal for example. The kind of homosexual who likes to prong others. For such a homosexual like the dike has set up a Chinese wall against the waters of wombivity. Their active "male" giving is the defense against an intolerable taking. And as I wrote in the last installment, a "habit" is overcompensated because the Juggler has decided not to allow *that* exhausting conflict to be active, but instead will deal with the disadvantages in another way. So the active homosexual has a deep enormous dread of becoming a passive homosexual. Yet because he sees women as bigger givers than himself, women are closed off too. Same with dikes. They despise womanly Lesbians, they hate men because they believe men are bigger givers than themselves.

645 THE BURGLAR WITH HIS half-insights, his Germanic Vummmmm! always yammers about the basic masochistic passivity—case closed, human being impossible! But passivity is masochistic only in the eyes of the sup. The man of the distant distant future will be a taker. The closer man approaches to the infinity of God the more he will live in passivity, thought, pleasure, and space. Indeed no human can enrich himself without returning and dipping into the lore of the mind-body. It is the source of all creativity available to us, outside of what we intuit from nature when we personify it. For indeed man is a part of nature and so can comprehend nature by understanding himself. As, for example, the way I now understand animals so much better than before. To be ashamed of one's passivity is to cripple one's capacity to give. Those nights in bed where I not only give but where I take, receive, lie passive before Adele are always the prelude to rich activity for me on the following day. Let me fight or seek to repress my sexual impulses and I am nervous and depressed in the morning.

But I have one basic difficulty in sex. I truly hate to accept the orgasm too early. So I delay it, and the result is that my orgasms suffer. Lately, I have found a compromise. When it is coming I relax, I let it take me like a wave, and so it is often better. But I suspect that until I am ready to enter the act of love ready to come so soon as the orgasm takes me, I will never have the full symphony of an orgasm. However, I accept this too for I would not like to lose the joys of loving for an hour or more.

646 THE PHALLIC NARCISSIST (WHO cannot take) says, "I shot in her." The cock is a rifle. The gentler man says, "I came in her." The "I," the part of the person which is in the world, the skin, also was passive, also entered the woman.

The shitter is the one to beware. "I got off my rocks." ROCKS! Unless he sees it as rockings. I've never used the expression.

647 ALL DAY I HAVE been holding back a part of this journal. It comes down to the feeling that Bob Lindner gave me a pain in the ass last weekend. He acted like a shy sexy teasing society bitch who gave you the sexual come-on when you'd given up, and threw her manner at you when you advanced. Bob, whose virtue is that he has not frozen himself into authority, is not a Burglar, suddenly put on the psychoanalytical mantle, and all weekend, except for rare moments, had a healthier-than-thou attitude. What gave me the pain in the ass was that I was not interested in who was healthier. We're both healthy, we're both sick, each in our own ways. But Bob who knows so Goddamn well that his lacks, his shlumper ness, his sly (but heavy) manipulations, his hang-dogness, his fear of authority, his half-works, his games with Johnnie, his guilt about it, his guilt about every fucking thing was hanging on to all those things. I will not bother now to recite his virtues. I've been doing that long enough in this journal. What infuriated me was that he fought me all weekend when he knows so very well, or should by now that I don't seek to make people my creatures, that the idea of total victory is so unpleasant to me that I always give away victories as I get them, and that a man who confesses a fault to me opens in me the desire to confess ten of my own faults. No doubt he'll call all this paranoid projection. But he can't have his cake and eat it. He cannot see me as enormously intuitive and blindly paranoid—each when he chooses to call it so. Obviously there will be times when he thinks I'm right when I'll be wrong, and vice versa. If I didn't like him so much, if I didn't feel so psychically close, as if we were the two talented Jewish sons of the same family, the older brother I never had, I really would be tempted to slug that sly stealing cocksucker. One day he'll realize what he really has on the ball, and then he'll surprise everybody, including me. The greatest arrogance is to assume that one knows the potentialities of one's dear friends and one's mates. If one knew them then they hardly would be big potentialities. But I do hope that the next weekend we spend together isn't pissed away by Bob exhausting himself before it begins. And the bloody arrogance of the Lindner. "Don't write novels, write expository works." "Adele, let me tell you my ideas about painting." When it comes to painting he can't tell an ass-hole from an appetite. I much prefer Johnnie's aggression. She comes out with it, she slams it down, she invites you to sock her back. She says, "I think smoking marijuana is going into a dirty urinal." So you can talk about it. You can fight about it. But the Lindner tries to play chess. He talks about marijuana as if it were a charity case and he's the kind matron who accepts all, even dirty children—one can always wash their ears. When the kid says, "Get your fucking finger out of my ear," Mother

Superior Bob shrugs sadly and says, "The poor neurotic child, I was trying to help it." In a way I have more respect for Johnnie than for Bob. She doesn't pretend to be helping you when she feels like whamming you with a plate. Her aggression is her health. One of these days I hope the Lindner realizes that his aggression-conceal-ments make him act like Uriah Heep.

648 THERE, NOW, I LIKE him again. The sculptor in me, the Hous(e)man sees the beautiful ad under the slob-snob.

652 I HAVE A FEELING that the choices of homeostasis have to be seen dynamically rather than as an instantaneous statis-tical opting for the best alternative. The sup and the er war with one another, but they war in many ways. They have trench-warfare (depression); they have great advances and great retreats, break-throughs, concessions (finally the life of the body is at stake and only the most powerful er or the most powerful sup will say, hang it all, kill the body). Very often the victory of a sup results in a relaxing of sup, and vice-versa. My sup against being a rebel relaxed when I made the concession of a good apartment, good clothes, and selling *Naked*. I'm no longer so covetous of celebrities because I haven't alienated myself from them in the way I live. I can gratify the sup which says make money because the er now knows what to do with it—which it didn't five years ago. And so forth.

What I also feel is that the sup and er carry on intelligence and counter-intelligence, and that they go in for feints and deceptions, so that one of the meanings of a test-situation is that one discovers, that is one's sup or er discovers, that there were tricks up the other's sleeve. Which is why we sometimes avoid test situations. The sup or er expends energy-anxiety to keep the other from knowing. Er energy is lerve, sup energy is *serve*, or verve and serve. For example, my er was working for a long time in this journal by furnishing all kinds of hints and opening in my typing errors. But today is seems to me that I get nowhere investigating my typing errors. For example "stiuation" for situation which conveyed nothing to me, it merely distracted me from my thought. So the sup has started to trick the er. But the er is very strong today, so it takes the trick and gives back counter-trick, perception. The examples of verve and serve energy expenditures on wasted objects is of course endless. But one of the tricks of er or sup is to indulge the other, catch it off-balance. Thus, the er tricks the sup in the case of a minister or priest by letting him rant and roar in the pulpit about the sin of sex. To his sup horror and his er glee he finds himself buggering a choir boy ten minutes later. His serve got too complacent, and wham went the verve, off to the races.

Now, I don't think that there is an uncontrolled war except perhaps in psychosis. The ego which I prefer to call the Juggler decides which ball to keep in the air. The juggler's aim is to keep the human as healthy as possible, and so he listens to his two advisers. The counsel from the sup and the council of the er. And they take many forms, they are respectively Judge and Highwayman, Pope and King, clerk and beggar, benevolent social modesty and roaring sadist (these two gentlemen the juggler accommodates with a sigh—Ah, well, malice again.) And the need when one is developing to accept each emotion, each depression, each hour of energy and each hour of fatigue is that neither sup nor er can be denied, even when one is growing stronger—that is, becoming more consciously powerful. So, with the great expenditure of verve which goes into these journals, follows the depression of serve. But tomorrow or the day after when it comes I will accept it, I will relish in it instead of trying to overcome it by force. The more I accept my depression the faster I'm out of it, because depression like the elaboration of trenches thrives on resistance.

Each moment of existence the Juggler works, juggling a thousand things in the space of a heart-beat. But if we include the buried body decisions, then truly the work of the juggler in an instant is infinite.

653 WHAT OCCURS TO ME is that there may be a "death-instinct"—that the er deep within it knows that there is the hereafter of entering infinity, and when it has been mutilated by the sup it shrugs its shoulders and says, "To hell with advancing this fragment of the infinite—I return to the infinite." And it welcomes "death" which is eternal life. Although I suspect the Hindus may be right and just like the fucking army one comes back from a patrol merely to be put on K.P. Which introduces reason and the sup. To build society, to have men act in life, it is necessary that the sup penetrate the deepest reaches of the er and induce the counter-conviction, that there is no life after death and so one must do all one can now. To build a society one must believe in zero after death. Hence the sup while punishing man enables man to raise himself to the infinite. And that is why the sup (read the Super Ego) mysteriously relents at times. It knows that if it goes too far, the er will give up, it will begin to long for death. So the sup as well as the er is a preserver of life. And that is why a genius needs a sup to match his available er (for all people have vast er—what differs is the amount available). If the genius did not have such a sup he would become a Taker and not a Maker-Giver. (Is this the effect of the Roximyl? I'm so tolerant today. I see good in everything. Except for passing rage at the Lindner. But notice the mellowness of this note now that I gave vent to my irritation.)

654 OVER THE WEEKEND I took many notes, and had a host of word echoes. In the reading dingus on *Omnibus* I noticed something with interest. They showed pages to read and gave you various times. To my pleasure I noticed that I was now a slower-than-average reader, I who as recently as two years ago had the fastest reading rate Fig Gwaltney ever came across in the Nelson-Denny test which I at the time called the Motherwell-Ginsberg test—how revealing. Anyway, they had a dried up old prune of a schmoo talking about how to increase one's reading speed on *Omnibus* and he talked about all the blocks to quick reading. One stops too often on each word, one reads words backwards, *at least children do* (Dr. Pruneface said so). (God and dog—which the old bugger commented on) in short one does not "absorb" rapidly. Then he talked about modern reading methods. My suspicion of them is well-founded. To grasp the word as a whole is to lose the richness of a word. Modern reading methods make experts, they do not make artists. For the expert is capable of taking the mass and giving it a name, a one—he has sublime disinterest in understanding-taking, he is interested in nomenclature-one-giving. So my poetic insight about academicians seems to have confirmation. To become an academician, an expert, one must amass mountains of "knowledge" which means one must read quickly. But to read too quickly is to get the gist and not the orgasm—geist. (The artist has the ability to take the one and make it enormously various, the opposite of the expert, the critic, the academician. All those latter gentlemen seek answers. The artist seeks questions. This I learned from Malaquais, who once said in a passion, "There are no answers. There are only questions.") So, the academician is drawn to the subject which intrigues him least—in other words, he can read it the fastest because he finds it the least disturbing and stimulating. He takes less as he reads so he can read efficiently. Which is why editors often get little out of a book—they read too quickly.

February 22, 1955

657 TODAY, I'M COMPLETELY DOWN. The sup depression came on last night after rereading the journal for the day and being struck forcibly by the fact that it all seemed far less profound and much more "gushy" than I had thought. Particularly the enthusiasm about having my ass whipped. In bed last night that seemed really *de trop*. AND TODAY, I regret the note about Bob, although of course it served its purpose. I vented the spleen I felt, and today I like him as much as ever. But will he like me? The balance between obeying one's swings and social consideration is of course the great difficulty.

662 THERE IS ONLY ONE revolution—the sexual revolution.

663 THE REVOLUTIONARY AND THE mystic. Each are against society, but the mystic leaves society, the radical returns from his deep hell to leave a social portrait of the future which society in its retreat from advancing man will in time come to adopt as a defense. (Symbolically, the miner-radical lives in hell, the mountaineer-mystic in heaven.) Our resentment of mystics is not altogether unjust—they have left us; they have refused to add that particular perversion (into words) of their thought which might be a step-hole in the wall for men to come.

664 TIME. OUR IDEA OF it is very crude, for just as society has flattened the infinity of wealths through the unit of currency, so the clock chokes our appreciation of the varieties of times. The clock-present is a skin, no more, it is merely overt time, present time, an attempt to postulate a *material* time. Such items as the newspaper, the commodity, the mass media, TV especially, are the overt act, the social defense against the expressive er. What we may say of overt time is that in the act of its birth, its presentness in relation to clock-time, it is in a deeper sense come to us from far in the past. The state of the total of emotions of all men is a far closer approximation of "present" time. Not their acts—which belong to the past, are merely fruitions of emotions and needs out of the past. Deeper in man's unconscious sooner or later to come to consciousness in the future.

Actually there are wave phases to time, parallel expansions and contractions which bring us closer to the nature of it than the unilinear concept. As a practical example let me draw time for the writer. His present is unverbalized thought, his immediate future is the unexpressed but *verbal* idea. Further future is talk. Then the note. Then the article, or the finished product, and if that is ahead of the social limb of society for which it is intended, it fails to expand overtly until the "thought" of man (not the idea—that comes later with the critical evaluations) reaches it. If it is behind, if one's thought to work progression succeeds for groups one does not wish to reach, groups who are behind the "center" of the artist's aim, then one has created a false art-work, no more than a past product even as it was conceived as a future one.

In political economy one can see this better. Money is the unilinear adjunct of unilinear time, social time. Thus, the essential condition of individual existence which is that the relation to the "norm" on any given quality of experience we live in future time or past time—we are twenty-first century in our sex-expressions, say, and eighteenth century in our reasoning methods, or whatever, or whatever—this condition, this existentialism of living across a spectrum of time is muddied by unilinear money, for finally there is not a consumer body as such, there is rather a congery of consumer-coteries, and products which are conceived for one coterie (one consumer-position in relation to time) often reach a coterie more to the future or more to the past relatively. The only limitation is that commodities too advanced must fail, as must commodities too far behind the most retarded consumer-coteries.

665 THUS, THE FUTURE EXISTS materially in the thought-idea flow of man at actual past which we conceive inaccurately as clock-present. Put most crudely—what we think today is what in some form we do tomorrow.

The past, the social concretion, vanishes slowly. The horror of the past as Marx saw is that it is the dead incubus on the body of the future which lives in the present. One returns to the past, one studies it best in order to interpret and increase one's sensitivity to the future. It is worth approaching the past only if one wishes to draw from it a finer extrapolation into the quality and quantity of the future.

666 THE VALUE OF COMMODITIES is that they give us power. The only legitimate power. Passive power. To wit, power for ourselves, rather than the power which is domination of others. The aim of man is to increase his own power. In the domination of others we diminish our true power for we can be enriched only by taking, and the domination of others is giving which if it predominates too totally can only exhaust the man who has social power. History as opposed to the distant and perhaps unattainable Hissoul, is the story of the attempt of man against society to convert domination into power.

667 HAS ANYONE REMARKED THAT bebop is the first popular and tentative expression of Joycean language. "Gimmerhereson sonomove that avocado sauce with the reekiefookies." Which is why I prefer it to "cool" which while technically advanced is nonetheless a retreat from a more advanced state of perception to a more elaborated but retrogressive-in-time social production.

674 WHEN I TAKE LIPTON'S I am free of guilt. Hence I understand. Guilt is the inverse function of understanding. The academic compulsive is the guilt-ridden man who never has the faintest understanding of the subject to which he has given his life. When an academician begins to understand his subject (as indeed often happens) he solves a thousand other mysteries at the same time. In a funny way, I was the academician of sex while I was writing *The Deer Park*. *The Deer Park* is authoritative (indeed, author—iative) on sex, but doesn't understand it at all. And too the author is the authoritarian, the man who does not understand, which is why authors are invariably such horses' asses.

677 SHAKESPEARE IS THE DECADENT genius of the Elizabethan period. All geniuses anticipate the decadence to come, and yet retain the vigor of the Make-Give era, the expansive era in which they live and work—they cast forward into the decadence which will follow much to Enter and much to Take. It is therefore so fitting, since the decadent genius always casts a multiple set of interpretations that Shakespeare's name has so many spellings and his identity, his legitimacy, are in question.

681 ADELE, AS ONLY I have seen her, has the weird potential of becoming a hipster-lady. It's not likely but she could actually m.c. a radio program someday which would be Tallulah or Faye Emerson hipsterized.

682 THE SALESMAN HAS TO sell—no matter what it is. He sells good as eagerly as evil—which explains the enigma of Collie Munshin to me. He sells Elena, he sells Eitel—indeed Eitel gets close to him when Eitel has decided psychically to buy.

683 THE FOOT-NOTE LEADS INTO the earth. There is a terror in footnotes for they suggest the indefinite expansion of a point. They are the scholar's timorous tap on the door of the artist.

684 I GLIMPSE A FORM for *Antacid Analgesic*. It could start as a play, dialogue and actions. An unplayable play for it would include a masturbation, a fuck, and an orgy, probably in the form of Two, Three, One. Then, next, it would be a novel. Then an expository essay—"The Psychology of the Orgy." Then ???? the heart of the book, written in double and triple and n-parallel lines which come together and fall apart, as opposed to the punning condensations which Joyce used. Until finally, at the end, it must *degenerate* into handwriting, picture scrawls, non-objective scrawls, and mathematics. Yessir, we end on H_2O.

687 I CAN HARDLY COMPLAIN about Adele's alternate love and rage toward Susie, for Adele unconsciously was acting out upon Susie the way I act toward Adele. And Susie in turn would act toward me as Adele acted toward her. What characterizes that three-way daisy chain is that I call the tune for Adele, she called it for Susie, and Susie called it for me. The way I felt it at the time was that Adele was unreasonable in her swings toward Sue, and Sue gave me the time of day when Sue felt like it.

688 I SUSPECT THAT THE frequency of sound has some relation to the depth of one's unconscious. As frequency is stepped up, so the notes rise. At infinite frequency there would be an infinitely high note. Low notes are progressively more conscious. The lowest note of them all is the single grunt of the bull-ape. In life, the high-pitched voice seems hateful to us, the low-pitched voice draws us forward. Women who are drawn to men with low-pitched voices like Gary Cooper sense a deep tenderness in such a man as well as outer male strength—they are drawn to the combination of inner vulnerability and outer force. Women who are drawn to men like Truman Capote with his high-pitched shrill are drawn by the outer vulnerability and the inner steel, hatred, etc. Bisexuals with their inner and outer vulnerability and strength invariably have voices which are alternately high and low pitched. Brando for example. Myself. Adele. Tallulah, Millie, etc.

The high note is a Taking (small symbol giving—point of the universe) however.

The low note is a Give (large symbol of little). A legitimate swelling up of the ape-principle which is half of our motive power.

691 LAUGHTER. WE LAUGH WHEN we recognize a great thought and immediately conceal it. The longer we laugh the more the thought persists, and *helpless laughter* is the anxiety that the thought will never go away. Which is why we feel so good after laughing for minutes at a time. We have succeeded in blurring the magnitude of the thought, but the beauty and danger of the insight remain as an echo within us, we have glimpsed a fabulous cavern of being, and it leaves us content that that exists within us. People who never laugh are occasionally totally inert, but much more often are people with such a cruel sup that they dare not laugh—their large but whipped er would destroy them if it could appear. A man who does not laugh is either a saint who lives in thought rather than society, or else is a man close to suicide, murder, or death.

But there is the critical passage in laughter from Enter-Take over the fence to Make-Give. And it is hurdling this fence which creates the dialectical antithesis. Thus enter and take swell the thought, but the moment we start to laugh, that is to make and give a sound, we have given antithesis to thesis, we have converted thought into a greatly diminished idea. It is the gap between thought and idea which is enormous in laughter that creates the laughter, the muscular ripple, the release of muscular tension. Which occasions the notion that thought exists in our muscular tension, and idea is the release, the expansion of muscular contraction. This seems to be true for me. When I cannot sleep it is because I am churning with thought. As I convert it to idea, as I verbalize silently, the tension diminishes provided each new idea is not good enough to encourage more thought, more muscular tension. I ideate so profusely on Lipton's because my natural state is one of great muscular tension. Lipton's in releasing muscular tension demands speech. My yap yap yap is the health of my body—I ought to learn to dance. But then I wouldn't ideate as much.

Serious people are serious when they give ideas—the relation between thought which is comparatively small and idea which is comparatively large (almost equal to the thought) make them sober and grave. What they dredge up from themselves has the capacity to be realized as a social artifact. But when I diea (ideate means die?). When I ideate I alternate between intense seriousness and sudden high pitched laughter. The reason is that my thoughts are forever sweeling (swilling?) into something enormous, and so my laugh goes up—it's a wail of hatred that I'll never be able to ideate such a beautiful thought.

Thus, in laughter, the laughter is the S—expressed making-giving defense against the er-impelled enter-take of an advancing thought.

That is why dirty jokes are invariably funnier than "clean" ones. The sexual truths are the universal truths. Off Lipton's I roar with laughter at Legman's Limericks. On Lipton's I read them seriously, gravely, sadly, wisely, and joyously.

694 MORE ON LAUGHTER. A baby walks across a room for the first time and laughs in pleasure when it reaches its mother's arms. Why does it laugh? Because the discrepancy between thought and idea is immense. The baby may say OOOOOO, but its murky vast thoughts have elaborated a universe of space, of its own changing relationship to its environment because it can now give walking, it can locate, its relation to the world has been drastically and dramatically altered. So it laughs in the relief of repressing such a vast thought. Or it weeps if it cannot repress it. And weeping is often the expression of the throbbing of a thought which cannot be suppressed until the muscular tension is expressed/released through tears. Laughter and weeping are very close. If er consciousness persists we weep, if sup consciousness takes over we laugh. Often we do both. We laugh until the tears come. But this is always in the condition of sustained laughter, the joke we cannot stop laughing at. Hence, if a substance in tears is an anti-cancer agent, what is suggested about cancer is that like all disease only much more intensely so, it is the product of a frightfully cruel repression, a condition of muscular or tissue *tension* which cannot be released. Hence, Reich's cancer biopathy may actually have done a lot.

695 Exhi*liar*ATION AND DEPRESSION IN writing. (Do I think I'm just a big liar in all this journal?) At any rate: the reason exhilaration is the sign generally of poor writing is that our thoughts are large, so large that the critical estimator of how closely they are embodied in the idea-act is overwhelmed by the happy emotion of the thought. So we think we are uncovering worlds, and the next day, rereading, the thought virtually absent, we find that the idea-act we have made is crude and doesn't even awake echoes of what we felt yesterday. Often we bounce too far in the direction of disappoint-ment, for what we feel as nothing on the second day may still have enough idea-elaboration in it to arouse some thought in the reader.

On the other hand, writing from depression we feel depressed because there is little thought in us. (There and their mean the same thing.) Very little thought-energy which is not lost in trench-warfare. So what little there is, is ideated very carefully. The result is that the idea-net when reread opens more thought to the writer than when he actually wrote it. His own ideas which often are crude expres-sions (although carefully worked) of thoughts whose depth in him he does not suspect, become recognizable as such years later.

Therefore, a mild flat mood is best for me in writing. Lipton's stimulates too much, and it takes at least three or four days for the total effect of the stimulation to wear off. Hence, if I wish to write a novel I had better get off it and go through some dreary plodding months. When I get too depressed to write, I can always take a week or two off, Lipton up, and Lipton off, and start working again.

696 THOSE PERIODS IN HISTORY which mark the advance of reason are periods in which great popular artists appear, and there is rough general agreement on what is art. Periods like today where reason has exhausted itself as a valuable mode of perceiving reality are periods where the coterie artist flourishes, and there is rough general disagreement. It has to be this way, and there is no need to complain. Reason has produced its opposite, special and often exclusive coteries of sensitivity, private languages. The lingua franca becomes progressively more non-existent. We are in a flourishing decadence, a contractive period. Out of it, if we are not destroyed, will come expansions we can barely glimpse, and new great artists. But the trend in history—as a natural law of development—is for artists to become progressively less great in relation to the greatness of their audience. We can hardly have an Aeschylus today, nor next century for that matter. Nor probably ever again. And that is to the good. As Malaquais once said—I quote him haphazardly—"The ultimate aim of art is that man himself become the work of art."

697 IN THE COURSE OF this journal I have been elaborating a more and more private jargon. It is necessary. For me to understand the phenomena I am trying to understand I must create my own conceptual words. To use the conceptual words of others is to maroon myself in pseudo-rational processes rather than to depend on my intuition. My capacity to do something exceptional comes from the peculiar combination of powerful instincts face to face with my exceptional detachment. I am one of the few people I know who can feel a genuinely powerful emotion, and yet be able to observe it. This is what I must depend on, instead of violating my capacities by trying to make the rational scholarly effort to illumine my understanding of other men's jargons. Instead of poring (pouring) over all the relevant books, and there are five hundred I "ought" to start studying tomorrow, I do better to "waste" time and discover things for myself. The only things I've ever learned have been the things I've discovered for myself.

698 IDEAS AND THOUGHT. WHERE Bob Lindner is wrong about the novel is that he doesn't understand the peculiar communicating power of the novel. The novel goes from writer's-thought to reader's-thought by the use of an oblique (obliging) symbol, expression, or montage. It does not enter the more paralyzing process, more accurately limiting process, of converting thought to idea in order that the receiver can then try to let the idea enter in order that he take thought. Which is why I cannot write a novel when I know what I want to say. It comes out too thin, too ideated. My best scenes are the ones where I didn't know what I was doing when I did it. Few artists have ever been able to work on the thought-idea-thought interchange. And their weakness was often there, as Gide for instance. I must always tackle the novels I do not understand. Which is why Lipton's has stripped me of my next ten years of books. The ideas here would have come out obliquely in the books I blundered through. Now I have to take an enormous step, and my capacities may not be equal to it. Still, I don't regret the too-quick opening, the great take of these past few months. I had to, for my health, and besides one should always try for more, not less. That's the only real health.

March 4, 1955

701 THIS IS GOING TO be tough today because I've bought an electric typewriter and I'm more concerned at the moment with mastering it then with saying anything.

702 LAUGHTON CAME TO TOWN over a week ago and I spent seven days in a row talking about *Naked* to him. Now's not the time to go into all that, although it was very rich (I wrote rocy—rocky) and then left me with a bad depression which I'm just beginning to come out of. Today I felt a deep strong need to work at this Journal as if it is not enough for me to think or even to speak silently, but that instead I must write down what I think, and thereby find the release. This undoubtedly has something to do with the difficulty of self-analysis. One must emphasize it. It is not enough merely to consider oneself passively, to "think" about oneself. Instead one must have the *muscular* expression (I wrote ex ression—excretion). (Do intellectuals hate sports, sweet, etc. because muscular expressions are excretions to them or is this true only for me?) Anyway—there must be a physical overt act be it speech or writing (finger movement) before anxiety is released. I have done an enormous amount of thinking in the last few weeks, or rather in the two weeks or ten days since I've last worked on the Journal, but I've also been in the worst depression yet these last couple of days and I suspect that a good part of it was due to the fact that moving my fingers, "writing," is an exceptionally important and anxiety-releasing muscular activity for me. More than that, writers finding themselves unable to work on the typewriter return to an earlier finger activity, to wit they hand-write.

704 SHIT SHIT SHIT SHIT shit shit The muscular frustrations of the keyboard are inhibiting three-quarters of my thought. I'm going to try to get away from my self-consciousness about fingering.

705 I DO WANT TO say a few things about love which I believe I'm beginning to understand. The key to love is that love like all fixed decisions of the juggler (always read The Gambler for The Juggler) is a habit. Thus in the dreary daily couplet dialogue of marriage where one mate or the other says, "Do you love me?" and the other answers automatically, emptily and unenthusiastically, "Yes. Of course," the answer is not a lie. The key to habit as I've said already is that the juggler makes a decision to freeze some part of the responses in order that juggler-energy be saved from constant decisions in that expression. So to be in love is to freeze, to make a habit of a situation—the juggler has decided that it is too exhausting for the nervous system and for himself to be constantly exploring the state of love—one could do little else—and for himself to be constantly exploring the state of love—one could do little else—and so like all habits what is most true of two people who are in love is not whether they are enthusiastic or depressed about the love (habit) at the moment but whether they are preparing or not preparing to alter it. Most of the time they accept the habit like all habits, and so they do not lie when they say "Yes I do love you," no more than they would lie if they answered "Yes I'm still smoking." (This typewriter is just driving me nuts—I'm losing a beautiful set of notions.)

What distinguishes love from other habits is that an enormous amount of sup-approval and er-need can collaborate on the concept. The sup demands order and sex-repression or else society cannot be built, the er demands sex for the health of its nervous system— ergo orderly sex is One-Marriage. Of all the working compromises between the drive of the sup to suppress the passivity wombishness of the sex need in the er and the er desire to be orgiastic despite the dictates of the sup, the idea concept of love is accepted by most people. It is a compromise between two basic and polar irreconcilables which is why we adore love so much, seek for it so absorbedly, and experience so much anxiety at the thought of losing it or altering it. But married love is not natural love, it is concept love. Natural love is the reverse of a habit, it is an ebb and flow, it exists and does not exist as the child feels it or does not feel it. Nothing is so painful to a child as to be reminded that it was good and loving but an hour ago. The child cannot comprehend why it is now asked to pay allegiance to a feeling which has left it. The adult on the other hand is far more concerned that the decision to be in love which like all habit-decisions is over-compensated, that is over-established, be not shaken, for nothing is more exhausting to the capacity to work, to accomplish, to move easily through life than a constant juggler-anxiety about whether to alter the love habit or not.

So seen in this way a lot about love becomes understandable, that is married love. It accounts for the virtuous sensations one knows when one *feels* in love with one's mate; it also accounts for the depression one knows when one does not feel in love. The habit is threatened, and when a habit is broken the juggler goes through a mad few weeks or few years, so the depression about not being in love is very powerful—the juggler is drenched in gloom and generating all the depression he can, sup depression and er depression, sup rage and er rage, he wishes to confuse the system, knock it out, for depression usually keeps people from taking a new step—they feel everything is too hopeless to act.

Truly what a dilemma it is. No wonder analysts look for happy marriages to end their cases. What can be said of a happy marriage is not that it is "happy" but that it is a powerful and temporarily undefeatable habit which acts benevolently upon the system—a minimum of energy is wasted on the sex vs. order imbroglio, and a maximum is therefore available for work enjoyment etc. But the trap is that the orgiastic impulse has so worked itself into the consciousness of our time that the "happy" marriage becomes more and more difficult to maintain. Ironically more and more energy must go into maintaining the habit, over-establishing it, as opposed to the minimum of energy comparatively which existed in the nineteenth century. So, the state of marriage itself ceases to be a social habit which has total sup approval. The irony today is that an active powerful man is beginning to think there is something wrong with him if he does not wish to cheat on his wife, and indeed he is right—monogamy is one of the most ridiculous and utterly conflicting one-concepts which society has placed over the er.

And that is one reason why the reactions on *The Deer Park* are so wildly different. *The Deer Park* threatens the love-concept habit; hence people react to it not as a book but as a potentially habit-smashing experience. Which would also account for why so many homosexuals have liked it. Their juggler love habit casts have much less to lose from accepting the book.

706 IN THE INTERIM WHILE I was not working on this journal I thought more things than I could possibly begin to sketch in many weeks on these pages. There is no use even trying to recapitulate them, but philosophically one vast problem I've gotten into is the business of what is ethical conduct. And I suspect that the answer is that one must always do what one feels like doing subject of course to keeping out of danger most of the time (danger, ranger, manger, changer). But to act well toward one's friends when one does not feel it is the height of arrogance among other things. For we are making the assumption that we know what is good for them, what they need. And it is a reflex of life that we learn from hostility being expressed toward us as much as learn from love being expressed toward us. Each has its value, each contains its potential benefit—to maintain cordial relations with friends when one does not feel cordial is merely to deaden the relationship and introduce large elements of mutual deception in it. As Bob Lindner said to me some time ago, a lot of people are going to be hating you soon. That may well be true, but what is far better that I like myself—that is my health—and since I have always been a rebel and have always found the meaning of my life and the most intense sense of my own existence at those moments when I rebel with some size and confidence, so I have been hampered and fucked up in the past by my overanxious desire to be loved. These days I give much less of a fuck whether most people like me or not, and the result is that to my amazement I am far more capable of handling myself. For example Laughton and I worked together very well for the whole week—it was a collaboration in the best sense and that was the first time in my life that I was able to work with a man whom I felt was an equal. Also a thousand other things that have been going better together with a price. My depressions when they come these days are pretty Christ-awful. They come invariably late at night and I sit alone in the living room—that too-white too bare living room—and feel empty and dull inside and I wonder if I am completely deteriorating, and if everything in the journal is an hysterical attempt to hide how desperate I am. But these days my depressions always but always come when I am low in energy, in lerve. Last year I could be full of energy and still be very depressed.

707 ALSO I HAVE BEEN going through terrifying inner experiences. Last Friday night when I took Lipton's I was already in a state of super-excitation which means intense muscular tension for me. When the Lipton's hit, and it hit with a great jolt, it was my first in a week, I felt as if every one of my nerves were jumping free. The amount of thought which was released was fantastic. I had nothing less than a vision of the universe which it would take me forever to explain. I also knew that I was smack on the edge of insanity, that I was wandering through all the mountain craters of schizophrenia. I knew I could come back, I was like an explorer who still had a life-line out of the caverns, but I understood also that it would not be all that difficult to cut the life line. Insanity comes from obeying a hunch—it is a premature freezing of perceptions— one takes off into cloud even before one has properly prepared the ground, and one gives all to an "unrealistic" appreciation of one's genius. So I knew and this is my health that it is as important to return, to give, to study, to be deprived of cloud seven as it is to stay on it. One advances forward into the unknown by going forward and then retreating back. Only the hunch player decides to cast all off and try to go all the way. What I ended up with was a sort of Existentialism, I imagine, although I know nothing of existentialism (Everybody accuses me these days of being an existentialist). Anyway, the communicable part of my vision was that everything is valid and that nothing is knowable—one simply cannot erect a value with the confidence that it is good for others—all one can do is know what is good, that is what is necessary for oneself, and one must *act* on that basis, for underlying the conception is the philosophical idea that for life to expand at its best, everybody must express themselves at their best, and the value of the rebel and the radical is that he seeks to expand that part of the expanding sphere (of totality) which is most retarded. Deep in the vision action seemed trivial which is why I knew the cold graveyard of schizophrenia. Out of the vision I had a happier tolerance. I could deal with people like Catholics and *saidsists* sadists because I was not worried about who would win the way I used to be. And indeed I learned the way to handle sadists—there are only two ways: One must wither be capable of generating more force, of terrifying them (I have a story I have to tell Bob when I see him) or else one must dazzle and confuse them. Lulu up against one of the great sadists, Herman Teppis, comes off with a part victory because she has given all her energy to confusing and startling him.

708 TONIGHT PEOPLE ARE COMING over and we'll have a Lipton's party. I half don't want it. Last weekend with its Lipton's carried me flying half-way through the week and dumped me in depression these last two days. Now I'm finally coming out of it and it'd be interesting to see how I would act next week. But on with the fuckanalysis.

CORRESPONDENCE

BETWEEN NORMAN MAILER AND ROBERT LINDNER

INTRODUCTION

L*ipton's Journal* CANNOT BE fully understood outside of Mailer's friendship with Robert Lindner. We are lucky to have the bulk of their correspondence and can thus get a glimpse of the texture of their relationship.

Lindner came into Mailer's life at a particularly difficult time—a period in which he was still reeling from a formidable blow to his ego after the failure of *Barbary Shore* and was writing his new novel *The Deer Park* under a cloud of uncertainty. This might have been a good time to consider turning to a psychotherapist for help. So, perhaps it is not surprising that after reading *Prescription for a Rebellion*, Mailer felt compelled to write to the author. On November 18, 1952, he sent his first letter to Lindner, opening the gate to an intense and fertile friendship that lasted until Lindner's untimely death in February 1956.

The letters follow a certain rhythm. At first, they discuss literature, their work, and their ideas. But as their affection for each other deepens Mailer will turn to Lindner for advice and feedback, while Lindner will reach out to Mailer for help in the craft of writing or of artfully navigating the publishing world. They call each other "hermano" or "brother of mine." They meet in person as much as possible and nurture their friendship with animated discussions about politics, psychoanalysis, philosophy, their wives, and their own psyches, usually over a quart of whisky. Kindred spirits, they are joined by their belief that people can transform themselves, become bolder and more creative, and that society itself can be renovated. Both are tremendously ambitious and competitive, but their spheres of interest are adjacent, partially overlapping, and thus Mailer does not have to worry that Lindner will outshine or supplant him as a literary force. They critique and encourage each other's work and are candid without being competitive.

The tenor of the letters varies through time but the first two years, up to the rejection of *The Deer Park* by Rinehart, and the beginning of the journal, is a time in which Mailer's trust in Lindner and appreciation of his fine mind only grows. Lindner at times acts as an older brother, at others as a therapist. In many letters we see a devoted friend expressing his love and need for Mailer's affection, and his admiration for the writer's talent.

Once he begins writing the journal, Mailer, not one to easily open his most intimate thoughts to another, sends Lindner the pages as he writes them to get his feedback.

By this time, Mailer is smoking marijuana seriously. He believes weed will take his psyche to places he might otherwise not discover. But marijuana, aside from opening his mind, excites him and plunges him into a state of relentless insomnia. He regularly downs one or two Seconal to sleep. He wakes up in a barbiturate fog and pops a bennie to give him a lift; he drinks cup after cup of coffee to wake up, and usually smokes two packs of cigarettes to help him think. Marijuana comes later in the afternoon, especially on weekends, together with a good daily dose of alcohol. Lindner is concerned. He is convinced the drugs have transformed his friend's personality, turning him aggressive and paranoid. He disapproves of the marijuana experiment and is convinced it is taking Mailer to dangerous places. Although Mailer agrees on this point, he sees it as something he must do to reach the untapped regions of himself— to get close to his genius, to become not only a better writer, but a great one.

By the time Mailer stops writing the journal, in March 1955, his relationship to Lindner has cooled. He is no longer comfortable about revealing his most intimate thoughts to his friend. He resents Lindner's criticism and is disappointed he has not understood the importance of his marijuana adventure. Mailer, now protective of his intimacy, asks for the pages—his friend returns the manuscript.

In an interview with J. Michael Lennon in 2007, shortly before his death, Mailer says:

> And then what happened is that I started smoking marijuana
> and then the marijuana took over. And then came a time
> when that marijuana became King Marijuana. It determined

everything, including my friendships. If you wouldn't smoke marijuana, if you wouldn't go on a trip with me, you weren't my friend. And he was aghast. He was aghast on several counts. One of them was selfish. As a rising analyst, he could hardly be caught having a friend who was not only a huge smoker but had turned him into one. So, he had to be self-protective. He had his family, after all, his reputation and everything. So, he was not moving on that. And so, he'd try to write me lectures. Those lectures used to drive me wild because I was not about to be lectured to. The wild side of me would come out. It was like, "If you don't like my smoking, go fuck yourself." I was wild. "This is my inkling if you're not with me, you're not my friend." He was upset, I think, by seeing an ugly and ruthless side of myself that he was perhaps not wholly prepared for until then. In other words, I was not as nice a guy as I had seemed. And from my point of view, he was not as generous a guy as I had thought. And so, this began to poison our relationship to a degree.

During the second half of 1955 their correspondence dwindles, the visits become less frequent, and by the end of the year Mailer is hardly present. Lindner's ailing heart takes a turn for the worse. Mailer says of Lindner's death:

He was in his early forties, and I talked to him on the phone one day and he said, "There's nothing they can do; I'm going to die." And he burst into tears. And I was so cold and so full of anger at where we'd gotten and when I look back, it was one of the most unpleasant moments in my life. I didn't feel a fucking thing for him. I felt contempt that he was weakened. You see, my feeling was: "We're soldiers and if we die, we die." I have that feeling now; it's a lot easier now, I can assure you. But I remember not being sympathetic. Going through the dull motions of being sympathetic, the way one does when one's not there with a friend, and not really giving him what he needed. And I didn't believe he was going to die. And then, some weeks later, he died. And that was one of the great blows of my life because I couldn't believe it. And then I felt woe, and then I felt contrition.

A week after Lindner's death, in March 1956, Mailer writes in his *Village Voice* column:

One of my really good friends died last week at the age of 41. He was Robert Lindner, the psychoanalyst, and he had been suffering from a heart ailment for many years. . . . Bob Lindner was so good a friend that I simply have no heart to write about him now. I should go on at length about his charm, his generosity, his intellectual curiosity, his foibles, his weaknesses, his kindnesses, his ambitions, his achievements, his failures, and his great warmth (he was truly one of the warmest people I have known).

Mailer was deeply shaken by his friend's death and was aware he had let his "hermano" down when he most needed him. We can only imagine that with Lindner's death, Mailer also lost a voice of reason at a time when he fought with many of his close friends and traveled to that dangerous territory, the land of madness, he had written about in his journal.

THE LETTERS

Dear Dr. Lindner,

I WISH I HAD BEEN able to write you a long letter on your book at the time I finished it a month ago (unfortunately I was pretty much caught up in the business of finishing a first draft of my own) for the ideas and criticisms I had about *Prescription for Rebellion* were far more sharp and for that matter passionate than they are now. But the thing which is most important is to write to you, because I think you've written a bad book, and I think it's a thundering pity when so much of what you have to say has not been said, and should be said in the very best way.

First of all, I think I'm very angry at you. I read the first fifty pages or so with quite a bit of excitement, and I had the feeling that here at last was an analyst who had the courage to attack everything that I have found most dispiriting in psychoanalysis: to wit, almost exactly as you say, that this most radical body of new information has been perverted into a kind of sophisticated *pater-familias*, and that the body of therapy moved in exactly the wrong direction. I suppose what I hoped for among other things, was a detailed analysis of all the problems of therapy, and how they would be treated concretely in an analysis which was concerned with rebellion rather than adjustment. Instead I think you deserted what was the bedrock of your book and went off on a series of rather fantastic excursions, so at the end one has found in three hundred pages, a summation of psychoanalytical schools, a theory of history (in twenty pages) a prescription for the world's ills, a singularly bombastic attack on Marxism, a call to action which must apologize for its penury, and pages and pages of—to be brutally frank—the sort of exhortative prose that one associates with such books as *Peace of Mind*. The worst of all is that when you are done, I for one had no idea at all of what one is supposed to rebel against. It's all very well to talk about the limiting triangle, but rebellion as a way of life consists of choosing a thousand courses, each for something specific. How one can speak of rebellion without speaking of society is utterly beyond my comprehension. For example, one must finally believe that American society is either capable or not capable of continuing to function, or think that the optimum society for man must be equalitarian and libertarian (my conception of socialism) or that such distinctions and such goals are ill-founded. One must feel that a society which warps, corrupts and "adjusts" its members must either be destroyed, or to the contrary modified.

To be a rebel without ever posing these problems, is like being an analyst without studying Freud. I was a little aghast that a book which calls itself *Prescription for Rebellion* and fulminates against adjustment, never attempts to give more than a few passing epithets to the society which demands adjustment. It seems to me that you come out by the same door as all the adjustment analysts. "Arise ye wretched of the earth—you have nothing to lose but your toilet training." Let me make this clearer. What is your rebel's view toward marriage? Toward sex? Toward family? Toward capitalism? Toward society? Toward war? Toward all the terrible and very definite problems of such things as Korea, the defense of the West, etc. etc. I don't ask that you write a political or a sexual treatise, but I wonder why there is no window in your view which includes such matters. I don't even know how you can differentiate yourself from so many of the analysts I know, intelligent liberal men, whom you would claim promulgate the adjustment fallacy. It seems to me they would be quite justified in saying, "So far as I can make out what Lindner is saying, his idea of rebellion is the same as our idea of adjustment. We, too, want people to be spontaneous, healthy, constructive, tense, critical, etc. etc."

There's no getting around it. If you are really a rebel, and you really preach rebellion you've got to end up with something a little more startling and unpalatable than "let's try to improve the level of school teachers."

Moreover, I resented the ambitiousness of your book. A theory of history if it is to be something other than cocktail party talk must be more than grandiloquent and confined to twenty pages; an attack on Marxism if it is to be other than fashionable has to be a little bit more precise than (I quote approximately) "his economic theories have long been disproved." How have they been disproved? By whom? By what economic data? If you're going to be truly serious and truly ambitious, you owe it to yourself to study economics, and to be able to disprove a book like *Das Kapital* concretely and not condescendingly.

I consider myself to be a rebel and a radical, an anti-communist radical who believes that both the Soviet Union and the United States are both driven by insoluble economic problems toward war, a war which may destroy civilization—I tried to express those ideas in my last book, *Barbary Shore*. Since I consider myself neither a True Believer, "proletarianized" nor "adjusted," I must say that you alienate a very large part of your small audience when you make attacks so clumsily on Marx and company, that I really wonder whether you have read *Das Kapital*, whether you're familiar with the tragic history of the Russian Revolution, have grappled with the kind of things Reich engaged in *The Sexual Revolution*, or if your ideas on revolution as opposed to rebellion come from no higher source than Philip Wylie or someone like him. I will add in case you may think that this is only in response to my Marxist fanaticism that I was terribly disappointed in your book long before you got around to disposing of Father Karl.

I don't pretend to know all the answers, or to be less pompous, I'm not asking you to write the kind of book which will accord exactly with every one of my ideas as they exist at this moment. What I do ask is that you be truly serious, and that you keep to what you know, and that when you attack, you know what you are talking about because it comes from your experience and your study. Many years ago I worked in a mental hospital for about a week—I could stand it no longer—and I was very excited about what you had to say about methods of treating the insane, for at the time I was horrified by the callousness of the doctors, and the roaring brutality of such therapy as the hydro baths. I assumed that my reactions of disgust and horror were perhaps misplaced for I knew so little about the subject and was so inadequate for the job of an attendant. In your chapter on how psychotics are treated, I was able to learn something, and something well worth-while—you gave an important confirmation and extension to my experience, you taught me something. And the reason was there you knew what you were talking about both by experience and study. [. . .]

Most of all, what I would like to do, is argue and discuss with you sometime. Do you ever get to New York? My phone number is SP 7-3572, and my address is 41 First Avenue. Perhaps we can get together, and perhaps we can learn something from each other. There are very few of us, and therefore we must be very critical of one another, and more than good in our actions and words.

Yours warmly,
Norman Mailer

Dear Norman (the way you close your letter permits this):

I WAS VERY GLAD TO hear from you about your impressions of Rx, but I wish you had written when—as you say—you were more passionate about this book. As it stands now, I can hardly make out your meaning. You raise hell with me in one place for being too ambitious in this book, and in another for not committing myself to absolute statements on the nature of our society and my position on every social matter conceivable. As to the latter, either you're a poor reader or I'm a lousy writer—for I believe my attitudes on all of these matters are absolutely clear and unequivocal. Certainly, they are very much like yours—but in my case not (I think) founded on faith.

To answer your statement that I am writing of things of which I have no knowledge—this I must deny. My reading and study have been, I suspect, about the same or more extensive than yours, and if you will inquire among mutual friends (I'm sure we have many) you will learn of my participation since 1932 in every progressive movement on the record short of the Party. But, of course, this is an absurdity—your throwing one book at me, and I shouting, "I read it and this one, too." The point is that I've honestly made a deep study of the matters I've written about and my decision to reject Marxism (among other things) was determined by knowledge and whatever uses of reason I've been capable of.

You have made a major point when you object to the way in which I handle the two chapters on theory of history. I am not speaking of your dismissal of the worth of this theory because of the brevity of treatment—we both know that length and validity are not independent. That brevity, however, was determined by the fact that I had to present the theory—to me it seems intrinsic to my purpose in the book—but avoid turning my book into a study of history. In the condensation, however, I made enough mistakes of presentation to justify your criticism.

My pique with you, Norman, comes from your easy dismissal of the prescriptive part of the book. You burn me up when you compare these pages with Liebman's Peace of tripe. I think what you want from me here is the substitution of propositions and proposals lifted from the body of what I am convinced is half-assed social theory and grafted onto or in to the personalities of men and their social structures. I can't do this that you seem to want of me because I'm convinced against these items as solutions—and to me they are the unpsychologic formulas my prescriptive ingredients appear to you.

There's lots and lots more to say. I'll wait for a further note from you or, lacking that, my next visit to New York. I get there every month or so and will be coming up soon. You can be sure I am eager to talk about all of this and more with you. As you write, there are not many of us and the few we are should be particularly hard and demanding on each other. If we are going to make of ourselves any kind of instrument for tomorrow, the refining process has to be done by us or else it will be done to us.

Best wishes,
Bob
Robert Lindner

P.S. Send me a copy of *Barbary Shore*. You refer to it in your letter, but I never read it. By the way, I'm doing a book now of which the first section is devoted to a discussion of Marxism and the psycho-analysis I made of a party member not long ago.

Dear Bob,

I HOPE YOU'LL EXCUSE THIS long delay, but things have been kind of up in the air. I've started working on the second draft of my book, and the first month on a book (as I said this second draft is virtually a new book) is the worst kind of hell I know. If anything drives me to analysis in the near future, it's going to be exactly that depression, ambivalence, anxiety, etc. etc. etc. which just comes upon me, predictably as a railroad schedule, whenever I start. Indeed at the moment this second draft strikes me as being conceivably a roaring error. No sooner had I gotten into it, than a whole set of ideas occurred to me on how to save the first draft, and I'm still debating whether to go back to that—hence the non-appearance of my promised manuscript in your mail. Will you be patient on that? I feel at the moment as if it would be very bad to have anyone read that first draft, for I'm so susceptible to opinion at the moment that I think a man I picked off the street to read a page of mine could depress or elate me according to his reaction. And since your reaction would be far more important to me than that, I think it best to bull through this on my own for the next few months.

Lamont mentioned to me that you had remarked how much you had enjoyed our luncheon. Well, I did too, Bob, and I hope we can make it a regular function on your trips to New York. In fact I'm looking forward to your next appearance. There are so many things to talk about. One of the things I'd like to go into with you, are the curious psychological prerequisites for writing a novel in the first person or the third person. I've been very aware of it the last few weeks, for there have been alternate days in which I've written in first person, third person, and finally both, and think I have a certain small knowledge of why.

I read your article on the gambler with very great interest, and I thought it a sound convincing piece of work—the necessity to both win and lose, finally to lose if sanity is to be maintained, seemed exactly right to me vis-à-vis my "friend" "Bernard." I found that something happened in me too while I was reading. I had always felt about Bernard that it was a question of character as well as neurosis, and that there was something unpleasant about him above and beyond his gambling. While I read your monograph a fund of rare compassion for him began to form in me—I understood suddenly how terribly compulsively neurotic Bernard is, how helpless he is, and I felt more tender toward him, understanding for perhaps the first time—this may sound odd—that he is merely a sick man and not a despicable man, and that he has suffered the most. Incidentally, I never met his father, and he rarely talks about him, but his father is apparently or was like the father of Ralph, stern, cold, unfeeling, and it's quite possible Bernard hated him. One difference, however, is that Bernard started gambling before his father's death.

The amusing part of the article to me were the various interpretations advanced on gambling (i.e., not by you, but your patients). Psychoanalysis is so often in danger of explaining the soul by listing the features of the soul, so that I suspect on almost all the "delinquency" symptoms—homosexuality, alcoholism, gambling, dope, sex perversion, etc—the explanations are in danger of being merely big-word substitutions for the commonfolk's little words—which indeed you practically say yourself. I remember that once after Bernard wrote me a chatty little letter in which he asked virtually in passing for several thousand bucks—it seemed that if I didn't get it to him in forty-eight hours his bank account would explode—I flipped my lid and wrote him back that he had been masturbating all his life, and it was about time he quit. Thus my perception was equaled only by my stupidity, and as an amusing footnote to it, Bernard succeeded in punishing me by running the debt up to five thousand dollars. Also his answer to my letter was livid, the only time he has ever in my memory been abusive in a letter. Well, that for that.

How does your work get along? I'd love to read your manuscript if you ever feel the need or desire. As soon as I'm somewhere on this draft, I would still like you to see my first draft. Let's get together soon.

My best to you, Bob,
Norman

Dear Bob,

I'VE BEEN PUSHING HARD into the book, mainly by an act of will, because now that I'm near the end, time just seems to drift. I guess what it comes down to is that I just don't want to finish it because then what will I do next? The problems of the unemployed man. In a way I almost wish you hadn't liked it so much because now I feel less drive to improve it—my feeling is pretty much one that it has good structure and just needs a new coat of paint. Telling Amussen did no harm except for the tender vanities involved over there—when I see you I'll tell you how funny the whole thing was, because before you spoke to Ted the situation there was very complicated, and now it's probably even more complicated. Anyway, we'll have a laugh over it. There's been something I've been meaning to write to you about for a long time, and I've let it rest to see if I would cool down in my feeling about the matter. But since I still feel the same enthusiasm, I guess it's safe to broach it now. Going to that prison, Bob, was truly a central experience for me. I had the feeling that for the first time in years I'd found something which excited me basically. I believe I mentioned in passing something about doing such work to you, and I know I mentioned it to Johnnie, but anyway, thinking about it at length, the following set-up has occurred to me. I want very much to work on some sort of interviewing level in prisons for six months say after I finish this book. Not necessarily to write a prison novel, but the feeling I have is that I'm running dry of personal experience and life experience, and that it's time to fill the well again. (Fill the pen again!) And the women fascinated me even more than the men because I know so little about women from lower income levels. What a way to describe them! But you know what I mean. So I suggest this as something which might be of interest to you, and possibly of mutual benefit—I know it'll be of benefit to me. That is, that I work as your assistant over at that prison on a full-week basis, possibly doing some sort of research for you that you don't have the time to do personally but would like to see followed up. As far as pay goes, I don't care about that particularly because I'm still relatively solvent, and I'd rather do the sort of work I want to do rather than take pay for something which interests me less. Possibly a sort of social counseling job to the girls or whatever would be feasible. I can see any number of aspects to this which are impractical or worse for you, and there probably are difficulties I don't even know about, but I thought I would throw it out to you, and when we get together next time we can go into it at length. Also, you'll know how you feel about it at that time.

Incidentally, I met an actor named Neville Brand who's quite a fantastic character. He was one of the five or ten most decorated soldiers in the last war, and he's a big oaf of a man in appearance, but with it all is surprisingly intelligent, sensitive, and articulate. On top of it all he's been analyzed for years now and has that tender somewhat muddled surface personality that people in analysis often have. Anyway he worked in a picture called *Riot in Cell Block* 11 which he says is the best (if not the first) prison picture ever made. It's coming out this week in New York, and I aim to see it early. Neville put in about two weeks in Folsom Prison before the picture, and spent something like eighty hours with a homicidal psychopath who he says was just brilliant—a cell-block leader. He talked all night about prisons, and he apparently had an experience something like mine. He said that the moment he walked into Folsom he thought to himself, "I'm home." Brand, by the way, read all your books in boning up for the role, and would love to meet you. I took the liberty of telling him that if he's ever in Baltimore he should look you up cause I think you'll find him very interesting indeed. He's the only man I ever met who's not only a hero, but has imagination as well. We talked about *Rebel Without a Cause* and he thinks Walter Wanger might be interested because Wanger since his four months in jail has been completely hipped on the subject of prison. If you have an agent, it might be well for him to contact Wanger, or if you wish, I could get you a Hollywood agent easily enough. I've been trying to remember if the *Rebel* screenplay belongs to you now or is still in Jerry Wald's hands.

Adele and I are having a tremendous party this Saturday, and if there's any chance of you and Johnnie being in town, we'd love to have you. Actually, it would be a waste. I'd be greedy for your collective company and have to share the two of you with seventy others. But, still I throw this out in case you might be in town.

I'll be seeing Ted Amussen tomorrow and will be giving him your regards. Do give my warmest to Johnnie, and say hello to Marged, Jean, and the boys.

As ever,
Norman

Dear Norman,

J UST RECEIVING YOUR LETTER was a great relief. I feared that I had
spoken out of turn with Ted, and your slight delay in answering
my note made me somewhat concerned.

About your book—Norman, it is so good, and has such potential,
that I have to urge you not to compromise on it. I've given it a lot
of thought, and I really think just a "new coat of paint" is not sufficient—at least not for you. To fail to give it the intensive attention it
requires in this final draft would be to commit a really grave literary
sin, but more than this, a crime against yourself. So please keep
pushing.

Johnnie told me about your talk with her on the topic "whither
Mailer," and so your remarks about putting in six or so months of
work in a woman's prison didn't surprise me. During the last few
days I've given the matter a lot of thought—and I think something
can be arranged when you're ready. Whether it can be done here,
near or in Baltimore, will have to be explored further. I don't know,
because the local situation is kind of snafued and riddled with a
curious brand of politics. For our sakes, we'd like to have you around
it could possibly be arranged. But on the other hand, the opportunity may not exist here, and if it doesn't, there is an alternative that
may be quite satisfactory. I'll go into the details with you when we
get together again. Meanwhile, I think you can rest assured that the
idea—so far as I can see—is excellent and possible of realization.

About Neville Brand and the possibility of pushing the *Rebel*
screenplay—I'm delighted you talked with him and anxious to meet
him. After I received your letter I wrote to Kay Brown at M.C.A.
(they were the agents for the sale of the screenplay that terminated
in an inconclusive stalemate) and asked that all outstanding copies
of my script be turned over to my agent, Ivan von Auw at Harold
Ober Associates. Then I wrote to Ivan and asked him to consider

getting in touch with Mr. Wanger. Warner Brothers, you see, own the motion picture rights and I (with Budd Fishel) wrote the screen-play, which anyone who makes the picture has to use. If Wanger or anyone else wants to buy the rights from Warner, I'm sure they'll sell. For my part, I think an arrangement about the screenplay can be made through the Ober office.

I wonder, Norman, if Brand would want to suggest *Rebel* to Mr. Wanger? An approach from that side would light a fire under the whole matter. I'd personally like to see the picture made, since it is a valid study of the subject and the only truthful representation of prison life I've come across. By the way, apart from all of this I hope Brand and I can get together. He sounds interesting and the kind of guy I'd like to know.

You'll be glad to know that I've done an intensive editorial job on the four stories of my book and followed your good suggestions as closely as I could. Jeanne (who sends her love, natch) is busy re-typing the manuscript in final draft, while I'm finishing the remaining story. I hope to be out in about two weeks, including the preface. Last week I talked with Ted by phone and discovered he had no changes to suggest, so I'm readying final copy. It will be a relief to get the book out so that I can get on to the next job.

Come soon, Norman. I'll be in New York within the next three weeks and certainly expect to see you and meet your friends. But you should arrange for an early and long visit here. We want you. Meanwhile, our love,

Bob

Dear Bob,

I'M ANSWERING THIS IMMEDIATELY because I'm going away skiing from March 5 to about March 16, and I'd like to get an answer from you before then. The first thing is your mention of coming into New York sometime in the "next three weeks," and I write this to ask you if it's possible to make it after the sixteenth because Adele and I would love to give a party for Johnnie and you, and also have you as our guests if you don't mind our place. (I mention the place because as I may have told you it's situated in a slum, and the building itself is a tenement.) In our apartment it's rather pleasant—although a little deficient on privacy since the rooms are partially partitioned rather than separated by walls—but there are beds for you and it's really nice. However, a great many of our friends are kind of appalled by the neighborhood, and it may be that Johnnie or you might be also—*sans façons* as Don Beda says—What I'm trying to say is that honest and clean I'm not trying to discourage you from staying with us because I would love that, and on the other hand am also trying to say that I will not be offended if you would prefer something a little less extraordinary. But, anyway, staying with us or not as you choose, could you make it for after the sixteenth?

The other thing I'd like an answer on is your warning that "a new coat is not sufficient." I've been going over the prose of the book with a really fine comb, and that makes a big cumulative difference. Also, I've added a few little bits. But I take it that the criticism you have is more one of lacks in *The Deer Park* than of excesses. So far as I can list them, the things you felt should be improved were (apart from the beginning on which I intend to do work) a larger role for Dorothea and more resolution of her action; the presence of Pellito as the "stereotype of evil," fixing the orgy, and improving Sergius' character.

I agree with all those criticisms you have, but up to now with the exception of orgy which has to be redone and the last two chapters (I read it over again today), I just don't have any ideas on how to improve, enrich, and just generally spark up the things we talked about in the above paragraph. But what I also felt in your letter is that there are many other criticisms which you felt and did not have time to express when we were running to the train. And if they are definite in your mind, Bob, I would appreciate your telling them to me no matter how discouraging I may find them. It may be that I need a little shock to generate my imagination, but whether that be so or not, and even possible or not, I have the feeling on the book that while on the whole it's very good there is something missing in it which keeps it from having real stature. This could come of course from the boredom and patience and depression of going over the thing sentence by sentence, but I did sense a somewhat similar feeling in your last letter, and if you feel explicit about it, I'll appreciate what you have to say no matter how severe.

Neville Brand is out of town now, but he ought to be back sometime in the month, and we plan to get together. I'll be only too happy to sic him on to *Rebel*. What I feel may be worth considering is to have him read the screen-play. He's extremely intelligent for an actor as I've said, knows a lot about prisons as a layman, knows a lot about analysis, having been analyzed these many years, and so if he liked your script as I'm certain he would, he would be anxious to get Wanger to do it, possibly with the idea of him playing the part. (Although he's very big and brawny, perhaps too much so.) I saw *Riot in Cell Block* 11 the other day, and it is really good, Bob, amazingly good. One cannot call it great because there is finally not enough penetration into character, but I had the feeling it was one of the most honest movies ever made, almost completely without sentimentality, and its emotion impact I found enormous. Make sure to see it from the beginning for it's a picture which builds all the way. If you want Neville to read the screenplay, should I tell him to call up Ivan von Auw, or for that matter I can do it myself. But let me know.

I have an article coming out in the next *Dissent* which ought to get things cooking a bit on the magazine. Did you get a copy of the first issue? [. . .]

My love to you and Johnnie,
Norm

Dear Norman,

I T WAS GREAT TALKING with you the other night. I hope you understood what I meant when I said I'd been having trouble writing. It is simply that my letters have been composed under the shadow of our private talks when you were here—and I couldn't, for some reason, keep out the pompous and pedantic tone. Recognizing this, I've now made the decision not to write about those matters—to save them, that is, for personal meetings. This has removed the blocks, and now I'm able to continue our correspondence.

For some strange reason I've been feeling lousy these last weeks. My gut has been kicking up—a most unusual thing—and I've twice had a swelling on my lips. The guys I've talked to have this "angioneurotic edema," a condition due to a specific allergy or sensitivity to something (a food or?), plus a condition of tension. You're supposed to take anti-histamines for this kind of thing—but the last time I did they made me feel worse. Today my lower lip looks like I've just been made an honorary Ubangi. My private opinion is that this business may be related to my conflict over smoking. For some time I did great—but within the past few days I've slipped, and although I stay under 10 butts a day it still is the wrong thing. But if it isn't the cigarette thing, it must be a food—and I'm damned if I can figure this out. In any case it can't be something a few hours of analysis won't clear up. Meanwhile, as usual when there's something physically wrong with me, my chronic feeling is one of anger, anger at this frailty in myself.

I think you, too, react to illness or physical weakness with anger, don't you? Which brings me to your liver. I've made inquiries, based on the very little you gave me, and I've learned that your condition is not to be taken too seriously. Apparently, you've been making excessive demands on a biologically slightly inadequate organ, and there is hardly any question but that a period of relaxed pressure on this organ will restore its proper function. Until I learned this, I did worry somewhat. Now I'm even glad of it, glad because the drinking (so you've said) has been eliminated.

You know, Norman, I haven't been completely truthful with you (or Adele) about the drinking. I've honestly been concerned with it, mainly because I've noticed that rather than relaxing you, it seems to create more and more tension, and tension of a specific kind. By this I mean that it draws you away from people, breaks communication a little bit. This happens, of course, with every drinker, but you seem to get there a little more rapidly than most others. Also I think you've used the drinking for bad reasons—it wasn't *emergent*, that is, growing out of a personal or party situation; but with you, the personal or party situations *came from* the drinking. Do you understand what I mean? To hell with it. We'll talk soon.

As I told you over the phone, I'm in a kind of limbo these days. I don't feel like doing anything, and I lend myself only reluctantly to my work, finding very little pleasure in it and pushing every day away or behind me. I think I get this way about this time each year—a kind of immense intellectual and (what?) spiritual fatigue seems to engulf me. I get jaded and bored very easily, have a minimal attention span, jump from one small enthusiasm to another, and largely hold secret converse with myself. I think what happens is a consequence of not having a framework or pattern for my ideas. When I am doing a book—or even writing an article—the ideas that occur to me during the time are employed somehow (and also everything I read). In this post-book, pre-book period they are necessarily unattached; they occur, I react—and then they dissipate. I guess this leaves me with a feeling of worthlessness: I'm, somehow, then, loose and become *disengagé*. I know the solution is to begin a new project, even if only in thought; but right now I just don't feel like it. Perhaps when the unattachment increases to a point of real discomfort—or when these blasted psychosomatic things *really* get my goat—I'll do the necessary.

We've been seeing no one of any interest. Yesterday we drove out to Edgy Berman's farm, and Phoebe (they both send remembrances) showed us a wonderful piece of property near them. It has a small waterfall and a narrow stream running through it. I've been wondering about it as an ideal spot for a long cherished dream of mine—a small weekend house. We think it may be possible to widen the pool to a real swimming place and dam up the stream at the further end. Then we could build a house above the water, stock the pool with bass or trout. Maybe this is the place we can write the Mailer and Lindner books from in a couple years—with time out for swimming or skating or fishing! In any event, I'm more excited about this than I've been about anything recently—and maybe it will go through.

About *The Fifty-Minute Hour*, I guess I've written it off now. Lerner's preface, as I said, is terrific. He's done exactly what I hoped—described the book as writing in a new literary genre, and emphasized the intrinsic excitement of the stories. Ted and Dudley feel there is a chance of having a selling success—for a change—and I'm sure that if Ivan brings off the *Harper's* thing, we'll get off to a good start. The "concerning" part—at least until reviews come in— is over. But it isn't over for me (curiously, do you think?) about your book. I find I get more exercised about *Deer Park* than about my own book. Your report about the conference with Stan and Ted was much too brief; I hope you'll expand when you write. What irks me is this: that the reaction of Stan is likely to be the reaction of any publisher I can think of (did you say this or am I being bright?), and at least at Rinehart's you have a friend at court. It has probably taken courage for Ted to stand up for you as he did. But what's to be done? Will Stan give the book what it should have if he continues to feel the way he does? Does it *really* matter? And then I'd like to ask you about your own feelings regarding the two scenes that seem to be the big thorns for Stan. I recall when I read the orgy scene, I told you it left me with a feeling of dissatisfaction. I thought your own doubts about it were showing at that time, and I remember saying that I thought you should either do it or forget it. Now I think it would be a serious artistic error (and a compromise that might harm you) to drop the scene; but I do believe it has to be really written, in detail, full orchestra. (Of course, I don't know if you've done more with it since I saw the manuscript in January.) As for the Teppis scene, when we talked about it last time you convinced me it was essential *stat*. I remain convinced—the scene is tightly and intrinsic (if not, perhaps, entirely necessary) to the portrait of T. But on this I'd bet a house Stan can be convinced.

It is, finally, distressing to think that we'll be out of personal contact for the next few months. All of us will, of course, be thinking of both of you every day. Believe me, it will be the one blot on our own vacation. We'll be leaving for Low House on July 31st—just previous to that, when I get your Mexico address, I'll send you the address. I'll hope, too, that you might realize on the off-chance and join us there late in August. At least let me consider this improbability a possibility.

Much love for both of you from all of us,
Bob

Dear Bob,

T HE TRIP TO MEXICO keeps getting put off. I've just finished typing my book today after thirteen consecutive days of work— about twice as long as I thought it would take—and then next week is going to be full of the old ripperoo with Stan [Rinehart], so that if all goes well we'll take off either before or directly after next weekend. And when we get to Mexico I'll write you again. If something comes up where you want to send me a line, send it care of Beatrice [Silverman] Sanchez, Eligio Ancona 85-12, Mexico D.F. Actually I don't think we'll be there before the second or third of July.

Amigo, I'm afraid we're a couple of *alta kakes*. (Lippy and Liver). Actually I appreciated your scouting around to find out about my condition which is not bad as you say, and I've been dieting very carefully, amazing myself with my capacity to stay off alcohol, sugar, bread, etc. All the things I love so much. I guess the idea of "severity" can be carried over to other things. I winced as you described the lip symptoms. How unpleasant that must be. You know, Bob, part of your depression—obviously large parts — are the cigarettes, and the aftermath of forty stuff (my after-thirty jag carried on for months), but I wonder if a big part isn't the author's equivalent of post-natal depression. I know that every time I've finished a novel I've been in a state of purposelessness and vague anger and irritability for quite a while afterward. Sometimes it takes a few months to set in, sometimes not, but it's quite possible that a writer feels unconsciously that his works are his children—I remember you telling me that there's embryo envy or impregnation envy or something of the sort in the male psyche, and since it takes a man with a big load of the feminine in his nature to be a serious writer, perhaps the depression has to do with some recognition that the literary foetus is finally literary and not a foetus. I don't know, but since these games are fun, note carefully: swelling of the lip (lip equal to vulva) (vulva terminus of womb) ergo you are still carrying the symbolic pregnancy you hate to relinquish. Forgive me for the above but it was such fun I had to go through with it. Do present it to Arthur Mandey as my latest "contribution" to psychoanalysis. I'm certain it'll get him agitated enough to chew up an extra box of Dexamyls.

Congratulations on the Lerner. Despite my mild antipathy to Lerner I'm genuinely glad he gave you a good preface, and as a matter of fact I like him a little better for it.

The problem of the ORGY. Ugh! I ended up cutting the orgy to the bone so that all that remains is a sort of vague idea of what's going on. And if necessary I'll cut it completely. The reason for cutting it completely is that the chapter will actually be improved because of the sense of what happened at the orgy will come through in the subsequent Eitel-Elena dialogue, and as a matter of fact it will seem even more evocative and orgiastic that way. I'd do it before submitting to Stan except that if I do, he's going to demand other cuts, and I need something for bargaining. You're quite right that I feel the orgy is a failure, but Bob I've shot my wad on it—I cannot make it better, I even hate writing the Goddamn thing, and there are times when every author has to recognize that certain things in his book have to remain infirm because he lacks the talent or imagination to up them. Your suggestion that I write the orgy in full I just can't follow. I don't even know if you're right in the abstract, but in the concrete it's equivalent to having the book either (1) unpublishable or (2) banned upon publication. Now if I had set out to write a book which would be privately printed, that would be something else. The entire book would have been different, in style, conception, everything, and if I'd been a braver bigger writer possibly I would first have conceived it that way. Except I'm not quite sure because finally *The Deer Park* is about morality and what is love, what is sex, etc. rather than what is fucking. And therefore to stick in one chapter on an orgy which is written to the hilt would be out of line with the rest of the book. I've got a strong sense of when I chicken out, and I really don't feel Bob that I'm compromising here. The book is going to be hated, reviled, stomped on, etc, I believe, because it's a disturbing book as I wanted it to be, and the orgy is more a function of the plot than a part of the essential meaning. Don't worry about my compromising with Stan. I'm prepared to walk out of Rinehart if he doesn't see the light, because although having Ted in my corner is fine, I believe there are better houses for me. This of course is *confidential, vieux Lippé.*

I don't know if I follow you on the business of my drinking. Since I've been without it at a couple of parties I've noticed that my anxiety is if anything greater, and that I feel very withdrawn from people. You're quite right that a part of me disconnects when I get drunk, but another part connects, so that often I act drunk the way I would like to act sober. Sometimes emotions like love are much easier for me to feel strongly when I'm strong—sometimes of course vast detachment, but as you say this is more to talk over that to write about.

Re: Stan, there's something very peculiar going on in him. I even have a hunch that in some cockeyed way he sees my portrait of Teppis as a portrait of him, and this hurts all the benevolent *pater* paternalism on which Stan runs his business, his house, and his heart. He keeps claiming the book will be banned because of the Teppis scene which I think is a little alarmist, but anyway that I'm not going to take out. Even before Stan saw it, I took the descriptive edges off it so that the reader will have no more than a sense that something perverted happened, but whether it was fellatio, urinatio, coming in the pants, or just twitching will be left to the readers own predilections and antipathies which I think is artistically more valid because the essential relation of Teppis to his "love" objects has not been obscured at all, and as Cy [Rembar] said, "Why set cock-sucking back ten years?" by which he meant that the connotation of the scene made fellatio the villain rather than Teppis. Anyway, Stan saw the revised version, still hates it, and next week the battle of the blow-hards starts. My guess is that I will gain my points and stay at Rinehart. If you don't hear from me until I get to Mexico that will be the case. If something more dramatic or final occurs I'll drop you a line.

There's a small chance we'll see you and Johnnie this summer, Bob. If Mexico hits us badly, and if Bea is real bitchy to Adele we may not stay as many months as we planned, but this is all speculation now. Adele is in fine shape albeit a little depressed by her twenty-ninth birthday, today, and sends her love along with mine to you and Johnnie and the kids.

We miss all of you too, *hermano*.

Love
Norman

Brother of Mine:

IT IS TO BE hoped greatly that this my letter finds you and your liver happily well. O *Normano mio*, we are indeed *hermanos* now, I having, but minutes past come from the consultation of the professor of skins, wherefrom emerged I with the list of a diet excluding all the pleasures and delights of the gut—including the press of the grape and the vine's fruit.

The affair began with the lip of mine, as I have informed you by an earlier post, and am itching of the skin in various places, and, sadly, the manifestation of that upon the skin said by all to be of the nature of "hives." Following the initial seizure of me by these portents and symptoms, there passed some days, when in this fashion once more I was taken.

There was I, then, on the day of Saturn of the last week, in repose following my labors, at rest (I repeat) in the house of me, sampling slowly of a brew much in repute and admired by the natives of this region, compounded of substances to the number of two, hyght "gin" et "vermouth," in a formula of mathematic relations "six-to-one." Of a sudden there overcame me, your brother, in the region of the mouth of mine, especially the underpart, a curious perception of heat and vibration, after which there did appear a swell, or fullness, thereof, which, to my distress, persisted through the long night. Accompanying this occult untowardness, even more unbelievable, a furor of the insides of me came to pass, with nauseation and mild vertigo attending. Thereafter misery companioned me until bedding hour, the which was on that occasion delayed far into birthtime of the day subsequent by wasteful converse and further draughts of the self-same empoisoned brew, at intervals of a certainty prescribed, I know not how, yet assuredly be the (incomprehensible) rituals of the region, and upon the invitation, graciously rendered, of natives, oddly comparisoned (I tell you for your instruction) and outdecked with fabrics suited to the sultry climate of that night, assembled in a conclave composed of various tribes to fashion a thing called (by these the natives) a "party," the which was not in any place to be seen, although my search for it occupied, when the lip of mine allowed, the whole of the night. Sleep arrived, then, and upon the morrow, such is the bounty of the saints, a properly proportioned visage was returned to me in the glass.

Of a minor degree, since, has this distress pursued me, your brother, until this moment of writing. I have, as written, attended the professor of skins following matins of this day. He, the professor, advised, first, a purging of the bowel, and thereafter also, the regime of the monk, happily confined to that which passes into the body by the mouth of me, for a period of weeks, reasoning thusly: that unfriendly spirits have in me lodged and made me to be of a sensitivity profound, and a responsiveness, to an irritant which, in time, through a famous method known abroad as "progressive elimination," may be apprehended and indicted.

In resignation the, I surrender to the saints and the professor of the skins.

Given this date, hyght above, by the hand of the signatee below. Nihil obstat. Imprimatur. Nertz!

Roberto el labio

* * *

Dear Norman:

I HAVE SEPARATED THE ABOVE report on the state of my physical body from the rest of this, chiefly to confound our biographers—whose existences I do not ever for a moment doubt. If they can dig the styles involved and their sources (I date such biographers about a hundred years hence, a few decades after an Orwellian debacle during which all traces of previous cultures will have vanished ((except our works, of course)) and the language will have degenerated into a series of melodious grunts (((except in the case of a handful of scientists who will by then have uncovered a Rosetta stone enabling such masterworks as *Naked* and *Prescription* to be read)))—if they can, I say, they'll deserve the right to write about us.)

To continue. Apart from all these horrors there is little to report from the Baltimore front. The thing that may amuse you is that Ivan enclosed a letter from Gollancz in which the dear old boy reports that he turned down the stories in *The Fifty-Minute Hour* originally because he "came to the conclusion that there was something wrong with the book. I can't clearly explain my feeling: I think I might perhaps put it, in a Jewish phrase which Lindner will understand, that it was not quite Kosher. Or, to put it in another way, I had the feeling that the investigations had been "done up" a bit—that there were points at which the science merged into fiction." "But," the dear old boy continues, "I may have been quite wrong—in any event the thing was of fascinating interest—and I should certainly like to get another opinion. So please send the typescript over to me . . ."

Apparently the Lerner preface whetted old pip-pip Victor's appetite again, and we are going to comply with his request for another look-see. In responding to Ivan about this I took the occasion to point out that everything about the stories is true and factual, but that, of course, they have been "fictionalized" to give the necessary dramatic tension. I rather expect that V.G. will decide to buy—but if he doesn't Ivan assures me that almost anyone else in England will.

So far as the business with *Harper's* is concerned, apparently they have not yet completed their mind-making up, and I anticipate that it will be another couple of weeks before we hear from them.

Some further small bit of news is that we went last night to hear Freddie Weisgal play at a local beer joint, to which I will have to take you when you come down again. Before deciding to do this, Freddie came to my office for an off-the-cuff opinion on whether or not his practice would suffer—or his reputation as a lawyer be hurt—but doing this I neglected to point out to Freddie that little damage to his legal reputation would be possible under the most extreme circumstances. However, I did feel he had somewhat of a point. I related the story of the man who complained he had been a tailor 40 years, and no one ever called him Schneider on the streets, yet for "zaging" one little "bein," the whole world thereafter called him "cocksucker." Fred got the point.

Soon after you receive this letter I expect that you will be off for Mexico, and I confess to envying you greatly this time of leisure. Me, I will be sweating out a living over a hot couch for another 6 or 7 weeks—and probably nursing my hives—until the first of August. [. . .]

Bob

Dear Bob,

I REALLY ENJOYED YOUR MASTERPIECE, and think that the grievous
affliction of the lower lip had its one compensation in those pages
of incomparable (shall we say Gregorian?) rhetoric. Anyway, Old
Lippy, I hope this finds you in good health for I write in bad health.
To begin with I developed the cruelest case of the piles driving
down here, especially on those days through the Middle West and
Texas where the temperature went above 100 and I did my seven
hundred miles without stopping. And what a curious drive is that.
Up at midnight and drive through the dawn (the best part) and then
through the morning and the hot noon and the burning afternoon
until we stop at four or five and collapse on a bed. Then, in Mexico
where we arrived two weeks ago (after a week at my friend's in
Arkansas) I had to desert that liver diet until we found a house, and
of course came down with one of my bitchy sore throats which has
lasted a full week now and won't go away until I get more of this
home cooking—boiled beef and proteins etc.

But the house we've found is really extraordinary. It's an old
Spanish colonial which is like a fortress, indeed looks like a jail from
outside, and inside has the most beautiful garden, an enormous
living room, with a ceiling over twenty feet high and old timbers
exposed, and all kinds of rooms and balconies and a fabulous
dining room which looks like something out of a Dutch painting—
honey-colored woods, with green ceiling and massive but cheerful,
and wonderful furnishings with Spanish antiques—a fine line of
furniture in its time, and one great added charm which is all kinds of
child's surprises, so that you turn on a faucet here, and there in the
garden a little fountain begins to flow, and orchids grow on the trees,
and there's a cobblestone patio in the back, and internal windows in

rooms which look down on other rooms, and a solarium where you can sun bare-ass of which there is no greater aphrodisiac—it's cool, doc. And all for 1500 pesos a month or $120. But of course we had to look and look to find this place.

Things at Rinehart turned out beautifully. Ted gave the book to the other young editors in the place and they all turned in enthusiastic reports and so Stan would have had to buck his editorial department and instead retired into sulky silence, not even seeing me the last day I was there. And Ted plans to push the book in February—its new publication date. They accepted the book as it stood, and I in delight offered to take out the page on the orgy at which point Ted looked at me somberly, soberly, and said, "I sure wish you would, Norman." So it's out. And frankly I'm glad because it was bad writing as it stood, and the orgy will be larger now since people will imagine it. But the big surprise for me was Ted who stayed strong as a rock all through it as I believe I wrote to you.

Right now I sit and read novels and study Spanish and think a little. I'm very tired and drained intellectually, exactly as you felt last June, but the consolation is that a book may be on the horizon—at least I feel ideas coming together and so enthusiasm, and the vague glimmering of a theme. But I'm not going to rush it at all. The prison work still appeals—just how easy is it Bob to get a job as some sort of counselor or whatever in a men's prison? Is it the kind of thing you can get by just applying? Also, did I write to you about *Break Down the Walls*? I thought it quite disappointing, and you're quite right about his borrowing from *Stone Walls* only I wish he'd borrowed more. I then read another book by Martin, *Why Did They Kill?* [1953] and thought that was first-rate.

Adele is painting, and Susie stays with us overnight every now and again, and I feel love and pain always in my relation with her, for Susie is so gaminish and delicate and odd and fey, and I can feel neurosis building in her from day to day yet feel not only incapable of halting it, but often think I can contribute greatly to it myself. But at her best, Susie is a bright spot. I feel good that soon you'll have your long-awaited and much-deserved vacation, and we'll be thinking of all of you on Long Island. Give our love to Johnnie and to the kids, and my best to Jeanne, and let me hear from you. Do you feel closer to starting a novel? The novel, I should say. We miss you, old Lippy.

Till October,
Norman

Normancito:

D ON'T TELL ME WE'RE not simpatico! I had hardly finished a letter
to you when yours arrived. We were overjoyed to hear from you,
but are now distressed to learn about your health. Have you considered returning for treatment? Or can you get what you need where
you are? Please, man, take care—it's important for everyone that you
remain well—or at least well enough to get done what's yours to do,
including having a good time.

As for me, mysteriously, I have had little or no further trouble,
lip-wise or hive-y. Whether the blasted thing has run its course, or
my psyche has undergone some occult kind of reorganization, I
don't know. In any case, I'm eating almost everything (although I
remain leery of—and avoid—tomatoes, berries and cheese) without
ill effect. Physically, then, I'm in pretty good shape. Except for heart
trouble, cancer, leukemia, and tuberculosis I have fewer complains
these days than I had when I last wrote. Mentally, I continue
dull. Although I've read a lot—much. An occasional idea, yes—but
nothing that sticks. Nevertheless—and I think only you can understand this—I feel yeasty. Stuff is moiling and brewing deep down.
Occasionally, with what reminds me of a bubble's burst in a cauldron
of some thick liquid, an etwas (sentence, thought, vagrant phrase)
rises to the surface, breaks, then settles—So maybe there's a thing
happening that will start me soon on the book.

Your news about *Deer Park* is warming and exciting both. When I
got the catalogue two weeks ago, I observed there was no announce-
ment of your book, I worried about what had happened. Your letter
calms—apparently all has ended well. As for the orgy scene, I agree
its elimination is artistically necessary and that the book will profit
from the deletion.

Parenthetically, the "Jet-Propelled Couch" will be in *Harper's* in
abbreviation in December and January. Ivan concluded the arrange-

ments last week. We think they've done a fine editorial job and its appearance there will help *The Fifty-Minute Hour*.

We leave for Long Island on July 31st. Please copy this address and phone number and put it where you'll be reminded of me (us) constantly. May I suggest Adele's beautiful butt? [. . .]

To both of you from all here, much love,

Your
Lippy
the labile lover of labia

Dear Bob,

I'VE BEEN SORT OF saving up and looking forward to this letter, and in fact meaning to write to you for some time now, but I got side-tracked into doing an article for *Dissent* which began as a book review of *Individualism Reconsidered* by David Riesman, and ended up going to fourteen pages, and including *The Lonely Crowd*, and all in all getting ambitious. So three weeks were devoted pretty exclusively to that.

We've been having a quiet time here, Adele painting, and I studying Spanish a couple of hours a day, and readings novels with an occasional trip thrown in. I think normally a life so inactive would pall, but I've been getting a succession of ideas for a long novel and a short novel which have been exciting me—how exciting ideas always are before you have to start shaping them to words— and so a lot of these quiet days have passed with considerable internal excitement. However, I do miss the rhythms of New York at times—and the excitement of talking to good friends at my three hundred word a minute rate. The friends we have here are all nice enough, but on the home lot I'm afraid they'd belong to the second string.

In reading your letter I see you've been having etwases too. Eppis is an etwas. But truly there ought to be a better word than etwas for something so marvelous, and there are times when I think that outside of screwing at its happy best, there's no kick like an etwas.

I was very pleased to read the news about "The Jet-Propelled Couch," and I'm delighted for you. The sign of how good it is that *Harper's* got off their fat ass of precedent to print it. And of course we salute the passing of the third floor labia. What's the matter, Ginso, you wanta lose your practice scoring your patients?

Susie (my daughter) has been with us a fair amount of time, and I have the cockeyedest relation with her. I'm kind of nuts about her for she's a subtle, charming troubled child with a little old lady's face and a grave manner which when it cracks under laughter gives her glee a peculiarly poignant (at least for me) quality. And of course her Spanish accent slays me. But with it, she's often remote and not often very affectionate, and do my damndest I can't get as close to her as I'd like. The irony of my "seductive" personality is that children aren't taken in by it. Not my own child anyway.

The other child is painting well, and our fights are occasionally heroic farce in their magnitude, but what saves it is that we always feel so bruised and tender when they're over, like the kid knocking his head against the wall because it feels so good when he stops.

Also we've discovered the joys of "tea." This I'll expound to you when I see you, and if you read me a psychoanalytical lecture I'll call you an old reactionary. But if you have any good doctor friends who are a little less inspirational and hortatory than Arthur M., I am curious to know what the physiological action is, whether it's harmful over extended periods, etc. My knowledge of it is that is does no harm at all, but I don't know how reliable it is. One thing, I find it far less wearing on the system (no hangovers) than whisky. Anyway, old buddie, do subdue your panic reactions about my going straight to hell—why does everybody see my early doom? when I know that I'm just a simple middle-class Jewish boy and never to anything to excess, and when I see thee I will explain the pleasures of the pipe.

Cy phoned a couple of days ago, and mentioned that you were all going to phone me until he wisely dissuaded you via expense. Of which I approve. I would have been so horrified at the expensive connect between minutes and money that I would have been able to say nothing. Anyway, I'm glad you felt like calling.

It seems as if the deal on *Naked* is going to go through, and to Adele's amazement, I feel absolutely flat about that. I suppose what depressed me is that at least half of me, hopes for the day when I'll be poor, faced with the real realities of life, and therefore able to write better. Which is probably nonsense, but the ideas and passions of college, like art in a garret and traveling the wide world of adventure die very hard, don't they amigo?

Everything seems routine now at Rinehart on *The Deer Park* that just as it was hard to write, so will its publishing life be full of episodes and near-catastrophes. Now the bitch is in England, where they like it, but as I understand from Cy, Cape wrote Ted something to the effect that I sure was a novelist but that little old *Deer Park* might need "a fig-leaf or two." Fig 'em. I mean it.

About my health—it's fine. After a month of laying off completely, I've been drinking sparingly and feel no compulsion about having to have stuff. Of course we haven't been meeting many strange people and that could be part of it too. Incidentally, it just occurs to me, I think it would be better, Bob, if you don't mention the marijuana because you know how that kind of story will spread about me.

At the moment we plan to start back in slow stages somewhere around the middle of October, but that date is very elastic. I think though that the emphasis would be more on leaving earlier than later because we just aren't that nuts about Mexico, and the altitude demands an average of nine hours of sleep which of course I resent.

We think often of you and Johnnie enjoying the sun and the water at Low House, and regret that we miss visiting you this summer. Maybe next. Anyway I hope this finds you and the blonde beauty in the best of health, and give our hellos to the kids.

Did friendship take with the Rembars? I'm sure it did.

Adele sends her love to which I add mine.

Norm

Hermano mio,

Now, AT LAST, I take my pen in hand (I'd take my secretary, but she's otherwise engaged) to write to you. Why I haven't done so before—there are many reasons, but most of it has been sheer laziness. Anyhow, I don't like to write letters to you, Chico—I'd rather speak direct—man talk. Letters embarrass me. And who knows? They're even saying Freud and Fleiss had a mad affair!

We returned to Baltimore last week, worn out from violent vacationing. Now I'm back at work, slaving over a hot couch and chasing a buck here and there. Actually, I've hardly dug in, and don't expect to—really—until next week, when I return from a quick trip to New York. I have to go there to meet and talk with the people who are arranging a lecture tour for me in California begin-ning November 1st. You did not know this, Ginso, so I'm telling you now. On November 1st, we go West for about two weeks. Anyhow, previous to seeing these birds about the arrangements and details, I have to talk with Ivan. Always (you know) with an eye to the main chance, I'd like to see if there's a possibility to have the articles (lectures) commissioned by someone, or gather them into a fast small book. So when I get back (from N.Y.), I'll have to hustle to put the stuff down on paper.

So much to tell you—and so much I want to know about you, Cholo. I think the state of our souls needs examination and discus-sion over a quart of whiskey. Hurry back, Pal.

Which brings me to what you are doing. I like the fact that you are having etwases, that you are thinking about two novels, that your liver is lively, your gonads sizzling, and your asshole is tight— But, *amigo querido*, this flirtation of yours with the gage—this I do not like. Not because it may mean early doom or residence in some Yiddish purgatory—that would be okay since then we'd share hellroom together—but because the winding of the self should take place from the inside. A theory I'll discuss with you one night soon.

By the way, I don't know if you know yet about the love affair between the Rembars and the Lindners. It's a fact, anyhow. On Friday, when I get to New York, I'll be calling Cy—and getting what news he has of you. Perhaps he'll tell me then about the *Naked* deal. And when you get rich, Chazar, I'll take the Jaguar on the left.

Christ! I miss you.

The jacket came from Rinehart for the 50 minute job. I don't know what to make of it—or how to think of it. Everyone says it's "striking, vivid, attention-getting."—Me? I think it looks like something that's been cooking too long.

How's my Peruvian Yenta? If I thought you knew where to do it, I'd ask you to kiss her for me.

All of us enjoy good health. Maybe that's why I feel so bad.

Adios, marica,
Robert, *el toro dé Latrobe*

Dear Bob,

J UST A SHORTIE TO tell you what a good time we had, and to let you
know that there's no news on the big thing yet. I've submitted
it [*The Deer Park*] simultaneously to Knopf and Random House
(please don't mention Knopf, nor for that matter that I'm in the act
of changing publishers) and in a funny way I'm hoping that both
houses don't want the book with equal enthusiasm, mainly because
I had to use such pressure to make them both agree to the simulta-
neous business that it's going to leave me with an enemy when I turn
one down. I'll let you know as soon as there is news. Maybe by next
Monday.

My inner life continues with much stimulation. I've gotten on
to something in advertising which I believe is pretty big. It's the
old thing I discovered from Lipton's that tremendous truth is to be
found in the cliché if you crack open the shell. As a matter of fact I
feel a little bit these days as if I'm a man from Mars. I walk around
(even when I'm not taking Lipton's) really listening and concentrating on what I hear. On exactly what is said. It's amazing what
one discovers if one only listens. And of course my great mental
weakness in the past has been one of not concentrating. Now I feel
as if everything I see, do, feel, and hear, is in italics.

By the way, I'm a little pissed off at you for your attitude on
Lipton's. Mainly at the element of condescension, the feeling that
you know me. Like Gide I scream! Please do not understand me too
quickly. If our activities were reversed, I would be extremely interested in what you had to say, and what you thought about it. And, by
the by, I don't ascribe magic powers to Lipton's. For anyone to get a
radically new insight, some sort of magic or catalyst—if you will—is
necessary, be it love, liquor, psychoanalysis, religion, or what have
you, and this happens to be mine. You can of course be right, and I
think no better, hear no better, etc., but why be sure ahead of time?

Do you know everything? Am I that simple? There exists the danger in you, Bob, and I say this to a beloved friend, that you can end up as some sort of avant-garde *paterfamilias*. One is either truly radical or merely a liberal with muscles.

Anyway, when next I see you, I have three large subjects to expound on—1) The artist and psychopathy, 2) Advertising and the modern state, 3) The illusion of psychoanalysis. Where and when did the German lecturer come to birth in me. But do remind me because I really have so much to discuss.

[. . .]

Con amor,
Norman

Dear Norman,

THE FACT THAT YOU left a number of things around the house is good evidence that you want to come back, so I hope you will make arrangements soon to return. We need to sit down and talk a little bit more about Lipton's. It may be that a part of my reaction toward it is determined by preconceptions and prejudices—these leading to concern when any of its celebrants are so close to me. In any event, I do want to discuss the ideas you talk about.

We've had a lot of excitement here because of the piece in this week's *Time*, and the coincident publication of "The Jet-Propelled Couch." All sorts of amazing things have happened as a result of the *Time* piece, not the least of which is an immediate decision by Ted to bring out the lectures as a small book by spring. Before I do the final draft I am terrible anxious to have you go over the manuscript with me—or by yourself—so that I can take care of the rough spots you mentioned. I'd be enormously grateful for this and also for some assistance in completing the homosexuality piece.

I also want you to do me a more immediate favor, and that is to write to Rinehart immediately after you see and read your copy of *The Fifty-Minute Hour*. If you can give them some statement to be used for advertising, I'd be in your debt. In addition to you, I have asked that a copy be sent to Bill Styron, from whom I would like the same thing—but only if he feels the book deserves his praise. Moreover, if you can think of anyone to whom complimentary copies should be sent, that is to say anyone who can assist in promotion, I would also appreciate this.

I am full of appreciation today as you see—but nonetheless, the inner man is still somewhat apprehensive about everything. What I need is a few hours with you over a couple of drinks. Many issues have been raised about my ideas in various editorials all over the country and in columns such as those now being run by Max Lerner in the *New York Post*. I'd like to talk out and re-evaluate some of the ideas before heading into the final draft of the essays—and you're it.

When you find out about Christmas, please let me know, and also what yours plans are going to be for the celebration of the New Year. Since I have to see Ted and a few other people, I intend to come to New York within the next few weeks, but will let you know further about this in my next.

I haven't said anything about *The Deer Park* in this note simply because I am awaiting word from you. Nevertheless, my concern with the matter is very deep, and I think of it constantly. You will be interested to learn that in the two or three letters I've had from Ted Amussen since you were here, he never fails to express his "numbness" and general despair over what's happened. I get the feeling that he is truly disturbed and regards the whole affair as a great fiasco and deep personal blow. This despite the under-side of his character which you and Johnnie so well delineated.

Don't fail to write soon and let me know what's going on and what your plans are. All of us here send love to all of you.

Bob
Robert Lindner

Dear Bob,

MORE NOTES FROM THE journal. I don't intend to keep sending this
stuff to you, having respect for your time among other things,
but I do believe these notes clarify a hell of a lot I said before. On
Note 56 you will find a blurb for *The Fifty-Minute Hour*. The correc-
tions come for an interesting reason. I wrote the blurb before I
reread the book in its published form. Reading it, I liked it considerably better than the first time, particularly Charles, Mac, and
Anton—Kirk is about the same, but you know how enthusiastic I was
about that. I'd really be very excited about the book if it weren't for
two literary faults of yours, one overcome by discipline; the other
perhaps psychically more serious. The first is just your style which
at its worst gets down to pure cornball, Bob. But this is just wasteful.
You should make the effort yourself, but after I go over the lectures,
let us say. For if I give them a week, I think I can show you what I
mean. My editorial principles are very close to Orwell's, even though
when I write I'm guilty of many lapses myself. And this you can
learn. Charley Devlin once went through a book for me (*Naked*) and
I learned an awful lot from him.

Perhaps you don't like the blurb. If you don't, I'm willing to write
something shorter, vaguer, and more complimentary cause I would
like to help you sell books. But I do have this conviction that the
evaluative blurb as opposed to the laudatory blurb actually interests
people more. They're given five new classics every week, and so a
blurb which is not simply dithyrambic catches their eye more I think.

The other difficulty is something we must talk about carefully.
In short what it comes down to is that your endings tend to be
wandering and uneasy. I suspect, although I may be wrong, that it
comes from being at the cross-roads of your ambition. On the one
hand you want to be a great man; on the other you want to be a
celebrity here and now. Your contempt for the thinking of celebrities

keeps you from really serving the pablum which is requisite, but the tendency in all your thought which is to go out very far, very wide, with nothing but your speed and your sincerity to protect you is something you probably hesitate before. So, the equivocation which probably expresses itself in the ends and the endings.

My own affairs, alack, alay. As of today it looks like I can't get together with Knopf. I really believe they want to do the book, but Blanche Knopf seems almost irrationally terrified by the thought of the book being prosecuted. I cooperate with them to a point. I took out sentence after sentence which might be construed as sexually gratuitous. I went far because they were willing to leave the Teppis scene intact. But finally it came down to cutting passages which involved the motivation of characters. And this I can't do. It's the heart of the book. The worst of it, is that gossip has made the book seem so pornographic that by the time it goes to six more publishers, somebody is going to have to believe it's the best thing since *Remembrance of Things Past* before he's willing to publish it. Bob, it looks like *The Deer Park* is in for a long haul. But of course I have the ace in the sleeve of finally publishing it myself, no matter the cost. What the hell did I sell *Naked* for, if not to have such options? Anyway, I'll give you no more day by day communiqués until a contract is signed. For, frankly, it's like being on an elevator. Yet, deep-down, a part of me is delighted. I must have done something to get people that upset.

Reading *Fifty-Minute* made me realize something again about you. You're such a manipulator of people. I suspect my notes have not been answered because you're worried about me, and you're trying to think of the thing to say which will move me in the direction which is best (by your lights) for me. If it is true . . . oh, Bob! Just tell me what you think straight out. Don't manipulate me. My mother is the great one of all time, and I have enormous sensory apparatus toward that.

How's about getting some mescaline, kid?

Love,
Norm

Dear Bob, in fact, Dear Dear Bob,

H APPY NEW YEAR. AND what a year this new one is going to be. I've
decided to send you one-half of the journal, my carbon. Please
keep it in some safe place. And as I add to it, I'll send you more. The
part you haven't read starts on page 19. And I think it carries along
much of what I had before, and expands it.

Incidentally, try not to read it critically. That is, don't pick out
such and such items as good, others as bad, etc. I'm putting it all
down because I want the record. As I read it over, there is hardly
a note which could not be improved, or indeed expanded into an
essay. So, the thing is very crude. But I don't want to stop to polish
now. And I want the wild with what is less wild because some of the
wild ones become less wild as I expand them subsequently. Viz the
saint-psychopath thing. Essentially I started it by saying, saints and
psychopaths are brothers. But, by now, I feel I'm pushing it into a
new view of personality.

If you don't have much time, and want to read the homo-erotic
corollary, it is in Note **139**. If you have time, I suggest coming to it
naturally.

Brother, one thing. You must suspend your caution or we'll get
nowhere. So much of your thought is now in mine. Truly I'm not
competing with you. Don't look at me that way in my relations with
you—it's beneath us. I send you these notes because deep in me I
feel that you're the only person who can understand me right now
intellectually, just as Adele is the only woman who can understand
me intuitively. Which is why the two of you are so drawn to each
other and so jealous of each other. (Don't forget you called her the
Peruvian Yenta.)

I'm mailing the blurb to Dudley Frasier. I would have made it
bigger, but truly, Bob, I couldn't. You can go so very far that some

day you'll look back on *Fifty-Minute Hour* as one of your last stands or retreats before the big kickoff.

I'll try to make the flight for the 13th.

Answer this at your leisure. Unless something goes wrong, we'll be skiing from the Second of Jan. to the Fifth or Sixth or Seventh.

Much love,
Norm

P.S. Don't forget your depression at reaching forty. That was you telling yourself that you haven't gone far enough.

Dear Bob,

SOME MORE OF THE journal. I think a few of the items you'll find attractive.

Your reviews were excellent I heard, and I congratulate you warmly, old friend. Naturally, I've seen none of them, everybody somehow taking it for granted that I would see them in some mysterious fashion in Mexico, but when I see you in Baltimore, we'll be able to go over more of them. I hope the book does well. Bob-bo.

I've had a turn of luck with *The Deer Park*. G. P. Putnam's is taking it, asking for no changes I do not consent to make, paying the full royalty (confidential) and have agreed to a first printing of 25,000 copies. But I'm such a pig and unregenerate egotist that the news which greeted me upon return from Mexico left me flat. I was so geared for a fight that I really felt a little disappointed. Which I guess proves what a saint-psychopath I am at bottom. Interestingly, Cy was somehow left a little flat too. Anyway, the contract is to be signed in a few days, and the book is tentatively set for August publication. What excited me much more was your message about Ivan. Does he really think it's my best book? (I do.) Somehow, what with Ivan being so right and so quietly helpful in the shadows, I came to wait more and more anxiously for what he would finally feel when he read it. I think nothing would have upset me more than Ivan not liking it, and so I felt a real burst of joy when Adele gave me your message. What a good bastard you are to know the pleasure such news would give me.

Mexico was rough on me, but I'll tell you about that when I see you. One day I literally had to fight off weeping twice while I was with Susie because of the pain of leaving her. And the weight she carried in her heart and the wisdom. She fell asleep the night before I left, the last time I would see her, and I think she knew that it was far better to be unconscious when I left than to go through the pain of the scene. I really think she loves me, and I want no one to love me more than I want Susie to. Unrequited love thing maybe.

Anyway, write soon, amigo, and I hope we get together soon. I am indeed looking forward to it very much.

Love,
Norm

Normano mio:

TRIED TO CALL YOU last night but you were out—or perhaps (I can see you) reclining with your feet up in that wonderful chair while that gadget of yours poured out the music. Wish I'd been with you.

What I wanted to tell you was that I'm glad about the Putnam thing. I want to see *The Deer Park* behind you. As you so correctly saw—long ago—it was a phase, a necessary step in your development. It now needs to be solidified in print—(which is really the way an artist buries, successively, each of his selves), then mourned (the critical and public reception), finally forgotten by being absorbed. Now that this is well on its way, you're free to grow a new self.

Which leads to the Journal.

Norman, buck-o-boy—I can't tell you how excited I am about it. I wait from day to day to get the next installment, and find myself almost totally absorbed in following its development. Some of the ideas I hate—most I love—but all of them fascinate me. Occasionally, reading it, I find myself leaping ahead in my mind—or arguing fiercely as if you were present. Our next meeting should detonate an explosion that will probably tear up 53rd Street and route out some of the whores in the St. Regis.

As for me, I'm kind of in a fallow period now, intellectually; but emotionally I'm sizzling on some griddle of curious design. Things I can't write about have been happening to me, and the shape of that griddle is burning hieroglyphs on my soul.

The success of the book—or what looks like a success—and the fuss my lectures have been kicking up all over the place, have made me excited and tense—But the yin of this yang is a new level of consciousness—almost a new birth, with a fermentation being prepared in another recess of my mind. I'm getting ideas again, *hermano*—and, as you predicted, dangerous ideas.

How perceptive you are! What genius (I mean it) lies in your intuition of my growth (?) from psychopathy to sainthood, badness to goodness, dishonesty to truth! The whole story, which I must now resolve to tell you some day, will confirm you down to the very misspellings of the words you used. I'm going to try to call you again tonight, comrade—becaus I'm tired of writing letters these days and because I need the more direct contact. Also, I have to come up to New York for a few hours next week to talk to the moguls who are planning to do an *Omnibus* dramatization of the J. P. Couch—which means a few hours we can tear up together. Meanwhile, pal, go *go*, Go . . .

Yours,
Bob

Dear Norman,

I HAVE BEEN SO TREMENDOUSLY excited about the last two install-
ments of the Journal that I can hardly wait to talk with you about
them. I want to urge you very strongly to re-read *Rebel Without
a Cause*—forget the expository material and read only Harold's
productions. Moreover, I think it is imperative that you follow
up your insights on the sexual life of saints, by getting hold of St.
Theresa's books and whatever other writings of this kind you can
find. Huxley's *Devils of Loudun* will also give you some important
leads.

As usual I don't have time for a real letter, but I have to tell you
that I actually anticipated your situation with *Dissent*—after reading
the last issue I determined not to renew my subscription for the
exact reasons you describe in the Journal. Which brings me to Note
344, which, I think—if developed—would say the first significant
words on the whole problem.

So far no word from my brother or about a brief trip to New York
next week. Will let you know as soon as I can.

Love,
B

P.S. Just received a wire stating that Mannie, my brother, will be
here for the weekend. Will call you early next week to arrange for
your coming down next weekend—Great!

Dear Norman,

I T'S BEEN SO LONG since I heard from you that I've begun to wonder
why. I called you when I was in New York last week—almost
continuously (as Edna must have told you)—and since returning to
Baltimore a number of times, including last night. It did occur to me
that you may have gone on the ski trip you talked of taking—and
maybe that's why there've been no notes from the journal, no letters,
and no calls.

It occurs to me that there may be a change of climate in our
relationship. I don't feel one on my part—but perhaps, after your
last visit, you do. According to the notes, once you expressed your
peeve, you purged yourself of ill feelings. I can only hope that this
is so. For my part, I think that if there is any difficulty between us,
it is put there by your insistence on projecting some of your doubts
about the "new" self you are discovering on me. I wish I knew how
to get you beyond this—how to convince you of my total acceptance.
But, at the same time, Norman, I feel your pressure to, somehow,
close me off. Take that matter of painting. You and Adele insist I
know nothing about it, and I'm content to let you think that—both
of you—if you wish. But when I try to tell you, not what I *know* about
it, but what I think of it, you accuse me of lecturing on painting. And
yet I have stood by both amused and a little appalled when Adele has
pointed out a picture in a book to you and said, "Don't you think I've
been getting a few effects like this?"—so I have seen and heard the
evidence from both of you that what I wanted to discuss with you
then—the absence of *ideas* from non-objective painting—you charge
me with gratuitous and pompous "lecturing." So also with Lipton's.
Do you want a one-way street, Chazar? Look, I'll take—willingly,
happily—all you have to dish out; but don't sulk when I show I've got
a few stray bits of guts, too.

Ah, well—enough of that. If it's there, we'll both know it—or sign off.

The last few weeks have been disturbing and distressing ones. The death of a close friend set the tone for a whole series of disappointments. Although the book is doing alright, it is just about limping along, and will continue that way unless or until I can get Rinehart to do more advertising. They've been content to see it move at about 600 to 1000 copies a week on what they call "word of mouth" and excellent reviews. What it wants, of course, is a goose. That goose would have been provided by the *Omnibus* program—which fell through. Yes, my friend, I've been fucked but regally—with all the trimmings—and I want you to be among the first to know about it. Seems that when the final decision had to be made, the medicos on the board of the Ford Foundation ruled that it would be regarded as an unfriendly act by the medical profession if I, a psychologist, talked about my work and my thinking to twenty-one million people. The implication being that I'm a charlatan and a quack. So they gave me the knife—and that, too, is that.

They've been other disappointments and shocks, too—but this above was the worst. I wanted this thing, not for what it would do for me, but for what I could do. Do you understand?

I've missed you, Norman—what gives?

Yours,
Bob

TO NORMAN MAILER
MARCH 15, 1955

Norman:

EITHER YOU WROTE THOSE two notes in a paranoid fog created by the week—or you're deliberately provoking a break—which I, for one, don't want.

It could only be some kind of madness that would even let cross your mind the thought that I'd copy or have copied your Journal. No one has ever seen any of it. When the envelopes arrive, they are given to me sealed—and when I've read them, they're put, by me, in a place where no one but myself can have access to them. But if you don't trust me, boyo, say it straight out and you can have back, pronto, the whole works.

And about my talking about the Journal—I don't know what you mean. Believe it or not, I haven't said a word about it to anyone, except that once in a conversation with Wylie I said, in connection with a matter we were discussing (homosexuality, I think it was), that you had some intriguing ideas about it which I knew about because you showed me some notes you were making for a treatment of it in a book someday. I never—and if you don't believe me, Norman, that's your privilege—told a soul that you're keeping a journal.

I have talked a lot about *Deer Park*—to Ted, Ivan, Paul, Phil—everyone. I've said that it contains insights and perceptions that startled me, originating as they have from someone so young and so essentially inexperienced as you are.

And now to the matter of cross-fertilization or inter-fecundation. If you're so goddamn jealous of your ideas, keep them to yourself. I'm not so sure I'd miss them, anyhow. And observe, friend, I haven't used them so far. As for my ideas, you're welcome to them—whether we remain *hermanos* or not. I don't regard my thoughts as particularly precious and certainly have no necessity in me to hoard them.

As for your ideas, the truth about them is that, at present, they're really no more than interesting—worth talking over, considering, discussing. And where in hell do you get the megalomaniac notion that they're anything more than, in most cases, tentative propositions? To my mind some of them are good—that is, worthy of more thought. Some of them stink—that is, they're not worthy of development. Many of them are certainly not original—although you think they are, and many of them are screwed up.

I've refrained from commenting on every item in the journal purposely—and have discussed only a few of them with you purposely—because I've recognized the fact that you are concerned at present primarily with getting them down, getting them out of you, for later and calmer consideration. I'm astounded that now you seem to think of them as etched in granite, imperishable, monumental.

Finally, pal, I'm worried about you—and after these two letters, I think I have a reasonable cause for concern. There's a nastiness about them, Norman—they're like steeped in a stew of guilt and shame, a self-loathing. You're begging for a swift kick in the ass, you want me (someone) to stop you. You would feel justified and fulfilled and righteous if I responded in the way you half-want me to—if I told you to stuff it. And you would feel just about the same if I took these mouse drippings of yours and covered my head with them. I'm not going to do either. If you have the guts and I hope and think you have, you'll pull out of this and take whatever profit there may be in it. If you don't nobody's lost anything anyhow.

Sure, Norman, I'm a square and you're the king of the hipsters, I'm a stumble-bum and you're a genius, I'm a liver-lip, and a crook, a con-man, a gentleman, an old maid, a cliché artist—and you're the hep-boyo, the kid with the always open fly, the ace dong-wielder of all time, the glorious gourmet of gage . . .

Wise up, cocker,

Love,
Bob

P.S. Let's try to get together on a date for you to come down—if you want to, that is.

Dear Norman,

YOUR MANUSCRIPT IS BEING mailed today and should reach you
before the end of the week.

I am very glad that you are planning a visit to Baltimore, since
I think that only face-to-face will we be able to straighten out the
difficulties between us. Unfortunately, your visit here will have to
be delayed until after the middle of May, since I am committed for
every weekend between now and then and will very likely be in
California between the 11th and 17th of May.

I think one of our main troubles is that I haven't been completely
honest with you. I have pretended to sympathy with the whole
Lipton's deal that I really don't feel, and I think this pretense has
blocked basic communication and placed our relations in a false
light. Maybe this is what gives you the impression of "manipulating."
More than anything I want to be brothers and friends with you, and
I've missed you these past weeks. I think I have had too little trust in
your tolerance of my radically different concept of this whole matter
of Lipton's, and that I conceded initially there and, later, all over the
place until I became enmeshed in my own contradictions. I hope
I have underrated you, and that it's now possible to eat off clean
dishes.

Things here are in somewhat of a mess, and I don't have an
opportunity to write the long and more personal letter I hope to get
around to within a few days.

Meanwhile, love,
Bob

Dear Bob,

JUST A NOTE TO tell you how good I think our evening in
Philadelphia was. It was really very good for me and I want you to
know what a friend I think you are. I won't say more now because
I'm going blind getting *The Deer Park* ready for the printer and I'm
typing this out in a hurry.

Right now it looks like I'll be in California around the 1st of June,
so schedules look contradictory, eh Bobbo? Let me hear what your
schedule is—as I remember it was May 9th.

Love for the interim,
Norm

Dear Bob,

I CAME OVER TO MY studio today to do some work and found a letter from you which must have crossed mine. So since I'm not in a working mood, I think I'll write you a long one—there was so much I wanted to tell you the other day when we met in Philadelphia, and of course I was in bad shape—the cigarette withdrawal deal was hitting me in full force and I was just churning with anxiety. But one of the things that I believe has happened to me is that to a certain extent by the aid of Lipton's and other things I can pick a given direction for a week or more, assuming of course that I am not compulsive about the Lipton's, about which I'm not altogether convinced—the problem of course is that the internal world of L is so much more exciting, charged, and fabulous than the everyday world. However I suspect that I have certain built-in mechanisms which regulate the whole thing for when I push L too hard, I begin to lose its advantages. My weight goes down, my confidence goes down, my anxiety state takes away the pleasures of my sensitivity and I find in myself the desire to build up again. So for instance these days after a particularly active exhausting and debilitating (let it stand) week, I've been concerned the last couple of days to take care of myself and I'm building up, eating carefully, off L and off Seconal, and feeling relatively strong, calm, and with a desire to build weight and physical strength. Part of the problem over the last month was that I was working very hard on *The Deer Park* and in order to cut it up and go through it with a scalpel revealing what I had come to see was the core of the book under the surface moralizing, I needed the particular heightened sensitivity of L plus Seconal. But since it had to go on for too long a period of times, I wore myself down, and began to live too much on nerve and in anxiety. However, despite your skepticism I do believe in the self-analysis. What has happened to me is that I learned to get into my unconscious, to live there, to explore my conflicts, and what conflicts they are and when I come up for air, I find that over the long haul I do feel stronger, more confident, and more aware. One thing I think you have to realize about me is that I do contain a scientist in myself, a doctor if you will, and in a peculiar way the transference you speak of consists of a continuous internal dialogue between the doctor and the patient in me, and I'm far from sharing your idea that I'm merely entering my neurosis. In the act of entering it I discover all kinds of reasons and underpinnings to my neurotic habits of which I've been intellectually aware for years—but in seeing the restricting and compulsive character of them I realize the necessity to change. So I go out in the world in the following few days and as if I were a gambler I tackle little situations where I would have lost in the past and where I now feel I may be able to win. Sometimes I win and sometimes I lose—the victories are important, because the essence of changing a habit is to have a life-victory rather than a life-defeat. Defeats as I know you know merely send one running back to the habit. But I can take defeats better these days because the longer I go on with this self-analysis, the less I see it as a problem of will or pride, and more a business of patience, of digesting losses and trying to understand victories and what happens much more often—draws and partial victories. The bad part of it is that when I get too deep in L I feel at times an incredible anguish—I am not able to communicate, I feel burning desires to reach across to people, my paranoid urge to fuse is almost unlivable, and I have to wonder at times if I'm going mad. That scares me, and I pull up, and begin to build up again. But the process is fascinating.

One thing I've come to feel very strongly is that *The Deer Park* has to do well at least so far as I can affect its fortunes. I've learned about myself that I simply do not have the strength to do it all alone with the will and the pride of a Joyce. If I'm going to be able to express the very far removed but nonetheless potential genius in myself, I have to have certain victories along the way for victories nourish one, they allow new habits if one is ready to make new habits, they create a climate for one's thought—at least all this is true for me—when I feel most strong and confident, so I also feel most ready to tackle more, be more outrageous, bold, and creative in my thinking. Defeats shake my grasp on confidence. Some time I have to show you the reviews on *Barbary Shore*. They were vicious, Bob, and I believe I was unconsciously petrified when I understood how much I was hated, and how little capacity I had to fight back. Now, I think I know how to fight, and I want *The Deer Park* to succeed, because if it does I think it'll make a legend which will aid me greatly. You know—seven publishers turned it down and it turns out to be a small classic. The only thing I can see stopping it from success is a climate of unanimously bad reviews, and that I'm determined to prevent if I can. What I intend to do is to fuck all pride and stand-offishness and approach in the most canny way about twenty-five to fifty important writers—it I can get quotes from about four or five of them before the book comes out, I believe that people will wish to read it even with bad reviews, and moreover I suspect that a lot of reviewers in New York will not quite dare to attack the book as viciously as they did *Barbary*. So, Bobbo, I want to ask you for a favor in line with this. When you meet Huxley and Isherwood, I would like you to talk about the book a little, just enough to whet their curiosity, for they are two of the people I'm going to approach. Isherwood knows me slightly, and Huxley I met once, and I believe they're both sympathetic to me as a writer. Any anyway give them my regards.

I think I ought to try to explain something to you about how I feel about mysticism. You see the irony is that I don't like it, it's uncongenial to me, and when I talk to other mystics I get a pain in the ass. Nonetheless I find myself drawn to it *malgre moi*—at some of the deepest states of sensitivity I've entered the psychological reality is so intense, so self-evident that it's far easier to believe in a mystic entity or whole than to posit a totally imaginary and unreal construction. In other words what the realist calls imagination, I find myself believing is reality for I can hardly comprehend the experience as being one of artificial and baseless construction. One thing I have come to feel very definitely, and about this we would have to talk endlessly, is that there is such a thing as a death-instinct, that deep in our biology, perhaps in our cell-life itself, there is the knowledge that we do not die as such but instead enter the universe, and so when life becomes unendurable, or when our energy is worn out, death literally calls—we know it is not death but some new state of being. I know that I've found that this makes an enormous amount of sense in understanding things like suicides, murders, self-destructive activities, etc., provided of course that death itself is understood as a good or a partial good. To posit, as I believe Freud did, a death-instinct which leads merely to oblivion, makes far less sense in terms of human conduct. The life instinct as I see it depends of course upon a relatively powerful ego with its counter-part of relatively low sensitivity. For the state of high sensitivity with its almost telepathic awareness of other people's unconsciousnesses is not easily endurable what with one's awareness of danger, hostility, etc. etc. To me, mysticism is a call to death, and since I enjoy life much more these days, at least a good deal of the time, the liver in me, the novelist, the scientist, etc. is torn between leaving sensi-tivity and its quick concomitant of knowledge for the pleasure of just enjoying things. Anyway we have to talk about this.

A word about the Journal. I haven't written anything on it that you haven't seen. Looking back on it now I believe that much of its composition was a first outpouring and dissolution of my old intel-lectual baggage as if before I could enter my unconscious, I had like most intellectuals in analysis to go through an enormous sympa-thetic discharge of intellectual concepts—the doors to my uncon-scious always having been guarded by my intellectual barriers. These days I don't think as a Journaleer—instead of being confident and manic in my intellectual notions I have been testing some of the general assumptions I came up with in quiet ways and that has been secondary to work on *The Deer Park*, general self-analysis, etc.

Norman

Dear Bob,

T HAT WAS A GOOD talk we had on the phone and I wish we could get
together soon. Everything is in a jam here. I'm working overtime
on *The Deer Park*, trying to do the impossible, alternate critical
detachment with creative immediacy—very close to the psychopathic, you know—and somehow pull off a small miracle which,
between us, I doubt if I will do. Still, the book will be a little better
and I'll have learned something in the process, I hope.

You sounded very tired on the phone and while I know your
amazing capacity to recuperate quickly, I hope that you will take
your simple bodily needs into account and take off a few days now
and again over the summer, whether your patients get p.o.'ed or
not. I've been living for a good many months now pushed past the
normal output of my energy, and it can set up a vicious circle.

Let me hear from you when you get a chance. I know you're very
busy and your correspondence must be heavy, but if you have an odd
moment drop a note.

Love,
Norm

Dear Norman,

THE DAYS GO BY and I find myself more hard pressed for time to write to you. Today I'm cutting through the crap to do what I've been wanting to do for weeks—spend a few minutes with my brother. Bingo, I have missed you. Actually, my inability to write has not been due entirely to other preoccupations, but due to the fact that—I've been—as you seem to sense—close to illness with exhaustion. About two weeks before I went to California I picked up a viral infection. Out there I seem to have been able to pickle it in alcohol and burn it to an ember with the excitement. On my return it flared up—busting out this last week with severe gut pain, agonies in my back and chest, and a sort of quacking ague. Over the weekend I loaded myself with stuff and slept almost continuously. Today I'm better—and even have a few ideas. I hope I've got it licked—because despite my notorious hypochondria I resent, hate, despise the weaknesses of my body.

Genug!

I got back on the book this morning. There remains to be done only the homosexuality paper, the one on character-and-politics, and a general introduction. Rinehart announced it already for January, and I've agreed to talk on it at Town Hall on Feb. 8. So I've got to hustle to get the ms. in.

The homosexuality paper, in its original form, now seems gibberish to me. I'm going to tear it apart and put it in the perspective of the book, the perspective of conformity. Now I believe immersion in negative rebellion, the compromise between the protestant, evolutionary instinct and the conformist pressure on the erotic desires. Immersion is a way of conforming—and whereas I once thought social attitudes were changing, I now no longer believe that's so—what's happening is that our anti-sex culture is forcing more and more persons into homosexuality, in negative rebellion, and the [garbled] now, becoming prevalent, is becoming the new conformist pattern. As you see, the whole thing isn't entirely clear yet—but the golden nugget is in there someplace. I hope to dig it out in the next few days.

With the book out of the way—I hope in a few weeks—I'm going to knock off writing for the summer. I'll devote myself, I think, to pushing the schemes for realizing something from previous work, and maybe the new house. About the former, it looks like the plans to rush into production of television films based on *The Fifty-Minute Hour* will have to be delayed. The problem now seems to be that "spots" on the networks for the next year are all contracted for, and it will be at least a year until room can be made for the program. Meanwhile, abstracts are (so Harold Ober says) being drawn with Maxwell for me to do something similar (provide story synopses and be consultant) for him beginning now. I've stalled about it as long as I could, but it looks like the chips are down now and I've got to act. I may have to go out to Lost Angeles again soon to get the final details settled—but I'm not going without a real commitment.

The house we're moving into in August represents something big for all of us. As far as I'm concerned, I'm intending to use it for a real change in my style of life. I'm hoping to alter the pattern somewhat . . . but this is something we'll be talking about.

You'll be surprised, I know, and maybe a little chagrined, to learn that I've resigned from my state job as of July 1. No more prison work—and I'm going to miss it. But I had to do it. There was a major change made in the fiscal set-up of the state, a change that would bring my work under the direction of department agencies and people unfriendly to me and my methods. I would be forced, if I remained, to give up my independence and put in a very subordinate position. The best (actually the only) solution was to resign. This I did—although it means reducing my income by about 5 thousand a year—which, however, I can easily make up elsewhere if I wish.

Again—*genug!*

Now what of you? When I talked with you, and from your note, I gathered you are literally re-writing *Deer Park*. I hope it's going well and I'm very eager to see where you come out. As I promised I would, I've been talking it up everywhere—trying to create where I can an atmosphere of excited anticipation. For myself, you know I can hardly wait for its publication.

Jeez, Norman—these pages hardly scratch what I have to tell you and what I want to talk with you about. We've simply got to get a few days together. Let me know when you'll be ready to come down. If I can get this bug out of me and start percolating again, I'll be in shape to make some plans. Certainly you've got to get here before you go West.

Cy and Billie will be coming down this weekend. Since we're not going to Long Island this summer, this visit will have to do all of us for the good times together we should be having in the next two months. Maybe we can fix it for a weekend in August in Amagansett.

Write when you can—but make it soon.

Love,
Bob

Dear Norman,

PERHAPS YOU WILL FORGIVE my silence when you learn that all the nightmares have finally had triplets and have caught up with me. As of this writing, I am a patient at John Hopkins Hospital, where they are going to try to give me back my tight ass hole. There is nothing more to say, except love.

Bob

P.S. Last week I was a patient at the Johns Hopkins in New York and Billie and Cy came to see me at Johnnie's urgent request, since she needed Billie. I asked them not to disturb you with all this worry, and that's why you weren't told. I would be very grateful to you if you would call them and tell them what's happened.

(Dictated but not read or signed.)

And then what happened is that I started smoking marijuana and then the marijuana took over. And there came a time when that marijuana became King Marijuana. It determined everything, including my friendships. If you wouldn't smoke marijuana, if you wouldn't go on a trip with me, you weren't my friend. And he was aghast. He was aghast on several counts. One of them was selfish. As a rising analyst, he could hardly be caught having a friend who was not only a huge smoker, but had turned him into one. So he had to be self-protective. He had his family, after all, his reputation and everything. So he was not moving on that.

And so he'd try to write me lectures. Those lectures used to drive me wild because I was not about to be lectured to. The wild side of me would come out. It was like, "If you don't like my smoking, go fuck yourself." I was wild. "This is my inkling if you're not with me, you're not my friend." He was upset, I think, by seeing an ugly and ruthless side of myself that he was perhaps not wholly prepared for until then. In other words, I was not as nice a guy as I had seemed. And from my point of view, he was not as generous a guy as I had thought. And so this began to poison our relationship to a degree.

And then as time went, we drifted apart a bit because of it. And then he began to get ill. He had a problem; he often said to me "I'm going to die young." What it was is he had high blood pressure, which was hard to reduce because the medicines used to reduce it widened the hole in one of the heart valves. This was at a point when they couldn't operate on heart valves. Today I'm sure he'd be alive. But in those days, he had this problem. One medicine he needed was there to kill him on the other side. So at a certain point it got hopeless.

He was in his early forties and I talked to him on the phone one day and he said "There's nothing they can do; I'm going to die." And he burst into tears. And I was so cold and so full of anger at where we'd gotten and when I look back, it was one of the most unpleasant moments in my life. I didn't feel a fucking thing for him. I felt contempt that he was weakened. You see, my feeling was: "We're soldiers and if we die, we die." I have that feeling now; it's a lot easier now, I can assure you. But I remember not being sympathetic. Going through the dull motions of being sympathetic, the way one does when one's not there with a friend, but not really giving him what he needed. And I didn't believe he was going to die.

And then, some weeks later, he died. And that was one of the great blows of my life because I couldn't believe it. And then I felt woe, and then I felt contrition. And then I remember at his funeral, his memorial service, I remember speaking and talking about him and creating a sensation at the memorial service because I was talking about all his many wonderful qualities and I said, "And on top of all that, he was a rogue." Whohooohoo went through the audience at the memorial service. There's his wife, his widow and all. But it was true; he'd have fucked anything with legs that really wanted him. His children were affected terribly by the death. They adored their father.

I didn't know them well enough to know if they adored him more than they adored her, but it would be easy to make such a statement because she was more forbidding. She had a strong disposition; she had a very strong sense of what's was right and what's wrong, whereas he was more adaptable. I'm sure she got into more intense set-tos with the children than he did, whereas he was their Papa and they adored him. So they may never have recovered altogether. It was really tough.

ENDNOTES

INTRODUCTION

VII   *Lipton's.* The original typescript is in the Mailer archive at the Harry Ransom Center, University of Texas–Austin. This edition was prepared from the carbon copy, which Mailer gave to Lennon in the early 2000s.

VIII   **"The White Negro."** First published in *Dissent* (summer 1957), it was reprinted in *Advertisements for Myself* (1959). In both it contained the same subtitle: "Superficial Reflections on the Hipster." City Lights Press in San Francisco published it as a pamphlet in 1959, and reprinted it perhaps a dozen times into the 1970s. The cover was a reverse negative shot of an archetypal hipster, rumored for years to be Paul Newman, but identified as photojournalist Harry Redl.

VIII   *Cannibals and Christians.* The conflicting forces in *Cannibals and Christians* mirror the homeodynamic-sociostatic opposition in *Lipton's.* The Cannibals are the forces of reaction stretching from the Republican Party to "the ghosts of Nazis"; the Christians are the party of revolution and change, and cover the spectrum from L.B.J. to Mao Tse-tung. *The Armies of the Night* is as searching a self-analysis as *Lipton's,* and the best presentation of Mailer's ultimate political identity as Left-conservative. The nice Jewish boy from Brooklyn is again the "despised" self-image. *Ancient Evenings* is, among other things, a further exploration of Mailer's interest in the double or hidden meanings of words, first essayed in *Lipton's.* *Harlot's Ghost* presents an elaborate rethinking of the duality of human identity, discussed at length in *Lipton's,* as the Alpha-Omega theory of Kittredge Gardiner, a CIA analyst.

X   **Freud and Marx.** Mailer discusses the need for "a radical bridge from Marx to Freud" in *Advertisements*, p. 365. Mailer's second novel, *Barbary Shore* (1951), contains his most extended comments on Marx and his followers. See his brief essay, "Freud," written around the time of *Lipton's*, in Mailer, Norman (2013), *Mind of an Outlaw*. New York: Random House, Sipiora, Phillip, ed.

X   *Prescription for Rebellion.* Dr. Lindner's fourth book was published by Rinehart and Co., on May 27, 1952. His first book, *Rebel Without a Cause: The Hypnoanalysis of a Criminal Psychopath* (1944) was sold to Warner Brothers and made into a 1955 film of the same title starring James Dean, although the title is the only connection to the book. Lindner wrote or edited a total of seven books. His last, posthumous book *Must You Conform?* came out on May 1, 1956.

XI   *An American Dream.* Shago Martin, an extraordinarily talented jazz singer who has a relationship with Cherry, the girlfriend of the novel's protagonist, Stephen Rojack. Mailer's fourth wife, Beverly Bentley (1930–2018), had a long-term relationship with Miles Davis before she met Mailer.

XI   **Stitt.** Mailer was friendly with Sonny Stitt (1924–1982), one of the greatest bebop jazz saxophonists. Stitt's iconic 1956 recording of "Autumn in New York" was played as the audience filed into Carnegie Hall for Mailer's memorial, April 9, 2008.

XII   **Marlon Brando.** Mailer met Brando (1924–1984) in Hollywood in 1949, and saw him on and off over the decades. He reviewed *Last Tango in Paris* in the *New York Review of Books* (May 17, 1973), rpt. *Pieces and Pontifications* (1982). After inserting a small piece of paper in front of his teeth, Mailer continued to give imitations of Brando in *Waterfront* (1954), which he saw just before he began *Lipton's*.

XII	**Hilary Mills.** Mills, Hilary (1982). *Mailer: A Biography*. New York: McGraw-Hill. p. 129.
XIV	**Richard Poirier.** Mailer met and became friendly with Poirier (1925–2009), who reviewed several of Mailer's books and wrote what is still the most probing and elegant critical study of Mailer, a 1972 volume in the Viking Modern Masters series, *Norman Mailer* (1972).
XIV	**comment he made.** From "Rugged Times" by Lillian Ross (*New Yorker*, October 23, 1948). Reprinted in Lennon (*Conversations with Norman Mailer* [1988, University of Mississippi Press, pp. 12–13]). *The Naked and the Dead*, published on May 6, 1948, remained on the *New York Times* list for sixty-two weeks, until the summer of 1949, and for nineteen weeks was number 1. *Barbary Shore*, published on May 24, 1951, made it for three weeks, and then sank like a rock. It received the worst reviews of any of Mailer's forty-odd books. *Time* called it "paceless, tasteless and graceless."
XV	***Dissent.*** Mailer was on the editorial board of this leftist journal from the early 1950s to the mid-1980s, and contributed several essays and reviews to it.
XV	**"Quickly."** Mailer's column ran from January 11 to May 5, 1956. He retired from his column over a dispute about the copyediting of his column. The majority of the columns are reprinted in *Advertisements*.
XV	**Jules Feiffer.** One of the greatest American satirists, Feiffer (b. 1929) is also a novelist. His strip *Sick Sick Sick* ran from 1956 to 1997 in the *Village Voice*. See Mailer's comments on Feiffer in an interview with Lennon, and Feiffer's on Mailer in Olshaker, Mark (2014). "Walking into the Zeitgeist: A Conversation with Jules Feiffer," *The Mailer Review*. 8 (1): 21–51.
XVI	**he said later.** See Stratton, Richard (November–December 2004). "Norman Mailer on Pot." *High Times*. pp. 44, 88.

ENTRIES

4/3   **Stanley Rinehart.** President of the firm of Rinehart and Co., Stanley Rinehart Jr. (1897–1969) wrote a letter comparing *The Naked and the Dead* to the work of Hemingway and Dos Passos that was printed on the dust jacket of the first edition. But in late November 1954, with an ad for *The Deer Park* already published, Rinehart canceled the novel's publication after Mailer refused to cut a sexually explicit scene. Later, Mailer sued and received the remainder of his advance for the novel.

4/3   *The Deer Park.* Mailer's third novel, *The Deer Park* (1955), set in a Palm Springs–like resort town in southern California where the elite of the film world go for relaxation, deal-making, and various shenanigans, revolves around the choice faced by a leftist film director, Charles Eitel: testify before a Red-hunting congressional committee or lose his prominent position in Hollywood. Mailer began final revisions on *The Deer Park* immediately after the four months he was writing *Lipton's,* and includes in the journal comments on his aspirations for the novel and his plans for its characters in future works.

5/4   **The Concentration camp novel.** Titled "The City of God," and begun in the early 1950s, it was never completed; only a fragment exists in the Harry Ransom Center at the University of Texas–Austin, home of the Mailer Archive. Initially, Mailer's setting was a Soviet concentration camp; he later changed it to a German camp (see entry **471**). He finally published the novel, his last, *The Castle in the Forest,* in 2007.

6/4   **apprehension of the universe.** The richest exploration of Mailer's views on the pre-knowledge of children is in the novel fragment "The Book of the First-Born," as yet unpublished.

6/4   **Susie.** Susan Mailer, the only child of Mailer and his first wife Beatrice Silverman, and the oldest of his nine children, was born in Hollywood, August 28, 1949.

7/4   **Herbert A.** Mailer met Herbert Aptheker (1915–2003), a blacklisted communist intellectual and historian of African Americans in the United States, through mutual friends associated with *Dissent*, a leftist, anti-communist journal launched in 1954. Mailer served on its editorial board for over twenty years.

8/4   **In modern jazz.** During the 1950s and 1960s, Mailer went to clubs in Greenwich Village and heard all the great jazz musicians: Miles Davis, Charlie Mingus, Dizzy Gillespie, Dave Brubeck, Thelonious Monk, and Sonny Stitt, who became a friend. In both *Lipton's* and "The White Negro," jazz is linked with marijuana, sex and the lives of hipsters in the demimonde. Miles Davis, who had a long relationship with Mailer's fourth wife Beverly Bentley (1930–2018), was a model for Shago Martin, the jazz singer in *An American Dream* (1965).

9/5   **Thoreau's beautiful remark.** The most quoted line from *Walden; or, Life in the Woods* (1854) by Henry David Thoreau (1817–1862).

DECEMBER 8, 1954

13/7   **Romain.** A prolific French novelist (of Litvak origins), Romain Gary (1914–1980) was also an aviator during World War II and a postwar diplomat. Mailer met him in Paris in 1947–1948, and became reacquainted with him when Gary headed the French delegation to the United Nations in the early 1950s.

14/7   **her across my lap.** Adele Morales (1925–2015), who he married in April 1954, was Mailer's second wife. The mother of his daughters Danielle (b. 1957), and Elizabeth Anne (b. 1959), she separated from Mailer in early 1961 a few months after he stabbed her with a penknife, just missing her heart. He pled guilty to felonious assault and was given a suspended sentence. They divorced in 1962.

25/9 **opposite echo.** A great deal of *Lipton's* is given over to Mailer's theories about the hidden meanings and relations between words. Although his linguistic theories are wrong-headed, his ruminations demonstrate his desire to peel back reality to reveal the hidden structures of social existence embedded in language.

26/9 **extraordinary quality.** Mailer was intrigued by the possibility that television's monotony had a deadening effect on viewers. He explored his ideas on the medium in a long essay in *Esquire* (November 1977), titled "Of a Small and Modest Malignancy, Wicked and Bristling with Dots," reprinted in *Pieces and Pontifications* (1982).

31/10 **The saint and the psychopath are twins.** Here is the first mention of a linkage that obsessed Mailer for decades, a belief, as he put it in *Existential Errands* (1972), that "the saint and the psychopath were united to one another, and different to the mass of men. They were closer to existence. They shared a sense of the present so powerful that memory, caution, precedent, tradition, commonplace, project, and future enterprise were nerveless before the sense of the present in their mind and body. In their most incandescent states, they existed for their next breath, and so were indistinguishable from one another." He planned to use his ideas on this duality in a thousand-page book titled *A Psychology of the Orgy*. Mailer drew on his definition of the psychopath a few years later in "The White Negro," which is arguably the greatest fruit of *Lipton's*. In the opening of the essay, he states that the psychopath seeks to "explore that domain of experience where security is boredom and therefore sickness, and one exists in the present, in that enormous present which is without past or future or planned intention." It is easy to find dozens of passages in *Lipton's* that resurface conceptually or syntactically or both in the essay.

35/11	**Bob's.** Robert Lindner (1914–1956) was a prominent Baltimore psychoanalyst and writer. Author of several books, among them *Rebel Without a Cause* (1944), *Prescription for Rebellion* (1952), *The Fifty Minute Hour* (1955), and *Must you Conform?* (1956). Initially Mailer and Lindner were drawn together by their disgust with Senator Joseph McCarthy's hunt for Communists in government, and the dull fog of conformity rolling over the country, as well as distaste for President Eisenhower (who Mailer thought was "awful, because he was so middle-of-the-road American"), their relationship deepened when they recognized their similar ambitions and how they might help each other. Mailer and Lindner had a close friendship for four years, until Lindner's death in 1956. While Mailer was writing *Lipton's*, he sent Lindner chunks of the journal to discuss when they met. See also the Introduction to the Mailer/Lindner Correspondence in this volume.
37/12	**Marion Faye.** Mailer's antihero for a post-Hiroshima world in *The Deer Park*, Faye (son of Dorothea O'Faye, a former singer who presides over a drunken salon in Desert D'Or, Mailer's name for Palm Springs, California), is the archetypal hipster. A bisexual pimp and drug dealer, he is the novel's dark conscience, the polar opposite of Charles Eitel. Mailer planned to use Faye as a centripetal character in the seven novels that he planned and failed to write as sequels to *The Deer Park*.
39/12	**Mendes-France.** French Minister of Foreign Affairs, 1954–1955, Pierre Mendès-France (1907–1982), wrote an account of his 1941 escape from a Vichy prison, "Escape: How I Fled to Freedom," in the December 24, 1954, issue of *Collier's*.
43/13	**Rhoda L.** Lifelong friend of Mailer's sister Barbara, Rhoda Lazare (b. 1926) was introduced to her husband, Daniel Wolf, by Mailer.

45/16   **Spengler is a great writer.** Mailer read the two-volume masterwork *The Decline of the West* (1932) of Oswald Spengler (1880–1936) while overseas in World War II, and admired its sweeping exposition of world history, one that rejected a linear progressive view of social development in favor of a cyclical interpretation of the rise and fall of civilizations.

46/16   **Brubeck and Desmond.** Dave Brubeck (1920–2012), a composer and pianist, and Paul Desmond (1924–1977), a composer and saxophonist, were key figures in the West Coast cool jazz movement of the 1950s, playing together as members of the Dave Brubeck Quartet from 1951 to 1968.

53/18   **Millie.** A friend and distant cousin of Mailer's, Millie Brower had the lead in his 1947 experimental film, *Millie's Dream.*

54/19   **Danny.** A close friend of Mailer's in the 1950s, Daniel Wolf (1915–1996), the cofounder of the *Village Voice*, introduced Mailer to his second wife, Adele Morales.

54/19   **Bea.** Beatrice Silverman (1922–2016) was Mailer's first wife. They met when she was a student at Boston University and he was at Harvard. They married in 1944, and their only child, Susan, was born in 1949. After their divorce in January 1952, Silverman moved to Mexico, married Steve Chavez, and became an MD psychiatrist.

57/20   **the hipster.** Someone who is "hip," or in the know, especially about jazz and bohemian life. The term goes back to the 1940s, when it was used to describe white youths who were followers of black jazz artists. Later, it was popularized by Jack Kerouac, Allen Ginsberg, and Mailer to describe alienated individuals, mainly living in New York and San Francisco, who had their own argot and ethos. In a short piece in *Advertisements for Myself*, "Hipster and Beatnik: A Footnote to 'The White Negro,'" Mailer distinguishes between the beatnik and the hipster. Both believe, he says, that "society is the prison of the nervous system." But while beatniks are attracted to mysticism and a contemplation of the mysteries of the universe, hipsters are more competitive, and ready to juggle "the perils of getting your kicks in this world, against the hell (or prison) of paying for them in the next." Mailer's beatniks are left-wing and generally pacifist; his hipsters, whose "psychic style derives from the best Negroes to come up from the bottom," are open to violence, seek power, and are generally apolitical. He ends by noting that "for years now, they have lived side by side, hipster and beatnik, white Negro and crippled saint."

60/21 **Antacid Analgesic.** It is unclear if Mailer understood how and why these two drugs are combined in medicines such as Alka-Seltzer, the antacid protecting the stomach from the pain-killing ingredients in the analgesic. It is likely that he conceived of the drugs as opposed in ways that mimic the struggle between soul and society that he elaborates on throughout *Lipton's*.

64/23 **Ernie Kovacs.** One of the pioneers of television comedy, Kovacs (1919–1962) was irreverent, improvisational, and satirical. In a series of weekly programs and specials in the 1950s and 1960s, his wildly varied sketches breached the fourth wall, taking the camera behind the scenes and into the street. His work influenced the formats of many future comedy series, including *Rowan & Martin's Laugh-In* and *Saturday Night Live*. Mailer praised the unscripted and unhackneyed television antics of Kovacs, George Gobel, and Steve Allen in his February 22, 1956 *Village Voice* column.

DECEMBER 29, 1954

77/28 **the word Red in American political life.** The Second Red Scare from 1950 to 1956 (the first took place in the years 1919–1921) was characterized by rabid anti-communism and the hunt for communist sympathizers, as well as strong anti-Stalinist movements. Joseph McCarthy (1908–1957), Republican senator from Wisconsin, was the leading red-baiter of the period. Mailer took part in the struggle against McCarthy and his followers, for example, aligning himself publicly with blacklisted Hollywood actors and writers.

78/29   **Sergius.** The narrator of *The Deer Park*, Sergius O'Shaugnessey, is a veteran U.S. Air Force pilot who flew combat missions in Korea. After his discharge, he settles in Desert D'Or, where he has an affair with movie star Lulu Meyers.

79/29   **Lulu.** Lulu Meyers, a Hollywood actress in *The Deer Park* who was once married to Charles Eitel, aspires to be the most popular actress in America and has an affair with Sergius O'Shaugnessey through most of the novel.

79/29   **"And I realized . . ."** The long paragraph following these words describing how Lulu's life had become nothing but a series of screen images was intended by Mailer to be used in the final draft of *The Deer Park*, and echoes of it can be seen in chapter 17. Mailer discusses the impoverishment of the lives of movie stars again in his biography of Marilyn Monroe, *Marilyn* (1973).

83/29   **Elena.** Elena Esposito is the lover and later wife of Charles Eitel in *The Deer Park*. Their love affair is one of Mailer's finest fictional creations. Mailer based her character on his wife Adele.

84/30   **Don Beda.** A minor character in *The Deer Park*, Don Beda is a wife swapper who, along with his wife, Zenelia, takes part in an orgy with Eitel and Lulu.

85/30   **My mother . . . my father.** Mailer's mother, Fanny (1891–1985), the hardworking motor of the family, held down various jobs until she was in her seventies. His father, Isaac B. ("Barney") (1892–1972), an accountant, was a secret and unrepentant gambler for all of his married life who was bailed out many times by family members. Mailer admired his rebellious secret life.

85/31   **the Yipper.** An unknown reference.

86/31   **Jean Malaquais.** A Polish Jew (real name Vladimir
Malacki) whose parents perished in the Holocaust, Jean
Malaquais (1909–1998) was a veteran of the Spanish Civil
War. Mailer has often said that Malaquais influenced
him intellectually more than anyone else. They met in
Paris in 1947 and became close friends a year later when
Malaquais was translating *The Naked and the Dead* into
French. Malaquais and his first wife Galy lived with the
Mailers when they spent a year in Hollywood, 1949–1950.
During their time together, Malaquais, who wrote several
novels, informally tutored Mailer on leftist thought and
the history of the Russian Revolution. See Mailer's "My
Friend, Jean Malaquais," an introduction to Malaquais's
1954 novel, *The Joker*, rpt., *Pieces and Pontifications*.

94/31   **(another adventurer).** Mailer's fascination with spies
and counterintelligence reached its apex in 1991 with the
publication of *Harlot's Ghost* (1991), a novelistic depiction
of the history of the CIA from the end of World War II to
the death of President Kennedy. He claimed, and believed,
that some of his furtive extramarital romantic entangle-
ments in the 1980s while he was writing the novel gave
him psychological purchase on the double life of spies.

104/33   **sending his journal.** Mailer did not add Faye's journal
to the final draft of *The Deer Park*, which he completed
in the summer of 1955. Over the next six or seven years,
however, he made a few half-hearted attempts to write a
sequel to the novel, and Faye's notes on his experiments
with marijuana in prison are part of these unpublished
fragments.

107/34   **Teddy Pope.** In *The Deer Park*, a handsome gay actor
who is forced to play straight, masculine roles by the
homophobic Hollywood film industry. At one point, his
producer, Herman Teppis, tries to force him to marry
Lulu Meyers. Mailer admitted and rejected his earlier
antigay bias in an essay, "The Homosexual Villain,"
that he wrote shortly after completing *The Deer Park*

for *One: the Homosexual Magazine* (January, 1955), rpt. *Advertisements for Myself.*

DECEMBER 31, 1954

125/37   **Joyce . . . Proust . . . Mann and Gide.** Four of the great novelists whose company Mailer in his thirties hoped to join. Dostoyevsky, Stendhal, Tolstoy, Kafka, Faulkner, and Hemingway were also part of his desired peer group. See *Advertisements for Myself,* 477.

128/38   **tape recorder.** Mailer did buy one, as later notes indicate. A few of the recordings can be found in the Mailer Archive at the Harry Ransom Center, University of Texas at Austin.

132/39   **Brando. Bankhead. Taylor.** Three major actors who Mailer admired and saw on Broadway: Marlon Brando (1924–2004) in *A Streetcar Named Desire*; Tallulah Bankhead (1902–1968) in *The Little Foxes*; and Laurette Taylor (1883–1946) in *The Glass Menagerie.* Mailer met Brando during the year (1949–1950) he spent in Hollywood trying to write screenplays.

138/40   **Devlin.** Charles Devlin was an impecunious leftist writer who lived in the roominghouse at 20 Remsen Street in Brooklyn where Mailer had a studio and wrote the bulk of *The Naked and the Dead* (1948). Mailer was grateful for his help in editing *Naked* and said so in the novel's acknowledgments. Their letters often contained insults, but their friendship persisted. Devlin was the physical model for McLeod in *Barbary Shore* (1951).

140/40   **Wilhelm Reich.** An Austrian psychiatrist and psychoanalyst who worked with Freud, Reich (1897–1957) was the author of many clinical works, including *The Function of the Orgasm* (1942). He fled to the United States when the Nazis came to power. His eccentric and controversial theory of orgone energy, and the phone-booth-size orgone accumulators he invented, got him into legal trouble, and he was sent to federal prison, where he died. Mailer was influenced by Reich's ideas about sexual repression and character armor and built his own orgone box.

141/41   **Eitel.** Charles Francis Eitel (I-tell is the pronunciation), the protagonist of *The Deer Park*, is a blacklisted film director, who names former communists to a congressional committee.

141/41   **Teppis.** Herman Teppis, the head of Supreme Studios in *The Deer Park*, is an unscrupulous movie producer who manipulates actors for his own benefit.

147/42   **dial NERVOUS.** In the 1950s, and perhaps earlier, one could get the correct time by dialing this word, as confirmed in Norman Vincent Peale's *The Amazing Power of Positive Thinking* (1952).

150/42   **kicked off hipsterism.** Mailer was perhaps the first writer to apprehend the causal links between the bomb, the concentration camps of Nazi Germany, the Black Power movement, and the sexual revolution, as delineated in "The White Negro." The opening sentence reads: "Probably, we will never be able to determine the psychic havoc of the concentration camps and the atom bomb upon the unconscious mind of everyone alive these days."

155/43   **send him these notes.** Mailer sent Lindner a sheaf of pages from *Lipton's* perhaps every two weeks or so, and Lindner would reply in the letters included in this edition, over the phone, or in person when they met in New York or Baltimore. Lindner was Mailer's one-person audience for *Lipton's*, as well as his informal analyst, as noted in the introduction.

155/43   **Rosen.** A physical therapist, Marion Rosen (1914–2012) created the Rosen Method of psychological therapy, a program of therapeutic posture, breathing, and bodywork exercises that purportedly helps patients access their unconscious more easily.

156/43   **Verlaine and Rimbaud.** Paul Verlaine (1844–1896), a major symbolist poet, took in Arthur Rimbaud (1854–1891), an aspiring writer whose work prefigured surrealism, after he left home at the age of seventeen. The two men had a tempestuous drug- and alcohol-fueled romantic and literary relationship for two years. Mailer used their competitive/collaborative relationship, along with that of Marx and Friedrich Engels, as provisional models for his with Lindner.

156/44   **Gide.** A major French novelist and autobiographer, André Gide (1869–1951) won the Nobel Prize in 1947. Mailer cited the influence of Gide's *Corydon* (Paris: Nouvelle Revue Française, 1924) on his self-interviews collected in *The Presidential Papers* (1963) and *Cannibals and Christians* (1966). One of the epigraphs to *The Deer Park* is Gide's advice to his critics: "Please do not understand me too quickly."

156/44   **Ivan von Auw.** Literary agent (1903–1991) at the Harold Ober Agency.

156/44   **Gertrude Stein.** Mailer's opinion of Stein (1874–1946), one of modernism's major figures, fluctuated over the years. He wrote of her androgynous appearance and relationship with Picasso in *Portrait of Picasso as a Young Man.*

156/44   **Jonesie.** Mailer met James Jones (1921–1977) in 1952, shortly after he gave an admiring blurb to Jones's 1951 novel, *From Here to Eternity.* They became close friends almost immediately, in part because of the experiences they shared. Both were young and had written war novels set in the Pacific; both books had enjoyed fantastic sales and reviews; both became famous overnight. Mailer said later, "We felt like the touchdown twins." Although it would be brief, his relationship with Jones would be the most intense male friendship of his life.

156/44   **Johnnie.** Eleanor "Johnnie" Johnson (1910–1996) met Lindner while he was a graduate student at Cornell University. They were married in 1937. Mailer described her as "a sort of pepper pot blonde, pepper pot fire . . . full of strong feelings, full of love, full of lust, full of fire, full of the inability to pardon."

156/44   **Adeline.** A college friend of Mailer's sister Barbara at Radcliffe, Adeline (née Lubell) Naiman (1925–2011), was a junior editor at Little, Brown in 1946 when she heard about Mailer's novel from her. In January 1946, before he was discharged, she asked to see a rough draft, and in September, Mailer sent her the first 184 pages. She told her superiors it would be "the finest American novel to come out of the war."

156/44   **Gandy.** A painter known for sensuous, figural paintings done with impasto technique, Gandy Brody (1925–1965) met Mailer in the early 1950s, and visited him several times in Mexico.

156/44   **Miles and Barbara Forst.** Miles Forst (1923–2006), an artist and teacher, was an important member of the New York School of Abstract Expressionism. He and his first wife, Barbara, divorced after fourteen years of marriage.

156/44   **Mickey Knox.** Mailer met Knox (1921–2013), an actor, during his first trip to Hollywood in 1948. They became good friends and in June 1951, Mailer accompanied Knox on a cross-country drive to California. On the way to Hollywood they made a twenty-minute detour through Palm Springs, which Mailer was scouting as a possible setting for the novel that became *The Deer Park.* Mailer wrote more letters to Knox, a blacklisted actor and acting coach who lived in Rome for decades, than to anyone else except his first wife, Bea. See Knox's memoir, *The Good, the Bad, the Dolce Vita: The Adventures of an Actor in Hollywood, Paris and Rome* (2004).

156/44   **Toby.** Toby Schneebaum (1922–2005), was an artist, AIDS activist, and anthropologist who wrote a memoir, *Keep the River on Your Right* (1969) about his trip to Peru, where he lived with a cannibal tribe. Mailer wrote that Schneebaum, his New York neighbor, lent him Donald Webster Cory's

The Homosexual in America (1951), the reading of which led Mailer to revise his views on gays.

156/44 **Mike.** Mike Harrington (1928–1989), an American political theorist and the author of a groundbreaking study of poverty in the United States, *The Other America* (1962). Harrington and Mailer met at editorial meetings of *Dissent* magazine and became friendly.

158/45 **Croft.** Sam Croft is the fearless, sadistic platoon sergeant who contrives the death of Lieutenant William Hearn in *The Naked and the Dead.*

158/45 **Hollingsworth.** Leroy Hollingsworth is the FBI agent who interrogates the ex-Stalinist William McLeod in a Brooklyn roominghouse, the setting for Mailer's second novel, *Barbary Shore.*

158/45 **Lannie.** Lannie Madison is a deranged young woman of leftist leanings who interacts with the cast of characters in *Barbary Shore.*

158/45 **McLeod.** William McLeod is a former communist "hangman" who renounces Stalinism and preaches a variant of Trotskyism in *Barbary Shore.*

158/45 **Lovett.** The amnesiac war veteran and the narrator of *Barbary Shore*, Mickey Lovett carries McLeod's political message into the future.

160/46 ***Antacid Analgesique.*** Pondered and discussed for years, this behemoth was never written, one of several such works Mailer projected.

JANUARY 3, 1955

171/49 **Malraux.** French novelist and Minister of Culture under President de Gaulle, André Malraux (1901–1976) was one of Mailer's heroes when he was at Harvard. Malraux's *Man's Fate* (1933) was one of Mailer's models for his long story, "A Calculus at Heaven" (1944), reprinted in *Advertisements for Myself.*

171/49 **Gary.** Romain Gary, cf. **13/7.**

175/50   **Dizzy Gillespie.** Mailer heard Gillespie (1917–1993), one of the great jazz trumpeters and also a composer, many times in New York jazz clubs.

182/51   **Steve Allen.** A multitalented composer and comedian, Allen (1921–2000) was one of the creators of the television talk show. He and Mailer became friendly in the mid-1950s.

187/52   **Ted Amussen.** An editor at Rinehart and Co. for both Mailer and Lindner, Theodore Amussen (1915–1988) was instrumental in Mailer signing a contract for *The Naked and the Dead*.

187/52   **Stan Rinehart.** See **4/3**.

187/52   **John Aldridge.** A prolific literary critic and professor at the University of Michigan, Aldridge (1922–2007) had a warm relationship with Mailer for several decades. He gave thoughtful and generally positive reviews to most of Mailer's important books, but cared little for *The Deer Park*.

188/52   **Marilyn Monroe.** Mailer's biography of Monroe (1926–1962), *Marilyn: A Biography*, sold more copies than any of his other books, save *The Naked and the Dead*.

JANUARY 20, 1955

199/55   **Jewish middle-class.** In *The Armies of the Night* (1968), Mailer states that the only part of his personality he finds to be "absolutely insupportable" is "the nice Jewish boy from Brooklyn."

200/55   ***Dissent* vs. *Partisan Review* vs. *Commentary*.** Mailer wrote for these three major literary-political journals, all dominated in the postwar period by Jewish intellectuals he knew personally. He was well aware of where their editorial policies did and did not overlap.

200/55   **Carson McCullers.** A Southern gothic writer influenced by Faulkner, McCullers (1917–1967) memorably depicted eccentric and isolated characters in her novels, stories, and plays. Mailer admired her first novel, *The Heart is a Lonely Hunter* (1940).

200/55   **Paul Bowles.** A novelist and music composer, Bowles (1910–1999) lived most of his adult life in Tangiers, where he hosted several Beat writers, including Jack Kerouac, Allen Ginsberg, and William Burroughs. *The Sheltering Sky* (1949) is his finest novel.

200/55   **Truman Capote.** Mailer and Capote (1924–1984) became friendly in the 1960s when they both lived in Brooklyn Heights. Later, they feuded about whether Mailer had sufficiently recognized Capote's "nonfiction novel" *In Cold Blood* (1966) as the progenitor of *The Executioner's Song* (1979).

200/55   **vs. Jones and Early Mailer.** The literary divide Mailer notes was first sketched out by Philip Rahv in a 1939 *Kenyon Review* essay, "Paleface vs. Redskin." Henry James was the poster child for the palefaces and Mark Twain for the redskins. In Mailer's mind, he moved closer to the palefaces after *Naked*.

200/55   **Freudians, Reichians, Horneyans, etc.** There is no way to describe here the complex struggles between and among Sigmund Freud (1865–1939), the father of psychoanalysis, and his erstwhile followers, Alfred Adler (1870–1937), Carl Jung (1875–1961), Wilhelm Reich (1897–1957), and Karen Horney (1885–1952). Mailer was familiar with their writings.

200/55   **Lenin vs. Trotsky; Trotsky vs. Stalin; Stalin vs. Hitler.** Mailer was also familiar with the writings of Vladimir Lenin (1870–1924), the head of communist Russia from 1917 to 1924, and his ally, Leon Trotsky (1879–1940), who was assassinated by Lenin's successor, Joseph Stalin (1878–1953). These three Russians, and Adolf Hitler (1889–1945), are discussed endlessly by the occupants of Mailer's roominghouse cum debating club in *Barbary Shore* and in his final novel, *The Castle in the Forest* (2007), a well-researched fictional re-creation of Hitler's early life. The preponderance of Mailer's writing is situated beneath the overhang of the Cold War, most notably his 1991 novel of the CIA, *Harlot's Ghost*.

201/55   **the war within a man.** Mailer expanded this metaphor in a long self-interview in *Cannibals and Christians*, "The Political Economy of Time," where he says, "Form in general—now I let you in on the secret—is the record of a war." He continues, saying that this war "reveals the balance of forces, discloses the style of the forces, it hints at the move from potential to the actual." The lucubrations of this interview, and the one preceding it, "The Metaphysics of the Belly," are a mature ramifying of the jottings in *Lipton's*. See also Richard Poirier's chapter, "The Minority Within," in his seminal 1972 monograph, *Norman Mailer*.

202/55   **Mexico.** Mailer usually spent two or three months every year from 1952 to 1959, visiting Susan in Mexico, and usually bringing her back to the United States for a visit.

205/56   **John Walsh . . . Slim and Glenn and Clem.** Unknown.

208/58   **Styron.** One of Mailer's closest literary friends in the early 1950s, William Styron (1925–2006) became famous with his first novel, *Lie Down in Darkness* (1951). Mailer admired it, and also *The Long March* (1956). Their friendship collapsed over a demeaning comment Styron allegedly made about Adele, and they remained estranged until the mid-1980s.

208/58   **Juan Bilbao . . . Bette Ford . . . Pat McCormick.** Mailer met this trio at bullfights in Mexico. Ford (b. 1937) and Patricia McCormick (1929–2013) were the first American women bullfighters. Don Juan Bilbao was their manager.

JANUARY 24, 1955

216/61   **Seconal.** Brand name for Secobarbital sodium, a barbiturate used as a sedative and anticonvulsant. Mailer used this drug regularly in the early and middle 1950s.

217/61 **Larry and Barbara.** Mailer's sister, Barbara Mailer Wasserman (b. 1927) was married to Larry Alson (1920–2016), a writer and editor, from 1950 to 1962.

217/62 **Dave Kessler.** David Kessler (1889–1960), a candy manufacturer, was married to Mailer's father's sister, Anne (1889–1958). The Kesslers were fond of Mailer and helped with his college expenses. *Advertisements for Myself* is dedicated to them.

223/62 **Homeostasis and sociostasis.** Mailer presents this struggle as a crucial dialectic: the thesis is sociostasis, or the healthy balance of society, and the antithesis is homeostasis, or the individual essence that often stands opposed to social order and conformity. Mailer does not see sociostasis (literally "like standing still") as healthy, diverging from the original meaning, and privileges homeostasis as a more pure, natural, or Ur-state. In entry 245, Mailer replaces homeostasis with homeodynamism, suggesting individual expression and growth through movement or an active power that resists external oppressive forces.

223/63 **Randolph Bourne.** A progressive thinker, Bourne (1886–1918) wrote an anti-war essay in 1918, "War is the Health of the State."

224/64 **Planck's Quantum theory.** Max Planck (1858–1947) was a theoretical physicist who proposed that the energy of light is proportional to its frequency.

225/64 **for Army life.** Mailer, who served twenty-five months on active duty, part of it as a rifleman in a reconnaissance squad in the Philippines, often said he was ill-prepared for army life, and lucky to have survived the war.

225/64 **The small trumpet of my defiance.** On the next-to-last page of *The Deer Park*, Sergius imagines Eitel telling him that as an artist he "must blow against the walls of every power that exists, the small trumpet of your defiance."

230/66 **an earlier note.** See **205/56**.

231/67 **English is spelled so unphonetically.** The chief reason words in English are often spelled un-phonetically is that its word-stock, unlike those of French and Spanish, was drawn over several centuries from several languages, each of which has its own system of orthography and pronunciation, a process that continues.

235/68 **Laughton.** Mailer met Charles Laughton (1899–1962) in 1954, and over the next two years the great English actor and director tried and failed to write a screenplay based on *Naked*. Laughton directed the Broadway production of G. B. Shaw's *Don Juan in Hell* in 1951 and played the role of the Devil, with Agnes Moorhead as Doña Ana, Charles Boyer as Don Juan, and Cedric Hardwicke as the Commander, a production Mailer admired.

235/68 **Cummings.** General Edward Cummings is the semi-fascistic commanding general of US forces on the fictional island of Anopopei in *Naked*.

240/70 **Sheen.** From 1930 to 1968, Bishop Fulton J. Sheen (1895–1979), who had a doctorate in philosophy, appeared on radio and television offering humorous and thoughtful comments on modern life from a Catholic perspective. He is sometimes called the first televangelist.

242/71 **Bebop.** A jazz style of the 1940s and 1950s, and also the nonsense, or scat, language of hipsters and musicians. Mailer is referring to the latter definition here.

242/71 **P and B are sibling consonants.** Mailer is correct in linking P with B, and T with D in reference to where they are articulated, by the lips, teeth, tongue, voice box, etc. The first pair are bilabial (formed by the lips), and latter interdental (formed by the tip of the tongue and the teeth).

242/71 *Finnegans Wake* is the experimental serio-comic novel written by James Joyce (1882–1941) over two decades and published in 1939. Written in what Joyce conceived to be the language of the unconscious or the dream, it recounts the life of a Dublin family named Earwicker. Mailer regularly, incorrectly, inserted an apostrophe in the title, an indication of his unfamiliarity with Joyce's work at the time.

243/71   **homeodynamism.** In a physiological sense, homeostasis is the normal condition of the body regulated by bodily processes that maintain a dynamically controlled equilibrium that counteract external influences. Mailer uses it in a slightly different way as the "most healthy act possible at any moment for the soul" (223/62) that resists sociostasis, or conformity to the imposed behaviors of the external world. Here, Mailer substitutes homeodynamism as a more accurate word to express the possible movement of the force of creativity, vitality, and rebellion in the individual.

248/73   **in the bad man there is good.** This is "the minority within," as critic Richard Poirier referred to these opposed dualities; see "The Minority Within" in Poirier's 1972 monograph *Norman Mailer.* Many if not most of Mailer's characters were created in loyalty to this division.

250/74   **Bergler.** An Austrian psychoanalyst and early follower of Freud, Edmund Bergler (1899–1962) focused on masochism and homosexuality in his many books and articles. He believed homosexuality was a neurosis that could be cured, and saw homosexuals as unscrupulous psychic masochists. Bergler is Mailer's whipping boy in *Lipton's.*

250/74   **"There was that law of life."** One of the most quoted lines from Mailer's works, it is inscribed on his gravestone.

252/75   **Adeline.** See **156/44**.

252/75   **Jenny Silverman.** Mother of Mailer's first wife, Bea.

JANUARY 25, 1955

254/78   **Uncle Dave.** See **217/62**.

255/79   *The Deer Park* **published.** After being rejected by Rinehart in late November 1954, the novel was considered and turned down by six other publishers over the next six weeks before being accepted by Putnam's about two weeks before Mailer wrote this January 25, 1955, entry. He recounts the story of the novel's composition, rejection, and publication in a long essay in *Esquire* (November 1959), "The Mind of an Outlaw," reprinted in *Advertisements for Myself* as "The Last Draft of *The Deer Park*."

260/81   *Divorce Won't Help.* Bergler's 1948 book argued that divorce usually didn't solve the fundamental psychological problems of individuals.

264/83   **Cy.** Mailer's first cousin, Charles Rembar (1915–2000), was a prominent First Amendment lawyer who successfully defended the publication of banned books such as *Lady Chatterley's Lover* and *Tropic of Cancer*. He was Mailer's lawyer for over three decades.

271/86   **Norman Thomas.** A Protestant minister and pacifist, Thomas (1884–1968) ran for president six times on the Socialist Party ticket.

272/86   **Put Tolstoy into Dostoyevsky and Dostoyevsky in Tolstoy.** Mailer hoped to build a bridge between the social and natural worlds depicted in Tolstoy's novels, and the deep penetrations into psychic space in Dostoyevsky's. He wrote that all of the latter's novels could take place in "ten closed rooms." He saw the need for a parallel span between the external world of economics and politics in Marx and the inner world of dreams and the unconscious in Freud.

JANUARY 26, 1955

282/92   **McCarthys.** Senator Joseph McCarthy.

282/92   **Billy Grahams.** One of the most charismatic Christian (Protestant) evangelists of the past century, Graham (1918–2018) appeared on television and held religious rallies for seventy years, including some in England.

282/92   **Aldous Huxley.** A member of a talented and accomplished British family, Huxley (1894–1963), was a novelist and philosopher with an interest in the occult and spiritualism. His most famous book is *Brave New World* (1932), a dystopian satire. He died of cancer shortly after taking a dose of LSD on the day President Kennedy was assassinated, November 22, 1963.

283/94 **the rational saint sent out to find the good in monsters and psychopaths.** A prophetic statement. Mailer's fictional heroes and biographical subjects include monsters such as Hitler, criminals such as Stephen Rojack, Marion Faye, Lee Harvey Oswald and Gary Gilmore, and a parade of rebels and iconoclasts—Jesus Christ, Muhammad Ali, Pablo Picasso, Henry Miller, Marlon Brando, and Madonna, to name the most prominent.

285/94 **a vast conservative echo in me.** Another prescient statement; from the late 1960s on Mailer described himself as a left-conservative.

286/94 **Hiram Haydn.** A prominent figure in the postwar New York literary world, and longtime editor of *The American Scholar*, Haydn (1907–1973) was an editor at Random House when it turned down *The Deer Park*.

288/94 **"The Jet-Propelled Couch."** A chapter from Lindner's 1955 collection, *The Fifty-Minute Hour*. Each chapter of the collection is a case study of one of his clients. In this one, Lindner discusses a man who thought he was living part of his life on another planet. It appeared first in *Harper's*, December 1954. Lindner was a fluent writer, and his essay in an important magazine spurred Mailer's competitive instincts.

289/95 **Munshin.** In *The Deer Park*, Carlyle "Collie" Munshin is the son-in-law of Herman Teppis and is best known for pirating the scripts of others. One of Mailer's finest comic characters.

292/95 **the buried soul of man.** Mailer's intuition that there was a simple, underlying basis for all language is borne out to some extent in the linguistic theories of Noam Chomsky, who believes that human ability to use syntax is innate, and that the structures of all languages vary only in surface peripherals or "externalization." As Mailer says later on in *Lipton's* (395/133), "what I'm really trying to do . . . is psychoanalyze language." See Tattersal, Ian (August 18, 2016). "At the Birth of Language." *The New York Review of Books.*

307/99   **Rosicrucians.** Rosicrucianism is an international organization that claims access to ancient, occult wisdom. It includes teachings from gnosticism and other religions. The name derives from the symbol of a rose atop a cross.

310/100   **"The Bodily Function Blues."** Mailer belted out this song for his family and friends for decades. In 1995, he recorded it, and another song he wrote, "Alimony Blues," for Don't Quit Your Day Job Records.

JANUARY 27, 1955

320/105   **the Negro prejudice of Southerners.** Mailer's comment about the sex life of Southern Blacks resurfaced in 1957, when he challenged Lyle Stuart to publish a longer and more nuanced version of the idea in his monthly newspaper, *The Independent.* The resulting statement argues that "the white man fears the sexual potency of the Negro," and this leads to whites believing that "the Negro had his sexual supremacy and the white had his white supremacy." This insidious, unspoken arrangement allowed whites "symbolically and materially" to possess Negro womanhood, which, in turn, created a murderous rage among Blacks. Stuart sent Mailer's statement to William Faulkner, who replied that he had heard this idea expressed over the years, but never by a man, only by middle-aged women from the North or Midwest. Stuart published Faulkner's response and those of others, including Eleanor Roosevelt, W. E. B. Du Bois and Murray Kempton, in the March 1957 issue of his newspaper. But Mailer was not done. Being dismissed by Faulkner, a writer he revered, incited him to compose a much longer rejoinder. So he began "the trip into the psychic wild" of "The White Negro," and the publication of this essay in the summer 1957 *Dissent.* In 1959 it was published as a pamphlet by City Lights Press, and also included in *Advertisements for Myself*. It has been reprinted scores of times since then, and with James Baldwin's 1955 essay "Notes of a Native Son" is one of the two most debated and reprinted postwar essays by an American writer.

JANUARY 31, 1955

326/109   **McCormick.** A conservative from a wealthy Illinois family that owned the *Chicago Tribune*, Robert McCormick (1880–1955) ran the newspaper from the 1920s until his death. He was a fierce critic of President Franklin Roosevelt, and opposed US entry into World War II.

326/109   **Winchell.** A newspaper and radio gossip columnist with a huge audience, Walter Winchell (1897–1972) supported the New Deal, but in the 1950s took a turn to the right and praised the communist witch hunts of Senator Joseph McCarthy.

332/111   **psychopathy may be healthier than we think.** "The White Negro," from one perspective, can be seen as an extended commentary on this notion. For example, he states that the psychopath, or hipster, is "closer to the secrets of that inner unconscious life which will nourish you if you can hear it, for you are nearer to that God which every hipster believes is located in the senses of the body."

339/115   **Eva Peron.** The second wife of Argentinian President Juan Perón, Maria Eva Duarte Perón (1919–1952) became a cult figure in the Argentinian mind after her death.

339/116   **Elliot Kammerman.** Unknown.

340/117   **Herbert Aldendorff.** A New York City psychoanalyst. Connection to Mailer unknown.

353/122   **An article in *Life*.** "The Doping of Race Horses" appeared in the January 31, 1955 *Life* magazine.

358/123   **Maloney.** A writer friend of William Styron and Larry Alson (1920–2016).

359/123   **as if you were present.** See the letter dated January 27, 1955, p. 297.

359/124   **stimulate the artist.** Mailer never stopped stating that it was the work of other artists that gave him new ideas and impetus, and that he hoped that his had a similar effect.

368/125   **Nat Halper.** A longtime art dealer in Provincetown, Nathan "Nat" Halper (1907–1983), ran the HCE Gallery (named after H. C. Earwicker in *Finnegans Wake*) for many years. He published widely on Joyce, including *Studies in Joyce* (1973).

370/125   **The Burglar.** Edmund Bergler. See note 250/74.

379/127   **Bluebeard.** Mailer confuses Bluebeard with Procrustes, a son of Poseidon who, in the Greek myth, cuts off or stretches the limbs of travelers to fit the bed he offers them for the night.

379/127   **Booth.** Adele's analyst.

390/130   **Lewis Coser.** A sociologist, Coser (1913–2003) was also an editor at *Dissent*.

390/131   **Pure Food and Drug Act . . . What a perfect title.** Mailer refers here to the controversial suppression and incineration of books, pamphlets, and other materials associated with the orgone therapy of Wilhelm Reich by the U.S. Food and Drug Administration, which administers the Pure Food and Drug Act. Calling his therapy "a fraud of the first magnitude," the FDA convinced a court to ban Reich's materials. Clara Mabel Thompson (1893–1958), a mainstream psychoanalyst, and the followers of social psychiatrist Harry Stack Sullivan (1892–1949) sided with the FDA's actions against Reich. Reich continued to sell and ship his orgone accumulators, was convicted of contempt, and died in federal prison while serving a two-year sentence.

390/131   **Plastrik.** A history professor and former Trotskyite, Stanley Plastrik (1915–1981) was the secretary of the editorial board of *Dissent*.

390/131   **Molotov.** An old Bolshevik and close associate of Stalin, Vyacheslav Molotov (1890–1986) was the USSR's Minister for Foreign Affairs from 1939 to 1949, and from 1953 to 1956. He signed a fateful nonaggression pact with Hitler's foreign minister, Joachim von Ribbentrop, in 1939.

390/131   **Serge Rubinstein.** A wealthy Russian émigré and shady businessman whose father financed the last Russian tsar, Sergei Rubinstein (1897–1955) was murdered by strangulation in his New York City apartment. The crime is still unsolved. Mailer's interest in the case foreshadows his later interest in sensational crime stories.

390/131   **Howe.** Literary critic and founding editor of the leftist quarterly *Dissent*, Irving Howe (1920–1993) asked Mailer in 1953 to serve on its editorial board, which he did for three decades. Mailer published several essays in *Dissent*, including his most influential, "The White Negro" (1957). Perhaps Howe's most important work is *Politics and the Novel* (1957).

FEBRUARY 1, 1955

398/134   **taking a drink of water.** According to a Bolshevik theorist, Alexandra Mikhailovna Kollontai (1872–1952), "The sexual act must not be seen as something shameful and sinful but as something which is as natural as the other needs of a healthy organism such as hunger and thirst." Lenin repudiated this view, saying, "This glass of water theory is completely un-Marxist, and moreover, anti-social. In sexual life there is not only simple nature to be considered, but also cultural characteristics, whether of a high or low order. . . . Drinking water is, of course, an individual affair. But in love two lives are concerned, and a third, a new life arises, it is that which gives it its social interest, which gives rise to a duty towards the community." From Zetkin, Clara (2004). "Lenin on the Women's Question." Marxists.org. International Publishers. Retrieved April 3, 2021.

398/134 **The Kronstadt rebellion.** In the winter of 1921, a group of sailors and workers at the Russian naval base of Kronstadt revolted against the Bolsheviks. The uprising was swiftly and violently suppressed, and thousands were killed. Leon Trotsky was the leader of the Red Army at the time.

400/137 **Tex and Jinx.** John "Tex" McCrary (1910–2003) and Eugenia "Jinx" Falkenburg (1919–2003) were radio and television talk show hosts in the 1950s. *Break the Bank* was a television quiz show hosted by Bert Parks from 1948 to 1957.

400/137 **Brando imitations.** Mailer performed these for many years, drawing on the roles played by Marlon Brando (1924–2004) in three of his best films, *On the Waterfront* (1954), *A Streetcar Named Desire* (1951), and *The Wild One* (1953).

400/138 **last pages of a novel.** *No Percentage*, Mailer's unpublished novel written in 1941 when he was a sophomore at Harvard and set in Brooklyn and Long Branch, New Jersey.

400/138 **Jack Alson.** Father of Larry Alson, husband of Mailer's sister, Barbara.

400/139 **tzaddik.** A Hebrew term meaning a righteous or holy person.

404/142 **Chasidim.** A sect of Orthodox Jews that arose in Eastern Europe in the late eighteenth century. Mailer's scholarly grandfather Chaim Yehuda Schneider (1859–1928) was an ordained Orthodox rabbi, but anti-Hasidim in his leanings, believing that the sect put too much trust in their rabbis and not enough in the Talmud.

405/143 **God who gave Life.** An early, rudimentary statement of Mailer's belief in a divided universe, a semi-gnostic vision discussed at length first in a 1959 interview, "Hip, Hell and the Navigator" (collected in *Advertisements for Myself*), and most fully in a series of conversations with J. Michael Lennon in *On God: An Uncommon Conversation* (2007).

410/144 **Tito.** Josip Broz Tito (1892–1980), the leader of the Yugoslavian resistance movement against the Nazis in

World War II, and later the longtime president of his country.

411/144   **my father.** Mailer's hope that his father would stop gambling proved illusory. Barney Mailer gambled until the end of his life, and shortly after his death a woman presented his wife with his notarized promissory note for $26,000, which the family paid.

412/145   **the hammer I got on my head.** For six months in 1951 Mailer and Adele lived on Monroe Street on Manhattan's Lower East side. A gang of thugs crashed one of their parties and Mailer was hit in the head a couple of times with a hammer.

413/145   **R.P.** Unknown.

FEBRUARY 2, 1955

435/153   **quite un-publishable.** Mailer never changed his mind about publishing *Lipton's*, but he made up a set of index cards for the journal, and drew on them through the rest of the decade, most notably for "The White Negro."

435/153   **going over *The Deer Park*.** Mailer missed several deadlines for submitting the last draft to Putnam's. He finally completed it at the end of July, and then shed Seconal and Benzedrine in Provincetown while awaiting the final proofs. Back in New York, he made the final changes toward the end of the month after taking some mescaline.

FEBRUARY 7, 1955

446/158   **Theodore Reik.** An American psychologist, Reik (1888–1969) was an early and brilliant acolyte of Freud.

458/160   **Freddy Weisgal.** A prominent civil rights lawyer, Weisgal (1920–1971) was at one time an official in Israel's Ministry of Justice. The details of his disagreement with Lindner are unknown.

460/161 **John Huston.** One of the great figures of Hollywood's golden era, John Huston (1906–1987), directed nearly forty films and wrote the screenplays for most of them. His first film, *The Maltese Falcon* (1941), is generally considered to be one of the first and finest examples of American film noir. Mailer met him in Hollywood in 1949.

468/163 **Guinevere.** Beverly Guinevere McLeod, wife of William McLeod, runs the Brooklyn boardinghouse that is the setting of *Barbary Shore*. One of Mailer's finest comic characters.

471/163 **Kant.** One of the major philosophers of the Enlightenment, Immanuel Kant (1724–1804), made contributions to almost every branch of philosophical thought, including aesthetics. He opposed the idea, held by rationalist philosophers, that the infant's mind is a blank slate.

481/164 **JB.** Unknown.

490/169 **the first emotional apperception of form.** Mailer explores the infant-mother relationship with verve and humor in the as-yet-unpublished "Book of the First-Born."

506/173 **the sperm itself should be unaffected.** Mailer restated this in *The Prisoner of Sex* (1971): "Good fucks make good babies."

516/175 **Ellis.** Havelock Ellis (1859–1939), a British doctor who wrote extensively on human sexuality, including a six-volume work, *Studies in the Psychology of Sex*, published from 1897 to 1928.

526/175 **comprehend the universe whole.** At which point all dualisms, oppositions, duads, and polarities would disappear. Mailer knew that this final resolution was a distant event, and therefore resisted the Emersonian tendency to make one of two. Doing so would make him miss all the surprises of the dialectic that lay before him. He would "lose the tension which now furnished thought," as he states in 527.

528/177 **Rose.** Rose née Burgunder Styron (b. 1929), the poet and translator, married William Styron in 1953.

545/180   **my Wallace days.** In 1948, Mailer campaigned for Henry A. Wallace, the left-leaning candidate of the Progressive Party, who ran against Republican Thomas E. Dewey and Harry S. Truman, the incumbent and winner.

FEBRUARY 10, 1955

558/185   **leave it for the next.** Mailer took this advice and for the rest of his life worked on several projects simultaneously. Even when deep into writing a long work like *Ancient Evenings* (1983), he interrupted it to write an even longer one, *The Executioner's Song* (1979).

562/186   **. . . surrounded by an enigma.** A slight misquotation of Winston Churchill's description of the USSR: "a riddle, wrapped in a mystery, inside an enigma."

FEBRUARY 14, 1955

564/190   **Roxitchitl.** Unknown.

572/192   **qvatch.** Probably the Yiddish kvetch, to nag and complain at length.

574/192   *Ulysses.* At Harvard, Mailer read up through "Calypso," the fourth chapter of James Joyce's 1922 novel, which ends with Leopold Bloom relieving himself in the privy, and wrote a paper on the scene for one of his writing courses.

583/194   **Ferdinand in the ring.** Mailer refers to Monroe Leaf's 1936 children's book, *The Story of Ferdinand*, about a bull that will not fight the matadors or picadors in the bullring, and would rather smell flowers.

583/195   **El Loco.** Nickname of the Mexican bullfighter Amado Ramirez, who Mailer saw fight during his visits to Mexico. He wrote an essay, "The Crazy One," about Ramirez, published in the October 1967 issue of *Playboy*, rpt., in *The Bullfight* (1967).

585/195   **India's.** Unknown.

585/195 **Chassidility.** Refers to the Hasidic Orthodox sect; **tefillin** refers to the small leather boxes (also called phylacteries) containing verses from the Torah that observant Jews strap to their arms during morning prayers.

613/201 **Vance Bourjaily.** He wrote to Mailer in the summer of 1951 with praise for *Barbary Shore*, and they immediately became friends. Bourjaily (1922–2010), whose novels include *The Violated* (1958), introduced Mailer to John W. Aldridge, who coedited *Discovery*, a literary annual, with Bourjaily. Mailer's short story, "The Dead Gook," appeared in the first number in 1952, around the same time that Bourjaily introduced Mailer to James Jones.

FEBRUARY 21, 1955

622/204 **Indian Roximyl.** Unknown.

625/207 *Mutiny on the Bounty.* Charles Laughton (1899–1962) was Capt. Bligh in this 1935 film based on Charles Nordhoff's 1932 novel of the same name. Clark Gable played Fletcher Christian in the film, and was nominated, along with Laughton, for an Academy Award for best actor. Neither won, but the film won one for best picture.

625/207 **Keystone Chaplin films.** Mailer met Charlie Chaplin (1889–1977) in Hollywood in 1949 when the great actor attended his Christmas party, and he had the pleasure of introducing his parents to him.

629/208 *Naked* for *Naked.* In February 1955, Laughton spent a week with Mailer in New York City discussing how he might write the screenplay for Mailer's novel, and also direct it, but ultimately turned the project over to an associate, Paul Gregory, who botched the film version, which came out in 1958. See entry **625/207**.

629/208 **interview.** Mailer refers to his 1948 interview with Louise Levitas, "The Naked are Fanatics and the Dead Don't Care," collected in *Conversations with Norman Mailer* (1988).

640/212   *Omnibus.* An educational discussion program, hosted by Alistair Cooke, on network television from 1952 to 1961.

641/214   **profound line by John Dewey.** The exact quote is: "The bad man is the man who no matter how good he has been is beginning to deteriorate, to grow less good. The good man is the man who no matter how morally unworthy he has been is moving to become better." Mailer adapts the line in "The White Negro," as follows: "In the instinctive dialectic through which the hipster perceives his experience . . . one is forever moving forward into more or retreating into less."

644/216   **Toby.** See **156/44.**

644/216   **Gore Vidal.** Mailer met Gore Vidal (1925–2012) in 1952, and their lives intersected for the next sixty years, not only because they were East Coast novelists of the same generation, but also because they were gregarious, ambitious, ornery, and permanently critical of the imperialistic streak in American foreign policy. Mailer's surmise about Vidal's sexual preferences is borne out by Vidal's friend, archivist, and biographer, Jay Parini, in his 2015 biography, *Empire of Self: A Life of Gore Vidal.*

654/221   **Fig Gwaltney.** Francis I. Gwaltney (1921–1980) joined Mailer's unit in Luzon and they began a close friendship that continued after the war. "Fig," as he was called, also became a novelist and wrote a novel of Pacific combat titled *The Day the Century Ended* (1955). A professor at Arkansas Tech University, he introduced a local high school art teacher, Barbara Davis Norris, to Mailer in 1975. She later became his sixth wife and changed her name to Norris Church Mailer.

FEBRUARY 22, 1955

681/227   **Faye Emerson.** A film actress who made the jump to live television, Emerson (1917–1983), hosted a number of talk shows in the 1950s.

688/228 Millie. Millie Brower was a distant cousin from Long Branch, who was an actress and writer for the *Village Voice*.

MARCH 4, 1955

702/234 they hand-write. After Mailer completed work on *The Deer Park* (he typed the final draft himself), he began to write his work almost exclusively by hand, and continued to do so for the next half century.

707/238 Existentialism. Mailer came to his version of this philosophy via events in his life, the rejection of *The Deer Park* by Rinehart, for example, rather than his reading. Existentialism was thrust on him. In November and December 1960, when he was committed to the violent ward of Bellevue for stabbing Adele, he began to seriously read existential writing in Walter Kaufmann's 1956 collection, *Existentialism from Dostoyevsky to Sartre*.

LETTERS

NOVEMBER 18, 1952

248 *Prescription for Rebellion.* Dr. Lindner's fourth book was published by Rinehart and Co., on May 27, 1952. His first book, *Rebel Without a Cause: The Hypnoanalysis of a Criminal Psychopath* (1944) was sold to Warner Brothers and made into a 1955 film of the same title starring James Dean, although the title is the only connection to the book. Lindner wrote or edited a total of seven books. His posthumous book *Must You Conform?* came out on May 1, 1956.

248 *Peace of Mind.* In 1946, Joshua Liebman (1907–1948), a Reform rabbi, published the best-selling self-help book *Peace of Mind*. The book, a synthesis of religious wisdom and psychoanalytic practices, grew out of his sermons.

250 **True Believer.** A reference to the 1951 work of social psychology, *The True Believer: Thoughts on the Nature of*

Mass Movements by social philosopher Eric Hoffer (1898–1983); the book is a study of the forces that impel fanaticism.

250   **The Sexual Revolution.** One of the key works of psycho-analyst and sexual philosopher Wilhelm Reich (1897–1957), *The Sexual Revolution* (1936) argued for the establishment of "natural" sexual relations and the overthrow of puritanical laws restricting them.

NOVEMBER 24, 1952

252   ***Rx.*** Shorthand for Lidner's *Prescription for Rebellion.*

252   **the Party.** The Communist Party, which many American leftists joined in the 1920s and 1930s.

253   **Liebman's Peace of tripe.** See note **248**. *Peace of Mind,* November 18, 1952.

APRIL 15, 1953

254   **my book.** *The Deer Park.*

254   **Lamont.** John Lamont, a friend of Mailer's.

254   **the first person or the third person.** See Mailer's discussion of the opportunities and hazards of both points of view in *The Spooky Art* (2003), 84–88.

255   **your article on the gambler.** Lindner's classic article "The Psychodynamics of Gambling" was published in the *Annals of the American Academy of Political Science and Social Science* 269 (May 1950).

255   **my "friend" "Bernard."** An alias for Mailer's father, Barney.

FEBRUARY 16, 1954

257   **Amussen.** Ted Amussen was an editor at Rinehart and Co. for both Mailer and Lindner. See note **187/52**.

257	**even more complicated.** Mailer is referring to the building crisis at Rinehart over the purported obscenity of *The Deer Park*.
257	**a central experience for me.** Lindner took Mailer to a women's prison in Baltimore where he met some of the inmates. His abiding interest in prison life, which culminated in 1979 years later with *The Executioner's Song*, was kindled by this visit.
257	**Johnnie.** Lindner's wife. See note **156/44**.
258	**I work as your assistant over.** This job never materialized.
258	**Neville Brand.** A World War II war hero, Brand (1920–1992), made a score of films and television programs.
258	**the best . . . prison picture ever made.** A 1954 film produced by Walter Wanger (1894–1968), *Riot in Cell Block 11* was more realistic than most of this genre.
258	***Rebel* screenplay.** The 1955 film of this name borrowed Lindner's title, but there was no other connection.
258	**Jerry Wald's hands.** Wald (1911–1962) was a screenwriter and producer who won an Academy Award as producer of *From Here to Eternity* in 1953. He had no connection to the film *Rebel Without a Cause*.

FEBRUARY 26, 1954

262	**Don Beda.** Character in *The Deer Park* who organizes and participates in orgies. See note **84/30**.
262	**Pellito.** A minor character in *The Deer Park*.
262–263	**Sergius.** Sergius O'Shaughnessey is the narrator of *The Deer Park*; Dorothea and Pellito are minor characters.
263	**Neville Brand.** See note **258**.
263	**Ivan von Auw.** Literary agent (1903–1991) at the Harold Ober Agency who represented Lindner.
264	**an article coming out . . . *Dissent*.** "David Riesman Reconsidered," a review of Riesman's *Individualism*

Reconsidered (1954), appeared in the Autumn 1954 issue of *Dissent*; rpt. in *Advertisements for Myself*.

JUNE 7, 1954

266   **Edgy Berman ... Phoebe.** Unknown.

267   *The Fifty-Minute Hour.* Each chapter of Lindner's 1955 book is a case study of one of his patients. Journalist and educator Max Lerner (1902–1992) wrote the preface to the book.

267   **Ted and Dudley.** Ted Amussen and Dudley Fraiser were editors at Rinehart.

267   **Stan Rinehart.** See 4/3.

267   **the Teppis scene.** Depiction in *The Deer Park* of Herman Teppis, a Hollywood producer, getting a blow job. It caused Rinehart to cancel publication of the novel.

267   *stat.* A misspelling of "stet," a typesetter's symbol meaning put back in something crossed out.

JUNE 12, 1954

269   *alta kakes.* Old farts.

270   **Arthur Mandey.** Unknown.

270   **Lerner.** See note **267**.

270   **The problem of the ORGY.** There are indirect references in the closing chapters of *The Deer Park* to the orgies Esposito takes part in with Eitel, Don Beda, and his wife Zenelia. Marion Faye also becomes involved after Esposito leaves Eitel and moves in with him.

270   *The Deer Park* **is about morality.** Critical opinion has come around to the position that *The Deer Park* is not pornographic, and that Mailer was "a passionate moralist," as Brendan Gill put it is his *New Yorker* review (October 22, 1955). Malcolm Cowley, in his review (*New York Herald Tribune Book Review*, October 23, 1955), said the novel "is a serious and recklessly honest book about art." Later

criticism of the novel has focused on the weakness of the narrator, Sergius O'Shaugnessey, and the shifting point of view.

271   **vieux Lippé.** Old Lip.

JUNE/JULY, 1954

273   **32 Macajium 4159.** Lindner made up this date, and the fictional place from where he purportedly wrote this comic first part of this letter.

273   **hyght.** Unnamed.

274   **Nertz!** Nonsense.

275   **Gollancz.** A leftwing British publisher and humanitarian, Victor Gollancz (1893–1967) published work by Franz Kafka, Ford Madox Ford, and George Orwell.

275   **the Lerner preface.** See note **267.**

JULY 16, 1954

277   **at my friend's.** Francis I. "Fig" Gwaltney. See note **654/221.**

278   ***Break Down the Walls.*** John Bartlow Martin's (1915–1987) 1954 book about the riots in the State Prison of Southern Michigan at Jackson.

278   ***Stone Walls.*** Unknown.

278   **Jeanne.** Lindner's secretary.

JULY 20, 1954

280   *etwas.* Something.

280   **"Jet-Propelled Couch."** A chapter from Lindner's book *The Fifty-Minute Hour* appeared in the December 1954 *Harper's.*

AUGUST 19, 1954

282   *The Lonely Crowd.* David Riesman's canonical study of American character published in 1950.

282   **Eppis.** Unknown.

283   **the deal on *Naked*.** The film version was sold to a production company run by Charles Laughton and Paul Gregory. It was not completed and released until 1958, and received generally tepid reviews.

284   **Cape.** Jonathan Cape, the English firm that published *Barbary Shore*.

SEPTEMBER 15, 1954

285   **Fleiss.** Wilhelm Fleiss (1858–1928), a German medical doctor, was a close friend and collaborator with Freud and carried on a long correspondence with him. He is credited with giving Freud the idea of innate bisexuality, and also came up with theories that prefigure the controversial idea of human biorhythms.

285   *amigo querido.* Dear friend.

285   **gage.** Marijuana.

286   **Chazar.** A variant of Khazar, a Turkic people living on the southeastern border of Russia.

286   **50 minute job.** Lindner's forthcoming book, *The Fifty-Minute Hour*.

286   *marica.* Spanish term for a gay person, another of Lindner's jibes.

286   *el toro dé Latrobe.* The bull from Latrobe. Lindner's connection with this city in western Pennsylvania is unknown.

DECEMBER 7, 1954

289   **this week's *Time*.** "Rebels or Psychopaths?" an article about Lindner's views on juvenile delinquency, appeared in *Time*, December 6, 1954.

289   **"The Jet-Propelled Couch."** See note **288/94**.

DECEMBER 20, 1954

291   **Charles, Mac, and Anton—Kirk.** Pseudonyms for Lindner's patients discussed in *The Fifty-Minute Hour*.

292   **Blanche Knopf.** Wife of Alfred A. Knopf, founder of the publishing house of the same name. Mailer was wrong about her dislike of the novel. She admired it, he later learned.

DECEMBER 31, 1954

293   **blurb to Dudley Frasier.** An editor at Rinehart. Mailer's blurb was not used.

JANUARY 20, 1955

295   **G. P. Putnam's is taking it.** Walter Minton, president of Putnam's, paid Mailer a $10,000 advance for *The Deer Park*, a very high sum for that time.

JANUARY 27, 1955

298   **J. P. Couch.** "The Jet-Propelled Couch." See note **288/94**.

FEBRUARY 3, 1955

299   **St. Theresa.** A Carmelite nun and mystic, St. Teresa of Ávila (1515–1582) was canonized in 1622. Her religious visions of spiritual ecstasy have often been seen as orgasmic, as a look at Bernini's 1652 statue, *The Ecstasy of St. Teresa*, demonstrates.

299   *Devils of Loudun.* A 1952 nonfiction account by Aldous Huxley (1894–1963) of the mass hysteria and purported demonic possession of a convent of Ursuline nuns in the small French town of Loudun in 1634.

MARCH 14, 1955

300   **Edna.** An employee of the call-answering service that took Mailer's calls.

MARCH 15, 1955

302   **those two notes.** Neither the originals or carbon copies have been found; they may have been handwritten.

302   **Paul and Phil.** Unknown.

APRIL 25, 1955

307   **internal dialogue between the doctor and the patient in me.** One of the foundation stones of Mailer's self-understanding is the duality of his nature, actor and observer, analyst and analysand, leftist and conservative, family man and philanderer. His awareness of this division enabled and encouraged the books of the 1968–1975 period (most notably *The Armies of the Night*) in which he writes about himself in the third person. As he once put it, "There are two sides to me, and the side that is the observer is paramount."

308   **approach . . . about twenty-five to fifty important writers.** Mailer followed up on this idea, and sent copies of his novel to Hemingway, Graham Greene, Alberto Moravia, Cyril Connolly, Philip Rahv, Dwight Macdonald, James Jones, William Styron, Lillian Hellman, and several others.

308   **Isherwood.** Christopher Isherwood (1904–1986) was an English-American novelist and playwright known for his works exploring themes of identity, sexuality, and society, most notably in his collection of short stories *Goodbye to Berlin*, which inspired the Broadway musical *Cabaret*. Mrs. Guinevere in *Barbary Shore* was based in part on Sally

Bowles, one of Isherwood's characters in *Goodbye to Berlin*.
Mailer met him in Hollywood in 1949 or 1950.

308   *malgre moi.* Despite myself.

JULY 1955

311   **illness with exhaustion.** It appears that the root cause of
Lindner's declining health was congestive heart disease,
which he died of seven or eight months later.

311   *Genug!* Enough.

311   **back on the book.** *Must You Conform?*

312   **Harold Ober.** Literary agent (1903–1991) at the Harold
Ober Agency.

312   **Maxwell.** Unknown.

313   **Cy and Billie.** Cy Rembar and his wife. See note **264/83**.

ACKNOWLEDGMENTS AND APPRECIATIONS

The editors would like to thank the Mailer estate and Mailer family for their kind permission and encouragement in our work on *Lipton's*. Our efforts would have been fruitless had it not been for the indefatigable Donna Pedro Lennon and her careful transposition of Mailer's typewritten manuscript into digital form. In addition, we would like to thank the Norman Mailer Society, especially Bob Begiebing, Ron Fried, Maggie McKinley, Jason Mosser, and Phil Sipiora, for their scholarly insights and support of this project and of Mailer's legacy.

INDEX

A

Adler, Alfred x, 55, 335
Advertisements for Myself xii, xv, 318, 319, 320, 325, 329, 333, 337, 340, 343, 346, 355
Aeschylus 231
Aesop 28
Aldridge, John 52, 334, 350
"Alimony Blues, The" 342
Ali, Muhammad xi, 341
Allen, Steve 51, 326, 334
Alson, Jack 138, 346
Alson, Larry 61, 138, 174, 337, 343, 346
Amazing Power of Positive Thinking, The 330
American Dream, An xi, 319, 322
Americans xi, xv, 28, 74, 81, 93, 128, 171, 181, 249, 319, 320, 322, 324, 326, 332, 333, 336, 343, 347, 348, 351, 353, 357, 359
American Scholar, The 341
Amussen, Ted 52, 195, 257, 259, 260, 261, 267, 271, 278, 284, 289, 290, 302, 334, 353, 355
Ancient Evenings viii, 318, 349
Annals of the American Academy of Political Science and Social Science 353
Antacid Analgesic 21, 46, 192, 227, 326, 333

Aptheker, Herbert 4, 5, 117, 177, 322, 343
Aristotle 196
Armies of the Night, The viii, 318, 334, 359
Asia 142
"Autumn in New York" 319

B

Baldwin, James 343
Baltimore 182, 190, 258, 260, 275, 285, 295, 300, 304, 324, 330, 354
Bankhead, Tallulah 39, 227, 228, 329
Barbary Shore vii, 57, 65, 73, 242, 250, 253, 308, 319, 320, 329, 333, 335, 348, 350, 357, 359
Bea. *See Silverman (Mailer), Beatrice (Bea)*
Bebop 71, 338
Beda, Don 30, 41, 42, 262, 327, 354, 355
Beda, Zenelia 327, 355
Bentley, Beverly 319, 322
Bergler, Edmund ("The Burglar") x, 74, 81, 90, 125, 133, 217, 339, 340, 344. *See Burglar*
Bernini, Gian Lorenzo 358
Bilbao, Juan 58, 336
Bligh, Captain 207, 350

Bloom, Leopold 349
Bluebeard 127, 344
"Bodily Function Blues, The"
    100, 342
Bolsheviks 134, 136, 346
"Book of the First Born, The"
    321, 348
Booth 127, 344
Bourjaily, Vance 201, 350
Bourne, Randolph 63, 337
Bowles, Paul 55, 335
Bowles, Sally 359
Boyer, Charles 338
Brand, Neville 258, 260, 263, 354
Brando, Marlon xi, xii, 39, 137,
    228, 319, 329, 341, 346
Brave New World 341
Break Down the Walls 278, 356
Break the Bank 137, 346
Brody, Gandy 44, 332
Brooklyn Eagle 121
Brower, Millie 18, 228, 325, 352
Brown, Kay 260
Brubeck, Dave xi, 16, 17, 322, 325
Bullfight, The 349
Burroughs, William 335

C

Caine Mutiny, The 207
"Calculus at Heaven, A" 333
Campbell, Jeanne 278, 356
Cannibals and Christians viii, 318,
    331, 336
Cape (publishers) 284, 357
Capote, Truman 55, 228, 335
Carnegie Hall 319
Castle in the Forest, The 321, 335
Castro, Fidel xi

Catholic Church xii, 28, 29, 41,
    69, 70, 121, 130, 131, 142, 143,
    144, 152, 153, 238, 338
Central Intellegence Agency
    (C.I.A.) 319, 328
Chaplin, Charlie xi, 207, 210,
    350
Chasidim 142, 346
Chavez, Steve 325
Cherry 319
Chicago Tribune 109, 343
Chomsky, Noam 341
Christian, Fletcher 207, 350
Christmas Carol, A 49
Churchill, Winston 216, 349
City Lights Press 318, 343
City of God, The 321
Coca-Cola 53
Cold War 55, 336
Collier's (Magazine) 12, 324
Commentary (Magazine) 55, 334
Communist Party, The 252, 353
*Confessions of an English Opium
    Eater* viii
Connolly, Cyril 359
*Conversations with Norman
    Mailer* 320, 350
Cooke, Alistair 351
Cooper, Gary 228
Corydon 331
Cory, Donald Webster 332
Coser, Lewis 130, 131, 136, 344
Cowley, Malcolm 355
"Crazy One, The" 349
Croft, Sam 45, 68, 333
Cummings, General Edward 68,
    338

D

Das Kapital 250
"David Riesman Reconsidered"
 354
Davis, Miles xi, 319, 322
Day the Century Ended, The 351
"Dead Gook, The" 350
Dean, James 352
Decline of the West, The 325
Deer Park, The vii, xv, 3, 12, 20,
 29, 33, 41, 42, 57, 65, 67, 68, 73,
 74, 79, 89, 94, 95, 125, 126, 146,
 153, 160, 170, 209, 226, 236,
 242, 243, 254, 257, 260, 262,
 267, 270, 280, 283, 284, 287,
 290, 292, 295, 297, 302, 305,
 306, 307, 308, 309, 310, 312,
 321, 324, 327, 328, 330, 331, 332,
 334, 337, 339, 340, 341, 347, 352,
 353, 354, 355, 358
de Gaulle, Charles 333
de Sade, Marquis 33
Desmond, Paul xi, 16, 325
Devil 43, 73, 143, 157, 338
Devils of Loudun 299, 359
Devlin, Charles 40, 45, 61, 182,
 291, 329
Dewey, John 214, 351
Dewey, Thomas E. 349
Dexamyls 270
Dimmesdale, Reverend xviii
Discovery (Magazine) 350
Dissent xv, 55, 130, 131, 136, 264,
 282, 299, 318, 320, 322, 333,
 334, 342, 344, 345, 354, 355
Divorce Won't Help 81, 340
Don Juan in Hell 338

"Doping of Horse Races, The"
 343
Dos Passos, John 321
Dostoyevsky, Fyodor xi, 86, 329,
 340, 352
Du Bois, W. E. B. 342

E

Ecstasy of St. Teresa, The 358
Edna 300, 359
Einstein, Albert 64, 121, 157
Eisenhower, Dwight D. x, 216,
 324
Eitel, Charles 29, 34, 41, 227, 270,
 321, 324, 327, 330, 337, 355
Ellis, Havelock 175, 348
El Loco. See Ramirez, Amado
Emerson, Faye 227, 351
Empire of the Self: A Life of Gore
 Vidal 351
Engels, Friedrich 43, 331
England / English (people) viii,
 66, 67, 73, 81, 92, 95, 96, 97,
 101, 105, 125, 128, 146, 164, 180,
 186, 197, 210, 215, 216, 275, 338,
 357
Eros x
"Escape: How I Fled to Freedom"
 324
Esposito, Elena 29, 30, 51, 125,
 126, 227, 270, 327, 355
Esquire (Magazine) 323, 340
Executioner's Song, The 335, 349,
 354
Existential Errands 323
Existentialism 238, 352
Existentialism from Dostoyevsky
 to Sartre 352

F

Falkenburg, Eugenia "Jinx" 137, 346

Farrell, James T. 162

Faulkner, William 329, 334, 342

Faye, Marion x, 12, 20, 30, 33, 34, 35, 40, 41, 45, 51, 65, 68, 95, 324, 328, 330, 341, 355

Federal Bureau of Investigation (F.B.I.) 28, 70, 90, 333

Feiffer, Jules xv, 320

Fifty-Minute Hour, The 19, 43, 261, 267, 275, 281, 286, 289, 291, 292, 294, 311, 312, 324, 341, 355, 356, 357, 358

Finnegans Wake 71, 125, 192, 338, 344

Fishel, Budd 261

Five Spot xi

Fleiss, Wilhelm 285, 357

Folsom Prison 258

Ford, Bette 58, 336

Ford Foundation 301

Forst, Barbara 44, 332

Forst, Miles 44, 332

Francis, St. 142

Frasier, Dudley 267, 293, 355, 358

French Revolution 92

Freud, Sigmund x, xi, 40, 46, 55, 72, 86, 109, 158, 164, 170, 173, 178, 179, 249, 285, 309, 319, 329, 335, 339, 340, 347, 357

From Here to Eternity 331, 354

Function of the Orgasm, The 329

G

Gable, Clark 350

Gandhi 142

Gardiner, Kittredge 319

Gide, André xi, 37, 44, 232, 287, 329, 331

Gill, Brendan 355

Gillespie, Dizzy xi, 50, 322, 334

Gilmore, Gary 341

Ginsberg, Allen 325, 335

Glass Menagerie, The 329

God 10, 15, 19, 21, 22, 39, 40, 42, 64, 67, 68, 69, 70, 73, 81, 122, 136, 141, 143, 153, 156, 157, 178, 186, 192, 193, 199, 207, 208, 217, 221, 321, 343, 346

Goebel, George 326

Gollancz, Victor 275, 356

Goodbye to Berlin 360

Good, the Bad, and the Dolce Vita, The 332

Graham, Billy 92, 340

Greeks 196

Greene, Graham 359

Greenwich Village 322

Gregory, Paul 350, 357

Gwaltney, Francis I. "Fig" 221, 277, 351, 356

H

Halper, Nathan "Nat" 344

Hamlet 170

Hardwicke, Cedric 338

Harlot's Ghost viii, 318, 328, 336

Harold Ober Associates 260

Harper's (Magazine) 267, 275, 280, 282, 341, 356

Harrington, Mike 44, 131, 333

Harry Ransom Center 318, 321, 329

Hawthorne, Nathaniel xviii

Haydn, Hiram 94, 341
Hearn, William 333
Heart Is a Lonely Hunter, The 335
Heaven 41, 114, 115, 141, 152, 158, 181, 192
Heep, Uriah 219
Hegel, Georg Wilhelm Friedrich 72
Hell 41, 114, 115, 130, 141, 152, 153, 158, 181, 192
Hellman, Lillian 359
Hemingway, Ernest 69, 181, 321, 329, 359
Hindus 158, 220
"Hip, Hell and the Navigator" 346
Hitler, Adolf 40, 55, 86, 94, 124, 335, 341, 345
Hitlerism 114
Hoffer, Eric 353
Hollingsworth, Leroy 45, 163, 333
Hollywood vii, 258, 319, 321, 322, 327, 328, 329, 332, 348, 350, 355, 360
Holy Ghost 69, 139
Homosexual in America, The 333
"Homosexual Villain, The" 328
Horneyans 55, 335
Horney, Karen x, 335
Howe, Irving 131, 136, 345
Huston, John 161, 348
Huxley, Aldous 92, 299, 308, 340, 359

I
IBM 163
In Cold Blood 335

Independent, The 342
India 134, 195, 349
Individualism Reconsidered 282, 354
Isherwood, Christopher 308, 359

J
James, Henry 17, 335
Jazz Gallery xi
Jesus Christ 126, 142, 147, 237, 286, 341
"Jet-Propelled Couch, The" 94, 280, 282, 289, 298, 341, 356, 358
Johns Hopkins Hospital 314
Johnson, Eleanor "Johnnie" 44, 218, 219, 257, 259, 260, 262, 264, 271, 272, 278, 284, 290, 314, 331, 354
Johnson, Lyndon Baines 318
Joker, The 328
Jones, Ernest x
Jones, James (Jim, "Jonesie") 44, 55, 56, 69, 198, 331, 335, 350, 359
Joyce, James xi, 37, 42, 73, 125, 192, 227, 307, 329, 338, 339, 344, 349
Jung, Karl x, 55, 335

K
Kafka, Franz 7, 329, 356
Kammerman, Elliot 116, 343
Kant, Immanuel 163, 348
Kaufmann, Walter 352
Keep the River on Your Right 332
Kempton, Murray 342

Kennedy, John F. 328, 341
Kenyon Review 335
Kerouac, Jack 325, 335
Kessler, Anne 62
Kessler, Dave 62, 78, 337, 339
King and Queen of England 180
Kinsey, Alfred 166
Kleenex 212
Knopf, Alfred A. 358
Knopf, Blanche 292, 358
Knopf (publishers) 287, 292, 358
Knox, Mickey 44, 332
Kollontai, Alexandra
    Mikhailovna 345
Korea 249, 327
Kovacs, Ernie 23, 326
Kronstadt Rebellion, The 134,
    346

L
Lady Chatterley's Lover 340
Lamont, John 254, 353
"Last Draft of The Deer Park,
    The" 340
Last Tango in Paris 319, 329
Laughton, Charles xi, 68, 165,
    207, 208, 234, 237, 338, 350,
    357
Lazare, Rhoda 13, 195, 204, 209,
    324
Leaf, Monroe 349
Lenin, Vladimir 55, 134, 335, 345
Lennon, J. Michael iii, 243, 318,
    320, 346
Lerner, Max 267, 270, 275, 289,
    355, 356
Levitas, Louise 350
Lewis, Washington O. Q. 52

Liebman, Joshua 253, 352, 353
Lie Down in Darkness 336
Life (Magazine) 120, 343
Lincoln, Abraham 94, 142
Lindner, Johnnie 44, 218, 219,
    257, 259, 260, 262, 264, 271,
    272, 278, 284, 286, 290, 314,
    331, 354
Lipton's (tea, marijuana) iii, vii,
    viii, x, xi, xiv, xv, xvi, xviii, xx,
    xxi, 1, 3, 4, 8, 9, 22, 27, 33, 34,
    38, 40, 43, 48, 50, 51, 55, 61, 81,
    88, 89, 94, 110, 111, 118, 127,
    130, 136, 137, 146, 147, 153, 166,
    171, 172, 180, 181, 184, 190, 195,
    200, 201, 204, 205, 206, 214,
    215, 218, 226, 229, 231, 232, 238,
    239, 241, 242, 243, 245, 283,
    284, 287, 289, 300, 304, 306,
    315, 318, 319, 321, 322, 323, 326,
    328, 330, 336, 339, 342, 347, 357
Little, Brown 332
Little Foxes, The 329
Lonely Crowd, The 282, 357
Long March, The 336
Lovett, Mickey 45, 333

M
Macdonald, Dwight 359
Maddox Ford, Ford 356
Madison, Lannie 45, 333
Madonna 341
Mailer, Danielle 322
Mailer, Elizabeth Anne 322
Mailer, Fanny 13, 30, 61, 80, 82,
    83, 94, 105, 113, 127, 133, 138,
    174, 197, 292, 327

Mailer, Isaac B. "Barney" 30, 61, 80, 81, 82, 83, 84, 105, 115, 116, 127, 133, 138, 144, 145, 174, 255, 327, 347, 353

Mailer, Susan iii, 4, 7, 12, 17, 18, 62, 92, 227, 228, 278, 282, 295, 296, 322, 325

Malaquais, Jean x, 31, 40, 61, 85, 86, 88, 99, 103, 104, 115, 182, 221, 231, 328

Maloney, John 123, 343

Malraux, André 50, 119, 333

Maltese Falcon, The 348

Mandey, Arthur 270, 283, 355

Man in the White Suit, The 162

Mann, Thomas xi, 37, 73, 329

Man's Fate 333

Mao Tse-tung 318

Marilyn: A Biography 327, 334

Marion Faye 12, 20, 33, 34, 35, 40, 41, 45, 65, 95, 324, 341, 355

Martin, John Bartlow 278, 356

Martin, Shago 319

Marx, Karl (Marxism) x, xi, 9, 43, 72, 86, 93, 156, 158, 226, 248, 249, 250, 252, 253, 319, 331, 340, 345

McCarthy, Joseph 92, 93, 124, 135, 324, 326, 327, 340, 343

McCormick, Pat 58, 336

McCormick, Robert R. 109, 343

McCrary, John "Tex" 346

McCullers, Carson 55, 334

McLeod, Beverly Guinevere 163, 348, 359

McLeod, William 45, 65, 68, 329, 333, 348

Mendès-France, Pierre 12, 179, 324

"Metaphysics of the Belly, The" 336

Mexicans 55, 56, 195

Mexico 55, 89, 171, 209, 268, 269, 271, 276, 277, 284, 295, 325, 332, 336, 349

Meyers, Lulu 29, 35, 95, 163, 239, 327, 328

Miami Beach 51

Miller, Henry 341

Mills, Hilary xii, 320

"Mind of an Outlaw, The" 319, 340

Mingus, Charles xi, 322

Minton, Walter 358

Molotov, Vyacheslav 131, 345

Monk, Thelonious xi, 322

Monroe, Marilyn 52, 334

Moorhead, Anges 338

Morales, Al 91

Morales, Consuela 91

Morales (Mailer), Adele vii, xii, xiv, 7, 12, 31, 40, 44, 45, 48, 57, 61, 80, 83, 91, 103, 104, 113, 125, 127, 130, 131, 136, 137, 145, 146, 161, 163, 172, 174, 176, 177, 182, 191, 192, 193, 194, 200, 204, 206, 209, 211, 214, 216, 217, 218, 227, 228, 259, 262, 266, 271, 278, 281, 282, 283, 284, 293, 295, 300, 322, 325, 327, 336, 344, 347, 352

Moravia, Alberto 359

Moss, Reggie 10

Motherwell-Ginsberg Test 221

Munshin, Carlyle "Collie" 95,
  163, 227, 341
Must You Conform? 319, 324, 352,
  360
Mutiny on the Bounty 207, 208,
  350
"My Friend, Jean Malaquais" 328

N
Naiman, Adeline 44, 75, 332, 339
Naked and the Dead, The vii, xiv,
  46, 65, 68, 69, 120, 161, 165,
  208, 219, 234, 274, 283, 286,
  291, 292, 320, 321, 328, 329,
  332, 333, 334, 335, 338, 350, 357
"Naked Are Fanatics and the
  Dead Don't Care, The" 350
Nazis (Nazi Germany) 318, 329,
  330, 346
Negro viii, xi, xii, xv, 52, 105, 150,
  208, 318, 322, 323, 325, 326,
  330, 342, 343, 345, 347, 351
Nelson-Denny Test 221
New Deal 343
Newman, Paul 318
New York 89, 251, 253, 254, 258,
  261, 262, 282, 285, 290, 298,
  299, 300, 314
New Yorker, The 320, 355
New York Herald Tribune 207
*New York Herald Tribune Book
  Review* 355
New York Post 290
New York Review of Books 319,
  329, 342
New York Times 120, 320
Nixon, Richard 216
No Percentage xiv, 138, 346

Nordhoff, Charles 350
Norris, Christopher 162, 351
"Notes of a Native Son" 343

O
Ober, Harold 260, 261, 312, 331,
  354, 360
"Of a Small and Modest
  Malignancy, Wicked and
  Bristling with Dots," 323
O'Faye, Dorothea 29, 35, 262,
  324, 354
Olshaker, Mark 320
Omnibus 212, 221, 298, 301, 351
One (magazine) 89, 329
*On God: An Uncommon
  Conversation* 346
On the Waterfront 137, 346
Orwell, George 19, 274, 291, 356
O'Shaugnessey, Sergius 29, 33,
  34, 35, 45, 81, 263, 327, 337, 354,
  356
Oswald, Lee Harvey 341
Other America, The 333

P
"Paleface vs. Redskin" 335
Parini, Jay 351
Parks, Bert 346
Parliaments (cigarettes) 210
Partisan Review 55, 334
Peace of Mind 248, 352, 353
Peale, Norman Vincent 330
Pellito 262, 354
Pepsi-Cola 160
Perón, Eva 115, 343
Perón, Juan 343
Picasso, Pablo 331, 341

Pieces and Pontifications 319, 323, 328, 329
Planck, Max 64, 337
Plastrik, Stanley 131, 344
Playboy 349
Poirier, Richard xiv, xv, 145, 320, 336, 339, 347
"Political Economy of Time, The" 336
Politics and the Novel 345
Pope, Teddy 34, 70, 328
Portrait of Picasso as a Young Man 331
Prescription for Rebellion: A Reinterpretation of Psychoanalysis x, 242, 248, 249, 252, 274, 319, 324, 352, 353
Presidential Papers, The 331
Prisoner of Sex, The 348
Proust, Marcel xi, 37, 42, 73, 329
"Psychodynamics of Gambling, The" 255, 353
"Psychology of the Orgy, The" 227, 323
Publishers Weekly vii
Putnam's, G. P. (Publishers) vii, 79, 94, 162, 295, 297, 340, 347, 358

Q
"Quickly" xv, 320, 326
Quincey, Thomas De viii

R
Rahv, Philip 335, 359
Ramirez, Amado 195, 349
Random House 287, 319, 341

"Rebels or Psychopaths?" 358
Rebel Without a Cause 258, 260, 261, 263, 299, 319, 324, 352, 354
Redl, Harry 318
Reichians 55, 99, 209, 335
Reich, Wilhelm x, 40, 43, 113, 131, 193, 230, 329, 330, 335, 344, 353
Reik, Theodore x, 158, 169, 347
Rembar, Billie 284, 286, 313, 314, 360
Rembar, Charles "Cy" 83, 115, 271, 283, 284, 286, 295, 313, 314, 340, 360
Remembrance of Things Past 292
Renaissance 39, 143
Republican Party 318
Riesman, David 282, 354, 357
Rimbaud, Arthur 43, 331
Rinehart and Company (Publications) vii, x, 3, 52, 129, 162, 243, 267, 269, 271, 278, 283, 286, 289, 301, 311, 319, 321, 334, 339, 352, 353, 354, 355, 358
Rinehart, Stanley vii, 3, 52, 129, 267, 269, 270, 271, 278, 321, 334, 355
Riot in Cell Block 11 258, 263, 354
Rojack, Stephen 319, 341
Rollins, Sonny xi
Romain, Gary 7, 50, 228, 322, 333, 341
Roosevelt, Eleanor 342
Roosevelt, Franklin D. 343
Rosen, Marian x, 43, 330
Rosetta Stone 274
Rosicrucians 99, 342
Ross, Lillian 320

Rowan and Martin's Laugh-In 326
Roximyl 204, 221, 350
Rubenstein, Serge 131, 345
Russia 135
Russian Revolution vii, 134, 250, 328

S

Saturday Night Live 326
Scarlet Letter, The xviii
Schneebaum, Toby 44, 216, 332, 351
Schneider, Chaim Yehuda 346
Seconal viii, xii, 61, 88, 104, 118, 137, 153, 171, 184, 193, 201, 306, 336, 347
Sexual Revolution, The 113, 250, 353
Shakespeare, William 227
Sheen, Bishop Fulton J. 70, 338
Sheltering Sky, The 335
Silverman, Jenny 75, 86, 339
Silverman (Mailer), Beatrice (Bea) xii, 19, 31, 44, 80, 194, 269, 271, 322, 325, 332, 339
Sipiora, Phillip 319
Soviet Union (Soviets) 85, 122, 163, 166, 180, 250, 321
Spengler, Oswald xi, 16, 325
Spooky Art, The 353
Stalinism / Stalinists 28, 45, 114, 134, 135, 136, 144, 333
Stalin, Joseph 19, 20, 27, 28, 42, 45, 55, 85, 98, 117, 131, 135, 216, 326, 333, 335, 345
"Star-Spangled Banner, The" 51
Stein, Gertrude 331

Stendhal 329
Stevenson, Adlai 216
Stitt, Sonny xi, 319, 322
Stone Walls 278, 356
Story of Ferdinand, The 194, 349
Stratton, Richard 320
Streetcar Named Desire, A 137, 329, 346
Stuart, Lyle 342
Studies in the Psychology of Sex 348
Styron, Rose 177, 348
Styron, William 58, 123, 177, 289, 336, 343, 348, 359
Sullivan, Henry Stack x, 344
Susie. *See Mailer, Susan*

T

Tahiti 209
Tarot cards/readings 112, 128
Tattersal, Ian 342
Taylor, Laurette 39, 329
Tea-Time 209
Teppis, Herman 41, 95, 163, 239, 267, 271, 292, 328, 330, 341, 355
Tex and Jinx 137, 346
Thanatos x
Theresa, St. 299, 358
Thomas, Norman 86, 340
Thompson, Clara Mabel 130, 344
Thoreau, Henry David 5, 322
Time (Magazine) vii, 37, 70, 123, 155, 156, 186, 209, 289, 320, 358
Tito, Josep Broz 144, 346
Tolstoy, Lev (Leo) xi, 86, 329, 340
Tropic of Cancer 340

Trotsky, Leon 55, 134, 135, 335, 346

True Believer: Thoughts on the Nature of Mass Movements, The 352

Truman, Harry 55, 216, 228, 335, 349

Twain, Mark 335

U

Ulysses 192, 349

Union of Soviet Socialist Republics (U.S.S.R.) 345, 349

United Nations (U.N.) 21, 322

United States of America, The xviii, 67, 74, 92, 166, 170, 171, 250, 327, 333

V

Verlaine, Paul 43, 331

Vidal, Gore 216, 351

Village Vanguard xi

Village Voice xv, 246, 320, 325, 326, 352

Violated, The 350

von Auw, Ivan 44, 197, 260, 263, 275, 280, 285, 295, 302, 331, 354

von Ribbentrop, Joachim 345

W

Walden; or, Life in the Woods 322

Wald, Jerry 258, 354

Wallace, Henry A. 180, 349

Walsh, John 56, 336

Wanger, Walter 258, 261, 354

Warner Brothers 261, 319, 352

Washington Post 120

Wasserman, Barbara Mailer (sister) 44, 48, 61, 81, 83, 103, 105, 138, 139, 146, 147, 148, 174, 324, 332, 337, 346, 351

Waterfront 319

Weisgal, Freddy 160, 275, 347

"White Negro, The" viii, xi, xii, xv, 318, 322, 323, 325, 330, 342, 343, 345, 347, 351

Why Did They Kill? 278

Wild One, The 137, 346

Winchell, Walter 109, 111, 119, 343

Wolf, Daniel "Danny" 19, 40, 61, 83, 88, 137, 139, 195, 204, 206, 324, 325

Wylie, Philip 250, 302

Y

Yipper 31, 327

Z

Zetkin, Clara 345

Zola, Émile 162